D1563845

# Music and Ritual at
# Papal Avignon
## 1309-1403

# Studies in Musicology, No. 75

George Buelow, Series Editor

Professor of Music
Indiana University

## Other Titles in This Series

# Music and Ritual at Papal Avignon 1309-1403

by
Andrew Tomasello

UMI RESEARCH PRESS
Ann Arbor, Michigan

Produced and distributed by
UMI Research Press
an imprint of
University Microfilms International
Ann Arbor, Michigan 48106

Library of Congress Cataloging in Publication Data

**Tomasello, Andrew.**
Music and ritual at Papal Avignon, 1309-1403.

(Studies in musicology ; no. 75)
Revision of thesis—Yale University, 1982.
Bibliography: p.
Includes index.
1. Church music—France—Avignon—500-1400—History
and criticism. 2. Church music—Catholic Church—History
and criticism. 3. Liturgics—Catholic Church. 4. Papacy—
History—1309-1378. 5. Popes—Court. I. Title. II. Series.

ML3027.T65  1983    783'.02'6094492        83-18296
ISBN 0-8357-1493-4

For my mother

# Contents

# List of Abbreviations

| | |
|---|---|
| ADV | Archives départementales de Vaucluse |
| ASV | Archivio Segreto Vaticano |
| BEFAR | Bibliothèque des Ecoles Françaises d'Athènes et de Rome |
| BMA | Bibliothèque municipale d'Avignon |
| BMC | Bibliothèque municipale de Carpentras |
| CE | *The Catholic Encyclopedia* |
| Coll. | *Collectoria* |
| Grove 6 | *The New Grove Dictionary of Music and Musicians* |
| NCE | *New Catholic Encyclopedia* |

# Preface

Within the last fifty years, several authors have noted the turmoil that seems to have pervaded fourteenth-century society. And although it is meaningless to discuss whether or not this age was more or less calamitous than any other, the history of the Church clearly bears witness to unsurety as first kings, then cardinals sought to dominate a politically ineffectual papacy. The era is characterized by the prolonged residence of the Holy See in Provence and by the election and counter-election of rival popes. For almost one hundred years, western Europe turned its attention to a walled town on the eastern bank of the Rhône, the city of Avignon.

Some still view Avignon through the distorted glass of Petrarch's hyperbolic and chauvinistic prose, railing against the moral depravity of the Curia, quick to point to the popes as the incarnations of debauchery and wickedness. Despite the impropriety of the sojourn in Provence and ensuing Schism, Avignon was neither "sink of vice," nor "sewer of the world." And the willing presence of Italian, Spanish, and Netherlandish clerics in this city bespeaks nothing of "captivity."

Instead it is necessary that we see the first part of this era merely as a period of 65 years in which the duly elected Sovereign Pontiffs reigned beyond the Italian peninsula. And as those pursuing the study of higher civilizations, during the first decades of the Schism we must take the side of the antipopes of Avignon.

Papal Avignon was the focal point for all aspects of culture. The wealth and power which were concentrated within its walls attracted artists, poets, scholars, and musicians hoping to partake of this abundance. Avignon of the popes became an important musical center. What is known about the music of the papal ceremonies and feasts during the preceding centuries seems to indicate a strong Roman bias. But the removal of the Holy See to Provence, the domination by French popes, cardinals, and officials, and the endorsement of the Gallic nobility brought with it an influx of French and Netherlandish clerics into the courts and chapels of Avignon. The close interaction of the Sovereign Pontiffs with the noble houses of France effected an exchange of musical repertory and chapel personnel that ultimately resulted in northern influence on music at the Spanish courts and at the fifteenth-century pontifical court of Rome.

Unfortunately, much documentation for this period has been lost; and especially when working with the highest of ecclesiastical institutions, so much more concerning art and culture is left unsaid. But even ignoring these limitations the author does not pretend that this book tells the whole story of music and ritual at Avignon. Many stones remain unturned; many volumes of documents rest unopened. Instead of logging the polyphonic works that were sung in the presence of curial members, a task which will forever remain impossible, the study attempts to examine the liturgico-musical practice of the fourteenth-century papal chapel in its proper historical context. It owes much to the excellent work of Ursula Günther, Bernhard Schimmelpfennig, and countless scholars and archivists who, for the past hundred years, have helped clear a path through the wilderness.

Among those who have aided and encouraged this study there are a few to whom I must give a special word of thanks:

To Gail Hilson Woldu, Maria Germano, and especially to Heidi Kunz for assisting in the preparation of the manuscript. To Ora Saloman, Claude Palisca, and particularly to Craig Monson for reading the text and making helpful comments.

To Yale University and the Martha Baird Rockefeller Fund for Music, whose generous financial support allowed work on the original study to proceed uninterrupted. To Martin Stevens, Dean of the School of Liberal Arts and Sciences of Baruch College (CUNY), for the released-time grant which facilitated the production of the final version.

To Georges de Loÿe, former curator of the Bibliothèque municipale d'Avignon and to his staff for quickly and courteously responding to an interminable series of requests. To the Equipe de recherche (1057) associé du C.N.R.S., particularly Anne-Marie Hayez and Janinne Mathieu, for permitting easy access to their vast files.

To Bernhard Schimmelpfenning who graciously consented to read the manuscript and to offer suggestions and emendations. To Michel Hayez, director of archival services of the Archives départementales de Vaucluse, who gave invaluable direction when all roads seemed to lead nowhere.

To Craig Wright whose enthusiastic support sustained the original work and whose insight and guidance helped focus my blurred thoughts and clear my muddled prose.

# Acknowledgments

The author wishes to thank Georges de Loÿe, (Bibliothéque municipale d'Avignon for permission to reproduce the illustrations shown on pages 37 and 84, and Michel Hayez, (Archives départementales de Vaucluse) for granting the rights to publish the document on page 143.

Fig. 1.   The Mediterranean coastline of western Italy and southern
France during the late Middle Ages.

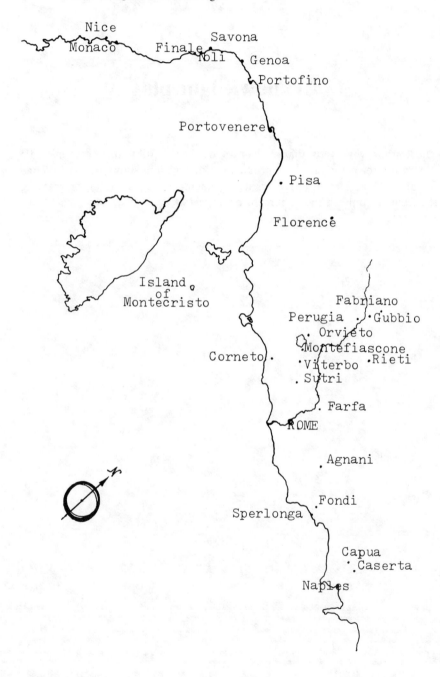

# 1

# The Popes at Avignon

The papacy of the twelfth and thirteenth centuries was an itinerant institution. Although the bishops of Rome were nominally located in the Eternal City, popes considered the world to be their diocese and, consequently, were not held back by the restrictions placed on other pastors. During the late Middle Ages, the pontiffs transferred their court as easily and as often as circus troupes paraded from town to town.

There were many established papal residences throughout Italy, though centered around Rome: Viterbo, Anagni, Perugia, Orvieto, Rieti, and Tivoli.[1] Moreover, there were additional towns, both on the peninsula and beyond, where pope and Curia established temporary and not-so-temporary residences. In fact, the popes who spent all or most of their time in Rome during this period are quite the exception. For the interval between August 1099 and January 1198, the vicars of Christ spent 55 years outside Rome, and 8 of these in France. From 1100 until 1304, approximately 122 years of the 204 saw the pontiffs residing beyond the walls of the Eternal City. The extreme example for such a practice is Pope Innocent IV (1243-1254) who lived at Lyon from 1244 until 1251 and spent only a very short time in Rome. Likewise, Pope Gregory X (1271-1276), who summoned a church council at Lyon in 1274, passed some time in France. Besides Lyon, Orange, Beaucaire, Valence, and Vienne all served as homes for the Curia. As astounding as it seems to us today, several popes of the thirteenth century never saw Rome at all.[2]

The reasons for these absences are often as scandalous as they are complicated. In no case, however, did the emigration of the Curia spell disaster for the papacy, neither did it curtail any of the authority of the bishop of Rome. For as the fourteenth-century apologists put it: *Ubi papa, ibi Roma;* where the pope is, there is Rome.[3] When the Court of Rome, as it was known, made its circuit, it wanted for nothing. The pontiff was accompanied by a great number of ecclesiastics, functionaries, and retainers. In addition, each cardinal residing with the Curia had his own retinue. When the pope entered a city, the population of that city swelled. Power, money, and those who sought both followed these ecclesiastics. Papal and Curial presence in thirteenth-century

Viterbo, for example, caused rents to double.[4] Similar increases were no doubt effected in other cities.

The itinerant pope and cardinals took their chaplains and clerks, as well as their servants, wherever they went. These chaplains participated in the liturgies of their masters, and to some extent they must have been responsible for the music of the service. Some of these clerics may even have provided musical entertainments of a less sacred variety for themselves or for their employers. During the conclave of Naples in 1295 that elected Boniface VIII (1294-1303), the following directive was given to the Sacred College:

> Singing, dancing, and other insolent servants are to correct themselves. If they do not, they will be removed unpardoned from the palace.[5]

Boniface himself ordained that clerics do justice to their rank in the following document of general import:

> Clerics who act as *jongleurs, goliardes,* or *bufones,* disparaging a good deal of their clerical standing, will be deprived of all clerical privilege. If they behave in such an ignominious fashion for one year, or if within a shorter period they fail to heed a third warning, this is the law.[6]

Evidently, to have elicited these admonitions, instances of clerics acting in a manner unbecoming to their position in the Church were commonplace.

When the pope was out of Rome, however, there were several things that he could not take with him, things indispensable to the execution of the liturgy as described in the ancient Roman ordos: namely, the stational churches and the *Schola cantorum.*

There were 42 stational churches throughout the city of Rome where the pope was expected to participate at 89 services held on 87 days of the year. The weeks of Lent, Easter, then Advent and Christmastide are the most complete in regard to these services. The liturgy involved the pope going in state from his residence in the Lateran Palace to the designated church, where all the titled clerics and faithful of the city awaited him. Here the liturgy was to be celebrated. On certain penitential days, for example, on the Rogation days, the entourage first went to a church where all were gathered to form a procession. The pope began the rites with special prayers that terminated in the *oratio ad collectam,* the prayer for the assembly. Then, led by a cleric bearing the wooden stational cross, the procession set out for a second church, chanting the litany of the saints that concluded with a three-fold *Kyrie eleison.* When the clergy and faithful arrived at the second edifice, the Mass for the day was celebrated.[7] It is obvious that when the pope was bereft of these stational churches, the processions could not have been carried out as they were described in the ordos. There is no evidence to suggest that such processions were in any way executed during those periods when the pope was residing outside Rome.

The second immobile institution was the *Schola cantorum*. According to the Roman ordos of the thirteenth century, it appears as though the *Schola* provided the music for the ordinary of the Mass and for some of the propers. However, when the pope was out of Rome, his liturgy had to proceed without this group and without its leader, the *primicerius*. Therefore, from most of the time after 1100 until the death of Pope Benedict XI in 1304, the *Schola cantorum*, instead of playing an integral part in Roman liturgy, was, in fact, not functioning at all. Its members remained at the Lateran Palace.[8]

## Clement V

After the death of Pope Benedict on 18 July 1304, the conclave was convened. But it was only after a year of argument and political machinations that the cardinals elected Bertrand de Got, the archbishop of Bordeaux, to be the bishop of Rome. Archbishop Bertrand was born in the city of Villandraut and received his education in the diocese of Agen. He went on to Orléans and then to Bologna in order to pursue his studies in canon and civil law. He held canonicates in turn at the cathedral of Bordeaux, Saint-Caprais at Agen, at Tours, and at Lyon though it is not known whether he ever made his residence at these places. He became vicar general to his brother Béraud, archbishop of Lyon and, in 1294, traveled to England on a mission of diplomacy. On 28 March of the following year, he was named bishop of Comminges and was raised to the archbishopric of Bordeaux on 23 December 1299. During his career, he and his family were held in favor by the king of France, and Bertrand himself came to be an influential figure at the French royal court.[9]

When notified of his election, the archbishop chose to be called Clement, the fifth of that name, and he arranged to be crowned at Vienne on the feast of All Saints (1 November). However, submitting to pressure exerted by King Philip the Fair, Clement was instead consecrated at Lyon on 14 November. After negotiations with Philip, Clement did not turn and head for Italy, but moved the Curia westward, into Gascony, where in mid-December he created ten new cardinals: one was English and the other nine were French. With two promotions similarly made in 1310 and 1312, the Italian majority in the Sacred College was no more. France had a sure grip on ecclesiastical power that it would not relinquish for nearly ninety years.[10]

Like immediate predecessors, Clement V was an itinerant pope, though he chose to do the majority of his wandering in the Comtat Venaissin, the area of papal states situated east of the Rhône River, south of Dauphiné. The Comtat was out of French royal territory, though just barely. Most certainly, it was not far enough away to be out of France's sphere of influence nor outside of the scandal surrounding such a close relationship between king and pope. Technically speaking, the area was within Provence, and under the protection of a vassal of the Church, Charles II of Anjou. The towns and countryside of

Provence, unlike Italy, were experiencing a period of peace and political stability. This, along with its location as a center for communications and international relations, made it of particular appeal.[11]

In March 1309, Pope Clement entered the city of Avignon, a town surrounded by walls of fortification, built on a rock. Considered another temporary residence, Avignon was, for this pope, just one in a long series of convenient stopovers far from Rome. While in the city, Clement made his lodgings at the Dominican monastery outside the walls.[12] Possibly, to provide larger quarters, a certain amount of remodeling of the monastery and cloister was done at the pope's expense.[13]

For his own liturgy, Clement must have made use of the small chapels that were part of the abbey, or perhaps he participated in services held in the Dominican church, the city's largest. We are certain that when King Robert of Sicily was crowned on 3 August 1309, and when Celestine V was canonized on 2-5 May 1313, Pope Clement officiated at the ceremonies held in the cathedral church of Avignon, Notre-Dame-des-Doms.[14] The pope remained but a short time in this city, preferring instead the other towns and castles of the surrounding Comtat.

Plate 1.    The cathedral of Notre-Dame-des-Doms at Avignon, north façade. A tower from the Palace of the Popes is visible in the background.

Clement V was an unpretentious man whose greatest fault perhaps was his excessive zeal to please the French monarch. He was a man of learning yet had little concern for the arts. At the Council of Vienne (1311-1312) he promulgated a constitution regarding the abuses in the performance of church music. He wrote,

> We are truly moved by a severe disturbance, which, because of the negligence of some rectors, is wont to foster much pestilence in our subjects as long as there is any hope of impunity. A great many ministers of the Church, having cast down the modesty of clerical standing, should be offering God sacrifice of praise from the fruits of their lips in purity of conscience and in devotion of mind. They presume to say or to sing the canonical hours either cursorily or syncopatedly, even intermingling a great number of extraneous, meaningless, worldly, and shameful texts. Or they convene late in the choir, frequently leaving the church before the end of the office, meanwhile carrying birds (or having them carried) and bringing hunting dogs along with them. Vested in the crown of the divine tonsure, they pretend to celebrate virtually nothing of the clerical militia, or they are present in a fashion undevoted beyond all measure.[15]

Again, as we have seen in the proclamation of Boniface VIII, the pope was concerned with those influences that the secular world had on the religious one. Especially important here is the remark made against a quick and syncopated manner of performing the divine office, a practice no doubt widespread among the clergy. While this may indicate no more than a lackadaisical attitude in the execution of the music of the divine office, the admonition against intermingling worldly and shameful texts with the sacred words is somewhat more provocative, possibly referring to the incursion of certain trope texts, farces, or liturgical dramas into the music of the Church.

The text continues with a passage directly relating to the musical practices of the Curia. It reads as follows:

> In sacred approbation of the Council we permit the following: Judging worthy, upright and fit that religious clerics as well as others, who are commensal domestics of the cardinals of the Holy Roman Church and of whichever pontiffs that are in grace and communion with the Apostolic See, can join them in the divine offices. They have the power to say that which those same cardinals or pontiffs rightfully say, and they are not required to say anything else.[16]

In this interesting passage we find conclusive evidence that the princes of the Church maintained their own households, supported their own chaplains, and celebrated the divine office independent of the papal liturgy. Clerics in the entourage of a prelate were required to recite the hours according to the usage of their employers, a "house usage" so to speak. During the course of the fourteenth century, these retainers and chaplains would be among the most highly skilled and educated men in the Curia and would make their patrons rivals of the pope as champions of art and learning.

## John XXII

When Pope Clement died, on 20 April 1314, the cardinals brought themselves to the city of Carpentras and locked the doors of the bishop's palace behind them. This began a series of conclaves which wore on for two years. After having transferred the site of the election to the Dominican monastery at Lyon, the cardinals only took one-and-a-half months to reach a consensus. On 7 August 1316, the Sacred College agreed on the cardinal bishop of Porto, the 72-year-old Jacques Duèse. He bore the name of John XXII.[17]

A sober and frugal member of the middle class, the new pope was born in Cahors and studied at Montpellier. He became archpriest of Saint-André at Cahors and later bore the same title at the church of Sarlat. He retained canonicates at Saint-Front of Périgueux and at Albi, and was later deacon of Le Puy. Jacques was consecrated bishop of Fréjus on 4 February 1300 and, eight years later, served as chancellor to Charles II, duke of Anjou. In a move that would subsequently change the course of history, Pope Clement translated bishop Jacques to the see of Avignon on 18 March 1310. Within three years he was raised to the cardinalate, first receiving the title of cardinal priest of S.Vitalis and then in May 1313, cardinal bishop of Porto.[18]

After his coronation at Lyon in September 1316, there was a marked shift away from the peripatetic tendencies of the Court of Rome. John XXII decided to transfer the Curia to the city of his former episcopal see, Avignon. Evidently he preferred not only the city but also his old home, the bishop's residence. For in October 1316, even before his arrival at Avignon, John began to transform the *domus episcopalis* into the *palatium domini pape*.[19] The episcopal residence was a fortress-like structure, essentially consisting of buildings arranged quadrilaterally around a cloistered area. Clement V once took refuge there when he felt himself being pressured by ambassadors of the king of France.[20] It seems likely that the buildings familiar to John may have provided him with some sense of physical safety.

It was the bishop's apartments and adjoining structures that were slowly transformed into a papal palace. The court of the cloister came to be called the *platea palatii*. The galleries above the court contained *tabulae pictae,* and on certain feast days it is believed that the pope preached to the populace gathered below.[21] The north side of the cloister was closed off by the two-story parish church of Saint-Etienne and by the buildings reserved for the provostry of the cathedral. In 1317 John had the parish moved to the nearby church of the Madeleine in order for the two-level structure to serve as the papal chapel.[22] Payments were made for the painting of Saint-Etienne, and remodeling was done in December of that year and in March of the next. Although the upper story functioned as the chapel proper, seats were made for the lower area indicating it had some other function.[23]

Fig. 2.   Palace of the Popes at Avignon.

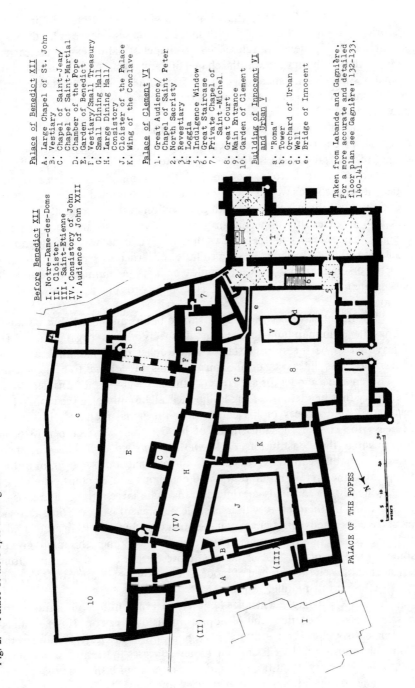

Before Benedict XII
I.   Notre-Dame-des-Doms
II.  Cloister
III. Saint-Etienne
IV.  Consistory of John
V.   Audience of John XXII

Palace of Benedict XII
A. Large Chapel of St. John
B. Vestiary
C. Chapel of Saint-Jean/
   Chapel of Saint-Martial
D. Chamber of the Pope
E. Garden of Benedict
F. Vestiary/Small Treasury
G. Small Dining Hall
H. Large Dining Hall/
   Consistory
J. Cloister of the Palace
K. Wing of the Conclave

Palace of Clement VI
1.  Great Audience/
    Chapel of Saint Peter
2.  North Sacristy
3.  Revestiary
4.  Loggia
5.  Indulgence Window
6.  Great Staircase
7.  Private Chapel of
    Saint-Michel
8.  Great Court
9.  Main Entrance
10. Garden of Clement

Building of Innocent VI
and Urban V
a. "Roma"
b. Tower
c. Orchard of Urban
d. Well
e. Bridge of Innocent

Taken from Labande and Gagnière.
For a more accurate and detailed
floor plan see Gagnière: 132-133,
140-141.

PALACE OF THE POPES

Besides Saint-Etienne, the pontiff might have celebrated in other oratories, since he had several chapels in the bishop's residence at his disposal. As early as 1237, there is a reference to a chapel of Saint-Jean in the eastern wing. In the southern wing was the chapel of Saint-Denis cited in 1264 and the chapel of Saint-Michel mentioned in 1185 and 1209.[24] Unfortunately, there is no documentation to show conclusively that any of these was in use during the papacy of John XXII.

Instead of building personal chapels, the pope spent large sums to construct or enlarge ecclesiastical edifices throughout Avignon. He built the chapel of Notre-Dame-des-Miracles in the southwest corner of the city. He either added chapels to or refurbished the Dominican, Franciscan, and Carmelite churches as well as the cathedral, Saint-Agricol, and the Madeleine. Not only was John preoccupied with the erection of these monuments, but he was also involved in supporting a great number of priests who, at papal expense, said Masses at these new altars.[25] While he was extravagant in sustaining Avignon's clergy, he seemed little concerned with providing himself a rich personal liturgy or with employing a large number of clerics to participate in papal Masses or offices. History records him as a man who lived in moderation.

John might have been a man of simple habits and tastes, but he was a strong ruler who maintained a hand in all aspects of papal organization.[26] He endeavored to be the spiritual father and teacher of all mankind, a *pastor universalis*.[27] As the successor of Saint Peter, his mission was to be a guide for the Church and a model for all. He reorganized his court and considered it so exemplary that in a letter to King Philip the Tall he counseled the monarch to restructure the services of his court using the papal model.[28] He tried to decrease the size of the households of his cardinals. In October 1316, he promulgated the constitution *De honestate cardinalium*. This document prescribes that the cardinals reduce the luxury of their courts and, among other things, that they retain no more than 10 chaplains and 20 courtiers.[29]

Evidently the cardinals continued to maintain large retinues and insisted on surrounding themselves with a sizeable number of clerics. Some of these must have been active participants in the liturgy celebrated within each family. If 10 was considered by the pope to be a reasonable number, this might give us some indication of the size of his own close circle of familiars, since John considered himself the paragon of moderation. However, many cardinals must have exceeded this number in practice.

John XXII strongly centralized church government by concentrating the power to bestow benefices and bishoprics in his own person. He maintained discipline through his constitutions, his legates, by means of synods, and by the Court of Inquisition. By carving out 16 new dioceses in the area south of the Loire, the Sovereign Pontiff augmented the number of bishops in that part of France and so hoped to stamp out heresy in Languedoc. This contributed to his goal of ecclesiastical domination, while adding to the burgeoning Avignonese bureaucracy. The pope outlawed pluralism by revoking the dispensations that allowed clerics to hold several benefices simultaneously, though this reform had no lasting effect.[30]

Out of this attitude and the desire to control all aspects of church life came the bull, promulgated in 1324/25, *Docta sanctorum Patrum*.[31] This document is a quite detailed enumeration of specific abuses in the practice of church music. It goes beyond either of those pronouncements made by Boniface VIII or Clement V in that it deals with certain techniques used in polyphonic music. But exactly as his predecessors had done, John treated the abuse that had historically perturbed popes, namely, the intermingling of the sacred with the secular. He specifically wished to proscribe the introdution of *hoqueti* into the *melodias ecclesiasticas,* the incursion of *tripla et moteti vulgares* on sacred Latin texts, and the use of anything but the tried and true *consonentie supra cantum ecclesiasticum.* The pope makes no pronouncement that such polyphonic practices were evil in themselves, but that they should not be introduced into the sacred services. Unlike his predecessors, John XXII goes on to specify the precise disciplinary action that was to be taken if this pronouncement be disobeyed.[32] It is only in the detail of this bull that John differs from earlier popes. But as we have indicated, detail and control were hallmarks of his papacy. When he died, on 3 December 1334, at age 90, John XXII left behind a clear set of decrees treating liturgical practice and a strong centralized church government firmly ensconced in the city of Avignon.

## Benedict XII

Against this backdrop, on 20 December 1334, the Sacred College of cardinals unanimously elected Jacques Fournier as Pope Benedict XII. Unlike his aristocratic and bourgeois predecessors, this pope had humble beginnings and had never known wealth. He was born in the town of Saverdun and, later, following the example of his uncle, he entered the Cistercian order. He first belonged to the abbey of Boulbon, but transferred to Fontfroide where his uncle, Arnaud Fournier, was abbot. He went on to study at the College of Saint-Bernard in Paris, where he received a doctorate of theology. By 1311 he had succeeded his uncle as abbot of Fontfroide and held this abbacy until March 1317, when he was consecrated bishop of Pamiers. Nine years later, he was translated to the see of Mirepoix, and within two years, he received the purple along with the title cardinal priest of S. Prisca.[33]

As a cardinal, Jacques Fournier was called upon to act as judge, and he was instrumental in stamping out heresy in France. As pope, he concerned himself primarily with restoring discipline among the religious communities. He reformed his own Cistercian order as well as the Benedictines and Augustinians. Only the Dominicans escaped censure; in fact, Benedict praised the purity of the Preachers and declared them to be at the head of all other orders. On the other hand, he was severely critical of the Franciscans and their lax conduct. In November 1336, he promulgated the bull *Redemptor noster* which prescribed constant attendance at the divine offices for the followers of Saint Francis.[34] This extremely important piece of information establishes Benedict as a man who considered the canonical hours to be an essential part of religious life. Holding himself as an example, the pontiff did not fail to strive for this ideal in his own practice. Thus, soon after his election, he reformed papal liturgical custom and established the *capellani capelle,* or chapel of twelve chaplains. The *raison d'être* of the *capella* was to say the *horas canonicas cum nota,* apparently a practice that had not been closely adhered to by the chaplains of John XXII. This papal chapel, first instituted in 1334 by Benedict as a renewal of monastic discipline in his own life, became the *capella pape* that later boasted having the composers Hasprois, Haucourt, and Johannes de Bosco among its members.[35]

Benedict did not limit his reforms to monastic communities but extended his control over the secular clergy as well. On 10 January 1335, he declared that those in the city of Avignon who held benefices *cum cura* were required to quit Avignon to begin their residence by Purification (2 February) and tend to the care of souls. The pope likewise set out to correct the innumerable abuses in ecclesiastic administration. He further concentrated power in the bishop of Rome by requiring all supplications for benefices be submitted in person and be approved and initialled by the pontiff himself.[36] Benedict was obsessed with the competence of his clergy, compelling all candidates for clerical offices to undergo an examination, and there is some evidence that he might have reviewed candidates personally. An anonymous chronicler relates a tale of how the pope interviewed a Brother Monozella, elected abbot of Saint–Paul–outside–the–walls in Rome after the death of the incumbent; Monozella had a reputation as a fine player of the lute and as a singer of *ballate.* The conversation is reported thus:

Monozella:  Holy Father, I have been elected abbot of San Paolo at Rome.

Benedict:  Do you know how to sing?

Monozella:  I do.

Benedict:  I mean secular songs [*la cantilena*]?

Monozella:  I know such songs.

Benedict:  Do you know how to play an instrument?

Monozella:  I do.

Benedict:  I mean do you know how to play the organ and the lute [*lo leguto*]?

Monozella:  Too well.

Benedict:  Is it thus that the abbot of the venerable monastery of San Paolo makes a clown [*buffone*] of himself? Get back there to your proper business![37]

Apocryphal though it might be, this story is in perfect agreement with the sentiments expressed by previous popes, namely, that never should the sacred and secular be mixed. Such practice by clerics evidently rendered them nothing more than buffoons in the eyes of the papacy if not of the faithful.

Though he lived an austere life, Benedict spared little expense in taking the decisive step that caused Avignon to become a permanent residence. On the site of the former episcopal palace, the pope erected an edifice worthy of the Roman Church.[38] In April 1335, work began to rebuild the chapel of Saint-Etienne that had come to serve as a papal chapel during the pontificate of John XXII.

The original two-story design was maintained, as the former parish church was lengthened eastward over the area once occupied by the provostry buildings. On 23 June 1337, the vigil of the feast of Saint John the Baptist, Gasbert de Laval, archbishop of Arles, consecrated the main altar. Although dedicated to God, the Virgin, and the Holy Apostles Peter and Paul, the chapel was named for Saint John. Work on it continued until November, and the payment for the glass windows was not completed until the end of 1338.[39] The chapel proper, or upper chapel, was the real pontifical chapel. The lower or "dark" chapel was soon deconsecrated because of insufficient lighting, and by July 1338 it was being used as a storage area.[40]

The Chapel of Saint John, an architectural oddity, was probably totally different from the restored version we find there today since, according to the accounts, it originally included round pillars, arches, buttresses, cross vaults, small naves, and a principal nave. The chapel was reworked in 1340-41 and possibly afterwards.[41] The version found today measures 38 × 9 meters and has a wainscotted ceiling in the form of a raised broken-barrel vault which was at one time probably supported by timbers. On the south wall is the doorway that leads to the upper gallery of the cloister where the papal Vestry was situated. Although it ceased to be used for ceremonies after the reign of Innocent VI, this chapel seems never to have been deconsecrated during the stay of the popes at Avignon.[42]

There were also smaller chapels in the new papal palace. One, which has since totally disappeared, was located near the apartments of the pope in the southeast corner of the palace and was in use after May 1337.[43] When the large Chapel of Saint John was undergoing construction, work on the Tour de Saint-Jean commenced. The roofing for this tower in the east wing was paid for in August of 1339.[44] Here we find two chapels. One is on the level of the consistory and also dedicated to Saint John; it measures 5.60 × 5.30 meters.[45] Directly above, adjacent to the Grand Tinel, is the chapel dedicated to Saint Martial; it measures 6 × 5.25 meters. In this upper chapel, the cardinals gathered to cast their votes in the papal election. By 28 December 1338 the altar stone for the lower chapel had already been procured; so it is probably safe to assume that both chapels were in use by the end of 1339.[46]

Near the hour of Vespers on 25 April 1342, Benedict XII died. He was laid to rest, as was his predecessor, in the cathedral of Avignon, Notre-Dame-des-Doms. Unfortunately for the Church, his far-reaching reforms of religious life were buried with him. Dispensations and favors were all too readily granted in order for his pronouncements to have any lasting effect. But, given the tenor of the age, the austere restrictions and complex laws were likely doomed from the outset. A rigid and complicated legal code could not remold a clergy accustomed to laxity.[47] Such seems to have been the case even with Benedict's own *capellani capelle*. As we shall see, his original conception of what a papal chapel should be was not able to long endure the weight of practicality. Happily for the history of culture, this frugal Cistercian left his successor coffers that were overflowing, a fortune to be spent.[48]

## Clement VI

On 7 May 1342, Cardinal Pierre Roger, archbishop of Rouen, was chosen to occupy the throne of Saint Peter. Pierre was born in Masmonteil, son of the Lord of Rosiers, a gentleman of small fortune. When he was only 10, in 1301, it was decided that he should become a Benedictine and be sent to the monastery at Chaise-Dieu. He came to the attention of the abbot who sent him to study at Paris in 1307. There, the future pope lived and worked for 16 years. Between 1321 and 1324 he became prior of Saint-Pantéléon, Savigny, and Saint-Baudil, though it is likely that he never did make his residence at any of these places. Sometime during his studies at Paris he came to be known at the French royal court. In fact, Pierre received a master's in theology through the intervention of King Charles IV in 1323 and taught at the University of Paris almost full time from this date.[49] On 23 June 1326, he was appointed abbot of Fécamp, a monastery enfieffed to Edward III of England in the diocese of Rouen, and was to spend the next 12 years in nominal pastoral care to several dioceses in the north of France. He was first named bishop of Arras on 3 December 1328 and, two years later, was translated to the archiepiscopal see of Sens. Then, one year after that, he was appointed archbishop of Rouen. Pierre's residence in these dioceses, however, seems doubtful in light of his extensive activity in the court of Philip VI.[50] In fact, his presence at Arras and Sens is documented only occasionally.

In 1328, Pierre Roger represented the king of France in bearing the citation of feudal homage to Edward III of England. There are several references to him acting in a similar capacity in 1331, when, as plenipotentiary of the accounts for Philip, he again took part in negotiations with the English monarch. In 1334 Pierre was an agent for the French king in his dealings with England, and he was also sent on a mission to interrogate partisans of Robert of Artois. After heading delegations to Avignon in 1332 and 1333 where he was very much concerned with the possibility of recapturing the Holy Land, he

Fig. 3.   Some cities relevant to the lives of the popes.

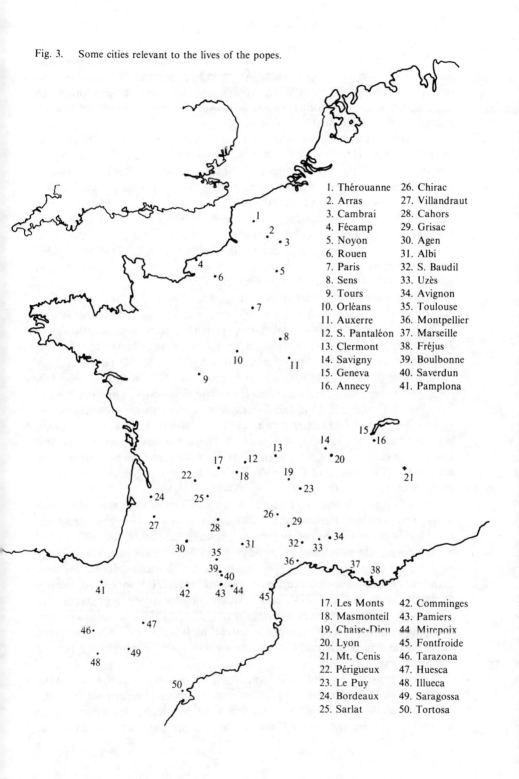

1. Thérouanne
2. Arras
3. Cambrai
4. Fécamp
5. Noyon
6. Rouen
7. Paris
8. Sens
9. Tours
10. Orléans
11. Auxerre
12. S. Pantaléon
13. Clermont
14. Savigny
15. Geneva
16. Annecy

26. Chirac
27. Villandraut
28. Cahors
29. Grisac
30. Agen
31. Albi
32. S. Baudil
33. Uzès
34. Avignon
35. Toulouse
36. Montpellier
37. Marseille
38. Fréjus
39. Boulbonne
40. Saverdun
41. Pamplona

17. Les Monts
18. Masmonteil
19. Chaise-Dieu
20. Lyon
21. Mt. Cenis
22. Périgueux
23. Le Puy
24. Bordeaux
25. Sarlat

42. Comminges
43. Pamiers
44. Mirepoix
45. Fontfroide
46. Tarazona
47. Huesca
48. Illueca
49. Saragossa
50. Tortosa

returned to Paris and there, on 1 October 1333, preached the crusade to king and court. The archbishop revisited Avignon as chancellor of France in 1334 after the death of Pope John XXII.[51] Three years later, he not only represented the king at Arras in a conference at which it is believed Edward III himself participated, but was sent yet again to Avignon.

Pierre Roger received the red hat as cardinal priest of SS. Neraeus et Achilleus on 18 December 1338, but his curial activities did not prohibit the continuation of a close association with the house of Valois. Royal accounts, in fact, indicate that the cardinal was paid 1000 *livres tournois* per year for his service to the king. After news of the death of Benedict XII reached Paris, it is said that Philip sent his heir apparent, John duke of Normandy, to Avignon, in the company of the dukes of Bourbon and Burgundy, in order to inform the Sacred College of his preference: Cardinal Pierre Roger. But before this delegation arrived, the conclave decided on the royal councellor, and he was crowned on 19 May 1342 as Pope Clement VI.[52]

Our picture of this new pope stands in marked constrast to that of his predecessor, for Clement was born to the manor. He was an aristocrat who begrudged himself none of the splendor to which he had become accustomed at Paris, and, now as Supreme Pontiff, of which he was deserving. After his coronation, two of the first payments he made were to musicians. On 26 May 1342, Jaquetus de Saychone, *ioculator* of the duke of Normandy, received 80 florins *pro se et aliis 11 joculatoribus cum diversis ministris*. On the following day, Petrus Guihoti de Morissono, *ioculator* of Peter duke of Bourbon, was given 5 florins, and G. Dassier, *minister sive ioculator* of the duke of Burgundy, was paid 15 florins, *pro se et aliis 2 sociis*.[53] This is the first payment of its kind known to have been made by a pope of Avignon, and, as a gift to the musicians attached to the legation of Philip VI, it bespeaks Clement's continuing link to the French royal court.[54]

The new pope's ongoing association with the city of Paris was manifested in other ways as well. Persons whom Clement came to know either while he was a student and teacher at the university or while he worked for the kings of France reaped the benefits of his good fortune. One of these men was Philippe de Vitry. We know that Philippe studied at the Sorbonne during the first decades of the fourteenth century as did Pope Clement. He worked as a *notaire* during the reign of Charles IV, held a royal office according to the records of 1328 and 1329, and continued as a *notaire* in 1337 and 1338. During this period, Philippe must have come into contact with the future pope on innumerable occasions and probably had a close relationship with Clement by the time of the coronation.[55]

As early as 18 July 1343, the composer and theorist was cited as one of the *capellani commensales pape*.[56] These commensal chaplains, distinct from the *capellani capelle* established by Benedict XII, were higher level ecclesiastics who acted as emissaries for the Curia. Philippe seems to have retained this title throughout the pontificate of his friend. Held in such high esteem by the bishop of Rome, the musician was raised to the see of Meaux early in 1351.[57] During these last 11 years, Philippe had not only been associated with the court of Avignon, but also had continued in service to the French monarchs as *maître des requêtes, maître de l'hôtel,* and *concillarius.* In addition, there was a close friendship between Cardinal Gui de Boulogne and the royal advisor, and there is even some evidence indicating that Philippe served as chaplain to the cardinal.[58]

It is not at all surprising, but, in fact, almost expected, that Philippe de Vitry would have written a motet honoring the accession of Pierre Roger to the throne of Saint Peter. The work, entitled *Petre Clemens/Lugentium,* must have been completed not long after the conclave of 1342. The text refers to the pope by name several times, playing on the coincidence of Cardinal "Pierre" taking the place of Saint "Peter" in changing his name to "Clement." The triplum begins with the words "Peter, you are clement [Clement], in fact as well as in name...." The text continues with an allusion to the event reported in John 1:42, where Jesus changes the name of his disciple Simon, to *Cephas*—the Aramaic word for rock—or, in Latin, *Petrus.* The words of the tenor more specifically identify this Pope Clement by stating that "Clement the sixth, through the morning ray of the Holy Spirit, divinely, is the wonder of the world ... The Supreme Peter [or Peter I], you desired not to be Peter II because you act rightly. You are clement, and so you said, 'Clement'...." The pope's magnificent exhortations to the French court calling for the recapture of the Holy Land are recalled in the motet, most vividly in the words, "Let sorrowful Armenia be consoled; and let proud Ishmael surrender [The Moslems consider themselves the descendants of Abraham through his son, Ishmael]; and let the Syrian desert flower; and let suppressed Israel rise once more." The work stands as a fitting monument to this teacher, ambassador, and Maecenas.[59]

Another person whom the Holy Father might have come to know well was Jehan des Murs. This music theorist and astronomer was a student in Paris in 1318 and spent much of his time there during the course of the next seven years. Documents reveal that he was residing at the Sorbonne in 1323 and 1324 and again in 1336 and 1337. The paths of Jehan and the future pontiff surely crossed, if not during the 1330s, then during the time when Pierre was a student, 1303-1323. In any event, the reputation of each man must have been well known to the other. Several decades later, on 25 September 1344, Jehan was called upon by Clement to help reform the calendar. The journey, financed by the pope, brought the astronomer to Avignon in 1345. Several years later, Jehan advised the pontiff on certain political matters based on astrological phenomena and was one of three men of science who drew up a treatise explaining the plague of 1348 by the conjunction of Saturn, Jupiter, and Mars that occurred in 1341.[60] Another of these savants in whom Clement was interested and one who also contributed to this explanation of the plague was

Levi ben Gershon. Levi, or Léon de Bagnols or Leo Hebraeus as he is also known, was the author of the work entitled *Guerres du Seigneur,* the astronomical part of which was translated into Latin at the request of the pope. This Jewish mathematician and philosopher, who spent nearly all his life near Avignon, was known to Philippe de Vitry. In 1343, at the request of the musician, he wrote *De numeris harmonicis,* a treatise that solved some problems of *ars nova* mensuration.[61]

The pontificate of Clement VI was a time of great patronage of the arts for pope and Curia alike. Cardinals maintained musicians, poets, and thinkers in their own households as did the secular princes. As already mentioned, Philippe de Vitry was, at one time, in the retinue of Cardinal Gui de Boulogne, and it was probably through his acquaintance with this prelate that he came to know the foremost man of letters of the time, Francesco Petrarca. Petrarch's family lived in the city of Carpentras beginning in 1313, while his father worked at nearby Avignon. He studied law at Montpellier and Bologna and later was in the service of Cardinal Giacomo Colonna at Avignon.[62] Here, in the church of the religious of Sainte-Claire, on 6 April 1327 he first saw his beloved Laura. During his lifetime he corresponded with Philippe de Vitry and another noted musician of the day, Louis Sanctus de Beringhen.

Louis, a singer in the chapel of Cardinal Giovanni Colonna, was, according to Petrarch, among the greatest musicians of that era. Though his knowledge of the musical arts suggested he be nicknamed Aristoxenus, Petrarch decided instead to call him "Socrates." To this "Socrates" then, Petrarch dedicated his first collection of letters. Although there is a short treatise extant on *musica sonora* authored by Louis, in 21 letters to him by the poet, music is not once discussed in any detail. Whatever his gifts may have been, he serves as yet another example of the many talented and educated men who were employed in or around the Roman Curia at Avignon.[63]

Further testimony concerning the position of the cardinals as patrons of the arts and as princes not reluctant to spend their wealth is found in an anonymous account of a grand reception and feast given for Pope Clement VI on 1 May 1343.[64] After spending more than a week visiting with various cardinals and having passed some time at his country palace at Pont-de-Sorgues, the pontiff traveled south to Montfavet, to the home of Cardinal Pedro Gomez. Here the cardinals and a great number of clerics awaited him. When the pope's arrival was announced, Cardinal Annibale Ceccano vested himself and, with 20 clerics, went in procession to greet the pope at the garden gate. With 16 cardinals joining the cortege, the papal entourage was escorted to the chapel. After pausing here to pray, the Holy Father retired to the apartments prepared for him. A brief interval elapsed, Clement entered the dining hall, and the feast commenced.

The meal comprised nine services of three plates each plus a dessert. After the third service, squires presented a castle constructed entirely of wild game as an intermezzo. This spectacle was accompanied by knights playing diverse instruments which, in combination with the sound of rejoicing, could be heard as far as Avignon, at least in the opinion of the witness.[65] After the fifth service, a fountain was brought out, from which flowed five varieties of wine. The structure was surrounded by a great variety of birds and fowl. Like the first intermezzo, this, too, was accompanied by the sound of men and instruments.[66] After the ninth service, came the sweetest tones from singing clerics, though the singers themselves were not seen. The account goes on to claim that all types of voices were heard, enumerating them as "deep, less deep, middle, small, and boys'" voices. The melody was said to have been so sweet that all ceased talking.[67]

How the chronicler knew that these unseen singers were in fact clerics could only be explained by the sound of what was sung. The text might have been in Latin, or perhaps the melody was a sacred one, or the music was in a style that was associated with clerics. It seems that this was quite unlike the music presented earlier for two reasons: first, there were no musical instruments involved in the music making; and second, the audience stopped their conversation, a point that the author clearly makes. The piece might have been polyphonic; it could have been a motet sung to honor Clement.[68] But if it were, it was most certainly not in five voice parts. It is likely, however, that men's falsetto voices and/or choirboys were part of this ensemble, certainly indicating that a polyphonic performance was highly likely. The fact that the clerics were not seen suggests that, although the music they performed was welcome at this feast, the sight of clerics at a purely secular celebration was not to be tolerated.

Besides the musical displays, other outlandish spectacles were performed for the Holy Father. At several times during the course of the meal, the hosts lavished their honored guest with expensive gifts. Such banquets may not have been frequent occurrences for Clement nor for any other Sovereign Pontiff, but they probably took place often enough to remind the popes that they were monarchs ruling a vast empire, and that the cardinals were their princes.

Clement's apparent willingness to be treated like a powerful member of the nobility may have contributed to his dissatisfaction with the papal palace. The building and grounds were likely spacious enough for the pope's immediate needs, but Clement's personal tastes, cultivated in the Ile-de-France, were soon revealed to be much more extravagant than those of his Cistercian predecessor. New construction begun on the palace at Avignon did not necessarily herald the replacement of existing chapels and halls, but instead brought an expansion of the territory claimed by the palace and an increase in the number of chambers. Just as the Benedictine palace included living quarters, halls for assembly, and the like, so did the Clementine. It is precisely those structures with which we concerned ourselves above to which we now turn our attention, namely, the papal chapels.

Soon after his coronation, the new pontiff ordered work to begin near the southeast corner of the quadrilateral that marked off the courtyard of Pope Benedict. Here, after 21 months' work, the Tour de la Garderobe received its roof in June 1344. Its uppermost story provided a small private chapel near the papal apartments dedicated to Saint Michael. In 1345 construction was begun on a new audience (the Great Audience) further yet to the south, over which another, much larger chapel was planned.[69] Though construction early on had proceeded rapidly, from mid-1348 until nearly the end of Clement's pontificate, an outbreak of the plague and its inevitable consequences drastically slowed new building. Consequently, this large chapel was not completed until 21 October 1351.[70]

Plate 2.    Addition of Pope Clement VI to the Palace of the Popes at Avignon, west façade.

To provide access to the new chapel from the Great Audience, a modern staircase, wide and well lit, was built. An innovation of the principal architect of the palace, Jean de Louvres, it incorporates several landings, the last of which is the parvis or loggia. Standing on the loggia, one overlooks the courtyard of the new Clementine palace by means of the Indulgence Window, so called because on certain feast days, the indulgences were pronounced from here to the faithful assembled below.[71] The Great Staircase was still under construction when the chapel was dedicated by Clement, All Saints' Day, 1352.[72]

Originally called the *capella nova* and dedicated to Saint Peter, it is today often referred to as the Clementine chapel. The structure measures 52 meters long and 15 meters wide, as wide as the principal nave of Amiens cathedral. The height, however, is a little less than half that of Amiens, i.e., 19½ meters. It consists of a singular rectangular nave with seven vaulted bays. The easternmost, or seventh bay, is somewhat narrower than the others and contains the doorway leading to the North Sacristy. This was the entrance used by the pope when he proceeded from his apartments to the chapel of Saint Peter. From the south wall of the sixth bay one passes through a portal that opens to the Revestiary in the Tour de Saint-Laurent. Here is where the prelate who celebrated in the adjacent chapel changed his vestments during the course of the ceremony. The tower was completed by January 1358.[73]

The seven-bayed chapel was divided by a low *cancellus* into choir and nave. Though no trace of the barrier's original position remains, during the seventeenth and eighteenth centuries there was a tall baroque screen situated between the fourth and fifth bays.[74] Historians of the Palace of the Popes have generally taken this to have been the position of the fourteenth-century *cancellus* as well, but they have admitted that such conclusions are provisionary.[75]

The choir itself was raised two steps above the level of the rest of the chapel. The area was covered by rush mats that were in turn covered with rugs.[76] Although the walls of the Chapel of Saint Peter were unpainted, the structure was not the bare stone cavern that stands there today. On the great feasts and celebrations it was decorated in a most sumptuous manner. The walls of the choir and possibly those of the entire chapel were covered with wall hangings. Eight great tapestries were purchased by Clement VI for his chamber and chapel in 1342.[77] The accounts of his successor reveal the purchase of two large tapestries, one depicting Saints Martha and Mary Magdalen and the other representing Saint Catherine, for use in the *capella nova*.[78] In 1355 there was a payment made to affix 52 *canne* (*canna* = approximately 1.975 meters) of board on to the walls of the chapel and from these, tapestries were to be hung. Fifty-two *canne* (approximately 102.7 meters) is about twice the length of the chapel (104 meters), therefore, the board might have run the length of both sides of the chapel. If this were the case, it would require that hangings would have been suspended below the windows on the south wall, a relatively small amount of surface area. Thus it is possible that the board and tapestries may have been set in two levels along each bay on the northern wall only. But whatever the situation, there seems to have been ample tapestry available to cover most of the bare stone walls.[79]

The richly decorated altar stood in the easternmost bay. Its stone, measuring approximately two by four meters, was consecrated on 19 October 1355.[80] The altar was surmounted by a tabernacle and probably by a crucifix and several statues. The inventory made in February 1353 makes mention of an altarcloth described as decorated with images and with the coat of arms of Clement VI. There was yet another altarcloth, one given to him in 1343 and embroidered by the queen of Naples herself.[81]

Although the vigorous campaign of papal building reached a peak with the pontificate of Clement VI, the bulk of the work was only completed after his death. According to his own words, he "lived as a sinner among sinners." According to historians, he was excessive, a blatant nepotist, but highly cultured, a great Maecenas. He left to posterity a "Mass in Time of Plague," a legacy of favoritism, and some of the greatest monuments of mid-fourteenth-century art to be found.[82]

## Innocent VI

Twelve days after the death of Clement, on 18 December 1352, at about the hour of Terce, the Sacred College named his successor: Cardinal Etienne Aubert.[83] Old and sickly at the time of his election, this native of the town of Les Monts stood in stark contrast to his predecessor. Much of his early career was spent teaching law at the University of Toulouse, and occasionally carrying out tasks for the king of France. On 23 January 1338 he became bishop of Noyon then, in 1340, was translated to the see of Clermont. Almost two years later he received the red hat of a cardinal, first with the title cardinal priest of SS. Johannes et Paulus then, in 1352, cardinal bishop of Ostia. Upon his succession to the throne of Saint Peter, he became Pope Innocent VI.[84]

Innocent's pontificate was a sad one. Like Benedict XII, this pope was a determined reformer of the religious orders. But unlike the great Cistercian abbot, Innocent did not offer himself as an example of religious discipline nor did he reform those institutions that touched his own life.[85] He was as harsh with offenders as Clement had been lenient. Left with little money in the papal treasury, Innocent had difficulty keeping what remained. He had neither the fortune at his disposal nor the vision to serve as a focus for the fine arts.

The principal cause of Innocent's penury was a costly war being waged in Italy. It so depleted papal funds that by 1357 the pontiff was complaining of poverty.[86] Works of art were sold rather than commissioned. In order to cut expenditures, the size of the papal household was reduced. One of the branches to be pruned back by these austerity measures was the pope's own *capella.* Although there had been between nine and twelve *capellani capelle* attached to the chapel of Clement VI, Innocent saw fit to retain only from eight to ten chaplains at any one time.[87] The city of Avignon was slowly recovering from the ravages of the plague of 1348 but had not yet reached the level of prosperity it had known previously. The little wealth that both the Curia and city possessed was then stripped away by marauding hoodlums, mobs of mercenaries disbanded after the English and French truce of 1357.[88] The populace from the surrounding countryside sought refuge within the partially completed walls of the overcrowded city. Through negotiations and the payment of 14,500 gold florins as tribute, the roaming gangs were sent away in late March 1361.

Though much damage had already been done, the worst was yet to come. Once again the dreaded plague struck the city on the Rhône. None went by untouched. No class was spared. Between 25 March and 25 July 1361, 17,000 people were reported to have died. This number includes 97 members of the curial staff, 9 cardinals, and at least 5 of the *capellani capelle*.[89]

It was, alas, not the best of environments in which to cultivate art and music. However, Innocent managed to have several monuments erected, most in Villeneuve. There in 1356, he founded a Carthusian monastery whose cloister and double-apsed church were consecrated two years later. In a side chapel of that very church, the pontiff was laid to rest after his death, 12 September 1362.[90]

## Urban V

When the college of cardinals met to decide a successor on 22 September, they had not foreseen that they would so quickly reach a consensus by naming Cardinal Hugues Roger to succeed Innocent. Hugues, brother of the late Pope Clement VI, chose not to accept the decision of his colleagues. In his stead, the conclave soon unanimously elected the abbot of the Benedictine monastery of Saint-Victor of Marseille, Guillaume Grimoard, to steer the bark of Saint Peter.

Guillaume was born to the lord of Grisac in 1310. His early studies were accomplished at Montpellier and Toulouse. He later attended lectures in these two towns and also at Avignon and Paris. He received the tonsure in 1322 and was on the rolls of the Benedictine priory of Cirac for much of his early life. After the doctorate of canon law was conferred upon him in 1342, he taught in various universities. Vicar general to Bishop Pierre d'Aigrefeuille at Clermont and Uzès, Guillaume was named abbot of Saint-Germain of Auxerre on 13 February 1352. On 2 August 1361, he was translated to Saint-Victor. Unlike his recent predecessors, the pope-elect was familiar with Italy, having been sent there on legations in 1352, 1354, 1360, and 1362. At the moment he was named Supreme Pontiff, the abbot was serving as nuncio in the kingdom of Naples. After arriving safely at Avignon, he was crowned Pope Urban V on 6 November 1362.[91]

History records Urban as a sensitive, humble, and pious monk, wise and meticulous. Guillaume Mollat, the renowned Avignon scholar, went so far as to claim that Urban had a "horror of luxury and ostentation."[92] In fact, he seemed to have a distaste for excess. For example, he kept only eight *capellani capelle* in service.[93] However, he managed to reach into the Church's coffers frequently in his support of teaching institutions, building projects, and music.

Soon after his election, Urban mandated that the lord of Montferrand distribute 100 florins to the royal *ioculatores* who accompanied the king of France on his most recent visit. Less than three weeks later, the pontiff gave a special gift of 30 florins to the *ioculatores* of the count of Savoy.[94] The pope was obviously neither averse to receive the homage of princes through the entertainments of their musicians, nor remiss in acknowledging them. Urban was quite attentive to his physical comforts as well. Behind the papal palace, the orchard and gardens were enlarged. Here the pope built a recreational gallery, replete with sumptuously decorated rooms and a tower. The place was nicknamed "Roma."[95] It is possible that Urban reserved this cloister-like area for private outdoor entertainment; however, both the design and nature of "Roma" lie in obscurity since virtually nothing of the structure remains.[96]

The Holy Father was a devoted patron of learning and became involved with numerous teaching institutions. He himself provided support for as many as 1,400 students. He sent seven boys and a music teacher to the *studium* at Toulouse especially to sing High Mass but also to study non-musical subjects;[97] on 25 April 1366, payment was made to a *magister* (teacher) and five *cantores* for expenses *apud Tholosam pro studendo.*[98] Another notice concerning musical education refers to a payment of 20 florins, 18 solidi to Petrus de Veza, *magister cantus* at the school of Saint-Germain de Calberta in the diocese of Mende. The sum covered his support for four months in providing *instructionem et informationem artis cantus* to the students that the pope maintained there.[99]

Besides endowing universities and *studia,* Urban was especially fond of providing support for monastic building. Perhaps his greatest achievement was the restoration of the abbey of Saint-Victor at Marseille. The pope, former abbot of the monastery, arrived at the port city in October 1365 to consecrate the completed work personally. It was a great day for the townsfolk. All work was forbidden, and all the citizens were to participate in welcoming the pontiff. The religious and secular officials gathered at the church of Saint-Lazare to await the illustrious donor. While the pope was making his way through the streets, he came to the Place d'Aren where the road skirted the sea. Here the head of the church witnessed a large flotilla of barges and galleys covered with branches and banners and on which men with musical instruments were positioned, playing for their visitor. Twice more Urban was saluted on his way: once, at the convent of the Trinity, the religious of Sainte-Claire led by their abbess sang for the pontiff; and a second time, when the abbess of Saint-Sauveur and her nuns stopped Urban and also honored him with their song. Each time he blessed them, and they returned to their convent.[100]

Although there is no record of Pope Urban bestowing anything more than his blessing to show gratitude for these musical salutes, according to the cameral accounts, he was not sparing with gifts more useful in this material world. In June 1365, for example, when the Holy Roman Emperor arrived at

Avignon, the pope, through Bishop Theodoric of Worms, gave 100 cameral florins to the *ioculatoribus domini imperatoris* with the stipulation that such money was to aid them in marrying off their children.[101] Early in 1367, Urban ordered that four francs be given to *quibusdam tubicinariis, qui venerunt obviam domini pape* at Nîmes, through which city the pontiff passed on his way to Montpellier.[102] Surprising the pope with musical salutes must have been a successful method of attracting the attention, if not the charity, of this much-traveled pontiff.

The most significant act of Urban's pontificate was the return, albeit temporary, of the bishop of Rome once again to the Italian peninsula. On 30 April 1367, the entourage departed from Avignon. They spent two nights at Pont-de-Sorgues and a few days at Noves, Orgon, Aix, and Marseille. On 19 May, the fleet set sail, docking at several ports along the way. By 23 May they had reached Genoa, from where they passed on to Porto Venere, Salsadas, Pisa, Piombo, until they disembarked at Corneto on 3 June. After making his way by land first to Toscanella then to Viterbo, the Sovereign Pontiff entered Rome triumphantly on 16 October 1367, the first that the Eternal City had seen of its bishop in more than three decades. On 20 December of that year, an entry in the accounts recorded a payment of 60 florins to *certis ioculatoribus* who came to Rome with Pope Urban.[103]

There were other types of musicians listed in the payment records as well. These were the watchmen or *gaychatores*. When Urban had lived in Avignon, he retained two watchmen for the tower of the Palace of the Popes as early as August 1364.[104] On 30 June 1367, Antonius de Sancto Marco and Silverinus de Alamania were paid their five florins per month each, for two month's service as watchmen.[105] At Viterbo, in late July, Johannes Alberto alias de Carpentorato was paid for his service there. The document specifies that he was one of the two watchmen who served in Avignon.[106] On 22 November, Johannes, called *olim trompette seu gaychator* of the palace, was paid for expenses incurred in going from Viterbo to Rome with the pope and for a *pennoncellus* that was attached to said trumpet.[107] Antonius and Silverinus continued to serve Urban through March 1368, when they were given their wages for standing guard *in campanili ecclesie Sancti Petri Rome*.[108]

While at Rome, the pope participated in numerous celebrations at Saint Peter's Basilica on the Vatican Hill where, unlike earlier popes, he preferred to reside. He also celebrated at the Church of the Lateran. Here in March 1368 he exhibited the heads, that is to say, the reliquaries containing the heads of Saints Peter and Paul. Following the tradition, on Laetare Sunday he gave the Golden Rose to a noble, this time to Queen Joanna of Naples. Since the king of Cyprus was also present at court, some of the cardinals murmured that such an honor should sooner have been bestowed on a king than a queen. Urban was reported to have responded by saying never before had an abbot of Saint-Victor been pope. Like his Roman predecessors, Urban preferred to spend his summers outside of Rome and, indeed, he passed much of the summer of 1368 in the city of Montefiascone.[109]

In November 1368, the Holy Roman Emperor, Charles IV, was in Rome where the empress was crowned.[110] The following year, the emperor of Constantinople went to visit the pontiff. After much difficult negotiation, Pope Urban succeeded in convincing Emperor John V Paleologus to renounce Orthodoxy and, in effect, unify the Eastern and Western Churches. On 21 October 1369, John made his declaration public by performing an act of homage to Urban. At Saint Peter's, John kissed the feet, hands, then the mouth of the Holy Father, after which Urban rose, took the emperor by the hand and intoned the *Te Deum*. This was followed by a solemn pontifical Mass that the pope himself celebrated and by a great feast that was held afterwards which the cardinals attended.[111]

But suffering the consequences of existing in the real world, the union of East and West was not long to survive. Nor was the sojourn at Rome for this Sovereign Pontiff. On 5 September 1370, the ships sent by the kings of France and Aragon, the queen of Naples, and the people of Avignon and Provence set sail westward and, 11 days later, landed at Marseille. On 27 September, pope and Curia entered Avignon with great ceremony. Not long after his return, Urban realized that his life was quickly drawing to an end. Thereupon he took up residence at the home of his brother, the cardinal of Albano and bishop of Avignon, Anglic Grimoard. Here in the episcopal palace, the Petit Palais, on 19 December 1379, Urban died.[112]

## Gregory XI

The Sacred College of cardinals met and, for a third time within 30 years, elected a member of the most prestigious of church families to the see of Rome. On 5 January 1371, Pierre Roger de Beaufort was chosen to be pope. During his reign, he was known as Gregory XI. The new pontiff was living testimony to the nepotistic abuses of his uncle Pierre (Clement VI). At age 11, young Pierre already possessed canonicates at the cathedrals of Rodez and Paris. In 1348, at 19 years of age, he was named cardinal deacon of S. Maria Nuova by Clement VI, one of his father's two younger brothers. His other paternal uncle, Hugues, had refused the tiara when it was offered him in 1362. His aunt Delphine was the mother of Cardinal Nicolas de Besse; and his cousins Cardinals Guillaume and Pierre de la Jugie were the sons of the youngest of the five Roger siblings, Guillemette.[113]

One of the first payments under Gregory was made on 22 January 1371 when he commanded that the *ioculatores* of the dukes of Anjou and Burgundy be paid 60 florins *pro dono speciali*.[114] A little over a month later, Johannes Wrioff, Fournerius, and Pontius de Francafort de Alamannia, *ioculatores* of the viscount of Turenne ( Gregory's nephew) were given a gift of 25 florins, 20 solidi from the papal treasury.[115] Immediately after the papal coronation, the cameral accounts often contain records of gifts to *ioculatores* of secular princes. This was probably the most likely time for feasting and celebration, before the pope settled down to take full command of the affairs of the Church. It was a time when the city of Avignon was filled with all manner of secular potentates, and these men of rank were accompanied by their personal bands of *ioculatores*. However, following the dictum not to mingle the sacred and the secular, the bishops of Rome themselves never supported any minstrels on a regular basis but rather paid them by means of a *donum speciale* on particular occasions.

One type of secular musician does seem at first to be above this rule, namely, the watchman or trumpeter. At least throughout the spring of 1372, Gregory retained two *gaychiatores* who served Urban near the end of his life.[116] Moreover, in September of that year, the pope supplied Raymond viscount of Turenne for his wars against the Lombards. The cameral accounts specify that his soldiers were to be accompanied by *1 trompeta et 2 ioculatores* at papal expense. We do not know if such civil and military musicians were ever used by the pontiffs for any purpose other than the one for which they were originally intended. However, in all the papal accounts, the distinction drawn between *ioculatores* and trumpeters places the latter in a special category, not quite as mean as their musician brethren.[117]

Another class of musician that should receive particular attention here is the choirboy. There is no indication that boys' voices were ever heard in the papal chapel during the fourteenth century. Neither is there any suggestion at this time that boy clerics were retained by the pontiffs for music making. However, if we are to believe the account of the great feast for Pope Clement VI cited above, boys' voices were heard among those of the clerics who sang for the Holy Father. Yet here it is not a question of papal singers but of singers in the employ of the cardinals. The evidence, therefore, suggests that cardinals may have had choirboys in their households. Notices from the pontificate of Pope Gregory bear this out. On 12 February 1371, Petrus Terrini and Johannes Batalha, *olim pueris sive cantoribus capelle pape dum erat cardinalis*, were paid for expenses in going to the *studium* at Montpellier. These two clerics were sustained at least until 1373, at which time Johannes was sent to study at the papal *studium* in Bologna. Martinus de Prato, a singer in the papal chapel, was often responsible for the financial arrangements regarding these two boys.[118]

If Pope Gregory maintained choirboys in his chapel when he was cardinal, it would not be foolish to suppose that at least some of the other churchly princes did as well. If the tacit rule excluding boy singers from the private chapel applied neither to members of the Sacred College nor, presumably, to bishops who were residing in Avignon, what then could we say about the employment of *ioculatores* at these courts? Would it not have been easier for these prelates to have acted as patrons of secular music and musicians that it was for the pope? Though it is tempting to answer such questions in the affirmative, the fact is that our knowledge of papal practices during the fourteenth century is scant, and, with virtually no documentation of the expenses of lesser prelates available, our hope of ever knowing anything substantial about the musical life surrounding the princes of the Church is slim.

Gregory XI, unlike his most illustrious uncle, found himself in a distressing financial situation, and he soon took action to curtail expenses. On 24 October 1372, the pope mandated that the office of *clericus capelle* be terminated.[119] The two clerics who held this post were not chaplains of the pope, but assistants in the liturgy who helped in the decoration of the chapel and in the execution of the service. Similary, the *capella commensalis,* another group traditionally part of the papal entourage, was no longer maintained.[120] These chaplains, who possessed a status greater than that of the *capellani capelle,* served as ambassadors and associates of the pope. Philippe de Vitry, we may recall, was a commensal chaplain of Clement VI. Though the *capellani commensales* were to dine with the pontiff on occasion and were expected to attend the papal liturgical service, they were evidently deemed expendable by Gregory. On the other hand, the singers of the pope, the *capellani capelle,* were kept at a strength of from 10 to 13 throughout Gregory's pontificate, a number that had not been attained since the reign of his uncle.[121] The singing chapel was considered so necessary to the execution of papal liturgy that, in spite of the financial hardships, it was well maintained.

As to the commensal chaplains, the liturgical duties they performed remain somewhat obscure. It seems as if at least part of their liturgical tasks involved saying Mass for the pope in his small private chapels throughout the palace. When the *commensales* were released, Gregory engaged individual clerics to celebrate in place of these chaplains. From May 1373 until September 1376, these priests were paid for their service *in capella secreta pape.* One of them, Petrus Bombarelli, said Mass each day in the Great Audience (beneath the Chapel of Saint Peter) for the *auditores palacii.*[122]

As a great patron of music, it is not surprising that Gregory should have had at least one motet addressed to him. This anonymous composition, preserved in the Chantilly manuscript and entitled *Pictagore per dogmata/O terra sancta, suplica/Rosa vernans caritatis,* calls for the return of the Vicar of Christ to Rome. The text has been carefully dissected and scrutinized by Ursula Günther, and only a few points need to be elucidated here.[123] The triplum alludes to the seven planets, though mentioning only six of them by name (Jupiter, Sun=Phoebus, Venus=Citerea, Mercury=Celenius, Luna=Cinthius). As Günther has indicated, the unnamed planet, Saturn, was the greatest of the gods during the Golden Age, before his fall from power. He was driven to Latium (the region on the west coast of Italy, south of the Tiber) where he created a new Golden Age. Günther has identified Pope Gregory with Saturn, because the return to Italy, the landing in Latium, and the attendant blessings

Fig. 4. The parallel drawn between the ancestry of the Roman
people and that of Pope Gregory XI.

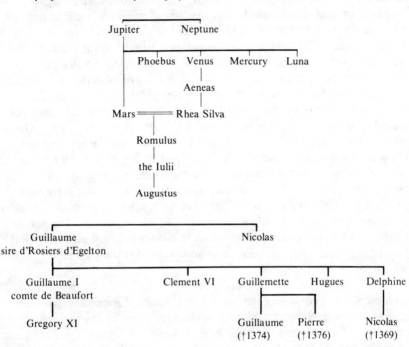

would effect the establishment of yet another Golden Age. Aeneas, the Trojan
hero, is brought into the text ostensibly as a parallel with Saturn, though it is
unclear from Günther's generally excellent analysis exactly how this
comparison works. To understand more precisely the references to Aeneas and
to the Golden Age, it is necessary to summarize briefly Virgil's *Aeneid*.

Aeneas was a noble Trojan, son of Venus and Anchises. During the fall of
Troy, he and his men escaped by boat, thereafter wandering throughout the
eastern Mediterranean, encountering innumerable obstacles and experiencing
countless adventures. On the island of Delos, the oracle of Apollo (Phoebus)
told him to go to the land of his forefathers, though the hero was, at this time,
unsure exactly where this would take him. After Aeneas spent some time in
north Africa where he tarried with Dido, Jupiter dispatched Mercury with a
message recalling the Trojan to his mission of destiny. Several times along the
way he was aided by the god Neptune. Eventually, he landed at the mouth of
the river Tiber. Here in the land of Latium, where once Saturn had established
his second Golden Age, Aeneas settled. Here he fathered the Latin race. After a
dozen or so generations, Rhea Silva was born to the hero's descendants and, by
the god Mars, she bore Romulus, the progenitor of the Roman people.[124]

In classical times, the Roman family of the Iulii claimed descendancy from Aeneas and Romulus.[125] Julius Caesar and his adopted son Augustus were members of that divine family and used these origins to their advantage.[126] Virgil was very much aware of the political ramifications of this myth for his emperor and, in fact, wrote the *Aeneid* as a tribute to the reincarnation of Aenean Troy, Augustan Rome.[127] But according to Virgil, this re-establishment of Trojan ideals was to bring about a new Golden Age, not under Saturn, but under Augustus Caesar. The key to this interpretation is found in the following lines of the epic: *Augustus Caesar, divi genus, aurea condet saecula qui rursus Latio regnata per arva Saturno quondam.*[128] Pope Gregory should not, therefore, be identified with Saturn, the father of Jupiter, as Günther asserts, but instead with the children of Aeneas, Romulus, and Augustus. The pontiff was to heed the admonitions of the gods, realize that he was dedicated to a loftier purpose, and set sail to Latium. Here he would establish the Golden Age—not of the deity Saturn, nor of the men Aeneas and Augustus, but the third—of God (*nam tertia fert secula auri*). The parallels in Christian belief are to the pontiff's goal in establishing not an age of God the Father, nor of the Son, but one thousand years of rule by the Holy Spirit, the Millenium.

The enumeration of the planets also relates specifically to this pope. The gods mentioned constitute part of a divine family. Jupiter, the *paterfamilias* and his brother Neptune, the god of the sea, stand in one generation. The children of Jupiter, namely Mars, the god of war, Phoebus, the god of light and of the Muses, and their brother Mercury, and sisters Venus and Luna stand in the next generation. Except for the goddess Luna, all these deities took some part in assisting Aeneas to reach his ultimate goal.[129]

There is a striking parallel to be drawn between the ancestry of the Roman people and that of Pope Gregory.[130] The pontiff's grandfather, Guillaume, sire de Rosiers d'Egleton, relates to Jupiter as the founder of the family, the *paterfamilias*. His great uncle Nicolas, archbishop of Rouen, finds his counterpart in Neptune. As this god assisted Aeneas in his journey, Nicolas must have aided Gregory early in his ecclesiastical career. Also Saint Nicholas, the uncle's patron saint, was the bishop of Myra who saved a ship from sinking and was widely venerated as the patron of mariners.[131] The parallel to Mars, god of war and father of Romulus, lies in Guillaume I, Comte de Beaufort, oldest male child of the sire de Rosiers and the father of Gregory. His uncle, Clement VI, the great patron of the arts, finds his counterpart in Phoebus, the god of light and protector of the Muses. The three remaining Roger siblings, two sisters and one brother, match the genders of the remaining gods. Venus, as co-ancestor of the race of Romans with Mars, might be Guillemette Roger, the mother of Cardinals Guillaume and Pierre de la Jugie, or Delphine, the mother of Cardinal Nicolas de Besse.

The text of the motetus calls for a recapture of the Holy Land which, while almost formulaic during the fourteenth century, is made more specific here by references to Gregory by name. The recapture of these eastern parts, terrain trodden by Christ and his apostles, is here a metaphor again for the "recapture" of Rome. In the line *Agar cognoscat aquilas,* "Agar" or Hagar, has several interpretations: first, as the mother of Ishmael, she is the ancestor of the Moslem people, and therefore she represents all of Islam; second, as Günther has indicated, she stands as the abandoned Jerusalem; and finally, as the Holy City, she is the personification of widowed Rome. The eagle (*aquila*) was the symbol of the Roman Empire, as exhibited in its standards. But after 1335, it became the emblem of the Holy Roman Empire as well.[132] In the line that follows, *Farfar delphini pinulas,* the author makes reference to the monastery of Farfa which lay in the diocese of Sabina, the Patrimony of Saint Peter, therefore in Latium. It was occupied by the Saracens in 861 and symbolizes both Islamic domination and the papal state itself.[133] The "boats of the dolphin" that Farfa is to recognize may be the ships of King Charles V of France who, as the dauphin (that is, dolphin), held as his heraldic symbol the principal element in the arms of Dauphiné before his coronation.[134] *Delphini pinulas* could also be a play on the name "Delphine," a popular name in the Roger family, that of Gregory's aunt and possibly also that of a grandparent.[135]

There are other uses of heraldic symbols in the motetus identified by Güther. At one point the author calls for peace between the "serpents" of the Visconti and the "roses" of the papacy. The tenor, *Rosa vernans caritatis,* also makes a reference to "the blooming rose of charity." Günther has made a strong case for the interpretation of the rose as a symbol for the papacy. As with all great works of art, however, this motet can bear interpretation on several levels. While applying generally to the papacy, and specifically to Gregory as the reigning pontiff, the rose also stands as the emblem of the Roger family. The coat of arms of both Clement VI and Gregory XI are identical and display six roses.[136] It is also worth noting that the middle French word for "a place covered with roses" is *rosiere* and that the *paterfamilias* of the Roger family was Guillaume, sire de Rosiers d'Egleton.[137]

The motet must have been written after the election of this pope (5 January 1371) but before 13 September 1376.[138] For on that day, Gregory set sail down the Rhône. His ships passed through the Durance, and he journeyed by land to Marseille. On 2 October, he once again took the water route and, not without considerable difficulty landed at Corneto on 6 December. The Curia remained here five weeks.[139] On the day after Christmas, according to the cameral accounts, a payment of 21 florins, 12 solidi was made to *omnibus trompetis* and to other *ioculatoribus existentibus in Corneto* as a gift given by the pope *pro festo Nativitatis Domini.*[140] On 13 January, because there was no bell at the palace in which Gregory was housed, 4 florins were paid to

Galeatrus, *trompator de Corneto,* and his associate doubtless for sounding the hours.[141] Four days later the Holy Father triumphantly entered the Eternal City to the sound of *trompatores* or *bucinatores* and *ioculatores.*[142] The city of Avignon had once again lost its pope.

## The City of Avignon

The *ville des papes* continued to survive, though certainly not in as much magnificence as when it was the seat of the bishop of Rome. Before the arrival of Pope Clement V in 1309, the town itself had been rather small in size. It was surrounded by a double wall dating from the previous century that enclosed within it from 5,000 to 6,000 inhabitants.[143] The population swelled the moment the pontiffs began to firmly establish Avignon as their principal residence and center of curial operations. As the great influx of people commenced, housing became ever more scarce and people lodged themselves in cabins along the narrow tortuous streets, along ramparts, and even in cemeteries. By the time the town completed its new walls during the pontificate of Urban V, it had attained a perimeter of four-and one-third kilometers and covered a surface of about six square miles. That made Avignon, after Paris, the second largest city in France.[144] Yet even with this increased area, the city was overcrowded. In fact, by the 1340s, the number of foreign inhabitants alone was reputed to have been 100,000.[145]

One entrepreneur who certainly benefited from the housing shortage and the concomitant increase in rents was Brocardus de Campanino de Pavia, *tactor instrumentorum musicorum.* Probably a player of stringed and/or keyboard instruments, Brocardus appears at least a dozen times in archival documents. The extant records give account of him as an innkeeper. He seems to have bought or owned as many as eight *hôtels* from 1336 until 1354 when he acquired an inn with a tavern. Though the documents yield no information concerning his musical activity, even after his death (ca.1363), his name continued to appear in the accounts as Brocardus, *tactor instrumentorum musicorum.*[146]

Petrarch called Avignon the most infected of cities. In fact, the twisting roads generally went unpaved except for the times of the great and solemn entries of emperors, kings, and princes. Crosses and wells dotted intersections, and the narrow streets were often partially or sometimes totally blocked by obstacles. Barricades, effectively fencing off access to public ways, were frequently erected by cardinals in order to connect the large sections of their palaces that were separated by intervening streets.[147]

The palaces of the members of the Sacred College, known as livreys, housed the princes of the Church and their retainers. To date, approximately 32 have been located within the city of Avignon, though few recognizable structures remain. The complex customarily consisted of two large buildings and a cloistered area. The cardinal's personal chapel was usually situated on an upper story. Here the prelate participated in a private liturgy with his chaplains, clerks, and other household members. Besides the livreys at Avignon proper, following the precedent of Cardinal Napoleone Orsini, several ecclesiastics maintained livreys outside the city walls. The most popular place for these suburban palaces was across the Rhône, on the territory of the king of France, at Villeneuve-lès-Avignon.[148]

Clement VI built his own suburban residence near that of Orsini, in the shadow of the Tour Philippe le Bel at Villeneuve. Beginning with this pontiff, and continuing up to the departure of Gregory XI, the popes of Avignon made a total of at least 34 stops here, some for as long as five months. There is frequent reference made in the accounts to painters and other artisans who participated in the construction and decoration of the palace. Besides the residence at Villeneuve, there were other papal retreats nearby, most notably at Châteauneuf and at Pont-de-Sorgues. Each had its chapel where the pontiff might participate with his chaplains in the liturgical services.[149]

In addition to those structures that were built at the instigation of pope and Curia, there were many other churches, chapels, and monasteries in the city of Avignon. Of greatest antiquity was the cathedral of Notre-Dame-des-Doms, where several times the ceremony of canonization took place during the pontificate of John XXII and where John and his successor, Benedict XII, were buried. Of the city's seven parish churches, three, Saint-Agricol, Saint-Pierre, and Saint-Didier, were raised to collegiate status by their respective donors, John XXII (1321), Cardinal Pierre des Prés (1358), and Cardinal Bertrand de Déaux (1385).[150] Many of Avignon's ecclesiastical edifices were rebuilt in the fourteenth century, testifying to the great influx of wealth that the city enjoyed during this period.[151]

Because of overcrowding, the cemeteries adjacent to the parish churches served as the only public spaces. At Place Saint-Pierre, for example, auctions were held and live animals sold over the shallow graves. On one occasion, pigs discovered and consumed the freshly-buried corpses of deceased parishoners. During the fifteenth century, cemeteries continued to serve as civic places. In 1470, the *Jeu-de-Sainte-Barbe* was performed in the cemetery of Saint-Symphorien.[152] Evidently, it was situations such as these, common throughout Europe, that caused the following general pronouncement from the pen of Clement V:

> Some clerics as well as lay persons, especially on the vigils of certain feasts while they ought to be present for prayer in churches, do not worship in them, but instead do licentious dances in the cemeteries of those churches, singing and performing many insolent songs [*cantilenas*]. From these violations of churches and cemeteries, shameful and varied offenses sometimes follow, and the ecclesiastical office has been very often disturbed, in offense of divine majesty and presenting scandal to the populace.[153]

Fig. 5.    The City of Avignon.
         (From George Braun, *Civitates orbis terrarum* (1572-1618;
         reprint ed., Cleveland: World Publishing Co., 1966), Vol.
         1, No. 13.).

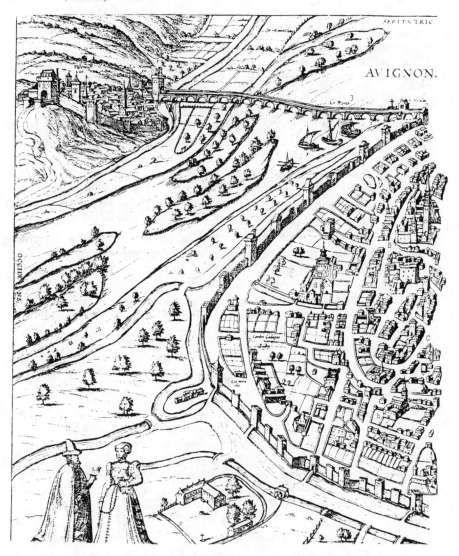

KEY

1. Palace of the Popes
2. Petit Palais (episcopal residence)
3. Pont Saint-Bénézet
4. Tour Philippe le Bel at Villeneuve
5. Studium (University)
6. Papal residence at Villeneuve
   (approximate position)

A. Notre-Dame-des-Doms (cathedral)
B. Saint-Agricol
C. Saint-Didier
D. Saint-Pierre
E. Saint-Etienne (formerly La Madeleine)
F. Saint-Symphorien
G. Notre-Dame-de-la-Principale
H. Saint-Geniès

a. Augustinians
b. Benedictines (Saint-Martial)
c. Carmelites
d. Dominicans
e. Cordeliers (Franciscans)
f. Sainte-Catherine (Cistercians)
g. Sainte-Claire (Poor Clares)

There were several large abbeys and convents in Avignon with their adjoining monastic churches. Royal and papal coronations occurred several times at the church of the Dominicans, the city's largest. It was in the church of the religious of Sainte-Claire that, on 6 April 1327, Petrarch reported to have first eyed Laura. Legend has it that she was buried at the church of Cordeliers (Franciscans).[154] More in the realm of fact, this place of worship was the first in Avignon to have possessed an organ. The records of the convent of the Friars Minor show that a payment of 7 solidi, 5 denarii was made in December 1359 for restoration of an organ. Again, in 1372, there is another account, quite detailed, citing further construction on the instrument.[155]

In 1372, the church and abbey of the Cordeliers served as the setting for perhaps one of the greatest spectacles the city of Avignon had ever known. Philippe de Mézières (†1405), chancellor of the king of Cyprus, was sent as a special ambassador to Pope Gregory XI. During his travels in the Orient, the king's representative had become a devotee of a popular Eastern observance, the feast of the Presentation of the Blessed Virgin (21 November), and in 1372 he successfully convinced the pontiff to adopt the custom in the West. That very year, in the church of the Cordeliers, the office was first celebrated. Although we cannot be certain, it is believed that a *representatio figurata* composed by Philippe was performed inside the church before Mass. Without doubt, it had been staged earlier in the city of Venice and was again performed in Avignon on 21 November 1385. Luckily, a detailed account of this most recent production has survived, written in the chancellor's own hand and providing remarkable details about the drama. It took place *in ecclesia Fratrum Heremitarum Beati Augustini Avenionensis,* the church of the Augustinian Friars.[156]

The cast of characters included two youths *pulsabunt instrumenta dulcia,* possibly organs. They were dressed *sicut Angeli* (white amices, tied by a stole at the neck, with a cross on the chest, red birettas with little fringes of multicolored silk, and wings), except the birettas were to be green, and they wore neither stoles nor wings. *Iuvenes* were called for because, beardless, they probably resembled angels at first glance. These musicians played during the processions and movements of the actors. All the characters were placed in an enclosed area outside the church, most likely, in the chapter house. Both the bishop who was to celebrate the Mass and all the participating clergy processed to where the players waited, accompanied by the sound of one cleric singing the *Salve regina.* When the little girl who had the role of Mary stepped out of the chapter house, the *Salve* ceased, and an angel interposed himself between the playing musicians. Then in a loud voice, he sang a *cantilena per modum rondelli...de Beatissima Virgine.* Philippe notes that the song was to be in the vernacular *ad excitandum populum ad devotionem.* It was performed responsorially between the angel who began it and the remaining eight angels.

Plate 3.     Vestiges of the church of the Cordeliers
at Avignon, the apse.

The youths continued to play until all the characters were in place on the stage
that was erected in the middle of the church. Each section of text was presented
by a solo voice. Immediately after the singing was completed, the instruments
filled the silences and accompanied the movement of the characters. At the end
of the play, two angels were to begin the *Veni creator spiritus* and the other
angels were to respond with the remainder of the verse. Again, the two intoned
the second verse, *Qui paraclitus,* and the others completed it in turn. The hymn
continued in this manner until it was executed in full. Philippe de Mézières was
careful to indicate that after the hymn was begun, *instrumenta amplius non
pulsabunt.* The detailed description of this performance indicates that the
musicians were in a special category of players, neither angel nor human. They
performed on their instruments to accompany the movement of the actors.
Only once did they play while there was singing, and the text of that song was in
the vernacular. When a piece from the established sacred repertoire was
intoned, that signaled the cessation of instrumental accompaniment.

Evidently, there must have still been an association between instruments of music and secular practice for such narrow limits to have been drawn here, and an *a capella* performance of all sacred Latin words was the rule.

There were several other grand spectacles that took place at Avignon. One merchant living in the city reported that in 1400 a dramatic presentation arranged by the duke of Anjou was performed. This, however, was eclipsed by a production of the *Representation of Troy* in March of the same year which boasted more banners and brattices than the ducal exhibition. Later, during the two days after Pentecost, a great passion play was produced in the city. It took place in the courtyard of the Dominicans. The merchant claimed that 200 men participated in this latest spectacle and that it was witnessed by 10,000 to 12,000 spectators. [157]

Avignon saw innumerable ambassadors of greater and lesser European powers come and go. Frequently, however, the potentates themselves arrived in the city to render homage to the vicar of Christ. During the pontificate of Urban V, John II of France, Peter of Cyprus, and Waldemar of Denmark were all simultaneously residing in the city on the Rhône. [158] And, as we have already indicated, they were often in the company of their minstrels and chaplains. This provided great opportunities for musical interchange between the members of the various households. The sacred and secular repertoire that has been called Avignonese or Avignon related might more accurately be seen as musical material simply transmitted and copied at Avignon.

Indeed, Avignon was at the narrow end of a funnel through which much of western culture passed. It was here that classical texts first were brought, before their ultimate journey to Italy. [159] Northern styles in sculpture and architecture were imported and so were Italian styles in fresco and miniature painting. [160] Several historiated manuscripts executed for individual popes and curialists are today preserved at the Bibliothèque municipale d'Avignon.

One missal, BMA, ms. 136 executed for Pope Urban V, was in use during the third quarter of the fourteenth century. Both the scribe and the miniaturist have been identified as Italian. [161] There are many representations of popes, bishops, and saints, all essentially of the same type. Since the facial features of these illustrations closely resemble those of Pope Urban, as preserved in his effigial sculpture, many of the miniatures have been taken by twentieth-century art historians to be portraits of the pontiff. Be that as it may, there is one historiated initial of particular concern. It appears on folio 152 and illustrates the *Te igitur* page within the canon of the Mass. The usual facing crucifixion is one of the four preceding folios that have been excised. The miniature is divided into two parts. The left section contains the "T" and the right, the "E" of the *Te*. The "T" stands in place of the crucifix before the altar, and that half depicts the Elevation of the Host. Within the letter "E" is a lectern and four singers. There is a book opened on the lectern, and the words [*S*]*anctus domin*[9] *deus* can be discerned. Above the words are marks that give the indication of

Plate 4.    Bibliothèque municipale d'Avignon, ms. 136, *missel:* fol. 152.

musical notation. Two of the four singers are in the background, almost obscured from view by the two in the foreground. Of these two, one is dressed as a priest (?) wearing a biretta on his head and having a red hood draped over his right shoulder. It appears as if, for purposes of clarity, the artist chose to vest him in a pink alb. The remaining singer is dressed in a white alb with a white linen almuce on his head. The index finger of his left hand is prominently extended, and his right hand is raised in front of his body with the palm facing upward, tilted somewhat towards the viewer, fingers bent. The mouths of both singers are slightly agape.

It is possible that the hand gestures indicate a method of conducting. The left hand might be providing the beat as it rises and falls. The right hand might be indicating some direction to the singers. This two-handed method of "conducting," with the left hand presumably providing a pulse of some sort, is seemingly depicted in several miniatures dating from the fourteenth and fifteenth centuries.[162] Although the illustration in BMA, ms. 136 is likely an accurate representation of singers at a lectern, we cannot be sure that it has any special relevance to the papal chapel; the artist may have simply recreated a stereotypical motif, without having seen a papal service.

In addition to the musical, liturgical, and artistic activities supported by the Roman Curia, the municipal government of the city of Avignon took part in providing the proper degree of splendor and solemnity for a given occasion. In September 1377, with no pope in Avignon, the town treasurers paid two florins to Petrus Fornerii *pro solvendo ioculatoribus et penoncellis* that were employed in the procession made to celebrate the peace between the kings of Spain and Portugal.[163] In 1390, when the king of Jerusalem and Sicily, Louis II of Anjou, left Avignon on 15 May, there was a great procession to the Dominican church. The *trompatores* who accompanied the procession received one florin, five gros, and an additional payment of two florins was made to Johannes de Carpentorate and his *socii*, to Guichardus and his *socii*, and also to Raynaudus and his *socii*.[164] Though the exact specification of their service is lacking, all these men may have been trumpeters, since Johannes de Carpentorate once served as *gaychator* of Urban V. A very similar payment (one florin, six gros) was made on 9 June to the *trompis et ioculatoribus*, and two florins to the three men named above, for the procession made in honor of the king of Navarre.[165]

The authority of the municipal government of Avignon extended to the organization of processions not only for those exclusively secular occasions. For this was a time when the sacred and mystical blurred the line separating things of God from things of Caesar. On Ascension Thursday 1390, the city fathers supported a procession in which the confraternities participated. Banners were carried, a standard with the papal coat of arms was displayed, and a cross, a representation of a tabernacle, and an *ymaginis* of the Virgin were all borne through the streets. They were accompanied by the *ioculatores cum cornetis et cornamusis* (paid two florins, two gros), *tubatores* and six *mimi* (paid one florin, six gros), and two servants who commissioned the *tubatores* (four gros).[166] But in spite of the potential and the wherewithal for musical patronage and creative stimulus, the city of Avignon was severely weakened by the loss of its pope.

Gregory XI died in Italy on 27 March 1378. The conclave convened on 7 April and soon decided on the archbishop of Bari, Bartolomeo Prignano. The Italian archbishop, employed in the Curia at Avignon, was long a familiar of Cardinal Gui de Boulogne and was well known to the electors. Eleven days after he was chosen to sit upon the chair of Saint Peter, Bartolomeo was crowned Pope Urban VI. In spite of the fact that drunken Roman mobs gathered outside the place of the conclave shouting "Romano lo volemo o almanco italiano," the participating cardinals wrote to the six others in Avignon that the decision was freely reached and unanimous.[167] The Sacred College was soon to declare otherwise.

On 3 May, in a public consistory, the new pope attacked the exhibition of laxity and luxury in the lives of the princes of the Church. He proposed limiting their allotment for food and prohibited them from practicing simony and pluralism. What was worse, he cited the faults of particular prelates and, in the process, mentioned individual cardinals by name. He found Cardinal Robert de Genève, for one, to be ribald and judged him unworthy of his promotion to the cardinalate.[168] Disgusted by such pontifical pronouncements, the members of the accused body repaired one by one to Anagni. By Pentecost (6 June), only seven cardinals remained at the Curia; by 24 June, all of them, save the four of Italian nationality, were gathered together in negotiation; and by 26 July, the entire college had convened at Vicovaro. In less than two weeks, they promulgated an encyclical casting anathema on the archbishop of Bari.[169] They declared his election void, and, in the city of Fondi on 20 September 1378, the cardinals voted once again in conclave. With three Italians abstaining, and one ballot cast against, twelve prelates agreed on a new Sovereign Pontiff: Cardinal Robert de Genève.[170] The Great Western Schism had begun.

## Clement VII

Robert was born in 1342 at the château of Annecy, the fifth son of the count of Geneva and Matilda de Boulogne. He was related to the French royal house on his mother's side. In order to more closely ally himself with the crown, he eschewed his family's coat of arms and instead bore as his device three *fleurs-de-lis*.[171] At age eight, he had been living on the banks of the Rhône in the household of his uncle, Gui de Boulogne, cardinal bishop of Porto. Thanks to the good offices of Gui, the young Robert, a member of the Franciscan order, became chancellor of the cathedral of Amiens, apostolic notary, and familiar of Pope Innocent VI. On 3 November 1361, he was named bishop of Thérouanne and was translated to Cambrai on 11 October 1368. But he rarely visited his sees, living for the most part at Avignon in the entourage of his uncle. When he received the purple on 30 May 1371 and the title cardinal priest of SS. XII Apostoli, he came to be known as *Gebennensis cardinalis*, the cardinal of Geneva. He was active in family affairs and spent some time in the county of Geneva during the several years subsequent to his reception into the cardinalate. On 27 May 1376, he was sent to Italy to govern papal lands, and he remained there until the notorious conclave of 1378.[172] When Robert was crowned pope on 31 October at Fondi, he chose—no doubt to ally himself more closely to the French monarch—a name that had been selected by two of his predecessors who worked at the royal court. To his supporters he was Pope Clement VII.

Meanwhile, in Rome, Bartolomeo began to dethrone the cardinals, excommunicate followers of the antipope, and, perhaps most detrimental of all, withhold prebends and benefices from members of the Clementine party. His French antagonists called him *stultus, dementatus,* and, at best, he was said to be of *duri cordis*.[173] Testimony provided by one Pontius de Curte, clerk of the chapel of Pope Gregory XI, presents evidence of Bartolomeo's schemes to ascend the throne of Saint Peter.[174] First, the archbishop purchased a house and vineyard in the Eternal City, *et fecerat se civem Romanum*. Then, when the reigning pontiff was yet on his deathbed, Bartolomeo *frequentabat consilia Romanorum* under cover of darkness. Whether this was true or not, the Roman pope had certainly been ambitious, and now he was prepared to fight to keep his tiara.

The schismatic Curia remained at Fondi until the penultimate day of March 1379. But because of military defeats at the hands of Urbanist mercenaries and for reasons of safety, the court later sought refuge in Naples. Clement stayed in the vicinity of this city until 22 May.[175] On that day, he set sail for the southern coast of France, his ultimate destination: Avignon.

On 22 June, two days after the new pontiff triumphantly entered the walled city on the Rhône, the town fathers paid 11 florins to the *ministrales* who participated in the celebrations both when the news of the pope's landing at Nice reached Avignon and at the time of his entry into the papal city. On that eventful day, the players went out far beyond the city's precincts and suburbs presumably to accompany Clement and his entourage in the procession. The minstrels participated in festivities that endured for at least two more days.[176]

Soon after Clement's arrival, the *ville des papes* regained its importance as a musical and cultural center. It was in August of that year when Duke John, heir to the throne of Aragon, asked his agent to find some good singers in Avignon, as he says, *per a servi de nostra capella*. He wanted them young, unmarried, and preferably able to play a musical instrument. He further specified that they bring a book of *cant de la missa notat e un libre* containing many *motets e rondels e ballades e virelays*. By October 1379, John had been able to procure seven singers.[177]

While at first one might assume that John was asking to be sent papal *capellani*, it was not the singers of the *capella pape* that specifically interested the duke. Surely any of the well-trained Northern clerics that filled the chapels of secular and ecclesiastical princes would suffice. Furthermore, there must have been a very great number of young, educated, and ambitious clerics who flocked to the revitalized papal capital in search of a patron, ready to travel to Aragon if but asked.

History records Clement's pontificate as one that tended towards the greatest show and splendor. His chapel was staffed by the largest number of commensal chaplains in the history of the Avignon papacy. His college of *cantores,* both in quality and quantity, had known no equal.[178] The important feasts of the Church and celebrations of the state were doubtless the most sumptous displays of the day.

The pontiff himself was a highly cultured man, of noble birth, and refined in his tastes. It was said that he *cantavit seu celebravit divina officia multum eleganter.*[179] Singers and other musicians found a willing patron and protector in this pope.[180] It is not particularly surprising, therefore, that in the several musical works whose texts deal with the schism, we should find three written in support of Clement's rightful place as Saint Peter's successor. *Courtois et sages,* attributed to magister Egidius, addresses the validity of the election.[181] Without mentioning the pontiff by name in the text, it reveals *le droit signour* elected *par comun sentir* in the acrostic *CLEMENS.* The ballade *Par les bons Gedeons* by Philipoctus de Caserta also chooses as its shepherd *le souverayn pape qui s'apelle Clement.*[182]

The Latin text of the ballade *Inclite flos* is less transparent than the aforementioned works.[183] Attributed to Matheus de Sancto Johanne, it takes as its principal metaphor the image of the pontiff as a flower. The flower may be the rose customarily associated with the papacy, or it may be the *fleurs-de-lis* in Clement's own coat of arms. The author calls the pope "the flower of Genevan origin whose sweet odor will cover the earth like a dew." He bids the beseiged antipope not to "bow to the slight breeze, for it is said: In adversities virtue is perfected." This last phrase, which recurs in each of the three stanzas of the ballade, is a paraphrase of 2 Corinthians 12:9, ...*virtus in infirmitate perficitur.*[184] The second stanza of the work goes on to claim that the Spanish garden is favorable to the flower. As Ursula Günther has indicated, this reference allows the work to be more precisely dated. Pope Clement only received obedience from Castile in May 1381, Aragon in February 1387, and Navarre in 1390. Therefore, the favorability of the Spanish could not be claimed before 1381.[185] The text of the ballade continues, "the cherished shrubbery of the Gauls, producing a garden with its extended arms." It is the garden of the Gauls, i.e., France, that since 1379 had protected and watched over this flower. The third stanza is substantially more difficult, and the text seems to have been corrupted with several vernacular spellings.

It begins with a reference to a mountain called *Encis.* This is possibly an abberation of Cenis (*Cenisius*), a high peak in Savoy bordering on one of the principal passes into Italy. The line that follows contains two possible Gallicisms. The editor of the text suggests that the words *veridicis...foncis* might have originally read *veriditas...frondis.* Although syntactically this makes for a difficult reading, the change from *veri-* (truth) to *viri-* (green) may, in fact be the more accurate interpretation. The second word in question is perhaps best read as *fontis.* The phrase might then translate as "For this mountain (or man) of the green spring, more just than the just, struggles on your behalf; by which favoring splendor, each, having been more quickly led for you, prostrates himself at your feet." The allusions made here may be to Count Amadeus VI of Savoy who, because of the monochromatic garb worn by the members of his court, was known as the Green Count. The father of the pontiff served as godparent to the count, and Amadeus long had close ties to the Genevan family.[186] He was in Avignon from 24 May until before 8 June 1382 to participate in the ceremonies making Duke Louis of Anjou the king of Sicily and heir to Joanna of Naples.[187] After his departure from Avignon, the Green Count undertook an expedition to southern Italy in order to aid the much beleaguered queen. While on his mission, however, Amadeus died, 1 March 1383.

If this interpretation is correct, then the ballade must have been written between the date of Castile's pledge of allegiance to Clement and the death of Amadeus, 19 May 1381-1 March 1383. It is possible that the final stanza was one hastily added for the festivities of 1382. Whatever the case, we do know that the composer of this work, Matheus de Sancto Johanne, was employed in the chapel of Pope Clement by the fall of 1382. Four years earlier he was serving as clerk in the chapel of Duke Louis of Anjou, and there is some evidence indicating that he worked for Queen Joanna as well.[188] It is certainly in keeping with contemporary political events and the career of Matheus for us to conclude that the ballade was composed in 1382.

Besides Matheus, Pope Clement employed several other composers in his chapel: Johannes de Altacuria (Haucourt), Johannes Symonis (Asproys), and Johannes de Bosco (Pellisson). Each might have contributed something to the polyphonic music performed in the papal chapel. However, the extant works attributed to these chaplains, with the exception of those to Johannes de Bosco, are all in the secular repertoire. Though we have no specific evidence to show that these chansons were written for the Court of Rome in Avignon, it is reasonable to assume that composers there were exploited for the more worldly applications of their art as well as for what they could contribute to the greater glory of God.

Although the illustrious antipope outlived the archbishop of Bari by five years, as Clement lay on his deathbed, a Roman counterpart sat on the throne in Italy. Boniface IX (Pietro Tomacelli), more tactful than Urban, won back many of the supporters to the Roman side and began to whittle away at the Clementine bases of power.[189] Not long after having uttered his final words, "Pour l'ame, pour l'ame, pour l'ame," on 16 September 1394, the French pontiff expired. The Sacred College, despite advice from Paris against it, convened for what would be the final conclave held at Avignon.[190]

## Benedict XIII

Twelve days after the death of Pope Clement, the electors agreed on the cardinal deacon of S.Maria in Cosmedin, Pedro de Luna. The cardinal of Aragon, as he was known, was born 62 years earlier in the town of Illueca to don Pedro Martínez de Luna and had blood ties to both the royal houses of Aragon and Navarre. Though he was most active in obtaining ecclesiastical posts on the Iberian peninsula, he spent some time at the universities of Paris and Montpellier. On 20 December 1375, after an illustrious career, he was raised to the cardinalate.[191]

In 1378 Pedro was at first a supporter of Urban VI but later took sides with the French cardinals. In the early spring of the following year, Pedro and

Cardinal Martin de Salva were sent to argue the Clementine cause at the courts of Castile, Aragon, Navarre, and Portugal.[192] During this 11-year absence from the Curia, Cardinal de Luna strengthened his bonds with these monarchs but particularly with his own king, John I of Aragon.

These close acquaintanceships resulted in the exchange of more than mere political and religious ideas. One of the commodities that was passed among these Spanish princes was the composer and harpist Jacob de Senleches, nicknamed *lo bègue* (the stutterer).[193] In the year the Great Western Schism began, Jacob was sent from Aragon, where he was in the employ of Duke John of Gerona, to the music schools of Bruges. During the following year documents reveal that he was under the protection of King John I of Castile. He appears to have remained in Castile for some time. However, a notice dated 21 August 1383 records a donation of *100 libras* made to Jacob by King Charles II of Navarre. At that time, the musician was in the service of *el cardenal de Aragon,* Pedro de Luna.[194] Although there is no further evidence of this service nor are there extant musical works whose texts might clarify this relationship, the fact does provide additional proof that while the popes never retained secular musicians in their households, it was permitted to the cardinals.

Ten years later, Pedro was serving as papal legate to France, Brabant, Flanders, Scotland, England, and Ireland, although his duties kept him primarily in Paris. He was an austere and sober man who kept the future Dominican saint, Vincent Ferrer, as his confidant and confessor. The coronation of the cardinal as Pope Benedict XIII was welcomed by the French crown and by the theologians at the University of Paris.[195] All that remained in order to end the schism was for both Pope Benedict and his rival to resign. However, this was not part of the Spaniard's plan.

Not long after his consecration as Supreme Pontiff, problems arose for Benedict. Bankers began to lose faith in him. The leaders of the secular Christian world were determined to put an end to the chaos. The lords of France, namely, the dukes of Berry, Burgundy, and Orléans, arrived at Avignon in the greatest magnificence to negotiate with the pope. They were accompanied by some 6,000 knights, and they each resided with a cardinal at Villeneuve. For several weeks, the dukes held public consistories and counseled with the princes of the Church at the Cordeliers.[196] But agreement was never reached. During the next three years, the stubborn Catalan was continually pestered by prelates and by secular and academic authorities to cede power to the Roman pope. Benedict was ever adamant in his refusal.

The plague struck Avignon during the year 1397/98, and the pope and Curia spent much of the time at Pont-de-Sorgues.[197] By the time they arrived back in the papal capital, the position of the Benedictine cause was considerably weakened. On 2 February 1398, Duke Philip of Burgundy and King Henry III of Castile offered an ultimatum to the pontiff: either reconcile with Rome or obedience would formally be withdrawn. On 27 July, the assembly of French clergy retracted its allegiance at the instigation of King Charles VI. On 1 September at Villeneuve, two royal commissioners publicly proclaimed that both French and non-French clerics would lose all rights to their benefices in royal lands if they remained faithful to Avignon. The following day, the greater part of the Sacred College transferred to Villeneuve.[198] Only five cardinals stood at Benedict's side. At this time also, Benedict was no doubt abandoned by most if not all of his *capellani capelle,* the singers of the papal chapel. On 30 November, Queen Marie withdrew the support of Anjou and Provence, and on 12 December, Henry of Castile did the same.[199] Only Aragon was steadfast in obedience to her native son.

Marechal Geoffroy Boucicaut and his troops came to the papal capital, occupied the city, and began to beseige the Palace of the Popes. But, holed up in the fortress-like structure, the pontiff was able to keep himself free from harm for several years.[200] During the time he was prisoner in his own castle, he no doubt continued in the rite and ceremony available to the bishop of Rome, though the splendor of execution was severely curtailed.

Slowly the tide of opinion turned back in favor of the *pape de la lune* as his detractors called him. On 28 August 1402, Louis II of Anjou returned Provence to the Avignonese authority.[201] Public opinion was shifting as well. But before the pope received the support of other princes, early on the morning of 11 March 1403, he escaped from the papal palace, and was never to return.[202] Ironically, on 31 March, the city restored its obedience to Benedict. Within a month, the college of cardinals and the house of Castile would return to the fold. And on 28 May, France would rejoin the camp of Pope Benedict.[203]

After the morning of his flight, the pontiff traveled by boat to Châteaurenard, then to Caumont, Cavaillon, l'Isle, and Carpentras where he spent six weeks.[204] By 12 July he was in his castle at Pont-de-Sorgues, and there were unfounded rumors circulating that Benedict was to bring the Curia back to Avignon.[205]

Departing from Pont-de-Sorgues once again in the company of his chapel singers, the pope began his peripatetic adventure in Provence and northern Italy. He passed through Châteauneuf, Salon, and Marseille. At Tarascon on 22 December, the Holy Father feasted with one of his staunchest supporters, Duke Louis of Orléans. Most of 1404 was spent in Marseille, but on 2 December the entourage headed for Nice in a journey that would ultimately take it to Italy.[206]

During the years that followed, Benedict continued to work for reconciliation while based in the northern part of the Italian peninsula. Yet support for his cause continued to wane. He made two trips in hopes of meeting with his rival, called a disastrous council at Perpignan, and eventually returned to his native Aragon. In 1409, several Roman and Avignonese cardinals convened a council at Pisa in hopes of ending the schism. All they succeeded in doing was to select yet another "pope," Alexander V (Pietro Filargo). The Holy Roman Church now had three Sovereign Pontiffs.[207]

By the beginning of the second decade of the fifteenth century, Benedict had lost virtually all support. In 1416, even his beloved Aragon abandoned him.[208] But it was here where Pedro de Luna continued to live, executing the rites and ceremonies that were the privilege of the bishop of Rome. He outlived three Roman popes, two Pisans, and at the time of his death in 1423, a more-or-less unified Catholic world had been rendering obedience to Pope Martin V (1417-1431) for over five years.

The seven popes and two antipopes who ruled their share of Christendom from Avignon were by no means rebellious, dissolute despots. Although deriving much of their political power from the Ile-de-France, they were first and foremost bishops of Rome. They carried on venerable traditions of the papacy as best as their surroundings would allow. This is not say that they were self-effacing ascetics. Indeed, they rivaled the most powerful secular princes in pomp, ceremony, and ostentation. While they themselves always eschewed direct patronage of secular musicians, the private and municipal players of temporal authorities were often handsomely rewarded for their service to the Holy Father. However, propriety permitted the open financial support of musical performance where it concerned the worship of God. It was here that the popes of Avignon left their legacy to subsequent Roman Pontiffs and to music history by establishing and fostering the *capellani capelle pape.*

# 2

# The *Capellani Capelle Pape*

By the time Pope Clement V first set foot within the walls of Avignon, chaplains of the pope had been participating in papal ritual for nearly 300 years. As early as the eleventh century, the Roman Pontiff sang his private offices in the presence of a sole cleric.[1] It was also during this century that Amatus, bishop of Silva Candida, is referred to as *capellanus domini pape,* the first man to be so called.[2] This prelate, the incumbent of a suburban Rome bishopric that was later to be united with the title of cardinal bishop of Porto, was doubtless one of the pope's closest advisors. Indeed, the first and most important papal servers must have been high ecclesiastics drawn from the innermost circle of attendants. By the late thirteenth century, besides the cardinals who regularly participated at the Mass and office with the bishop of Rome, there had developed a college of lesser clerics whose duties were more specifically liturgical. These men, the *capellani pape,* comprised the principal papal servers.

In the *Liber censuum* of the twelfth century, one first finds evidence of these chaplains involved in some singing during papal rites.[3] We know that they accompanied the pontiff and cardinals in the chanting of the *Te Deum* on the feast of the Exaltation of the Holy Cross (14 September)[4] and at the office of Easter. Late thirteenth-century ceremonials indicate that the *capellani* were responsible for the chanting of Matins and Vespers on Christmas and, led by the *subdiaconus,* they were to take part in the ceremony of papal consecration.[5] Their responsibilities were separate from those of the *Schola cantorum,* and whenever the Curia resided outside of Rome the *capellani* assumed some of the musical duties of the *Schola.*[6]

The earliest description of the office indicates that the *capellani,* or more specifically *capellani commensales,* were to live communally in a room called a *capellania,* and thus they were free to devote themselves to the execution of the divine office.[7] They were to go to the predetermined hall or chapel and say Matins at night, Mass in the morning, and Vespers in the evening.[8] They took turns carrying the processional cross. If requested, they were to accompany the chamberlain when he left the Curia on business and were to act as the pope's representatives. One among them, the *subdiaconus,* was to serve at solemn

Mass whenever the pope celebrated, and he was to read at table when the pontiff ate in the dining hall. From these *capellani,* a *presbiter* was chosen to make ready both the book of psalms used at Vespers attended by the pope, and the book of prayers used by the cardinal who served the pope at Mass and Vespers.[9]

Although meaner in rank than the cardinals, the *capellani commensales* of the late thirteenth century were nevertheless men of high standing. They were allotted a double ration of food daily, one for themselves and one for a servant, and they were provided the means to keep a horse. On the anniversary of the pope's coronation, Christmas, and Easter, they received two gold malachini each, as a special gift called a *presbiterium.* By the beginning of the fourteenth century, there were approximately 15 *capellani pape* assisted by a *clericus capelle.*[10] Lower in status, the *clericus* prepared the altar for the chaplains when they said Mass and Vespers, and whenever the pontiff himself celebrated, he assisted the treasurers (*thesaurarii*) in the deployment of the *iocalia* and *paramentum,* the ornaments and furnishings of the chapel. There was also a *hostarius capellanie* attached to the college who had care of the *capellania.* He called the chaplains to Matins, Mass, and Vespers, and he was also responsible for the candles and books used at the services.[11]

Matheus, first mentioned as *clericus* in May 1278, held this post both under Boniface VIII (1294-1303) and Clement V; the man who served as *hostarius* for both popes was named Giffredus. The tasks fulfilled by these two offices so resembled each other that from 1307 Giffredus was referred to as *clericus capelle.* From that point on, the office of *hostarius capellanie* never again appears listed, but instead we find two *clerici capelle.*[12]

By 1308/09, Matheus was succeeded by Thomas de Eugubio, who seems to have remained in papal service throughout the pontificate of John XXII. The other *clericus* at this time was Raimundus de Porta. Raimundus may not have been in the constant employ of the popes since payment notices for him are neither as numerous nor as regular as those for Thomas.[13] The duties of both men included the preparation of the chapel for the services and the provision of furniture, illumination and incense. On several occasions, the clerks were paid for having books rebound and for transporting the goods of the chapel.[14] The person who later came to be responsible for the *iocalia* and the books used in the papal chapel was Gaufridus Isnardi, named *capellanus pape* from 1320. He was also the *physicus pape* and, as such, belonged to the inner circle of papal retainers called either *presbiteri...,* *clerici...,* or *capellani pape intrinseci.*[15]

Among these *capellani intrinseci* were the camerals and administrators of the papal household, the papal scribes, and one Thomas Galli, *cantor pape.* Unfortunately, his duties as *cantor* are never specified in the cameral accounts. We do know that he was a priest and that several times he was responsible for acquiring the molds needed to make the *agnus dei.*[16] One of these references calls him Thomas de Capella. Therefore, it is safe to assume that on some level this *cantor* was associated with the papal chapel.[17]

Under John XXII the *capellani* still seemed to have been thought of collectively, though this does not imply that they lived communally or that they continued to carry out their liturgical tasks. In fact, in light of what was to occur upon the accession of Benedict XII to the throne of Saint Peter, the opposite seems to have been the case. As we saw in chapter 1, John XXII was more concerned with establishing chapels in the cathedral of Notre-Dame-des-Doms and in other regional churches than with building new oratories for his private and domestic use.[18] Totally consistent with this approach is the considerable number of payments made during his papacy to maintain these chapels and to have Masses said in them *pro papa*.[19] Therefore, as difficult as it may be to imagine, documentary evidence shows John XXII as a pope who not only had little interest in maintaining an active personal chapel, but who also may have delegated at least some liturgical services to clerics not associated with the papal household.

**Reorganization of the Chapel**

Immediately after his election on 20 December 1334, Pope Benedict XII effected a thorough reform of both Church and Curia.[20] In contradistinction to his predecessor, the new pope wanted all of his chaplains to recite the canonical hours *cum nota*. In addition, they were to sleep in a dormitory built expressly for them, and they were to dine with the pope. They would need nothing but food and clothing. If a *capellanus* required anything, he was permitted to request it of the pope, and of him alone.[21] Their number was fixed at 12, and they were not permitted to wear the rochet.[22]

In spite of these references to a reform, it appears as though a reorganization of the *capellani*, or more properly, *capellani commensales*, never actually occurred. What did in fact take place was the institution of a new chapel, a second group, which answered the demands of the pope. One of the first payment lists of this pontificate, dated 11 February 1335, includes the 19 *capellani commensales* and 1 *clericus capelle*, Thomas de Eugubio. But somewhat lower on the list we find payment made to another group, *12 clerici seu capellani capelle:*

  1) fr. Guillelmus Motonerii
  2) Petrus Sinterii
  3) Coleta
  4) Stephanus de Ucis
  5) fr. Antonius (for 42 days)
  6) Raimundus Servientis (for 9 days)
  7) Coumpanus de Cambello
  8) Guillelmus de Convenis

9)  Nicholaus Raimundi
10)  Raimundus de Anglade
11)  Johannes Gonterii
12)  Johannes de S.Quintino (for 9 days)[23]

Most of them were paid for the period beginning with the election of the pope, with one chaplain ostensibly added on the eve of the feast of Circumcision and two others added on Purification. An interesting, though admittedly unproven, hypothesis proposed by one historian suggests that Benedict might have been able to effect an immediate and nearly complete recruitment of chapel members by transferring them directly from a chapel that he maintained as cardinal into his new papal chapel.[24] We can, at this time, point to certain facts that at least partially substantiate such a claim.

Pope Benedict was a member of the Cistercian Order. He and his uncle Arnaud before him had both been abbots of the monastery of Fontfroide (in the diocese of Narbonne). The abbey came to be particularly favored by Benedict and, to a certain extent, remained so throughout the Avignon papacy. Two of Benedict's first chaplains, frater Guillelmus Montonerii and frater Antonius were, as was their patron, Cistercian monks closely associated with the monastery at Fontfroide. Their relationship with the new pope must have been closely established before his election.[25]

Another chaplain who may have had an earlier association with Benedict is Stephanus de Ucis from the diocese of Maguelonne. Besides his service as a papal chaplain, he worked in the *buticularia,* buying oil, wine, and salted meat for the papal household in 1335. Seven years later, he had custody of the objects kept in the lower treasury of the papal palace. He might have served Benedict in a similar capacity if he were associated with him before the abbot's accession to the chair of Saint Peter.

There were, in fact, several chaplains who were engaged in various nonmusical activities and who had a prior association both with the early *capella intrinseca* of John XXII and with the Curia much before Benedict's arrival on the scene. Johannes de Sancto Quintino, for example, was *serviens* on 3 June 1317 according to the financial records compiled under Pope John. The nature of the service is, unfortunately, unspecified. During the reign of Pope Benedict, Johannes performed duties outside the papal chapel. By 1336, he had already received the title of *scriptor* and was no doubt functioning in that office.[26] In 1339 and 1340, he was involved in procuring parchment from the city of Carpentras *pro libris pape transcribendis.* During the time of his service to the pope as *capellanus,* he is known to have been a protégé of the bishop of Uzès, Guillaume de Mandagout.

The chaplain Johannes Durandi also served the previous pope. In 1332/33 he likewise had received the title of *scriptor,* and the records tell us that he was not only a papal familiar but also a *clericus intrinsecus.* From at least 28 May

1333 until the death of John XXII on 4 December 1334, he was prefect of the papal library and was concerned with having volumes copied for the papal storehouse of books. After serving briefly in the papal chapel, he spent several years keeping account of vineyards at Villeneuve-lès-Avignon and purchasing wine for the papal household. The *capellanus* Raymundus Servientis might have been a chaplain of Jean Cojordan, bishop of Avignon, while at the same time serving Benedict. He was cited as familiar of the bishop, and thus might not have lived communally with the other papal chaplains.

The financial accounts show a clear distinction between the *capellani commensales* and the new *capellani capelle*. The latter appear in the first list considerably after the former but immediately before the group of *12 clerici intrinseci*. They were to be paid *4 grossi turonenses* each, per day, which is about half of the stipend given to a *capellanus commensalis* and about a third more than the wage paid a *clericus capelle* and a *clericus intrinsecus.*[27]

In the list of payments made early in 1336 we find thirteen *capellani:*

1) Petrus Sinterii
2) Stephanus de Utis
3) Raimundus Servientis
4) G. Convenis
5) Johannes Gonterii
6) Johannes de S.Quintino
7) Johannes Bertrandi
8) Bernardus Ademarii
9) Nicolaus Benedicti
10) Raimundus de Angladis
11) Johannes de Tregrossio (for 55 days)
12) Johannes Durandi (for 42 days)
13) Raimundus Seguini

Most were paid for the total number of days since the last account, 56.[28] In a document of 29 June 1336, the title of *cantor capelle* is given to a Cantonus Petri. His name again appears in the accounts from the following August, where he is designated as a *clericus serviens in capella* for the *capellani.* As *clericus,* he probably fulfilled functions similar to those of the *clerici* who were attached to the commensal chaplains, and therefore he prepared the chapel for service. Nothing is known about his activities as *cantor.*[29]

At this time too, Petrus Sinterii, who stood in second place on the original list of Benedict's chaplains, moves up to first. Here he remains in all subsequent rosters including this one from 1337:

1) Petrus Sintherii
2) Stephanus de Utis
3) Raymundus Servientis
4) Guillelmus de Convenis

    5) Johannes Gonterii
    6) Johannes de S.Quintino
    7) Johannes Bertrandi
    8) Berengarius Ademarii
    9) Nicolaus Bernardi
   10) Johannes de Cregossio
   11) Privatus Pastorelli
   12) Raymundus Seguini
   13) Raymundus de Angladis

This is followed in the accounts by a payment made to Cantonus Petri, *clericus serviens in capella.* Although a complete list of the papal chaplains is missing for the year 1338, we know from collections of papal correspondence that Johannes Gonterii, who had been with the new chapel from its inception in 1335, died before 7 July 1338 while residing with the Curia. The gap was probably filled by Johannes de Ayrolis who began his service with the *capellani* during the course of the year.[30]

   For the next several years, the composition of the chapel remains stable. Only the positions of the chaplains in the list change. The *capellani* in 1339:

    1) Petrus Sinterii
    2) Johannes de S.Quintino
    3) Johannes Bertrandi
    4) Johannes de Tregossio
    5) Privatus Pastorelli
    6) R. de Angladis
    7) Nicholaus Bertrandi
    8) Johannes de Ayrolis
    9) Berengarius Adhemari
   10) Stephanus de Utis
   11) Guillelmus de Convenis
   12) Raimundus Seguini
   13) Raimundus Servientis[31]

   Since 1336, the number of chaplains employed seems to have remained constant at 13, not 12, the original number proposed in the curial reforms. Apparently the position held by Petrus Sinterii, first among the *capellani,* had been indicating not only a hierarchical position but also a change in function. For beginning at this time, Petrus is sometimes referred to as *magister capelle,* and as such is responsible for the accounts and expenses of the chapel.[32] No doubt the presence of 13 chaplains in these lists reflects an arrangement of 12 full-time *capellani* plus 1 *magister capelle.*

   In 1341 we find the notice that 13 chaplains were paid, but their names are not given.[33] The following year, the name of Johannes de Lovanis replaces that of Berengarius Ademarii:

1) Petrus Sinterii
2) Johannes de Tregos
3) Privatus Pastorelli
4) Johannes de S.Quintino
5) Johannes Bertrandi
6) Guillelmus de Convenis
7) Raimundus de Angladis
8) Nicholaus Bertrandi
9) Johannes de Lovanis
10) Stephanus de Utis
11) Raimundus Seguini
12) Johannes de Ayrolis
13) Raimundus Servientis

Appended to these was the name of Cantonus Petri, *serviens in capella,* who was drawing less than half the salary of a *capellanus.*[34]

It is necessary to emphasize here that although the new college of chaplains was, by this time, well established, the old *capellani commensales* were by no means forgotten.[35] They continued to be recruited and maintained during the pontificate of Benedict XII. In all likelihood, they retained at least some of their former liturgical duties, especially on the solemn feast days.

It has been suggested that after the election of Benedict XII, and the subsequent construction of the papal palace, the pontiff moved his private liturgy from the cathedral into the newly constructed chapels. By divorcing himself from the chapter of Notre-Dame-des-Doms and the priests who celebrated there *pro papa,* Benedict may have again provided the *subdiaconus, clericus,* and *capellani commensales* with responsibility for carrying out some of the services.[36] Whatever the situation, very little is known about the private papal service in Avignon before 1334.

If we review what is known about Benedict's reforms, we may be able to postulate some of the motives for the establishment of a new chapel and draw a picture of the old *capellani* and their inadequacies. The thirteenth-century document cited above was more concerned with the physical needs of the *commensales* rather than with their liturgical service. The reforms of Benedict required that the new *capellani intrinseci* live in a *dormitorio,* probably indicating that the *commensales,* who were also supposed to live communally, were living in private quarters by the 1330s. The new group of servers was not only required to provide a physical presence at the services but were to recite the hours *cum nota,* a task at which the *commensales* may have been neither sufficiently trained nor particularly adept. They were not to be the papal ambassadors, not associates of the chamberlain, and accordingly, they received reduced stipends which prevented them from keeping servants. They were forbidden to wear the rochet, a vestment reserved for higher ecclesiastics, including probably the *capellani commensales.* They were to receive only food and clothing from their employer, basics beyond which the *commensales* probably requested. Implied also in these reforms are the liberties taken by the commensal chaplains in seeking and obtaining gifts and income from other sources. In so doing they allowed themselves to become beholden to others. This condition, combined with their duties as ambassadors, tended to remove them from the Curia and the center of papal celebrations. As time went on, the *commensales*, who originally might have substituted for the cardinals during papal services, evidently came to be higher ecclesiastics themselves and their appointment to the chapel, a greater honor. Accordingly, their capability in the routine liturgical offices ceased to be an important factor in their selection. The new chaplains were no doubt chosen because of their competence in assisting at the services. This would have included an ability to perform those portions of the services that were sung. They might also have taken over the duties of the Roman *Schola cantorum*.[37] If this was the case, then it would be to the chapel's advantage, if not to its very survival, for it to have included at least a few well-trained singers.

Although there is little more that can be said of the chapel of Benedict XII, it is evident that the *capellani capelle* generally tended to come from the south of France and some were probably first associated with his inner circle. Others had prior experience in the papal household, though not primarily as singers or servers at the divine office. They may have participated in this, however, as associates of the Curia. Judging from what has been gleaned from the financial records, we see that their day was not consumed by liturgical service, since they acted in other capacities as well.

Because they executed administrative and bureaucratic tasks for the Curia, we may safely assume that the *capellani* had received a significant amount of education. In spite of this, there is no evidence that leads us to suspect the chaplains of the papal chapel of 1334 possessed any special ability to sing the divine offices. The two factors that allowed them to be hired were first, their near continual presence at the papal residence and second, an implicit knowledge of Roman liturgy.

Benedict's experience as a monastic may have provided the stimulus for this personal desire to surround himself with a group whose *raison d'être* was liturgical service. His choice of the Cistercian order for his own life may have influenced his requirements for music and worship and led to the restrictions placed on the new body of chaplains. In spite of the intimate nature of this chapel, it continued to be maintained after his death.

## From Clement VI to the Plague of 1361

The first payments to the chaplains of Pope Clement VI were made on 3 August 1342:

1) Petrus Santerii
2) Johannes de Nobiliaco
3) Radulphus Ricardi
4) G. de Flandria
5) Matheus dictus Volta
6) Radulphus Tafardi, presbyter
7) Symon Mauricii
8) Johannes lou Camus (for 21 days)
9) Johannes de Tregos
10) Johannes de Sinemuro
11) Nicholaus de Nasiaco (for 8 days)

Also receiving wages at this time was Colinetus, *clericus capelle intrinsece.*[38]

Significantly, the *clericus* is here placed within the *capelle intrinseca.* Originally, during the pontificate of John XXII, this inner chapel comprised the closest papal familiars and included Gaufridus Isnardi and Thomas Galli among its members. But with John's successors, the *capella intrinseca* was the group of chaplains and clerks who were involved in the execution of a liturgy *cum nota.*[39] The *capellani* received *4 grossi turonenses* as before, and the *clericus* was paid half that amount. At the top of the list remained the name of Petrus Sinterii, *magister capelle pape.*[40]

For Clement's second pontifical year, 1343/44, the list of *capellani* remains essentially the same, again with Colinetus as *clericus capelle intrinsece.*[41] However, a list compiled 5 June 1344 includes only nine chaplains.[42]

For the year 1345/46, we know that a payment made to Petrus Sinterii included wages for himself and 12 others.[43] Though the account does not specify which chaplains were paid, from the papal correspondence it is evident that Stephanus de Chaulageto, Johannes Gervasii, Guillelmus de Flandria, and Johannes de Sinemuro were among them.[44] Similarly, a payment made to Petrus during the year 1346/47 shows that he was responsible for 11 unnamed *socii,* 10 receiving wages for 8 weeks, and 1 for 51 days.

In 1347, the papal chaplains were first referred to as *capellani et cantores capellae intrinsecae.*[46] This could possible indicate a dichotomy within the chapel itself: some of its members distinguished themselves as papal servers in both liturgical and non-liturgical spheres, while other members were recruited primarily for their ability as singers. In any event, the use of the word *cantor* unequivocally signifies that this chapel provided the music for the papal service.

One of the results of the outbreak of plague that swept through Europe in 1348 was a change in the personnel who staffed the pontifical *capella.* The chaplain Johannes de Sinemuro was dead before September 1348, when one of his benefices was requested by a new chaplain, Johannes de Bralli. Johannes de Bralli and Johannes Hyera had already entered the chapel as of 25 April 1348.

In the month of June, the names of the three new members appear: Johannes de Athies, Laurentius de Abbatisvilla, and Matheus de Barbino. On 9 August, Guillelmus Rastelerii joined their ranks. Besides these new chaplains, the *capella* included the *magister*, Petrus Sinterii, and probably Stephanus de Chaulageto and Johannes Gervasii. Privatus Pastorelli, who might have served as a chaplain of Pope Clement throughout his reign, died as a *capellanus* in 1348.[47]

On 25 June 1352, wages were given to *12 capellani capelle*, of which a certain one was paid for only four days of the previous eight weeks. There was also one *clericus* assigned to the *capella intrinseca* at this time, possibly Alanus Avis.[48] Several months later, on 10 November 1352, the last extant payment record for the pontificate of Clement VI indicates that 11 *capellani capelle intrinsece* and 1 *clericus* were in service.[49]

When Clement VI became pope, he maintained the same *magister capelle*, but except for Johannes de Tregos and Privatus Pastorelli, all the chaplains were replaced. While we can identify the dioceses of origin of the chaplains of Benedict XII to be of south or central France, those of Clement's chapel are decidedly more northern. Guillelmus de Flandria, probably from the city of Béthune (Arras), who served the pontiff while he was yet cardinal, became a *scriptor* soon after his reception into the papal chapel. Simon Mauricii was from the diocese of Paris, and Johannes de Sinemuro also had associations with the royal city. These two *capellani* might also have known Clement while he was working for the king of France. After 1345, yet another increase in the number of northerners serving in the papal chapel can be documented. The Picard, Johannes Gervasii, had risen to the rank of deacon at the collegiate church of Aire (Thérouanne). Johannes Clementis de Brullio was from the diocese of Tournai and held numerous prebends in the north, including the cantorate of Saint-Pierre at Lille. Probably as a consequence of the plague that struck Avignon, six new chaplains were admitted in 1348. Significantly, they had origins in only four dioceses: Thérouanne, Arras, Noyon, and Amiens. This turn to the north was to remain a feature of the Avignon papacy and, to be sure, continue for at least two centuries. Although it has been proposed that Clement became familiar with the talents of northern clerics during his episcopacy in Arras and Rouen, it is more likely that his use of northerners derived from the practice of the French royal court.[50]

Because of financial considerations, under Innocent VI a new chapel began to take shape, smaller in size than those of his predecessors. In the first payments of 1353, nine *capellani* received remuneration for the 56-day period and certain other chaplains were paid for 55 days of service. The number of *clerici* was raised to two, one of whom was employed for 47 days. It is highly likely that the number of *clerici capelle* was increased and that of chaplains decreased for reasons of economy, since clerks received half the wage of chaplains. The new *clericus* may have had a function similar to that of the *servitor,* and he may have replaced *capellani* such as Johannes Valentis who held both the office of *servitor* and that of chaplain of the papal chapel. Innocent seems to have sacrificed his *capellani* to the benefit of the clerks, though he may not necessarily have reduced the number of chaplains who were primarily singers.[51]

In 1355 Johannes Ademari had charge of a chapel that included Petrus Saumati, Guillelmus Lupi, Johannes de Venda, and Johannes Valentis, earlier called *servitor capelle intrinsece.*[52] On 3 June 1356, the *8 capellani capelle intrinsece* were each provided an "almuce of mottled and gray fur for various needs."[53] Fortunately, the names of these eight men are given:

1) Petrus de Moncolo   [Moncoulon]
2) Johannes de Ayras   [Attrebato]
3) Johannes Ademari
4) Johannes Valhant   [Valentis]
5) Petrus Bomarc   [Baniardi]
6) Petrus Montagut   [Saumati]
7) Guillelmus Lupi
8) Johannes Lavanta   [de Venda]

This is the only evidence of individual chaplains being provided clothing at the expense of the Apostolic Camera during the Avignon papacy.

We again find the *clerici* Alanus Avis and Bertrandus Majoris, along with Johannes Ademari, Guillelmus Lupi, and Johannes Valentis serving in the papal chapel during the year 1357. At the beginning of December, the cameral accounts reveal a payment made for 56 days of service to the 2 *clerici* (one, employed for 53 days) and 10 *capellani* (plus certain others paid for only 14 days).[54]

It seems clear from these notices that the number of *capellani* and *clerici intrinseci* must have varied greatly from week to week, if not from day to day. It is impossible to determine if certain singers were hired only for particular occasions, feasts, or seasons in order to bolster a small chapel, or if this fluctuation is indicative of a large chapel affected by absences of one sort or another. In any event, the relative stability in quantity and quality that was known in the *capella* of Benedict XII was not to be found in the chapel of Pope Innocent.[55]

## The Plague and Its Consequences

When the dreaded plague again struck Avignon in the spring of 1361, no group was spared, not even the pope's chaplains. During the months that followed the first signs of epidemic, several long-time chapel members died, though the vacancies were quickly filled by new *capellani.* Petrus Saumati was alive at the end of January, but dead by 25 April. At this time Egidius Quadrati, *capellanus capelle intrinsece,* requested certain benefices once held by Petrus. The master of the chapel is named in a supplication of 30 May, seeking the office of *scriptor* of penitential letters once held by Johannes Clementis de Brullio, left vacant by his death in the Curia. Johannes Ademari never realized the fruits of this office, because less than three months after he submitted his request, he was to suffer the same fate. Following his death the accounts of the chapel were kept by the new *magister,* Stephanus de Vergonio. By 19 August, Guillelmus Villart de Blano had been brought into the *capella intrinseca,* and approximately six weeks later Johannes Capel was received *in cantorem capelle.* This was the first time that an individual chaplain was called *cantor* since the induction of Johannes de Sancto Quintino into the chapel in 1336.[56]

According to documentary evidence, it is clear that the nature of the *capella intrinseca* began to change upon the appointment of chaplains who replaced those mortally stricken with plague. Experienced clerics were drawn from the "families" of the princes of the Church. Egidius Quadrati had been familiar of the late Cardinal Jean d'Auxois and might have been in the employ of another ecclesiastic in Avignon when called to papal service. Johannes Capel served in the Curia successively as familiar of the bishop of Como and of Cardinal Pierre la Forêt, before being received *in cantorem.* Philippus Servonhi was probably recruited from among the commensal chaplains of Cardinal Guillaume de la Jugie. It is likely that a number of other *capellani capelle pape* were brought in only after having distinguished themselves in service to the other members of the Curia.

## The Chapels of Urban and Gregory

On 11 November 1362, soon after the consecration of Pope Urban V, several new names appear: the chaplain Johannes Johannis, and the clerk, Walterus de Vastonia who probably replaced Alanus Avis. In addition, records bearing the same date show that Johannes Capel, Guillelmus Villart de Blano, Nicolaus de Bondevilla, Philippus Servonhi, and Walterus de Vastonia were also attached to the chapel. Although the specific information is missing, it is probably safe to assume that Stephanus Vergonio as *magister,* and Egidius Quadrati as *capellanus* both continued to serve in the chapel of Pope Urban. It is worth noting that, unlike Clement and Innocent before him, Urban V was apparently quite satisfied with the constituency of the *capella intrinseca* that he inherited. He not only continued to maintain the number of the *capellani* at eight, but even retained many of Innocent's chaplains in his own chapel.[57]

By 1363, the chapels of secular authorities as well as those of cardinals were providing experienced chaplains for the *capella pape.* Johannes de Heys de Rancovado, former chaplain of Raoul, lord of Louppeyo and governor of Dauphiné, entered the chapel of Urban. And in 1364, Dionysius Fabri, who earlier served in the apostolic palace as chaplain of Guillaume Rolland, lord marshal of the Roman Curia, was called chaplain of the papal chapel. On 26 January 1364 both Johannes Cossardi and Petrus Guermini were entered into the accounts as *capellani sive cantores*.[58] Johannes Cossardi had long been *precentor* of the chapel of Queen Eleanor of Aragon and therefore must also have been instrumental in the daily execution of the divine office long before his inclusion in the papal chapel. Petrus Guermini had seen service as a *subdiaconus* in the chapel of Cardinal Elie Talleyrand and no doubt also had substantial experience before he sang for Urban.

Stephanus Vergonio, *magister capelle* of Pope Urban V, disappears from the records in 1365 and seems to have relinquished his duties, if not his title, to Johannes de Ulmo. On 27 September, in the accounts of the chapel, Johannes was called *administrator capelle intrinsece pape*.[59] Within the first half of that year Johannes Petri, former *tenor capelle* of Cardinal Hugues Roger, and Johannes de Rancovado were mentioned as chaplains and singers of the chapel, the former on 19 May and the latter, one month later.[60] Only one new name, that of Johannes Monterii, appears on a list of six chaplains paid for their service 27 November 1365:

1) Nicolaus de Bondevilla
2) Johannes Monterii
3) Petrus de Quermini [Guermini]
4) Johannes Cossardi
5) Philippus Sernarii [Servonhi]
6) Johannes Petri[61]

On 30 April 1367, Pope Urban V left Avignon for Rome.[62] The next day Johannes de Ulmo began receiving a series of payments to cover the cost of moving those things that were necessary for the operation of the chapel first from Avignon to Marseille, then to Viterbo, and finally to Rome.[63] It is difficult to determine both the number and names of the chaplains who were in the employ of the pope at the time of his departure. Some *capellani* might have been recruited after the pontiff abandoned France. Theobaldus Furnerii, for example, was brought into the chapel on 27 October, 11 days after the pope entered the Eternal City.[64] Similar cases exist for both Thomas Tauri, who entered papal service in March 1368, and Johannes Lehoudain, who became a chaplain 17 April 1368, according to a document dated at Saint Peter's.[65]

There is also evidence, however, of several of the Avignonese *capellani* being at Rome. In November 1367, Johannes de Rancovado and Ancelmus Martini were reimbursed for the expense of renting two horses that were needed in going from Viterbo to Rome.[66] Johannes Johannis, while not called a *capellanus*, was in fact at Rome, acting as *elemosinarius* (almoner) in May 1368.[67] Johannes Petri, too, had made the trip to Rome, though when he died, before 29 August 1369 at the Apostolic See, he seemed no longer to be in papal service. Nicolaus de Bondevilla was cited in November as a chaplain of the chapel. The clerks Petrus Salteti and Pontius de Curte might not have journeyed with the pope in 1367, but curial documents show that they were both working in the Curia during the winter of 1369 and the spring of 1370, respectively. Whatever the exact situation might have been, the accounts do reveal that when Urban quit Rome to spend the summer of 1368 at Montefiascone, 12 horses were provided *pro 12 cantoribus.*[68]

The return of the Vicar of Christ to the Italian peninsula, albeit temporary, brought an essentially French Curia and a particularly northern *capella* to Rome. Here, the papal *capellani,* as well as those attached to the chapels of cardinals, must have been exposed to liturgical usages and ways of sacred singing that differed from those to which they were accustomed. The style of secular Italian music heard in the streets and courts entered the ears of these northern clerics. Similarly, some among them may have received an exposure to the unique notational system employed by the Italians in their mensural polyphony. Whatever new ideas these singers might have absorbed, they were not left to germinate and bear fruit in Rome. But, dissatisfied with the political climate in Italy, pope and Curia abandoned the peninsula and re-entered Avignon at the end of September 1370. Less than three months later, Urban was dead.[69]

Not long after the election of Gregory XI on 30 December 1370, the new pope filled his chapel. Johannes de Ulmo was officially given the title of *magister capelle* under the new pontiff, two days before the coronation, on 3 January 1371.[70] The same day, the following were admitted *in cantores:*

1) Robertus
2) Martinus [de Prato]
3) Richardus (I)
4) Radulphus
5) Thomas [Tauri]
6) Johannes Carnoten [Fillon][71]

On 9 January, several former members of Urban's chapel, who had since been engaged by Gregory, submitted supplications for benefices to the newly crowned pope: the *magister,* Johannes de Ulmo; the *capellani,* Philippus Servonhi, Johannes Lehoudain; and the *clericus capelle pape,* Theobaldus Furnerii. Within one week of filing the petitions, the following names were listed as having been brought *in cantores:*

1) Philippus Servain [Servonhi]
2) Ancelinus Martini
3) Johannes Houdain [Lehoudain]
4) Theobaldus Furnerii[72]

It is interesting to note that at this time Theobaldus seems to have been simultaneously *cantor* and *clericus capelle.* Earlier in his career he served as *capellanus* and also as *clericus*. His unique position in the history of the Avignon chapel, as one who simultaneously held both titles may be indicative of a flexibility in the office of clerk of the chapel during the pontificates of Urban and Gregory. The *clerici* might have had limited musical duties at this time, or, for that matter, throughout the entire Avignon papacy. Perhaps the clerks substituted for individual singers absent from the Curia or when the number of participating *cantores* fell below what was considered acceptable for a given celebration. Unfortunately there remains no financial account by which one may determine if and when the stipend received by Theobaldus changed with this alteration in status.

Contemporary with this development, the designation of *clericus capelle* became nonspecific. No longer do we find one set of clerks assigned to the *capella commensalis* and another to the *capella intrinseca*. Instead, starting in the late 1360s, there were only two *clerici* whose duty it was to serve both chapels. By 24 October 1372, however, the position of chapel clerk was suppressed for some unknown reason. An entry in the papal records states that, by papal mandate, the chamberlain suspended the *clerici* Petrus Salteti and Pontius de Curte, and deprived them of their wages until further notice.[73] This action along with the double title borne by Theobaldus may have been indicative of some changes in the organization of the papal chapel and in the assignment of tasks at that time. All this was probably precipitated by financial exigencies.

In 1372 Johannes de Ulmo was the master of a chapel that included at least Ancelmus Martini, Theobaldus Furnerii, Johannes Lehoudain, and Martinus de Prato. We know, too, that sometime during the year, a Johannes Colini was employed as *cantor,* for on 24 October he was deprived of his stipend because "he laid his hands on the *magister capelle*."[74] He continued his service throughout the first part of 1373, since extant records note his absence from 20 to 25 April of that year. By 5 June 1372, Johannes Ruffi de Roquignies was serving as *cantor capelle*. This singer should be identified with the Johannes Roqueni over whom musicologists have needlessly spilt much ink.[75] The accounts show that both he and Theobaldus departed 2 November and returned to the chapel six days later. The following year, these two are recorded as having similarly been absent from the Curia from 5 November until 11 November. This time they were accompanied in their absence by Guido de Lange, former *clericus capelle* of Urban V. In 1374, Theobaldus and Guido left the service of the chapel on 30 October, evidently not in the company of Johannes, for an unspecified period of time.[76] Unfortunately, the nature of these absences remains a mystery. It is possible that these men acted as representatives of the pope in diplomatic missions or fiscal affairs. Such was the case with Martinus de Prato, who, though not specifically designated as a member of the papal chapel during the year 1373 was, however, engaged in business undertaken on the pope's behalf.[77]

In the financial records of 1373, the *capellani capelle* are classified as *familiares*.[78] The term *familiaris pape* applied to all those who participated in the running and management of the papal household from the principal administrative clerks down to the scullions. The title had always applied to the *capellani* and *clerici* of the papal chapel, but only after 8 July 1347 was its use extended to include the *abbreviatores* and the *scriptores litterarum apostolicarum* and *penitentiarum*. Occasionally the privilege of being called a papal familiar was honorifically bestowed.[79] Therefore, those chaplains who served as *scriptors*, and for whom we do not find evidence of service in the papal chapel for any given year before 1347, but who are listed as familiars of the pope, undoubtedly continued to serve as chaplains throughout the period in question. For example, in 1345 Guillelmus de Flandria, both *scriptor* and familiar of the pope, was more than likely serving in the papal chapel, since he would have received the title of papal familiar by virtue of his service as *capellanus* not as *scriptor*. On the other hand, in 1352, the designation of Guillelmus as *scriptor* and *familiar* does not denote any association with the chapel, since after 1347 all *scriptors* were *ipso facto* familiars.

On 9 December 1374, *8 capellani capelle intrinsece* were paid for the entire preceding two-month period and five were given a partial wage, certain of these for 13 days. The payment was said to be similar to the one made 14 October.[80] Data on the personnel of the chapel is incomplete for the next several years.[81]

Although, as a rule, a number of chaplains were held over from the *capella* of one pope to another, the chapel was nevertheless subject to many variations in composition within each pontificate. The members of the chapel who seem to have provided the most stability were those who held the offices of *clericus* and *magister capelle*. In some sense, they must have preserved the traditions of the *capella intrinseca* and were no doubt able to pass them on to new *cantores* and future *clerici*. Once again, these practices were to make their way back to the Italian peninsula.

Pope Gregory XI was the only Avignon pope not to spend money on the enlargement of the papal palace, and he probably always considered the eventuality of a return to Rome. With the memory of the Blessed Urban still fresh in the minds of the faithful, on 13 September 1376 Gregory left the city of Avignon, ending what was the longest stay outside Italy in the history of the papacy.[82] We know for a fact that Gregory was accompanied by Johannes Ruffi de Roquignies and Johannes Volkardi from among his *capellani*, since they were both in the papal chapel during 1377; and Franciscus de Goano served the pontiff after his arrival in Italy. The exact fate of the other chaplains is unclear. There is, however, some evidence that eight of the men might have also made the journey to Rome. On 28 July 1377, payment was made to Bernardus Arnieu de Martegna for the fare of transporting 16 packages and 8 valets (*famuli*) of the chaplains of the papal chapel from Avignon to Rome.[83] There are several ways of interpreting this information: the *capellani* may have been allowed eight valets to serve them as necessary. Or each of the *capellani capelle,* if there were in fact eight of them, might have been permitted a *famulus* either expressly for this journey or as a rule. By this time in the history of the papal chapel, the status of the *capellani* could have increased to the extent that they were allowed to retain servants much as the *capellani commensales* had been able to do. If there were more than eight chaplains then in papal service, some might have had valets while others not. The evidence of assistants for the *capellani,* if such evidence could be found throughout the pontificate of Gregory, would help to explain the absence of *clerici* at this time. These assistants might have had some chapel functions that obviated the need for *clerici.*

The fiasco of the election of Bartolomeo Prignano and the subsequent counter-election of Clement VII that took place at Fondi on 20 September 1378 brought the papacy back to Avignon nine months later certainly in a temporal, if not spiritual sense. Of the papal chaplains at this time, we know of only one defector to the Roman camp: by 1380 Johannes Volkardi had become the master of the chapel for Urban VI.

## The Chapel During the Schism

In November 1378 Clement VII received the first supplications written in the city of Fondi by the members of his chapel. Franciscus de Goano calls himself chaplain of Clement VII and Gregory XI. One wonders if he also might briefly have served the Roman pope in a similar capacity. The other names found are those of Matheus de Longariga, Thomas Multoris, Simon Chauvin, and the familiars Thomas la Caille and Philippus Roberti.

The following *capellani* were paid on 19 September 1379:

1) Symon Haquetin
2) Philippus Roberti
3) Matheus de Longariga
4) Johannes de Moleio
5) Symon Chauvin
6) Ancelmus Martini
7) Franciscus de Goano
8) Thomas Multoris
9) Jacobus de Griseovillari
10) Thomas le Quaille
11) Henricus Poneti
12) Jaquetus (I)
13) Richardus (II)[84]

Henricus Poneti, appearing eleventh on this list, served in the papal chapel in November 1378 when he was referred to as *servitor, subdiaconus,* and *familiaris.* He continued in his service through the early part of 1379, and on 12

February 1379 he is found as *subdiaconus capelle* for the pope. This reference is somewhat misleading, since the office of subdeacon was linked to the *capellani commensales* as early as the late thirteenth century, and no such title was associated with the chapel of *capellani* or *cantores* that concerns us. But we can conclude that Henricus bore the title of subdeacon because of his rank in Holy Orders, and not because of his chapel functions.[85]

Symon Haquetin held the office of master of the papal chapel on 6 September 1379 and, as such, was responsible for distribution of the 215 cameral florins, 2 solidi, and 2 denarii paid to the chapel members.[86] The wage for service in the *capella* seems not to have been altered in any way since the first complete payment made in 1337 to 13 chaplains for a two-month period. On 17 September 1381, Johannes de Champiengyo and a Stephanus make their first appearance as *cantores*. The latter was the priest Stephanus Turqueti, called familiar and *capellanus capelle* in a document dated 14 October 1381.[87]

The payments made 30 October and 20 December 1382 contain complete lists of chaplains, and these are identical, save the reversed positions of two *capellani*. The later roster contains the following names:

1)  Symon Haquetin, *magister*
2)  Matheus le Longariga
3)  Ancelmus Martini
4)  Thomas Multoris
5)  Jacobus de Griseovillari
6)  Richardus (II)
7)  Henricus Poneti
8)  Johannes de Champieng
9)  Stephanus Turqueti
10) Guillermus de Ultraaquam
11) Bertrandus le Connoitie
12) Jacobus Ringardi
13) Matheus de Sancto Johanne[88]

This is followed by the reappearance of the names of Pontius de Curte and Petrus Salteti, reinstated as the *clerici capelle pape*.

The composition of the chapel seems to have remained constant for at least the next several months. Certain minor changes in orthography are to be noted in a list of 26 March 1383, the most significant of which is the transformation of Jacobus Ringardi to Jaquetus Ringardi.[89] It is possible, therefore, that the chaplain Jaquetus Ringardi named here is identical to the Jacquetus (I) who served in the chapel in 1379.

The subsequent payments for the year 1383 have been summarily noted in the documents, and they do not provide a full list of chaplains. Yet although we do not know the names of the men who served for the remainder of this year, a full complement of 13 *capellani* (12 *capellani* proper, plus the *magister*) and 2 *clerici* was in place.[90]

By 22 January 1384, Philippus Roberti, who served Clement at the beginning of his reign, was dead, and in June of that year we find Petrus Bataille referred to as papal familiar. The mention of Petrus would bear no special significance in and of in itself were it not for the fact that ten years later he would be found in the papal chapel. His appearance here in 1384 as familiar might have signified a brief participation as *capellanus*. During August of the same year, the composer Matheus de Sancto Johanne was called *familiaris* in a document that confers on him a benefice once belonging to Thomas la Caille, by then deceased.[91]

The master of the chapel throughout the late 1380s was Simon Haquetin.[92] He was engaged in the activities of the *magister* at least until 27 August 1388, and at the time of the last appearance of his name, 3 January 1389, he was still a papal familiar.[93] His successor was Johannes de Moleyo, chaplain in 1379, and again in 1384 and 1387. He served as *magister* from December 1388 until August 1392.[94] During 1387, Simon had an assistant, the priest, Petrus de Godescaut. Although his duties remain unspecified, this cleric bore the title, *servitor magistri capelle pape*.[95]

The renown of the *capella pape* had spread far and wide by the 1380s. King John of Aragon considered the singers of the pope to know the best motets and songs. The exchange of personnel between nobility and ecclesiastics that began in the 1360s continued at this time. The composer Matheus de Sancto Johanne was attached to the court of Louis I of Anjou and probably to that of Queen Joanna of Naples before his appearance in the chapel of the pope. The *capellanus* Johannes Lenfant served under Duke Louis as well. The composer Johannes Symonis is named in the papal documents first in the employ of the King of Portugal, then later in the service of the Angevin duke, Louis II. Thomas Multoris also seems to have been associated with the royal court of Portugal while he was serving as a papal chaplain.

During the first years of the 1390s, mention is made of several new chaplains in papal employ. In the record of payment to 14 *capellani* and 2 *clerici* made in May 1391, two names are cited for the first time: Johannes de Bosco and Raynaudinus de Hos [du Houx].[96] In July of that year, a Johannes Vitrassi [Vitrarii] is noted as being a papal familiar and chaplain. At the end of 1392, Richardus de Bozonvilla acts as substitute for the master of the chapel, Johannes de Moleyo.[97] This reference to an apparently new chaplain is most likely nothing more than the full name of the *capellanus* Richardus (II) who is found in service of the papal chapel from at least 1379. In the spring of the following year, the composer Johannes de Altacuria makes his first appearance as *capellanus pape,* and we find Guillelmus de Ultraaquam still maintaining his status as *familiaris pape.*

A document drawn up on 30 October 1393 and recording the payment to the chaplains and clerks yields the first complete chapel list since 1385.[98] In an action usually reserved for the master of the chapel, Stephanus Turqueti received the payment for the *clerici* Pontius de Curte and Petrus Salteti and for the 14 *capellani*:

    1)  Richardus   [Richardus (II)=de Bozonvilla]
    2)  Stephanus Turqueti
    3)  Guillelmus de Ultraaquam
    4)  Bertrandus   [le Convotie?]
    5)  Johannes Lenfan
    6)  Droynus   [Androynus?=Andrieu du Mor?]
    7)  Henrietus   [Scoenheze?]
    8)  Franciscus   [Johannes Franciscus?]
    9)  Johannes Lathomi
    10) Johannes Verrerii   [Vitrarii]
    11) Johannes de Altacuria
    12) Johannes Symonis
    13) Johannes de Boscho
    14) Raynaudinus   [du Houx]

In December 1393 and April 1394, Johannes de Moleyo is again called *magister capelle*.[99]

On 16 September 1394, Pope Clement VII died. His successor was the cardinal deacon from Aragon, Pedro de Luna. Elected on 28 September, ordained priest on 3 October, he was consecrated Pope Benedict XIII on 11 October 1394.[100] The first list of his chapel members was made on 5 October and stands as follows:

    1)  Johannes de Molleyo
    2)  Richardus   [de Bozonvilla]
    3)  Ancelmus   [Landeluy]
    4)  Johannes Lathomi
    5)  Johannes Rogerii
    6)  Johannes Vitrarii
    7)  Robertus Nyot
    8)  Johannes de Altacuria
    9)  Johannes Asproys   [Symonis]
    10) Johannes de Bosco
    11) Reginaldus du Houx
    12) Bataille   [Petrus Bataille]
    13) Hanetus   [Johannes Hanini]
    14) Jaquetus   [Jacobus Brisart][101]

On this same day, Petrus Salteti and Pontius de Curte were sworn in as *clerici capelle* for the new pope. The list begins with the title: *Cantores sive capellani capelle et quidam alii familiares et servitores.*[102] The status of the *capellani* as papal familiars was maintained throughout the Avignon papacy, just as their equation with *cantores* had been the rule since 1371.

A series of supplications submitted during the month of October 1394 corroborates much of the above information. Yet almost immediately after the date of composition of these requests, the make-up of Benedict's chapel was altered considerably from what it had been at the outset. On 13 October, Johannes Rogerii is referred to in a supplication as *olim capellanus capelle* [*pape*] *et servitor, nunc capellanus capele* [sic] *ducis Burgondie.* According to the evidence found in a rotulus submitted five days later by the same duke, Johannes Vitrarii had also entered the Burgundian chapel. In addition to these men, Duke Philip the Bold managed to acquire several clerics who had been singers in the chapel of the late Pope Clement.[103]

The well-documented interchange of personnel between the Burgundian and papal courts provides the most outstanding example of the position of the chapel singers at this time. It has already been shown that, early in the fourteenth century, papal chaplains often had previous experience serving cardinals and bishops residing at Avignon. After the deaths of their papal employers, some *capellani* reentered the chapels of other curial members. While comings and goings within the Curia occurred throughout the Avignon papacy, we can demonstrate like exchanges between the chapels of pontiffs and prelates and those of the secular princes taking place during the last third of the century. Indeed, toward the end of the 1400s there are indications that the singer's lot had become an increasingly independent one. Many of these men seemed not to bear allegiance to any one power or patron, but instead sold their services to various households and switched employers seemingly at will. The frequent interchange of *capellani* offered even greater opportunities for the diffusion of liturgical customs, polyphonic mass repertoire, and secular songs and motets.

On 21 October 1394, 6 of the remaining 12 chaplains of Pope Benedict XIII each submitted a supplication on behalf of a cleric of little status. Two of those named, Thomas Leonardi and Johannes Hobaut, stood as *familiares,* not of the pope, but of their respective patrons, the chaplains Ancelmus Landeluy and Richardus de Bozonvilla. Again, it must be stressed that there is no evidence that the 4 remaining supplicants were familiars of their chaplain-patrons (Johannes de Moleyo, de Altacuria, Symonis, and de Bosco), but since there was evidence of valets having been attached to the *capellani* as far back as the return of the papacy to Rome in 1376, it is possible that at this time such was the rule. If so, the support for these men did not come from the pontifical coffers but must have been supplied by the *capellani* themselves and by any ecclesiastical benefice and favor that they could have obtained through their influence.

The list of 23 December 1395 shows that 12 chaplains were employed, though only a few of the names are legible: Richardus de Bosanvilla, Anselmus, Johannes de Altacuria, Johannes Symonis, and Johannes de Bosco. For the wages due 15 January and paid 9 March 1396, we know only that Johannes de Altacuria handled the payment made to the 13 chaplains and 2 clerks. On 24 March, Petrus Capucii was admitted to the chapel, and the entry of 2 May 1396 for service rendered up to 12 April shows his name among those of the *capellani*:

1) Richardus   [de Bozonvilla]
2) Anselmus   [Landeluy]
3) Johannes Regem   [=Regerii?=Rogerii][104]
4) Johannes Vitirari
5) Johannes de Altacuria
6) Johannes Symonis
7) Johannes de Bosco P[ellisson] servit[105]
8) Johannes Aneti   [Hanini]
9) Jaquetus   [Jacobus Brisart?]
10) Guillermus Fabri
11) Petrus Capucii
12) Robertus Moti   [=Nioti?=Nyot]
13) Pontius de Curte   [*clericus*]
14) Anequinus Fabri   [*clericus*][106]

We know that Johannes de Bosco received the wages of 14 chaplains and 2 clerks on 19 July 1396.[107] The payment made 1 February 1397 for the 15 *capellani* and 2 *clerici* was likewise accepted by Johannes on behalf of the *magister*, Richardus. Johannes de Altacuria was given the wages of the chaplains and clerks in March 1396 and August 1397. During 1397 Johannes Hanini and the subdeacon Petrus Bataille no doubt served as chaplains.[108]

The account books for the time after August 1398 are, unfortunately, missing, and the curial records of supplications and letters provide little assistance since many of them are also lost.[109] Faced with the prospect of being deprived of the income from their benefices after the French crown withdrew its obedience, it is possible that some or all of Benedict's *capellani* deserted him, and in the list of 226 supporters of the pope named in Martin de Alpartil's *Chronica,* only the name of Johannes de Boscho is recognized by us.[110] The name is common enough not to be that of the papal singer, and such an assumption based on the coincidence of name alone cannot be made. In any case, there is no evidence precluding the possibility that all or some of the *capellani* abandoned the pope for the sake of their own safety. They might have remained in Avignon, though not in the palace. They might also have left the city, taken up residence at the place of their principal benefice, and fulfilled the *cura* of a rectorate, chaplaincy, etc. One chaplain who repaired to his principal benefice was the *magister capelle* himself, Richardus de Bozonvilla.

According to the extant notarial accounts for the chapter of the cathedral of Apt, Richardus began his residence as provost there at the latest on 4 June 1400, the year in which he is believed to have been named to this office.

Richardus is reported as having been present on more than 40 separate occasions over the next several years. His last documented presence at a meeting of the chapter bears the date 9 March 1403. Two days later on the morning of 11 March 1403, Benedict XIII escaped from the palace at Avignon where he was held captive. Neither he nor any other pope or pretender would set foot in Avignon again.

What happened to the remainder of the papal chaplains during the intervening years is not clear. Benedict regained enough political and financial support following his escape that within five months he was able to reassemble the greater part of the *capella* of 1396 in his residence at Pont-de-Sorgues. On Saturday 11 August 1403, the following members of the chapel were sworn in:

1) Richardus  [de Bozonvilla]
2) Ancelmus  [Landeluy]
3) Johannes Rogerii
4) Johannes Haucourt  [Altacuria]
5) Johannes Hasprois  [Symonis]
6) Johannes Vitrarii
7) Johannes de Bosco
8) Thomas Milonis
9) Bernardus  [Gralheri?]
10) Johannes de Cruce
11) Henrietus  [Pousardi?]
12) P. Salteti  [*clericus*][111]

At the end of September, while the pontiff was still at his castle at Pont-de-Sorgues, Gerardus Gerardi joined the chapel. On 13 October at Salon, a rotulus was submitted on behalf of the new chaplains, Johannes de Cruce and Petrus Sellerii. On this day, too, Johannes Broulette is first referred to as *capellanus capelle pape,* though he is only formally received into the chapel at Tarascon, 7 December 1403.[112] During his journey to the Mediterranean coast, Benedict evidently had difficulty in retaining old chaplains but not in recruiting new ones.

Jacobus de Massas [Macas] was sworn into the chapel on 13 January 1404, and a little over three months later the oath was administered to Petrus Selerii.[113] By 5 August, Reginaldus du Houx had left his post at Burgundy after the burial of his employer, Philip, and returned once again to serve as chaplain of the pope. On 24 September 1404 an entry for the remuneration of 11 *capellani seu cantores* and 2 *clerici* was composed, and the following list of 8 November yields the names of all the chapel members:

1) Richardus de Bosamvilla
2) Johannes Vitrarii
3) Johannes de Bosco
4) Regnadol de Houx

5)  Thomas Milonis
6)  Johannes de Cruce
7)  Bernardus Gralheri
8)  Gerardus Gerardi
9)  Johannes Boulette
10)  Jacobus de Macas
11)  Petrus Selheri
12)  Henricus Pousardi
13)  Petrus Salteti   *clericus*
*14)  Jacobus de Pratis   clericus*

The composer Johannes Symonis makes his last appearance in the records of Benedict XIII on 24 September 1404.

After the death of Richardus de Bozonvilla in the city of Nice, 29 January 1405, Gerardus Gerardi handled the accounts of the chapel as *locum tenens magistri capelle.* The information is somewhat sketchy for the next several years, since this was the time when the pope made his first voyage to north Italy. The chapel, which comprised 12 chaplains and 2 clerks on 24 April 1405, began to lose strength by the beginning of the summer. On 21 June while in the city of Genoa, Johannes Burec, Guillermus Epi, and Johannes Desrame were paid for their service as *cantores.*[115] It has been assumed that these three were members of the chapel, although this unique appearance in the accounts for each precludes a categorical statement to that effect. As in the case of Petrus Selerii, one who served in the papal chapel did not necessarily have to take the oath of fidelity to that office. It is conceivable that these three *cantores* were recruited from among the clerics of Genoa. It is likewise possible that the pontiff temporarily engaged a number of singers in each of the towns where he resided in order to bolster his weakened chapel. By 3 July there were only 5 regular members of the *capella,* possibly indicating that this was in fact the practice:

1)  Gerardus Gerardi
2)  Jacobus Macas
3)  Enricus Pusuardi
4)  Jacobus de Prato [*clericus*]
5)  Petrus Rosseleti [*clericus*][116]

On 8 July 1405 in the city of Genoa, Raymundus Arnulphi, a priest from the diocese of Limoges, was sworn in as *magister organorum,* and as such became a member of the papal chapel and received a chaplain's stipend.[117] This is the first reference to the office of the *magister organorum* in the *capella pape* that has come to light. It seems now necessary to assume that an organ was present in the chapel, in order to explain the presence of a man hired to regularly play it. This is not to preclude the possibility of the use of the organ in the papal chapel before this time; neither does it rule out the earlier establishment of the office of organ master, nor the possibility that a particular *capellanus*, besides being a singer, might have also played this instrument.

The mention of this apparently new office, *magister organorum*, may be indicative of a reorganization of the chapel offices taking place at this time. We also find the reference in 1405 to Pascasius de Briella, *scolaris capelle pape*.[118] Could he have been a choirboy attached to the chapel of Benedict? This sole reference allows us little further speculation. However, boy singers were very much a part of the chapel of the kings of Aragon from 1349, and this Aragonese pope, who drew much of his support and power from the Iberian peninsula, might also have been influenced in this regard.[119] The two *clerici* associated with the papal chapel were called *clerici cerimoniarum* beginning in 1405, offering further indication that a reform of the duties and titles of office in the *capella* of Pope Benedict was taking place.[120]

From papal correspondence dated 2 November 1405 we learn the names of two *capellani* then serving in the chapel: Nicolaus Vacherii and Johannes Broulette. When the pope was residing at Noli (Savona) during the end of June 1406, there was an outbreak of plague, and one of the chaplains died. A report from 27 June tells us that the fear of plague was so great among the papal singers after the death of one of their members they could not be found for Mass.[121] The next day the pope arrived at Finale where, because of the fatigue and absence of many of the singers, he could not hold papal Vespers.[122] In a document from 18 July 1406, we learn that a canonicate at Cambrai became vacant through the death *in loco de Finario, Saonensis diocesis,* of the *capellanus capelle,* Johannes Broulette.

The fear of plague, the instability in the location of the Curia which at this time was journeying through northern Italy and southern France, and the ever-dwindling power and influence of Benedict XIII did not deter the chaplains from acquiring prebended benefices. On 6 September 1406, chaplain Nicolaus Vacherii resigned a rectorate which then went to Petrus Selheri, papal familiar. Gerardus Gerardi acted as procurer in the transaction. On 10 September, Balduinus Piercoul who, before 1403, had long been serving in the chapel as *clericus, servitor sacriste capelle,* is noted as *servitor in capella pape.* By 30 November 1406, Johannes de Bosco, chaplain of the chapel, was dead, and Robertus Creque, *clericus capelle,* was seeking one of his benefices. Johannes might have passed on well before the date the supplication was written. And the very fact that he died as a *capellanus* suggests his death occurred between his last recorded appearance as an active chaplain, 23 September 1404, and 3 July 1405, the intervening period for which there are no extant chapel records.[123]

Pope Benedict was making his way back to France early in 1408, and in Porto Venere his chapel was staffed by a total of 11 chaplains and 2 clerks. Among *capellani* named during this period were Johannes de Manso, Johannes Foliomeri, Bernardus Gralherii, and Robertus Creque, formerly a member of the Aragonese royal chapel.

During the year 1408/09, the virtually powerless Sovereign Pontiff continued to retain six *capellani* under his *magister capelle* Gerardus Gerardi:

1)   Bernardus Gralheri
2)   Enricus Pousardi
3)   Johannes Vinyas
4)   Fericus Musilen [Nusilleti]
5)   Teodoricus Candelerii
6)   Johannes de Manso[124]

Though information about Pedro de Luna's *capella* becomes ever so rare after this time, we do know that he continued to maintain some semblance of a chapel for at least eight more years.

## The Office of *Capellanus* in 1409

Near the end of the account of François de Conzié that records much of the activity of Benedict XIII for the year 1406/07, there is a section listing the various offices of the papal household which outlines the specific duties assigned to each office holder. Dated 4 July 1409, it was written for the Pisan pope, Alexander V (26 June 1409-†3 May 1410), as a guide to building his court. The practice of Benedict was used as the model. There is one short chapter that concerns us here and is worth citing at length, the chapter entitled: *Capella.*

> Next, the Supreme Pontiff saw fit to have singers in his chapel; and among them there is to be one, who is called the *magister capelle* to whose office it pertains to direct and to govern all the others as much as it regards the service of said chapel. (The singers) who, on each day, with our lord (the pope) present or absent, ought to say Mass aloud in the chapel established for this. And they should sing both Vespers and Matins, if and when our lord should conduct them to the service mandated on account of the solemnity of the feast.
>
> Next, said *magister capelle,* if suited to this, ought to read the Bible at the mid-day meal in front of our lord and ought to say the blessing and to intone grace. And because of this, he should dine in the Apostolic palace but not sup there. If, however, that *magister* should not be so disposed, he ought to elect one of those singers who would do the abovesaid.
>
> Next, the number of said singers beyond the said *magister* seems to suffice at 12.
>
> Next, beyond the aforementioned, there ought to be two clerics, who are called *clerici capelle* or *ceremoniarum*. And thus in this chapel there are 15 persons, who should not see fit to eat in the apostolic palace, except on certain solemnities. They do, however, receive a certain stipend in cameral pounds, and they have their lodgings outside the palace.
>
> [Next, beyond said stipend, the Supreme Pontiff should give clothes to all on an annual basis.]
>
> Next, among those mentioned are priests who ought to say Mass in front of the pope on alternate weeks.

This early fifteenth-century description of the papal chapel agrees with the *capella* originally desired by Pope Benedict XII (1334-1342) in only one point:

there were to be 12 chaplains to sing the canonical hours (Matins and Vespers) for the pope. In most aspects, the nature of the chapel had changed. These changes primarily occurred for one important reason. Namely, Benedict XII did not effect a reform of his *capellani commensales* as he had originally intended but, instead, created a new chapel that in many ways replaced the commensal chaplains.[126] There are, in fact, several direct correlations between the two *capelle*. For example, they were both assigned *clerici* to serve within the chapel. Liturgical functions that had been carried out by the *commensales* at the end of the thirteenth century became the domain of the *cantores* by the pontificate of Benedict XIII. More than 100 years before Conzié wrote his description of the offices of the papal household, it fell to the commensal chaplains to celebrate Mass daily in front of the pope, if he did not celebrate. A chaplain, called *hebdomadarius,* was selected to perform the service for the week.[127] By the end of the Avignon papacy, such a task belonged to the priests among the *cantores, clerici,* and *magister.*

The replacement of the *commensales* in liturgical and in musical duties led naturally to an increase in status for the *cantores.* They continued to receive a stipend and probably clothing from the pope. However, by 1409, they no longer lived communally in a dormitory but probably in individual residences outside the palace. Consequently, they no longer ate in the Apostolic palace.[128] Since they received any number of ecclesiastical benefices *sine cura,* the potential existed for amassing considerable wealth.[129] With this increased income, they were in a position to retain servants and possibly to maintain small "families" of familiars. In 1377, as we have already noted, the *capellani* were permitted *famuli,* or valets, to assist them in the journey to Rome. This most certainly did not conform to the ideals of Benedict XII embodied in the chapel of 1334. Moreover, we know that by 1367 Johannes de Ulmo maintained a familiar, and, in 1394, two senior *cantores,* Ancelmus Landeluy and Richardus de Bozonvilla, were wealthy enough to sustain at least one familiar each. At this time, too, the chaplains had attained a position influential enough to enable them to sponsor friends and associates in soliciting benefices from the pope.

The fact is that by the end of the Avignon papacy the *capella commensalis* virtually ceased to exist. During the pontificates of Clement V and John XXII, before the founding of the *capella intrinseca* as a musico-liturgical institution, the popes maintained a maximum of 34 and 19 commensal chaplains, respectively. After the hiring of the singing chaplains, the recruitment of *commensales* continued in a similar fashion until the accession of Gregory XI. This pope brought only 3 commensal chaplains into the household during his entire pontificate. In 1372, he disbanded the *clerici capelle* entirely. He regularly paid several priests to say Mass in the various chapels of the Palace of the Popes instead of having a college of commensal chaplains for this purpose. Pope Clement VII reinstituted the title and received a total of 34 chaplains into his *capella commensalis.* These, combined with a great number of papal singers, must have made the liturgical service of this pope the most magnificent in the history of the Avignonese papacy. His successor, Pope Benedict XIII, on the other hand, seemed to use the title more-or-less honorifically.[130] By 1409, according to Conzié, the only *capella pape* was the chapel of *magister, clerici cerimoniarum,* and *cantores.*

The *capella* of Benedict XII in 1334 was a personal chapel that received the impetus for its creation in the austere tastes of its founder. It numbered Cistercian monks and household functionaries among its first members. By the time it had passed through the pontificate of Clement VI with its monarchic bent and close ties to the French royal court, the chapel had become a college of papal servers primarily drawn from the dioceses of the lowlands to the north. This practice continued throughout the Avignonese period and beyond. While Innocent VI and Urban V had no particular love for this *capella,* they continued to maintain it through dire financial hardships, drawing many of its experienced members from the chapels of curial prelates and secular princes. Though many of the *capellani* served the pontiffs as *scriptors,* almoners, and the like, by the last third of the fourteenth century the title *capellanus capelle* became synonymous with *cantor.* The sojourns in Italy of Urban and Gregory must have exposed the papal singers to musical and liturgical practices that had been previously unknown to northern, French-speaking musicians. When Clement VII brought the schismatic Curia and *capella* back to Avignon in 1379, he began what became the most impressive college of musicians and servers in Europe. During his pontificate and that of successor, Benedict XIII, the composers Matheus de Sancto Johanne, Johannes Symonis, Johannes de Altacuria, and Johannes de Bosco alias Pellisson all served as *capellani capelle pape.* The musico-liturgical traditions developed in Avignon, took root in the other papal capitals of Pisa and Rome, and flourished during the next century. It was from this practice of employing skilled composers at Avignon that grew the Roman chapel of international renown, one which ultimately attracted such luminaries as Dufay, Agricola, and Josquin.[131]

Fig. 6.   Personnel of the Papal Chapel.

| | Clement V | John XXII | Benedict XII | Clement VI | Innocent XI | Urban V | Gregory XI | Clement VII | Benedict XIII |
|---|---|---|---|---|---|---|---|---|---|
| *Capellani commensales* | 12-34 | 17-19 | 10-23 | 15-17 | 18-29 | 18 | 3 | 34 | 16 |
| *Clerici capelle* | 1-2 | 2 | 1 | 2 | 2 | 2 | 0-2 | 0-2 | 2 |
| *Capellani intrinseci** (cantores) | — | — | 12 | 9-12 | 8-10 | 8 | 10-13 | 12-14 | 3-13 |
| *Clerici capelle intrinsece* | — | — | 1 | 1 | 2 | 2 | *United to the clerici capelle* | | |

*Not including the magister capelle.

# 3

# The *Magister Capelle Pape*

The office of the *magister capelle pape* as it existed during the Avignon period has been a subject of interest for almost a century.[1] Its importance as it relates to later periods in the history of music is only significant as regards nomenclature, since the papal chapel at Avignon seems to have been the first institution to have had an office so called. The curiosity it has aroused is due more to the unfortunate similarity to the title *Kapellmeister* as it was used in eighteenth-century Germany and Austria than to any genuine interest in the development of the post at Avignon itself. It would, therefore, not be an entirely unfruitful endeavor to investigate both the duties of the office and the *magistri* themselves as they relate to our study of music at Avignon.

## Petrus Sinterii

At the outset of the establishment of the *capelle intrinsece* in December 1334, there was no provision made for the office of *magister capelle* nor was there any indication that such a title would have necessarily evolved. Not long afterwards, however, one chaplain, Petrus Sinterii, came to appear at the head of the list of *capellani*.[2] By 1341 this cleric had acquired the responsibility for the various expenses incurred in the chapel.[3] On 16 April 1342, for example, he was paid for the copper or brass case (*cassola*) that held the coals used in censing.[4]

The term *magister capelle* itself seems first to have been applied to Petrus in a document containing the accounts for the year 1340.[5] We know for sure that he officially held the title before 24 July 1342.[6] On 6 August of that year, however, he was called *capellanus capelle pape.*[7] One week later, as *magister capelle*, he was paid for repairs that he had made on the altar parament.[8] At this early stage, there was probably not much distinction between his chapel duties and the tasks of the other chaplains. He no doubt served during the Mass and the offices as was required of all *capellani*.

The notices reveal that most of the obligations of the *magister* were related to the purchase or the maintenance of the accouterment of the chapel. In October 1342, he was responsible for repairs made on the gold antependium that hung behind the altar.[9] He had a cathedra constructed in 1343, and in 1345, he was paid for two new lecterns fashioned for use in the chapel and for the repair of a third that was used on the altar.[10] He had old fabrics washed and purchased new ones.[11] He had certain vestments made.[12] He provided utensils such as *cassole,* candelabra, ampules for holy oil, and the like. Objects not in use were kept in storage under his custody.[13] He purchased the rush mats and the incense used in the chapel.[14] In sum, Petrus Sinterii functioned as a liaison between the Apostolic Camera and those innumerable merchants and craftsmen who flocked to Avignon to sell their wares and services. He was responsible for maintaining the chapel, for procuring the necessary items, and for keeping account of his expenses.

One of his primary concerns was the transportation of the trappings of the chapel. In late October 1342, Petrus was held accountable for transporting many boxes and furnishing to the papal chapel at Villeneuve-lès-Avignon.[15] The boxes probably contained furniture, tapestries, ornaments, and chapel books. The following April, the *magister* was paid for carrying the relics across the bridge, no doubt for the consecration of the altar in the papal chapel at Villeneuve.[16]

By 13 October 1345, Petrus was reimbursed for transporting objects both to and from the chapels in the cities across the Rhône.[17] In May 1350, the accounts reveal the more specific reference that he had *plures libros ad dicendum matutinas et officium in vesperas* carried to the chapels *ultra pontem* and *citra pontem* for the great feasts.[18] He had custody of the chapel books and was responsible for their repair and maintenance.[19] In February 1349, the cameral accounts indicate that he accepted payment *pro ligatura aliquorum quaternorum librorum capelle* and *pro cordonibus sive reyeriis pro libris capelle.*[20] At the death of Petrus Sinterii, which occurred before 20 November 1350, the tasks of the *magister capelle pape* must have been well defined.

## Stephanus de Chaulageto

Petrus's successor, drawn from among the *capellani* serving at this time, was Stephanus de Chaulageto. We have precious few references to him serving in his office. The records dated 13 February 1351 show that his duties likewise included provision of chapel furnishings. On that date, he received payment *pro 7 pannis magnis,* large drapes that covered the chapel benches *in quibus sedent cardinales.*[21] Significantly, the duties of the *magister* began to focus on those items of greater intrinsic value. Stephanus held a large, two-volume gradual in his possession, and several months before he died he compiled an inventory of the *iocalia et ornamenta* of the chapel. These *iocalia* were precious objects, not furnishings of wood or fabric but the gold and silver chalices, reliquaries, and statues.[22] Stephanus's term as *magister* was rather short compared to that of his predecessor. He died between 10 April and 25 August 1353.

Besides this shift to the more valuable items as his principal concern, the status of the *magister* vis-à-vis that of the other *capellani* underwent a similar redefinition. According to the cameral accounts dated 1 February 1353, a stoneworker was paid for building an archway near the well of the *camera domini Stephani magistri capelle*.[23] The notice yields the first evidence that any of the *capellani intrinsece* was not living in the common room, or dormitory, as decreed by Benedict XII. It is probably not without significance that the first indication of a private room for the *magister* appears at the time when certain portions of the Clementine palace were being completed. It was likely under the influence of Pope Clement's aristocratic ideal that the master of the chapel could be permitted the luxury of living alone.

## Johannes Ademari

Unlike the two who served before him, Johannes Ademari seems neither to have been a member of the papal chapel nor to have been in the employ of the pope before he began his tenure as *magister*. On 17 October 1354, Johannes was paid for the expenses of the chapel incurred from 12 September 1353 until 27 September 1354. His duties during this first year closely follow the precedents set by Petrus and Stephanus. He provided two pyxes for the hosts, a rope for the workings of the clock, one pound of incense, and some paper that was placed under the candelabra to catch the dripping wax. He also washed the albs and the amices, re-bound an evangel, had a key made for the chapel at Villeneuve, and transported those objects necessary for the operation of the chapel when the pope went to Villeneuve in April of that year.[24]

Not only was Johannes concerned with the expenses of the chapel but also with the custody and inventory of the vestments, furnishings, and *iocalia*.[25] In 1353, he took possession of those ornaments that were kept by Stephanus and by Petrus before him: paraments, chasubles, albs, and the *libri capelle*.[26] He drew up the following list of books in 1353, one representing the collection used in the papal chapel.

1) First, one book containing 7 masses (the first of which is for Easter) beginning on the second folio: *et terram.*
2) Next, another book of 7 masses (the first of which is for Pentecost) beginning as above [on the second folio]: *deinde dicat.*
3) Next, one legendary for Sundays and feast days, beginning as above: *accepturus est.*
4) Next, a notated antiphoner, beginning as above: *entem et nebula.*
5) Next, a psalter, beginning as above: *sanctis mereamur.*
6) Next, a text of the gospels, beginning as above: *desertum videre.*
7) Next, one missal, beginning as above: *am, ubi eum videbis.*
8) Next, one epistolary of little volume, beginning as above: *radix Yesse.*

9) Next, one book of new offices (the first of which is for Trinity) beginning as above: *de lumen cordibus.*
10) Next, a Roman ordinary, beginning as above: *R. bre Christe fili.*
11) Next, one epistolary, beginning as above: *bunt deus autem.*
12) Next, one missal, beginning: *dio templi.*
13) Next, one book of five masses (of which the first is for the Assumption of Mary) beginning as above: *sicut erat in principio.*
14) Next, another book of five masses (the first of which is for Trinity) beginning as above: *confiteor deo.*
15) Next, another book of four masses (the first of which is for the Purification of Mary) beginning as above: *Filio et Spiritui Sancto.*
16) Next, another book of five masses (the first of which is for the Innocents) beginning as above: *meam. Postea papa dicit.*
17) Next, another book of four masses (the first of which is for dawn of Christmas) beginning as above: *et nunc et semper.*
18) Next, another book of four masses (the first of which is for St. Andrew) beginning as above: *qui fecit celum et terram.*
19) Next, another book of four masses (the first of which is for the Annunciation of Mary) beginning on the third folio: *subsequenter dicant.*
20) Next, another book of five masses (the first of which is for Quadragesima Sunday) beginning as above: *tutem meam.*
21) Next, a pontifical, beginning on the second folio in red: *eum dicit antiphonam.*[27]
22) Next, one missal, beginning as above: *vatur preterquam.*
23) Next, one gradual, beginning on the third folio: *meam Deus meus.*
24) Next, one breviary, beginning on the second folio: *miserere mei.*
25) Next, one psalter *collectarium,* beginning as above: *autem constitutus sum.*
26) Next, one gradual beginning on the third folio: *letitia cordis nostri.*
27) Next, one breviary, beginning on the second folio: *orationem meam suscepit.*
28) Next, one book of new offices, beginning as above: *una trinitas.*
29) Next, one missal, beginning as above: *rideant me inimici mei.*
30) Next, one psalter, beginning as above: *tatis tue.*
31) Next, *flores sanctorum,* beginning as above: *ti tenebris.*
32) Next, a martyrology, beginning as above: *unde factum est.*
33) Next, one book of diverse masses (the first of which is of the saints whose remaining masses are contained) beginning as above: *tuorum N. et N.*
34) Next, one psalter, beginning as above: *mereamur aulam.*
35) Next, one historiated book containing the 7 states, beginning: *Adam in agro.*
36) Next, one book of diverse offices (the first of which is for Trinity) beginning as above: *summa deitas.*
37) Next, sermons, beginning as above: *unde debet.*
38) Next, one large illustrated book, beginning as above: *peccavimus domine.*
39) Next, one missal with the arms of Pope John [XXII], beginning as above: *deus qui labia.*
40) Next, text of the gospels with the arms of Pope John, beginning as above: *Ihesus dicere ad turbas.*
41) Next, one book of prefaces, containing the canon, beginning as above: *us ad te veniat.*
42) Next, one book containing the prophets that are read after the blessing of the paschal candle: *et appareat arrida.*
43) Next, another book containing masses of the saints (whose remaining masses are contained) beginning as above: *limus magestati.*
44) Next, one missal with the arms of Pope John, beginning as above: *et respice in faciem.*
45) Next, a martyrology, beginning as above: *epistola Chromacii.*

46) Next, one small dictionary, beginning as above: *sueverunt producti.*
47) Next, hymns and notated invitatories, beginning as above: *tur eminus sompnia.*
48) Next, a ferial psalter, beginning as above: *ite postula.*
49) Next, an ordinal or pontifical, beginning as above: *ut sicut similitudinem.*
50) Next, one notated collectary, beginning as above: *ecce dominus.*
51) Next, a text of the gospels, beginning as above: *scriptum est.*
52) Next, a legendary, beginning as above: *stolam quare pauper.*
53) Next, the prayers of St. Augustine, beginning as above: *in barbam barbam Aaron.*
54) Next, one small book, containing how the pope is to be served in the divine offices, beginning as above: *vel superpellicium.*
55) Sermons without covers, beginning: *hoc est unum.*
56) Next, one book containing the *formam hereticandi,* beginning as above: *ipsa villa que recipiat.*
57) Next, blessings for the entire year, beginning as above: *a delicto.*
58) Next, a beautiful epistolary with the arms of Pope John, beginning: *ficate eum omnes.*
59) Next, sermons, beginning as above: *et mittite in mare.*
60) Next, a pontifical, beginning as above: *auxiliante domino.*
61) Next, *flores sanctorum* in a beautiful volume, beginning as above: *petimus tamen in quarta.*
62) Next, one antiphoner, beginning as above: *venientem.*
63) Next, one breviary, beginning as above: *presta pater.*
64) Next, one legendary, beginning as above: *in sole et luna.*
65) Next, the *Constitutiones* against the heretics by Emperor Frederic [II], beginning as above: *suorum heredes.*
66) Next, one psalter, beginning as above: *et nunc reges.*
67) Next, a notated proser, beginning as above: *triis tuis.*
68) Next, a notated antiphoner, beginning as above: *domine quid.*
69) Next, one beautiful breviary, beginning as above: *ultra addentes.*[28]

Four points may be made concerning this list. First, the books themselves seem up-to-date. There is no indication that any of them was *antiquus* or *vetus,* adjectives that commonly appear in similar inventories.[29] In fact, just the opposite seems to be the case. There are supplementary volumes that contain the offices of the feasts most recently added, probably Trinity, Corpus Christi, and possibly those of newly canonized saints (9, 28, 36).[30] Therefore the books were no doubt in use and not stored in a treasury.

Second, the books are distinctly papal. While much of the material found in the papal libraries was acquired from the estates of deceased clerics through the imposition of the *jus spolii,* the right of spoil, many of the descriptions indicate that the volumes were compiled specifically for papal usage. For example, a number of books seem to have belonged to Pope John XXII and were at least bound or covered during his pontificate. They were still in use at the time of the compilation of the inventory (39, 40, 44, 58). Part of a rubric from one of the mass books is given as *Postea papa dicit,* testifying that this volume was likewise written for papal use (16). The same may be said for the Roman ordinary (10), the pontificals (49, 60), and the ceremonial that directs "how the pope is to be served in the divine offices" (54).

The third observation presents problems that are a bit difficult to resolve. In the collections of from four to seven masses (1, 2, 13-20), the great feasts of the year are included and probably some lesser masses such as the Common of Saints (33, 43). One may safely assume that these volumes contained the propers of the masses, whether notated or unnotated. But according to the passwords given in the inventory, at least seven of these books begin with the text of the prayers at the foot of the altar, namely, the Forty-second Psalm and at least the incipit of the *Confiteor*.[31] It seems odd that such texts would be included in collections of propers.

The presence of material normally found only once in a missal appearing at the beginning of these volumes indicates that each must have served as a partial missal. That is, the complete text of the propers must have been given, including the prefaces, and much of the ordinary must also have been included. These partial missals would have eliminated the need for transporting the larger and heavier complete missals whenever the pope went on a journey. They might have been less cumbersome whether used by the celebrant, the pope officiating from the faldstool, the cardinals, or the singers that were present.[32]

The fourth point is particularly important to this study. The inventory of chapel books lists no manuscript containing polyphonic music. This is true not only for this document but also for all similar lists compiled during the period of the Avignon papacy. Even those inventories of books left by members of the Curia after their death or seized by the Apostolic Camera under the right of spoil yield nothing with respect to polyphony. To be sure, there were books on music by ancient authors like Augustine and Boethius, and there were innumerable notated liturgical books such as those contained in the above document. However, from the more than 20,000 items noted in the book treasure, the absence of polyphony leads us to suspect that collections of polyphony were not the concern of popes, prelates, or ecclesiastical institutions but probably belonged to individual singers, composers, and theoreticians, and to those musically minded secular princes.[33]

During the early days of the pontificate of Pope Innocent VI, the *magister capelle* was still responsible for the transportation of the chapel items, principally between Avignon and Villeneuve, as well as for compilation of inventories. However, after the construction of the Clementine palace, the site for the celebration of the liturgy at Avignon often alternated between the two large chapels within the palace itself. In 1354, the *magister,* Johannes Ademari, was obliged to prepare the new Chapel of Saint Peter for the services on the feast of John the Baptist.[34] It is possible that the old Chapel of Saint John was the one being used at the time, and that the necessary furnishings and ornaments had to be brought across into the southern part of the palace. This was, in fact, the case at Christmas 1355 and again at Easter of the following year.[35] On 24 December 1356, Johannes was required to carry the *iocalia* into the new chapel (Saint Peter) where services were to be held until 6 January 1357; then they were to be returned to the old chapel (Saint John).[36] Evidently, two chapels were in use at this time, and it was the job of the *magister capelle* to tend to both.

At the end of April 1356, he was paid for the approximately 24 square yards (6 *canne*) of rush mats that were placed on the floor of the area bordered by the *parcus cantorum* of the new chapel and for a lock used there.[37] Between 5 August 1356 and 31 March 1357, Johannes had repairs made on the *parcus* of the old chapel and had a pulpit placed on it. He also was paid for a lock that was installed in the new *parcus*.[38] The cleaning of fabrics used in the chapels, the transportation of the necessary objects to Villeneuve, and the rebinding of at least 6 chapel books was also managed by the *magister* during this period.

Besides these outlays, Johannes dealt directly with those expenses incurred by the chaplains themselves. On 16 November 1355, he was paid for the pantries (*pro celariis*) of those homes at Villeneuve in which he and the other chaplains of the *capella intrinseca* were quartered from Easter (5 April) until Michaelmas (29 September). The master of the chapel was probably also responsible for the payment of wages to the chaplains, as one would suspect from his premier position on the payment lists and from the frequent absence of all other names, save his, from these lists.[39]

According to the accounts, the duties of Johannes extended to the papal treasure. In August 1357, he took possession of the *iocalia* that belonged to the late cardinal deacon Gaillard de la Mothe and sent them to storage in the *parva capelle tinelli magni*, the Chapel of Saint-Martial. Later that same month, Johannes was called upon to weigh the precious items once belonging to another deceased cardinal, Bertrand de Déaux.[40]

Between April and the end of December 1357, evidence shows that the chapel at Pont-de-Sorgues was in use.[41] It was the *magister*'s duty to transport the paraphernalia of the chapel there and back by horse-drawn wagon. He was responsible for the preparation of the chapels "beyond the Rhône" and the smaller chapels of Saint-Jean and Saint-Martial as well as the larger chapels in the Papal Palace at Avignon.

## Stephanus de Vergonio

After the death of Johannes, which occurred before 24 July 1361, his office was taken over by Stephanus de Vergonio who remained as *magister capelle* only a few years. On 19 August 1361, he was also cited as *helemosinarius*, or almoner, responsible for acts of charity mandated by the pope. It is possible that he held this title before the death of his predecessor. He certainly would have had experience in keeping records and in handling sums of money. In any case, we can be certain that Stephanus was not a member of the papal chapel before his

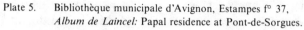

Plate 5.    Bibliothèque municipale d'Avignon, Estampes f° 37,
*Album de Laincel:* Papal residence at Pont-de-Sorgues.

appointment as *magister.* The several accounts compiled during his brief tenure as master of the chapel are unworthy of mention. He seems to have retired from papal service and spent the rest of his days as a well-prebended cleric.

### Johannes de Ulmo

On 12 June 1363, Johannes de Ulmo was admitted as *capellanus* of the papal chapel.[42] He served for several years under Stephanus de Vergonio, but when the latter, for some unknown reason, abandoned his duties, Johannes took over the functions of the *magister,* if not the actual title. As *administrator capelle intrinsece pape,* he received payment on 27 September 1365 for a number of small metal objects that were probably used in the chapel.[43] The term *administrator* was no doubt applied because, despite the absence of the *magister,* his duties—especially those of administration—had to have been carried out; and since for whatever reason the title of *magister* still belonged to Stephanus, it could not even unofficially have been given to Johannes de Ulmo. By the end of June 1366, however, the full title of master of the papal chapel was applied to him.[44]

We have witnessed the activities of the *magister,* not only in transferring the essentials from the Chapel of Saint John to the Chapel of Saint Peter and back, but also in transporting these items the greater distance to the chapels at Villeneuve-lès-Avignon and Pont-de-Sorgues. The management of such moves seems virtually insignificant, however, when compared with the expedition that was about to take place. By the beginning of 1367, Pope Urban V had decided to return the papacy to Rome. It was the job of Johannes de Ulmo to oversee the transfer of the objects of the chapel. Whether to assist him in the journey at this time or not, he was accompanied by a familiar, Stephanus Pictoris, cleric from the diocese of Sens.

On 19 February, Stephanus received payment for the expenses incurred from 7 August 1366 to 1 January 1367, as reckoned by the *magister*.[45] By mid-April, Johannes himself accounted for a portion of the costs of moving the chapel from Avignon to Montpellier.[46] On 1 May, with Stephanus present, Johannes received payment not only for those expenses already incurred in transporting the *necessaria* of the chapel, but also for future outlays.[47] The two worked together in early June, and it is likely that the *magister* was accompanied in Italy by his familiar during the summer months as well.[48]

When the Curia arrived at Rome, Johannes' major responsibilities remained the same. But instead of shuttling the trappings to and from chapels dedicated to Saint John and Saint Peter, the *magister* was paid in September 1367 for carrying the ornaments from the Basilica of Saint Peter to the church of Saint John Lateran. He also might have deployed the furnishings in the small private chapel at the Lateran, the *Sancta sanctorum*. The payment made at this time was compensation for all services rendered since 6 March, and it included the cost of receptacles for the chrism and a candelabrum used during the chanting of Matins during Easter week. He decorated a tower that was next to the chapel at Montefiascone and brought the ornaments to and from the church of Saint Margaret when the pontiff was passing the summer in that town. No fewer than 80 pieces of *pannos* were washed, 7 pounds of incense purchased, and lengths of cord and rope were bought for binding books, for ringing a bell, and for tying up the cases and bundles of the *necessaria*.[49]

Clothing and vestments worn by the chaplains were probably provided by the pope. Yet while there are many mentions of the washing and the repairing of ecclesiastical garb, there are scant references to the provision of new clothing. In 1356, eight chaplains each received an almuce of mottled gray fur for various needs.[50] On 5 November 1367, it was incumbent upon Johannes de Ulmo to have 15 albs made for the specific use of the *capella intrinseca*.[51]

In September 1368, the *magister* settled the accounts for the period between 10 October 1367 and 14 January 1368. This notice provides information on the valets or squires (*famuli*) attached to the papal chaplains. Because of the length of the journey and/or the status of the *capellani* at this time, assistants were assigned to them. They were no doubt responsible for those tasks beneath the dignity of the chaplains. At one point, it was their charge to have several horses reshoed. The physical extent of the paraphernalia might have necessitated their presence. One squire, for example, was sent to Rome from Viterbo with nine pack animals for carrying the vestments and ornaments of the chapel, a journey that took four days. These were transported in various ways at different places along the route to Rome. On one occasion the *famuli* carried 11 chests, brought from Viterbo into the chapel of the palace at the Lateran.[52]

Whatever the status of the *capellani* might have been, that of the *magister* was still greater. As was the case in Avignon, the master of the papal chapel was likewise provided a private room in the city of Rome. A notice dated 11 November 1369 testifies to the fact that Dominicus the roofer spent one day working on the roof of the chamber of the *magister*.[53] It is difficult to say whether or not the papal chaplains themselves continued to sleep in a dormitory as had originally been arranged in 1334. At Villeneuve, as we have seen, it was not exceptional to house the chaplain in various lodgings. Exactly what the state of affairs was in Rome, Avignon, or the cities in between is not known.

The next document referring to Johannes, one dated at Avignon, 3 January 1371, only provides a single piece of information: on that day, Johannes de Ulmo was received as *magister capelle* by the new pope, Gregory XI.[54] There are no published accounts citing his activities during the return from Italy, but they must have mirrored what preceded the Roman sojourn.[55]

One precept rules the late-medieval papal residence, be it Rome or Avignon, and that is that each papal capital served as a base from which the Curia was allowed to wander. As previously mentioned, before the election of Clement V in 1304, the popes spent the greater part of their reign outside of Rome, situated in towns scattered throughout Italy. As many of the notices concerning the *magister* testify, while the Curia was nominally located in Avignon, the popes might have been at Villeneuve-lès-Avignon, Pont-de-Sorgues, or at any of the cities nearby. This restlessness was likewise very much a part of Urban's brief and unsuccessful return to Rome, and there are two notices that concern us here which testify to this very fact.

On Thursday, 19 April 1369, the pope was in the city of Sutri, where Mass was celebrated in his presence, without doubt assisted by the papal chaplains. It seems that on this day, Johannes de Ulmo, the master of the chapel, inadvertently left his breviary (a volume covered with white linen) on the pulpit in the church of Sutri. Some time later, when he went to retrieve it, it was missing and presumed stolen. Another incident is reported as having occurred on 15 May of that year. While curial members were in the church of Montefiascone, a priest from the diocese of Mainz, one Johannes de Wymaria, "lost" his breviary *dum in dicta ecclesia dormiebat*(!). In each case, the chamberlain, Arnaud Aubert, decreed that the perpetrator, no matter what his rank may be, return said breviary intact within 30 days, under pain of

Plate 6.     The Tour Philippe le Bel at Villeneuve-lès-Avignon.

excommunication. These two stories underscore the importance of a liturgical book to a cleric and its intrinsic value.[56]

The papal volumes were kept in the treasury and, like plate and silver, often sold for hard currency when the coffers were low. They served as security for loans, as gifts, and as bribes. A typical book collection for a wealthy bishop numbered roughly 35. The average value of a book during the fourteenth century was approximately 33 grams of gold (9.3 florins), or one month's wages for a *capellanus capelle*.[57] The custody of the papal volumes was entrusted only to the most responsible of officials.

In March 1371, Johannes de Ulmo took possession of the images, reliquaries, tabernacles, ampules, thuribles, vestments, and paraments of the papal treasury. Part of his task was to compile an inventory of the books used in the papal chapel.[58] On 22 March, the following list was made:

An inventory (made 22 March '71) of the books in the custody of Lord Johannes de Ulmo, master of the chapel, follows:

1) First, volumes of missal books [*sic*], covered with red silk.
2) Two missal books, covered with green silk.
3) Next, two books, namely one evangel and the other, an epistolary covered with green silk.
4) Next, two complete missal books, covered with silk of various colors.
5) Next, another three missal books, one covered with blue leather, and the other with red leather.
6) Next, three epistolary books, and three other evangel books.
7) Next, one small pontifical book and one other book.
8) Next, another book of the prophecies on Holy Saturday.
9) Next, three complete breviary books.
10) Next, two breviary books, one of which is a moderately sized breviary.
11) Next, three books of collects.
12) Next, three books in which are contained the offices of new feasts.
13) Next, three gradual books.
14) Next, two large books, one of which comprises the antiphoner for the middle of the year.
15) Next, one other complete antiphoner book.
16) Next, three complete legendary books.
17) Next, four books of psalters.
18) Next, one book with notated hymns.
19) Next, one notated proser.
20) Next, one book of votive or special masses.
21) Next, one book of votive masses of the same size.
22) Next, one small book, where the rubric that it contains is: *Hec est forma hereticandi, etc.*
23) Next, one other notated book for the *Kyriel., Gloria in excelsis, etc.*
24) Next, one small book, in which are the prayers of Blessed Augustine.
25) Next, another small book in which are the blessings for certain feasts.
26) Next, two sermon books.
27) Next, one book which is called *Ordinarius.*
28) Next, one small book in which there are the imperial statutes against the heretics.
29) Next, one other book on the sermons, covered in leather.
30) Next, one other book on illustrated figures of Adam and Eve, etc.
31) Next, one small book of ceremonies: how the pope ought to celebrate and how cardinals ought to assist him, etc.
32) Next, a book of *flores sanctorum.*
33) Next, one other book called *Mathologium* [martyrology].

Next, Johannes de Ulmo said that in addition to the aforementioned books he had in his custody:

34) One book on the *flores sanctorum.*
35) Next, one book called *Mathologium.*
36) Next, another book on the hymns and antiphons of Blessed Mary.[59]

This list is not as descriptive as the one compiled in 1353, and Johannes de Ulmo was bent on identifying a book by its cover and not by the second-folio passwords as was Johannes Ademari. So although we cannot determine whether the same volumes were catalogued again in this later inventory, it is nevertheless possible to learn about the similarities in the two collections.

One group of books undergoes a change in the number of volumes catalogued:

| | **Entry Number** | |
| --- | --- | --- |
| **Title** | **1353** | **1371** |
| Evangel | 6, 51 | 6 (3 vols.) |
| Epistolary | 8, 11 | 6(3) |
| Collectory | 50 | 11(3) |
| Complete breviary | 24, 27, 63, 69 | 9(3) |
| Partial breviary | --- | 10(2) |
| Gradual | 23, 26 | 13(3) |
| Complete antiphoner | 4, 62, 68 | 15 |
| Partial antiphoner | --- | 14(2?) |
| Psalter | 5, 25, 30, 34, 48, 66 | 17(4) |
| Ordinary | 10, 49 | 27 |
| Pontifical | 60, 21 | 7 |
| Complete missals | 7, 12, 22, 29, 39, 44 | 4(2) |
| Partial missals | 1, 2, 13-20, 33, 43 | 1(?), 2(2), 5(3) |

These volumes tend to be large service books that contain material for the entire Church year. They may, in general, have received greater use, suffered more wear and tear, and, therefore, experienced a recovering, possibly one of those frequent rebindings for which the *magister* was responsible. Thick volumes might have been reduced in size to several thinner ones. Complete breviaries and antiphoners could have been broken down to smaller, more manageable partial volumes. Still other books, the ones that have been reduced in quantity, might have appeared in superfluous numbers in the earlier inventory and, hence, some of the volumes put into storage in the treasury.

The number of missals and partial missals seems to have undergone a change also. Though Johannes de Ulmo did not distinguish between the volumes as meticulously as did Johannes Ademari, he does note the difference between the *libri missales* and the *libri missales completi*. The total number of missals in use by the chapel was reduced from 18 to a number over 8, though, as expected, the complete missals are still rarer than the partial ones. The fact that the *magister* qualifies the description of the complete missals and uses no adjective to describe what we have assumed to be the partial missals shows that the complete missal was no doubt the exceptional book, at least from the point of view of Johannes de Ulmo.

The second group on the other hand, contains books that occur in identical quantity in the two lists:

| Title | Entry Number | |
| | 1353 | 1371 |
| --- | --- | --- |
| *Flores sanctorum* | 31, 61 | 32, 34 |
| Martyrology | 32, 45 | 33, 35 |
| Imperial statutes | 65 | 28 |
| *Forma hereticandi* | 56 | 22 |
| Prayers of Augustine | 53 | 24 |
| The seven states | 35 | 30? |
| Sermons | 37, 55, 59 | 26(2), 29 |
| Legendary | 3, 52, 64 | 16(3) |
| Prophets for Holy Saturday | 42 | 8 |
| Blessings | 57 | 25 |
| Ceremonial | 54 | 31 |
| Offices of new feasts | 9, 28, 36 | 12(3) |
| Notated proser | 67 | 19 |
| Notated hymnal | 47 | 18 |
| Evangel and Epistolary pair? | 40, 58 | 3(2) |

These volumes evidently comprise the thinner books or possibly those that were seldom consulted. In general, they probably experienced less use and, instead, served as reference books for the chapel. Although we cannot be certain, it is likely that these volumes are identical to their counterparts in the earlier catalogue.

There are several new categories found in the inventory of 1371 that are lacking in the one made 18 years earlier. The later list has two volumes of votive or special Masses (20, 21), possibly indicating an increase in the celebration of such Masses in the papal chapel.[60] The collection of hymns and antiphons to the Virgin (36) in the private possession of the *magister* might have contained the Little Hours of the Virgin. By the fourteenth century, the recitation of the little office had become an almost universal practice regarded as obligatory by all clerics, and therefore Johannes could have used such a book in his own personal devotion.[61] On the other hand, the book might have contained various texts collected as part of the growing Mariolatry with no other organizing factor. Unfortunately, we do not know if any of these volumes contained musical notation.

Another book used in the chapel in 1371, but seemingly absent in 1353, was a notated Kyriale (23). There is no indication that this volume contained anything other than monophonic mass ordinaries. If we are to judge from other Kyriales of this period, the papal volume was probably a rather small, not particularly uniform work. Its presence, however, points both to the concept of grouping mass ordinaries in papal practice, and to the necessity of such a collection in the late fourteenth-century papal chapel.

**Thomas Tauri**

The remaining accounts reckoned by Johannes offer little additional information concerning his duties in the *capella*, and by 23 May 1376 he was dead.[62] Significantly, his successor was drawn from among the members of the chapel. After more than eight years as a *capellanus* and *cantor*, Thomas Tauri drew up his first accounts as *magister capelle* on 12 June 1376.[63] His duties were typical of those performed by the *magistri* who preceded him. Although he was paid on 2 October 1376 for expenses already incurred and for future outlays *pro recessu*, the return of Gregory XI to Rome, no published account detailing the cost of the journey exists. Unfortunately, this is the last mention made of Thomas Tauri.[64]

**Simon Haquetin**

Our first reference to the master of the chapel of Pope Clement VII appears in a notice dated 6 September 1379. At that time, Simon Haquetin is recorded as having withdrawn a missal from storage in the *turri bassa*. Later that fall, on 24 November, he extracted a notated breviary compiled according to the usage of the Roman Curia and also a notated gradual, both *pro usu capelle dicti domini nostri pape*.[65] From this information we can conclude that in addition to the store of books kept for the chapel, the *magister* was able to draw upon the entire papal book treasure, much of which comprised spoils acquired from the private collections of deceased prelates. It is a distinct possibility that these three volumes were needed because all or some of the chapel books in use previously were at that time located in Italy, at the disposal of the chaplains of the Roman pope.

On 19 September 1379, Simon's name appears at the head of the list of papal chaplains. He served as *magister* until at least 27 August 1388, when he was given a receipt for the accounts he had rendered which he verified by an inventory of the *iocalia* and ornaments of the chapel.[66] Besides this continued concern with the treasure, the *magister* was still handling the wages of the chaplains. In December 1382 the payment for the service of the *capellani* and the *clerici* was given to *dicto domino Symone pro se et aliis recipiente*.[67]

The *magister capelle pape* came to be privileged among the members of the chapel. Besides living in private quarters, being permitted a familiar, and handling finances and treasure, the *magister* was assigned a special servant in 1387. Called the *servitor magistri capelle pape*, Petrus de Godescaut assisted Simon in matters pertaining to the chapel and was cited in service of the *capella* as late as 1394.

## Johannes de Moleyo

Simon, though still a papal familiar in early January 1389, seems to have relinquished his title by this time.[68] His successor was Johannes de Moleyo, who had served in the papal chapel as early as 1379 and who was again cited as *capellanus* in 1384 and 1387.[69] Nothing is known about Johannes before he began his tenure as *magister* in December 1388. He was called master of the chapel in August 1392, however, at the end of the year, Richardus de Bozonvilla, who had been serving in the chapel at least from 1379, substituted for him. The reason for Johannes' absence is unknown, as is the nature of Richardus's service at this time.[70] Although Richardus appears first on the list of *capellani* compiled on 30 October 1393, the chaplain Stephanus Turqueti was given the wages *pro se et aliis recipiente,* a function normally reserved for the *magister.*[71] In documents dated December 1393 and April 1394, Johannes de Moleyo reappears as master of the chapel, here he served at least until 21 October 1394.[72]

## Richardus de Bozonvilla

Sometime during the 12 months that followed, Richardus de Bozonvilla took on the title of the *magister capelle,* though it is difficult to say exactly when he assumed his duties. As early as 13 October 1394, when he was called *lector Biblie,* Richardus seems to have already assumed a function that was traditionally assigned to the *magister.* At least according to the description of the papal chapel composed by François de Conzié in 1409, reading the Bible at the papal meal was the charge of the *magister.* It must have been so by 1394.[73]

Another of the master's responsibilities came to be shared at this time. As already mentioned, the chaplain Stephanus Turqueti was given the wages of the *capellani* in place of Richardus. The frequency with which we find such an event taking place in the cameral accounts increases dramatically in subsequent years. In March 1396 and on 22 August 1397, Johannes de Altacuria performed this task. In July 1396, February 1397, and February 1398, Johannes de Bosco accepted the wages for the chaplains and clerics.

On 22 August 1397, part of the payment received (1 florin, 18 solidi, 9 denarii) was said to be the special stipend of the *magister.* It is uncertain exactly what the purpose of this small sum was; however, it probably was not a stipend. This amount given to Johannes for Richardus figures to 9 denarii per day for 57 days. Since the daily wage for a *capellanus* was approximately 80 denarii per day, this is too insignificant an amount to have served as a supplement to the *magister*'s wage. It is instead more likely a small reimbursement for chapel expenses. There is no indication that, at any time during the Avignon papacy, the *magister* received regular supplement as compensation for his extra duties beyond his wage as a *capellanus.*[74]

This practice contrasts with the procedure at other courts. In the ducal chapel of Burgundy, for example, the *premier chapellain,* the equivalent of the *magister capelle pape,* received 13 solidi, 4 denarii per day in wages, while the other chaplains had to be content with 8 solidi daily. By April 1391, the Burgundian ledgers indicate that the daily rate was increased to 1 franc for the *premier chapellain* and to 10 solidi, 8 denarii for the other chaplains.[75] Under the Pisan pope, John XXIII (elected 1410), the salary of the *magister* stood at 6 gulden per month, while that of the *capellani* was only 4 gulden for the same period.[76]

Although the wages of the papal *magistri* seem to have been incongruous with the duties and the power of the office, the recompense they did receive exhibited itself in other ways. Richardus de Bozonvilla, for example, as familiar and *scriptor litterarum apostolicarum* in March 1391, was accorded the right to dispose of the totality of his goods by means of a will, a papal privilege sometimes granted to prelates or curial officers. After his death, the Apostolic Camera seized sums that he had deposited both at the convent of Sainte-Catherine at Avignon and with his niece, amounting to some 2,000 écus.[77] This astronomical sum, amounting to over 15 years' wages of a papal chaplain, can easily be explained. During his career, Richardus held several important ecclesiastical benefices, and he was, no doubt, the best prebended of all the papal chaplains.[78] On 24 January 1405, five days before his death, he was granted by *motu proprio* a canonicate, prebend, and the precentory of the cathedral of Carpentras. At the time he was already rector of Saint-Julien at La Blachière (in the diocese of Viviers), canon at the cathedral of Cambrai where he was awaiting conferral of an official title, and provost of the cathedral of Apt. Richardus also maintained a familiar, Johannes Hobaut, who was with him in 1394 and who remained with him until his death. Evidence for this, for Richardus's having received the right to draw up a will, and for his wealth, is found in the following notice from the notarial acts of the chapter of the cathedral of Apt, dated 6 October 1406:

> ... Nicholaus de Hubantus, *scriptor* of apostolic letters, and Johannes Haubaut, canon of Embrun, executors, in the execution of the last testament in the name of Richardus de Bozonvilla, former provost of Apt... that said former lord provost, in his last testament, left for the purpose of one, two, or more anniversaries, one-hundred-twenty-five florins (*currentes*), which they have, in fact, deposited with consent of the chapter to celebrate the anniversary: a triple anniversary with vigils and nine lessons of the dead (namely, one 29 January, another 29 May, and another 29 September) for the souls of said provost... and benefactors of his aforementioned executors.[79]

## Gerardus Gerardi

After the death of Richardus, the title of the office was not given away so quickly. Surely the tasks for which he was responsible needed to be carried out.

Yet as late as three months after his death, the chaplain who filled in for him, Gerardus Gerardi, was only referred to as the substitute, the lieutenant of the master of the chapel (*locum tenens magistri capelle*). Gerardus first became a member of the *capella* at Pont-de-Sorgues on 29 September 1403, but he had been a familiar of Cardinal Guillaume d'Aigrefeuille in 1394 and might have had some dealings with the papal chapel before the date of his official reception. He came from the city of Saint-Dié in the diocese of Toul and could have been a protégé of Richardus who was likely from that area of France. Although Gerardus acted as a procurer in a transaction on 6 September 1406, the first reference to him as *magister capelle* appears in November of the following year. He served Benedict at least until 1416. The latest known reference to him dates from 1429.[80]

## Liturgical Duties of the Office

A thorough examination of the archival evidence shows that the post of *magister capelle pape* was essentially an administrative one. Previous studies have drawn much the same conclusion.[81] To support the claim that the office included important musical functions, scholars have placed great weight on a phrase contained in the document of Conzié that defines the responsibility of the *magister* as "to direct all the other *cantores* and to govern the service of the chapel." This single reference has been the sole basis for assigning musical duties to the *magister*.[82] All previous studies have ignored two important factors: first, the musical ability and liturgical experience of the *magistri*; and second, the limited nature of the sources consulted.

If nothing else, the *magister capelle pape* was first a *capellanus capelle*. That is, Petrus Sinterii was chosen for the chapel of Pope Benedict XII in 1334 not because of his administrative ability, but because he possessed whatever requisites and talents were needed to be a member of the chapel. Only several years after the institution of the *capella intrinseca,* did a need clearly arise for a master of the chapel. Therefore, Petrus did not act in an administrative capacity until well after he was admitted into the chapel. If we accept the fact that Benedict XII truly wished his chaplains to have the capability to sing Mass and certain canonical hours, then we must also accept the fact that Petrus, unlike many clerics (certainly the *capellani commensales*), was quite able at doing just that. In sum, the first *magister capelle* was chosen from a pool of *capellani* who had previously been selected for their ability to celebrate the divine service *cum nota*.

If we look for a moment at his successors, it becomes obvious that, for the most part, they, too, follow the precedent. Stephanus de Chaulageto was selected from among the *capellani* and had more than six years' experience serving in the chapel of the pope. Johannes Ademari and Stephanus de Vergonio (both appointed during the pontificate of Innocent VI) were, as far as we know, not papal chaplains before they were appointed to the office of *magister*. But Johannes de Ulmo was. He served in the papal chapel for more than two years before he became *administrator capelle*. Again, his musical ability must have reached the level of at least the lowliest of the *capellani*. The case is even stronger for Thomas Tauri who, while only having held the title of *magister* for two years, did spend eight years as *capellanus* and *cantor*. By the time he became master of the chapel, the musical ability of the chaplains and their principal function had affected the very title they bore: *capellanus* had become *cantor*. The point to be remembered is this: although the position of *magister capelle* itself did not require musical skills, those men who attained this post possessed them as a matter of course.[83]

At the outset of the schism, Simon Haquetin, about whom we know virtually nothing, served as *magister*. The career of his successor, Johannes de Moleyo, does conform to the notion that has emerged from this study. He first entered the papal chapel as a *capellanus* in 1379. Though his service to the pope might have been sporadic, he was brought back into the chapel several times before his appointment as *magister* in 1388. After serving nearly four years as master of the papal chapel and after some years during which his whereabouts are not known, Johannes was brought from Chartres, where he was *cantor* at the cathedral, to serve as *premier chapellain* of Duke Philip of Burgundy. His tenure here was evidently no more successful than it had been at Avignon, since he remained at the post less than a year. However, Johannes was rehired by Philip to serve in his chapel at the major feasts (*bonnes festes*) of the liturgical year, which he did until the death of the duke in 1404.[84]

Richardus de Bozonvilla only stepped into the role of the *magister* after 15 years as a singer in the papal chapel and, before that, 8 years in the service of a cardinal. He must have had some facility in the musical functions demanded of a papal chaplain, if not at the outset of his service as papal singer, then surely by the beginning of his tenure as *magister*. His long service to a cardinal may be characteristic of several, if not all, papal *magistri*. They might have distinguished themselves through employment in the chapels of churchly princes and lesser prelates. Johannes de Ulmo, for example, was a *cantor* in the retinue of Cardinal Elie de Saint-Yrieix for at least 8 months before becoming a papal chaplain. Gerardus Gerardi was associated with Cardinal Guillaume d'Aigrefeuille nearly 10 years before he joined the papal chapel as a *capellanus*. The unfortunate paucity of information concerning the households of many cardinals and most bishops could easily explain why some *magistri* seem to have been hired into the chapel with no previous experience.

The second important factor determining why the view of the *magister* as an administrator has held sway lies in the very nature of the sources consulted. A document that concerns itself with the reimbursement for the purchase of incense and cloth or with the payment of wages for services rendered is, by its very nature, a witness to a bureaucratic process. The *magister* appears as merely a bookkeeper because the preponderance of the extant documentation exists in the form of accounts and receipts. One strand of evidence that does not fall into this category is the often-cited passage from Conzié. In this we find the master of the chapel described as one among the singers (*inter eos*) who was to direct and govern their service in the chapel. Further light on this aspect of the *magister*'s responsibilities can be had from the papal ceremonials.

The greatest number of references to the *magister* are found in a ceremonial compiled during the reign of Benedict XIII (1394-1423).[85] Unfortunately, none of the passages that mention the master of the chapel is precisely datable. Moreover, because of the focus of the document itself, the *magister* is seen functioning on only a few feast days. On the feast of the Purification (2 February), candles are presented by the pope to the prelates and officials of the Curia.[86] When the pope begins the distribution of the candles, the *magister capelle incipit alta voce cantare: Lumen ad revelationem etc.*[87] The tapers are lit, the prelates and clerics are arranged in the proper order, and then, on word from the deacon, the procession begins. With that, the *magister capelle incipit cantare, que cantanda sunt.* That is, he intones the processional antiphons as necessary.[88]

On Ash Wednesday, when the pontiff begins to distribute the ashes, the *magister capelle incipit cantare: Inter templum et altare etc. V.*[89] On Palm Sunday, this document tells us, two of the *cantores* were to enter the church, *ceteris extra remanentibus,* and sing the hymn *Gloria laus* with the doors closed.[90] The doors are then opened, the procession begins, and all the necessary processional antiphons are sung. When all the verses are completed, the master of the chapel *incipit cantare: Ingrediente domino etc.*[91] What is meant here is that as the celebrant enters the church, the last antiphon, *Ingrediente domino,* is begun. The *magister* assured that the final melody was intoned at the proper moment.

There is a further reference to the *magister* in this document, and it is one of particular importance. It is included in the rubrics for Terce at Pentecost and, as with the previously cited passage, was written after the withdrawal of Benedict XIII from Avignon. The pope, already vested, goes to the church where the service was to have been held, and there receives the reverence of the cardinals. Meanwhile, the rubrics tell us, the subdeacon, acolytes, commensal chaplains, chaplains of honor, and the auditors of the papal palace vest themselves in surplices. The rite that is described, therefore, is one in which the upper-level chaplains, that is to say, the ones of higher status, and the *commensales* led by the subdeacon are the principal participants. The subdeacon was to intone the antiphon; then the *magister* was to intone the psalm, *Legem pone.*[92] The subdeacon then said the chapter, and the two acolytes chanted the responsory, *Spiritus Domini.*[93] No further mention is made of the *magister,* and the lower-level chaplains, the *cantores,* are not cited as participants in this service. This presents the unlikely possibility of the *magister* participating in the service with the *capellani commensales* and their *subdiaconus* but not with the singers. Curious also is the description of the *magister* participating only at Terce of Pentecost and not at any other of the canonical hours throughout the rest of the year. For a resolution to these problems, we must consult an earlier document, the ceremonial of Bindo Fesulani, composed ca. 1377.

This report tells us that at Terce of Pentecost, after the reverence, the pope begins the hour by intoning the *Deus in adjutorium.* Then he gives the incipit of the hymn but only after it is preintoned by one of the acolytes. The subdeacon commences the antiphon, the *magister* begins the psalm *Legem pone,* and the remainder of the hour continues as usual. The author of this ceremonial informs us that he provides a detailed description of the manner and form of the service because, on this feast, certain things are to be done *que non fiunt in aliis missis.* In fact, he reports to us that before other Masses, the pope *incipit tertiam sine nota.*[94] This immediately explains the presence of the *magister:* Terce of Pentecost was a *cum nota* service. Therefore, the presence of the singers and also the one "who was to direct them in the service," the master of the chapel, was required.

Though there is no indication of the master officiating at the hours of Vespers and Matins, we know that the *capellani intrinseci* were established for the express purpose of singing the canonical hours for the pope, as the manuscript of Conzié states, whether the pope is present or absent. Where the singers served, so did the *magister.* No doubt, when the full Curia and the *capella commensalis* were present, as is most often the case described in the ceremonials, the function of the *magister* in giving incipits was minimal. This is clear from the numerous references to the subdeacon and acolytes. However, since the singers were present, the master of the chapel must have been in attendance "to direct the singers." The *cantores* were certainly present at this service for Pentecost, and they might have been essential for the performance of certain chants, at least the psalm. The author of this ceremonial, however, was more concerned with the duties of the upper-level chaplains and the cardinals, while those of the singers went by unnoticed. The importance of the *cantores* and their *magister* in the execution of papal liturgy was mandatory when the *capellani commensales* were absent. The two popes to whom the presence of the singers was essential, therefore, were Gregory XI and Benedict XIII, who both maintained virtually no commensal chapel.

As with its successor, the ceremonial of Bindo refers to the *magister* on two other feasts. When, on Ash Wednesday, the pope begins to distribute the ashes, the *magister capelle debet incipere et cantare antiphonam: Imitemur habitu in cineram etc. et omnes alias antiphonas sequentes usque ad finem.*[95] It was therefore up to the master of the chapel to intone all the antiphons that were to be sung. The passage concerning the Palm Sunday procession also refers to the *magister,* though in somewhat vaguer terms. Here the service is described as taking place in the papal palace at Avignon. The procession is to advance to the door of the Chapel of Saint Peter, and then two *cantores* who are inside begin *Gloria laus*, which is sung *secundam dispositionem magistri capelle*. This probably means that the two singers were chosen by the *magister*, and that, as in the later ceremonial, the master intoned the chants and determined when the final antiphon, *Ingrediente domino*, was to be sung.

The document of Conzié also describes the office of the *magister* as including the task of reading the Bible at table during the papal meal. The early fourteenth-century ceremonial of Cardinal Jacopo Stefaneschi contains a chapter by Uguicio Borromeo de Vercelli written before 1329 and providing some information on this duty. When the pope had his midday meal, it was the job of the subdeacon attached to the *commensales* to request the blessing by saying *Iube, domine, benedicere* in a loud voice. After the blessing, the subdeacon was to go to the place designated (on the pope's right), seat himself immediately after the attendants begin serving the pontiff, and commence reading. The reading was to be distinct and appropriately slow, in the manner of a lesson from a nocturn. He should read continually while the pope is at table, except *quando papa bibit*. He was even allowed to pause two or three times at appropriate points during the meal. And once or twice the pope might see fit to give the subdeacon a little something from his carving table.[96]

The details of reading at table must not have changed very much during the 80 years before it is assigned to the *magister*. The first reference one finds to this task being specifically assigned to someone other than the *subdiaconus* is on 6 August 1353. In a supplication bearing this date, the papal chaplain Jacobus Comitis calls himself *capellanus . . . capelle intrinsece, ac lector Biblie coram [papa]*. There is a second appearance of such an appellation when Richardus de Bozonvilla refers to himself as *lector biblie pape* in a supplication from 1394. During the period immediately preceding the submission of this request, we find Richardus substituting for the absent master of the chapel and, as *lector Biblie*, he was permanently applying to himself some of the functions of the *magister*. A similar situation must have existed in 1353. We know that the *magister*, Stephanus de Chaulageto, was dead by 25 August 1353. He might, in fact, have died well before this date or might have been incapacitated due to illness. Before the appointment of Johannes Ademari as *magister*, Jacobus Comitis probably bore the responsibility of reading at the papal table. In any event, we know that by 1409 it had been firmly established as a duty of the master of the chapel, though he could designate a member of the chapel to substitute for him. This clause, yet unwritten, must have reflected a common practice by the mid-fourteenth century. It was most probably invoked in order to provide Jacobus and Richardus with their titles.

The only difference between the citation concerning the master of the chapel and the one regarding the subdeacon is in the type of material to be read.

That is, the *magister* was supposed to read the Bible at the papal table. This is corroborated by the citations to Jacobus and Richardus. But the earlier passage concerning the subdeacon states that the reading selected was to be either a legend or a history [of the saints], the homily of that day or of another day or feast, *si placuerit pape.* It is likely that, in spite of directions to the contrary, during the latter half of the fourteenth century as well as during the first decade of the fifteenth, the Bible was not the only material suitable for reading to the pope. When Johannes de Ulmo reported having a book containing selections from lives of the saints, a martyrology, and a collection of hymns and antiphons to the Virgin in his possession in 1371, could those have been the books from which he read to the pope? Obviously, we can never know the answer to this question. However if such material was the rule during the first decades of the fourteenth century, there is no reason to conclude that by the middle of the century it had been expressly forbidden.

At least on this account, the office of the *magister* was modeled on that of the *subdiaconus.* Though the subdeacon had extensive liturgical duties when the pope celebrated, such as vesting the Sovereign Pontiff, reading the epistle at Mass, censing certain prelates, and the like, he did have one discrete musical task as well. During Vespers at which the pope officiated, it was his duty to intone the first antiphon to the pope, who was then to reintone it.[97] This was the situation at least by ca. 1377. However, during the late thirteenth century, this task fell regularly to the *primicerius,* the leader of the *Schola cantorum.*[98] Since the *Schola* only participated in the offices if the pope was at Rome, it was most often necessary for someone other than the *primicerius* to perform this service for the pope. A ceremonial from the time informs us that if the Curia was not at Rome, the duty belonged to the *hebdomadarius* selected from among the commensal chaplains. Sometime before the beginning of the fourteenth century, the *subdiaconus* assumed a position of pre-eminence among the *commensales,* and he must have replaced the *hebdomadarius.*[99] Wherever the *capella intrinseca* replaced the *capella commensalis,* it must have been the duty of the *magister* to assume much of the role of the *subdiaconus.* As the new group grew in importance musically, the *magister* must have replaced the subdeacon in those more musical functions, especially those that he inherited from the *primicerius.* The service for Terce of Pentecost gives us some indication of the role played by the *magister* in the canonical hours. The citations for Ash Wednesday and Palm Sunday indicate that he was essential to the performance of processional antiphons. It is likely that in those ceremonies from which the subdeacon was absent and at which the *capella intrinseca* presided, the master of the chapel was even more important still. In the few references to his duties, we find him intoning antiphons and psalms, determining when certain of them should end and others begin, undoubtedly selecting the soloists from among the *cantores,* and, in general, performing those actions that are assigned to the *cantor* in modern liturgical books as well as those from medieval cathedral churches. It is not too difficult to imagine him acting in many more cantorial roles in the chapel of the pope.

During the Avignon papacy, the office of *magister* more than likely adapted itself to the talents of the man in office, to the capabilities of the *capellani*, to the liturgical requirements of the individual pontiff, and to the solvency of the Apostolic Camera. The lack of information concerning the previous experience of Pope Innocent's two candidates for the post (Johannes Ademari in 1353 and Stephanus de Vergonio in 1361) might be more closely related to the reduction in the size of the chapel and to a genuine disinterest in things musical than to archival lacunae. The success of Johannes de Ulmo and Richardus de Bozonvilla might have been a function of their liturgical experience and their willingness to delegate responsibility. The title *magister capelle pape* increased in importance during this period. An office that emerged out of liturgical and administrative necessity developed into a position of wealth and power.[100] The master of the papal chapel came to be a minor treasurer in charge of precious objects of the chapel. He was responsible for the liturgical and musical books that were used in the pontifical chapel and for transporting them whenever the pope traveled. He kept account of expenses and, for the most part, acted as paymaster for the *cantores.* Because of his service in reading during the papal meal, he was regularly permitted to dine in the Apostolic Palace. Several of the *magistri* were assigned servants to assist them in their chapel duties, and a few kept familiars. As early as 1353, the *magister* was permitted the luxury of having his own room. At the turn of the fifteenth century, the master had attained so elevated a position in the eyes of the pope that one was afforded a benefice at the rank of provost.[101] If the *capella intrinseca,* as a whole, underwent inflation in status and importance during the course of the Avignon papacy, the musical responsibilities of its members did not lessen any. In fact, the evidence points to the contrary. With the addition of new information indicating the active participation of the *magister capelle* in the chapel of the pope, it may fairly be said that the musical ability of the master of the chapel and his specifically musical responsibilities kept pace with those of the *cantores* throughout the reign of the popes of Avignon.

# 4

# The Liturgy of the Papal Chapel

## Papal Service and Ordos

When studying any aspect of the Middle Ages, we are ever confronted with the image of medieval man as a highly religious and ritualistic being. To his mind, the totality of existence was affected by the actions of an all-powerful God. It was therefore the duty of men not only to worship this God but to engage in acts of propitiation and gratitude as well.[1]

The pope stood at the apex of the ecclesiastical system that ordered man's religious sense and structured the cult. He was, to be sure, numbered among the most powerful of the European princes; but first and foremost, the Vicar of Christ functioned as the high priest, the greatest of all bridge builders between God and men, the *pontifex maximus*. In order to approach the music of the papal court in any realistic way, and to show the relationship between music and ceremony, one must first understand the liturgical framework within which these rituals were executed. Among the many types of documents that preserve the rites of the papal chapel, perhaps the most important from a purely liturgical point of view are the ceremonials.[2]

The ceremonials are among the oldest documents of the Church, and their early history is similar to the early history of many liturgical collections: obscure, lacking a visible beginning, and seemingly a mass of conflicting traditions. The first documents were but simple guides that contained the directions to be followed in the execution of the divine office and in the administration of the sacraments.[3] They preserve the order of service without giving the texts of the prayers.[4] Because the manner of worship, that is, the exact sequence of psalms, hymns, prayers, and the like, differs from rite to rite, the ceremonials for each usage vary accordingly.

The book that contained the order of service for the Church at Rome was called the *Ordo romanus*.[5] The earliest compilations of the ordos go back to the ninth century and reflect the practices of the previous century.[6] Comprising only the principal ceremonies, they contain the directions for the execution of the Mass, Baptism, ordination, dedications, and the offices of both Holy Week and of the great feasts of the Church year. Other ceremonies went unrecorded.[7] The ordos prescribe the usage of the pope as bishop of Rome officiating in his cathedral, Saint John Lateran, and had very little impact beyond the city of Rome itself.[8]

Situated near the Lateran Basilica was the papal palace, the official residence of the popes from the fourth to the fourteenth century. Within the palace was an oratory, dedicated to Saint Lawrence, that became filled with precious relics at least by the time of Pope Leo III (795-816). Called the *Sancta sanctorum,* it served as the private papal chapel. Leclercq calls it the pontifical chapel "par excellence," for only the pope had the right to celebrate Mass there, and he alone could give authorization for it to be entered.[9]

It is in the eleventh century that references to private papal service are first made. Pope Leo IX (1049-1054) was said to have recited the office in an oratory, no doubt the *Sancta sanctorum.*[10] At this time, too, we see the beginnings of a group of private papal servers who functioned in this chapel. Leo IX, for example, was reported to have been accompanied in the office *cum solo clerico.*[11] A bit earlier in the century, in 1026, we see for the first time the use of the term *capellanus domini pape,* here referring to one Amatus, bishop of Silva Candida.[12]

The members of the papal household did not have the same duties and purpose as a community of monks or canons, and the small, private oratory did not permit the same ritual as the cathedral. Consequently, the liturgy of the papal chapel diverged from that of the Lateran Basilica, the papal cathedral.[13] In addition, Roman practice was subject to a wide range of influences from without, not the least of them instigated by the eleventh-century Germanic popes. Many liturgical manuscripts of this time offer a liturgy adapted to and mixed with northern European practice.[14] By the mid-twelfth century, only the Lateran Basilica retained the ancient office of the Apostolic See. It is not surprising, therefore, that we find the first curial ceremonials in the twelfth century.[15] These documents are distinct from the ordos that preceded them since they were written to conserve the liturgy of the pope officiating in his small private chapel.[16]

Among the curial ceremonials, the first important collection is the *Liber politicus.* A few facts surrounding its authorship are worthy of mention. The text was written between 1140 and 1143 for the cardinal priest Guido de Castello by one Benedict, who refers to himself in the dedication as *beati Petri apostoli indignus canonicus et Romane ecclesie cantor.*[17] Duchesne, reading this inscription as "canon and singer of Saint Peter's of the Roman Church," believed the author to have belonged to a group of four titular singers instituted at the Vatican Basilica by Gregory the Great.[18] Bernhard Schimmelpfennig gives the more literal and, in fact, correct translation: "canon of Saint Peter's and singer of the Roman Church." In supporting this interpretation, he indicates that the Vatican Basilica would never have been called "Roman Church." Furthermore, he implies that the term "Roman Church" designates a specifically papal singer, and that Benedict may have belonged to a group of *cantores* —distinct from the *Schola cantorum*—who traveled with the pope when he was outside Rome.[19] If there actually was such a body, then the group established at Avignon in 1334 to sing the divine office in lieu of the *Schola* was not unique in this respect but, instead, may have been a manifestation of a time-honored, though infrequently exercised prerogative.[20] Whatever his exact duties, Benedict, as a compiler of a ceremonial, is typical: he observed and participated in the ceremonies of the Curia, he made note of the usages, and he then arranged these notes for use by a prelate to aid in the faithful reproduction of papal ceremony.[21]

## The New *Ordo Romanus*

At the beginning of the thirteenth century, there was a reordering of the liturgy of the papal chapel under Pope Innocent III (1198-1216). A new ordo was compiled during the last three years of his reign, and the other liturgical books used at court were revised during the late 1220s.[22] We do not know the exact nature of the revisions. The Curia, as it was, had followed the *cursus secularis* which presented a service that was not as long as the *cursus monasticus;* the revisions, precipitated by the exigencies of court life, tended to further shorten the papal liturgy. Private prayers and apologia that once filled the Mass were reduced. There is evidence that the papal chaplains eliminated the long pauses in psalm singing customary up to that time, and they may have increased the tempo of the chants. One liturgical historian has made the claim, though unsubstantiated, that this reform put an end to the creation of new tropes and sequences. Whatever the case may have been, suffice it to say, the papal service of the mid-thirteenth century took less time to perform than it did at the early part of the century.[23]

The brevity and simplicity of the service appealed to Francis of Assisi, and this abbreviated ordo was adopted by him and his followers.[24] Soon ordos based on the one developed under Innocent could be found among the Dominicans and Augustinians. The validity of the papal liturgy traveled as far as the monastic orders themselves.[25] The diffusion of the rites of the papal chapel was also hastened by the thirteenth-century wanderings of the Curia in northern Italy and into France. In 1337, when the pope was well ensconced in his tower at Avignon, the chapter of Notre-Dame-des-Doms met and ruled on the topic *De dicendo officium Romanum per personas ecclesiasticas dioecesis Avenionensis.* It ordained that since the Holy Roman Church was recognized as *mater et magistra,* owing to the presence of the Roman Curia and to the reputation of its *mores laudabiles,* all old office books of the diocese of Avignon were to be rendered *convenientes et aptos* to the use of the Roman Church and Curia.[26]

From the time of the first curial ceremonials, the texts had been acquiring an ever increasing level of specificity. The rubrics, or directions for how each ceremony was to be carried out, became more explicit. More types of ceremonies came to be included. By the end of the thirteenth century the documents included the rubrics for Church councils, and imperial and royal coronations. At the beginning of the fourteenth century they contained the order of service for canonizations and for the consecration of cardinals. The ultimate result was that by the turn of the fifteenth century, the ceremonials had become less collections of rubrics than diaries of the papal chapel.[27]

For this study, six ceremonials of the *capelle pape* were consulted. The two earliest collections date from around the middle of the fourteenth century. They were compiled by several scribes working at different times, but most texts essentially reflect the papal liturgy as witnessed by the cardinal deacon Jacopo Gaetano Stefaneschi.[28] The remaining four texts, each representing the work of lesser curialists, date from the period of the Schism.

1) Avignon, Bibliothèque municipale, ms. 1706.[29] Some of the texts come from the second half of the thirteenth century, while others may be dated as late as December 1352.

2) The collection known as *Ordo romanus XIV*.[30] Much of this complex ceremonial comes from the last part of the thirteenth century and one citation even as far back as the first half of that century. The latest addition is dated as having been made in 1474.

3) The compilation known as *Ordo romanus XV*.[31] Though collected in the late fourteenth century, it is based on texts from the middle of the century. Some of the material is the work of Petrus Amelii, *clericus capelle* of the Roman pope, Boniface IX. Most of the datable references are not relevant to this study.

4) The collection of Bindo Fesulani.[32] Compiled by a *secretarius* and chamberlain of Cardinal Pietro Corsini who, in 1378, was named *capellanus commensalis* of Pope Clement VII. Bindo claims to have witnessed events in Rome, probably during the pontificate of Gregory XI. All additions to his text seem to have been completed by ca. 1400.

5) The ceremonial of François de Conzié.[33] Successively bishop of Grenoble, archbishop of Arles, and later of Narbonne, he became chamberlain of Clement VII in 1383. For 50 years he stood at the summit of papal administration and finances in the household. Until 1409 he was in the service of the popes of Avignon, until 1415, the popes of Pisa. Later he served Martin V (1417-1431) and Eugene IV (1431-1447). His texts date from 1404 and 1416. They are important in that they are based more on personal experience than on exemplars.

6) The anonymous collection that dates from the time of Benedict XIII. Some of the material comes from the pontificate of Nicholas V (1447-1455).[34]

There are many different types of services described in the ceremonials, and there is some degree of flexibility allowed in the execution of each ceremony. The order of a particular service was often altered to suit the surroundings, the persons present, or the wishes of either the pope or the participants.[35] In some cases there was a pre-existing alternate form that could be drawn upon if circumstances allowed.

**Papal Mass**

The diversification of papal liturgical service is attested to by the variety of Masses available to the pope. The ceremonials draw distinctions between three:

1) Low Mass said by the pope, 2) the Pontifical Mass celebrated by the pope, and 3) the Mass that the Supreme Pontiff attended but did not celebrate, the *missa coram papa.*

## Low Mass

Unfortunately, no information is given on how the Holy Father was to say Mass privately nor what was available to him in the way of participants, since no ordo for private or ferial Mass was used at the papal court.[36] It was sometimes designated as a Low Mass, but more often all description is lacking. There are, however, sufficient references in the ceremonials to such a service, and we can make some supposition about its nature, at least as it was celebrated during the pontificate of Benedict XIII.

The *missa privata* was said by this pontiff *in sua capella* and is sometimes designated as being a Mass *de mane.* It is not public in any sense but is said *secrete* or *in secreto.*[37] Though it is not known who participated with the pope in the Mass, he was probably assisted by only one server.[38] Even if some *capellani capelle* or *capellani commensales* were present, as far as can be determined, the rite was never performed *cum nota.* It is frequently termed a *missa bassa* in the ceremonials.[39]

It is likely that such morning Masses were part of the daily routine of Benedict XIII, and it is probable that it was regularly celebrated by other Sovereign Pontiffs as well. However, the documents record Benedict reciting such a Mass on only a handful of feasts: Ash Wednesday, Quadragesima and Laetare Sundays, Tuesday and Wednesday in Holy Week, the feasts of Saint John the Baptist (24 June), Saints Peter and Paul (29 June), Assumption (15 August), Nativity of the Blessed Virgin (8 September), the Anniversary of the Pope's Coronation (for Benedict XIII, 11 October), All Saints' Day (1 November), All Souls' Day (2 November), and the First Sunday in Advent.[40] In 1412, when King Ferdinand of Aragon entered Tortosa where the Spanish pope was then residing, the prince, in the company of the Sovereign Pontiff, heard a Low Mass.[41] This case of a pope attending but not celebrating a Low Mass is exceptional and must have rarely occurred. A second example of such a service has been recorded: on 27 June 1406, with Benedict XIII at Noli, Low Mass was heard in the church of the Franciscans, *quia Cantores propter pestilentiam et mortem unius ex eis erant dispersi, et haberi non poterant.*[42] This notice leads us to suspect that the participation of the singers was required for the celebration of anything but a Low Mass.

## Solemn Pontifical Mass

The second type of service, the solemn Pontifical Mass celebrated by the pope, was the least frequent of the three modes of Mass. On certain days of the year, the bishop of Rome was expected to celebrate. However, there does not seem to have been any hard and fast rule requiring the pope to do so. If he did say the *missa magna,* it was imperative that several of the cardinals assist him in the vesting and in certain of the ceremonial actions. The prior of the cardinal bishops was bound to serve the pontiff on a predetermined number of feasts and whenever the Holy Father elected to celebrate personally. The ceremonials furnish a list of these feasts, and we may conclude that these occasions were the most likely times for the solemn Pontifical Mass. One document enumerates them as follows: the Third Mass of Christmas, Circumcision (1 January), Epiphany (6 January), Purification (2 February), Palm Sunday, Holy Thursday, Easter, Annunciation (25 March), Ascension, Pentecost, Saint John the Baptist, Saints Peter and Paul, Trinity, Corpus Christi, Assumption, Nativity of the Virgin, and All Saints' Day.[43] The prior cardinal priest, that is, the first ordained, was to serve as chaplain on all other days of the year but particularly on the two days after Christmas, Saint Stephen (26 December) and Saint John the Evangelist (27 December), the Easter Vigil service, and the first two Masses of Christmas (Midnight and Dawn). The enforcement of these stipulations, however, was likewise subject to papal discretion.[44]

The prior of the cardinal bishops placed the ring on the finger of the Sovereign Pontiff and assisted him in censing. This cardinal, accompanied by two cardinal deacons, was to join the pope in reciting the Gloria. The cardinal bishop held the missal *supra caput suum* while the pontiff read the prayer. He also censed the pope after the Gospel. The second of the cardinal bishops aided at the washing of hands, and both he and the prior assisted at the Elevation. The prior handed the *calamus,* or gold straw, to the pope by which he communicated from the cup. Both the second cardinal bishop and the third (or the prior cardinal priest) helped in the postcommunion ablutions.[45]

Conzié's document gives a more complete picture of exactly when Benedict XIII celebrated during the year 1406/07: Annunciation, possibly the first three Sundays of Lent, Holy Thursday, Good Friday, the Easter Vigil, Easter Day, Ascension, Pentecost, Corpus Christi, the three Masses of Christmas, Saint Stephen, Saint John the Evangelist, Epiphany (1407), Palm Sunday, Easter, Annunciation, Ascension, and Pentecost. This list corresponds by and large to the feasts at which the prior of either the cardinal bishops or the cardinal priests was supposed to assist.[46]

The *missa magna* celebrated by the pope was a sung Mass. Most curial officials were likely present, and the attendance of these cardinals, the commensal chaplains, and the *capellani* and *clerici capelle* was mandatory. These celebrations were no doubt marked by the presence of a large number of clerics, by the visual impact of the vestments, and by the elaborateness of the ritual.

*Mass Coram Papa*

While the ceremonials seldom report the pontiff's presence at a Low Mass, there are extensive rubrics for the Mass that the pope attended but did not celebrate, the *missa coram papa*. During this service the Holy Father is at his faldstool on the Gospel side (north) of the altar, the principal assistants seated on either side of him, the remaining cardinals on benches aligned parallel to the sides of the choir. There were certain more-or-less honorific duties that the pontiff had to perform when he presided, but most were left to his discretion. For example, if he decided to hear such a Mass on Holy Saturday (the Easter Vigil), he could have blessed the Paschal candle, *si vult*. It was his option to intone the threefold Alleluia.[47]

The cardinals, as well as the *capellani commensales,* were expected to attend these services. The pope was assisted by the *subdiaconus* and the *acolyti* of the commensal chapel. While the Gloria, Credo, and Sanctus were sung by the *capellani* standing at a reasonable distance away (*competenter distans*), the cardinals present were to leave their benches and form a semi-circle in front of the pontiff to recite these three movements simultaneously.[48] If specific cardinal-servers were not present at the Curia on the great feasts of the year, the pope himself was expressly forbidden to celebrate a solemn Pontifical Mass. Instead, he was obliged to hear a Mass *coram papa*. Such services took place both on greater and lesser feasts of the Church year.

Often the pope began his day by celebrating a private Mass in a small chapel; he then went to a large oratory that was available, where he elected not to celebrate pontifically but to hear Mass instead.[49] Extant records furnish the most detailed information concerning this type of service once again for the pontificate of Benedict XIII. During the year 1406, this Supreme Pontiff heard such Masses on numerous occasions. On Shrove Tuesday, for example, he rode to the cathedral of Savona where Mass *coram papa* was celebrated. He did the same on Laetare Sunday. On the following Palm Sunday, he attended a Mass that was said by the cardinal of Ostia.[50] On Trinity Sunday the archbishop of Vienne said the Mass; on the feast of the Baptist, the cardinal of Gerona was the celebrant.[51] The Vigil of Pentecost, however, was celebrated by one of the *capellani capelle,* that is to say, by one of the *cantores*. Like the solemn Pontifical Masses, such services were normally sung. For example, on the two days after Pentecost 1406, the pope heard Mass *cum nota . . . sicut solet facere diebus Dominicis.*[52]

There were other occasions that required the pontiff to attend a Mass which, for one reason or another, he himself did not celebrate. On Quasimodo Sunday 1406, one the the *capellani capelle* said his first Mass after ordination to the priesthood in the presence of pope and Curia. For this the chamberlain gave the unnamed chaplain 10 florins on behalf of the Holy Father.[53] This event is similar to the celebration of the first Mass of the chaplain Johannes Ruffi de Roquinies.[54] Low Sunday, outside of both the penitential season and Easter Week, was a day of little liturgical significance and seemed to be reserved for events of this sort.

There was further opportunity for Benedict to attend a Mass *coram papa*. When an important secular prince was present in the same city as the Supreme Pontiff, it was customary for the Head of the Church to worship with the dignitary. On Saturday, 5 June 1406, Benedict XIII heard a solemn Mass no doubt said in the presence of the ambassadors of the king of Cyprus.[55] In 1415, King Ferdinand of Aragon and his queen attended a Mass with the pope. This time, unlike the occasion in 1412 cited above, the service was recited *cum nota*.[56]

Before the last of the Avignon popes began a journey, it was his custom to hear a Mass.[57] He also attended Requiem Masses and exequies for deceased pontiffs, prelates, and nobles.[58] The Vicar of Christ was indisposed, and probably ill, on 1 January 1407 and consequently elected not to celebrate but to hear a Mass *coram papa*.[59]

There were, moreover, those times when, because of the lack of cardinals, the pope was actually unable to say a *missa magna*. On the feast of Saints Peter and Paul in 1406, Benedict was forced to say a *missa bassa* and then to hear Mass because the cardinals were absent. Again, on the following 15 August, the same situation obtained.[60] After the sickness and death of Cardinal Martin de Salva that same year, the members of the Sacred College, fearing the plague, were not available for the Mass of the Nativity of the Virgin. Consequently, the bishop of Nice said a *Magna missa coram papa*.[61]

When the Liturgy was celebrated in front of the Bishop of Rome, the eldest of the cardinal priests aided in the censing and the kiss of peace. But the ceremonials contain no rubric pertaining to the cardinal bishops that is at all comparable to those found for them in the solemn Pontifical Mass. Yet during the reign of Benedict XIII, the presence of the cardinal priest at Mass was not imperative, since, as we have seen, the pontiff was obligated to hear a Mass even when there was no cardinal present.

Most often, there is no record of who the celebrants were. Sometimes it was a cardinal or a bishop residing with the Curia.[62] Once it was the chamberlain.[63] And there are two occurrances of a *capellanus capelle* celebrating.[64] Indeed, according to Conzié's description of the *Capella*, it was the papal chaplains who were to take turns each week saying Mass *coram Domino nostro*, the pope.[65] It is not unreasonable to conclude from this information, therefore, that it was the exceptional case when a curial prelate celebrated for the pope. The norm, at least ca. 1409, was that the papal singers were generally responsible for saying the Mass *coram papa*. The document of Conzié further specifies that the *cantores* were expected to sing (*alta voce dicere*) Mass each day whether or not the Holy Father was present (*presente vel absente Domino nostro*). The singers of the pope must have been very active in the execution of papal liturgy during the first decade of the fifteenth century.

Though they were instituted at the Curia in 1334, the first references to the *cantores* appear in ceremonials dating from ca. 1377. The preponderant number of citations come from the greater feasts of the year, especially from those passages that outline the service for the Triduum (Holy Thursday, Good Friday, Holy Saturday). The rubrics for Holy Thursday indicate that on that day the singers were to perform the Introit without the Doxology. They were to sing the Improperia on Good Friday, at least the Tract, *Eripe me domine,* the Trisagion, and other antiphons used during the adoration of the cross. They provided the final *Amen* to the prayer after the *Pater noster* as well.[66] At the Easter Vigil, they participated in the procession of the Paschal candle which began at the entry of the church when the pope was outside of Avignon, but when he was in Avignon it started from the bay furthermost from the altar in the Great Chapel of Saint Peter.[67] While it appears as though the *subdiaconus* may have begun the chanting of the litany, the rubrics for the Vigil celebrated *coram papa* indicate that the task of singing the litany belonged primarily to the singers. As a group, they sang the Kyrie that followed.[68] The subdeacon or one of the commensal chaplains had the honor of intoning the Paschal Alleluia for the pontiff who then was to sing this song of praise. The verse, however, was performed *solempniter* by *duo cantores.*[69] These are all the references that mention the singers functioning at Mass in the chapel of Avignon.

Such citations furnish little more than what we know about the Roman *Schola cantorum* of the thirteenth century. Like the *Schola,* the *cantores* of Avignon were responsible for the Introit and the Kyrie on all days of the year, if we allow ourselves to extrapolate from those few references. They participated in singing the Tract of Good Friday and the Alleluia verse of the Paschal Vigil. It is safe to assume that they were responsible for chanting all the propers of each Mass, a task that might have been difficult, if not impossible, for the cardinals and commensal chaplains. They probably responded with acclamations such as *Amen.*[70] When appropriate to the liturgy, they no doubt sang the Kyrie, Gloria, Credo, Sanctus, and Agnus at Mass, and might have been the sole performers of these movements during the Mass said *coram papa.* We might recall that this was the Mass requiring all cardinals present to form a semicircle before the Holy Father to recite these texts with him while these movements were being sung. Moreover, at those Masses where there were no cardinals and few commensal chaplains present, whether documented (as in the year 1406/07) or not (probably when the pontiffs were at their residences in Villeneuve, Châteauneuf, or Pont-de-Sorgues, or perhaps during those periods of epidemic and plague) the burden of the liturgical service fell to the *cantores.*

This assessment of the participation of the singers in the papal chapel is corroborated by evidence drawn from the rubrics of Easter. Near the end of the pontificate of Gregory XI, the extensive lections of the Easter Vigil were customarily begun by an acolyte or by a clerk of the chapel (*clericus capelle*). The rest were recited by the *capellani commensales*. However, if the pope was not celebrating, that is, if the service was executed *coram papa*, the lessons were to be chanted *per capellanos sive per cantores de capella*.[71] This method of performing the readings was probably employed if and when the number of commensal chaplains was insufficient for the lections that were to be done. Another passage from the same ceremonial notes that if the pope did not celebrate on this day, the *clerici capelle* were to do the first two readings and the *capellani capelle* (the singers) those that remained.[72]

In addition to the two occasions in 1406/07 when Benedict attended a Mass celebrated by one of the *capellani capelle*, on the Monday and Tuesday after Easter this pope was expected to hear a Mass *cum nota cantatam per unum de capellanis sue capelle*. By analogy to Easter, the two days following Pentecost had like celebrations assigned to them.[73] On the commemoration of the election of Benedict (28 September) he was supposed to hear a Mass of the Holy Spirit *cantatam per unum de capellanis sue capelle*.[74] So while the curial prelates sometimes executed the Mass *coram papa*, it was doubtless the norm for the papal singers to celebrate these services. This is corroborated by the description of the office of *capellanus* outlined by Conzié, where the singers are held to take turns celebrating such Masses for the pope each week.

## The Canonical Hours

### Lesser

The importance of the *capellani capelle* in the execution of the papal liturgical services is witnessed in the descriptions of the canonical hours that were attended by the popes of Avignon. The lesser hours seem to have been seldom celebrated by the bishops of Rome. The rubrics for Lauds of the Vigil of Christmas assign the incipit of the first antiphon to the pope and those of the remaining antiphons (incipits) *per cardinales dicuntur non per cantores*.[75] The concluding *Benedicamus* was probably performed by acolytes from among the *commensales* or possibly by two singers bearing candles since it was to be done by *ceroferarii pape assistentes*.[76] Lauds of Holy Thursday are executed with the pope furnishing the beginning of the *Miserere mei* in a manner described in the ceremonial as *quasi legendo* with the remainder of the psalm provided by the *cantores*.[77] During the celebration of Lauds of Easter, it was the papal singers who were responsible for the execution of the antiphons.[78]

There is not a single reference to the hour of Prime in any of the documents. Yet whenever the Holy Father celebrated a solemn Pontifical Mass, Terce was said.[79] Before the popes settled at Avignon, it was executed thus: the papal entourage arrived in procession at the church where Mass was to be celebrated, the reverence was made by the cardinals and by the other prelates, and there, in front of the Sovereign Pontiff, Terce was recited *sine nota . . . cum capellanis* (or *ministris*) *suis*. On the feast of Purification observed at Avignon, the rubrics prescribe that Terce be done in the sacristy, the south sacristy or revestiary in the Palace of the Popes.[80] On Palm Sunday, the hour was said after the entry procession but immediately before Mass whenever the pope celebrated. It was customary before the Mass of the Day on Christmas.[81] At the Mass of episcopal consecration that took place in Avignon 19 December 1328, Terce was also said.[82]

During times of fast, both Terce and Sext were said before Pontifical Mass celebrated by the pope. At the Council of Vienne, both Terce and Sext were executed before the Mass on 16 October 1311 *quia dies ieiunii est*. However, on 3 April 1312 for the opening of the second session of the council, the rubrics indicate that Terce and Sext were to be said only *si placet*.[83] On Holy Thursday, before the Curia resided in Avignon, the office was performed *in camera*. However, if the Mass of the Holy Chrism was celebrated, then Terce was the only hour that preceded it.[84] On the Easter Vigil, if one of the cardinal deacons were to bless the Paschal candle, the Supreme Pontiff was expected to recite Terce and Sext *in camera*.[85] The usual time for the hour of Sext, however, was after the celebration of Mass, recited by the pope and his chaplains.[86]

Finally, there are only a few brief references to the hour of Nones made in the ceremonials. It was recited after Mass at the Council of Vienne, but on Good Friday and Holy Saturday it occurred before, not after, the solemn services. In the case of the latter celebration, while both Terce and Sext were to be said *in camera*, Nones was supposed to be said *in ecclesia* or no doubt in the Great Chapel at Avignon.[87]

Of the lesser hours, there is no indication that either Sext or Nones was ever performed *cum nota*. Terce was customarily recited by the Holy Father accompanied by his chaplains. It is probably that at these hours, the *capellani commensales* were to be the sole functionaries. The one feast that commanded a Terce *cum nota* was the celebration of Pentecost. This service has already been discussed in chapter 3, on the *magister capelle pape*.[88] The descriptions found in the ceremonials indicate that the master of the papal chapel participated in executing the psalm, *Legem pone*, though it is never specifically stated whether or not the *cantores* participated in this office. Benedict XIII took part in Terce of Pentecost on 30 May 1406 at the cathedral of Savona. According to Conzié, the pontiff began the hour *cum nota*. The *Auditores, Capellani Commensales, Magister Capelle*, and *Clerici cerimoniarum* attended *per modum chori*. On that day, two of the *capellani* said the psalm, the *Versus*, and the *Benedicamus domino*. This passage further explains that while the psalm was sung, Pope Benedict, *cum suis Cubiculariis, dixit . . . totam Tertiam submissa voce*, seated at his faldstool.[89] Two other ceremonials reserved the chanting of the short responsory and the *Benedicamus domino* to two acolytes bearing candles.[90]

Though we can unequivocally state that the *magister capelle* participated in Terce of Pentecost, such a claim cannot easily be made for the *cantores*. However, it seems that, although their services were not normally essential for the lesser hours of Terce, Sext, and Nones throughout the year, they most probably took part in this Terce along with the *magister capelle*.

## Matins and Vespers

Unlike the aforementioned lesser hours, the offices of Matins and Vespers were the exclusive domain of the college of papal singers. They fulfilled their functions in this regard as reported by the chronicles that outlined the reforms of 1334 and by the description of Conzié from 1409. At Matins of Christmas, the pontiff intoned the *Domine labia mea aperies* and the *cantores prosequuntur,* most likely by responding to the pope then by executing the Invitatory, *Venite, exultemus,* and the hymn, *Jesu redemptor omnium.* While the assignment of the readings is carefully laid out, nothing is said of the responsories. The execution of the music no doubt fell to the singers and the assignment of the incipits to the *magister.*[91] On an unspecified Holy Thursday, Benedict XIII, it is reported, *vult exire ad matutinas.* Though little information is given concerning this service, we know that the *cantores* participated and the cardinals did not assist the pope.[92] Conzié tells us that in 1406, the cardinals sat in the nave of the cathedral of Savona, the bishops and priests among them to one side and the deacons to the other. Meanwhile, Benedict *dixit Matutinum* with his cubiculars. This probably is similar to the performance of Terce of Pentecost, where the pontiff recited the text while it was simultaneously being sung. The same type of arrangement was prescribed for Good Friday and Holy Saturday.[93] Matins was heard by this pope on Pentecost, Trinity, Corpus Christi, Saints Peter and Paul, and on All Saints' Day. In 1406, Benedict heard Matins of Easter. This is worthy of note, given that he officiated at the vigil service.[94]

Matins for the bishops of Rome, therefore, seems to have been reserved for the most solemn occasions, particularly the Triduum and Christmas, though even in these instances it was likely the pope's prerogative whether or not to attend. According to Conzié, it was up to the Holy Father to mandate the chanting of Matins and Vespers if he deemed the feast of sufficient solemnity, though it was not obligatory for the pontiff himself to be present.[95] This is evidenced further in the numerous descriptions of Vespers and the variations in its performance found in the ceremonials.

Like the Mass, Vespers was a service at which the Roman Pontiffs were permitted either to celebrate or simply to be present. The most solemn of the offices were to be intoned by the pope and were usually those celebrated on the vigil of a feast, that is, first Vespers. They comprise Christmas, Pentecost, Saints Peter and Paul, Assumption, and All Saints' Day.[96] On these occasions the pope began the office by intoning the *Deus in adiutorium.* The subdeacon pre-intoned the first antiphon for the Holy Father who had the honor of formally giving the incipit. The second antiphon was intoned by the eldest cardinal deacon and the third by the eldest cardinal bishop. The senior cardinal priest provided the incipit for the fourth antiphon and the fifth was intoned by the second oldest deacon of the Sacred College. The chapter was recited by the highest ranking commensal chaplain, the subdeacon. One of the acolytes pre-intoned the hymn and the subdeacon pre-intoned the antiphon *ad Magnificat* for the pope, who gave the incipit for both these chants. While this antiphon was being sung, the Supreme Pontiff censed the altar. Accompanied by an acolyte, the cardinal bishop who began the third antiphon censed the pope, the cardinal deacon assisting the Holy Father, and all the cardinals who were properly vested. The subdeacon then performed the ritual in turn for the cardinal bishop and for the other prelates attending. Two acolytes removed the candles from the corners of the altar and stood before the pope while he recited the prayer.[97] Though the method of performance of the *Benedicamus domino* is not specified here, it is likely that it was executed by these two acolytes.[98] Finally, the pontiff himself was to give the concluding blessing.

During the reign of the last pope of Avignon, the pontiff seems to have usually officiated at first Vespers of a feast; while second Vespers, that is, Vespers of the day of the feast, was said *coram papa*. On the Vigil of Christmas, for example, the pope was expected to begin the hour with the *Deus in adiutorium*, to intone both the first antiphon and the antiphon *ad Magnificat*, to provide the incipit of the hymn, as well as to cense the altar and to recite the prayer aloud. Specific cardinals intoned the other antiphons according to their rank in the Sacred College. At the end of the service, *duo acoliti... dicunt Benedicamus domino*. On Christmas day, however, the pope did not do (*facit*) the office, but was only expected to hear it (*audire*). Even though the tasks performed by the Sovereign Pontiffs were exactly the same as at first Vespers, at the end of second Vespers, rather than acolytes, *duo de capellanis capelle dicunt: Benedicamus.*[99] On the less solemn occasions, the commensal chaplains were not the sole participants, but instead they were in part replaced by the *cantores*. On the Vigils of Epiphany and Purification the office was to be as on Christmas.[100] And the rubrics for the Vigil of the Annunciation indicate that Vespers was to be modeled on that of Purification.[101] The same distinction between first and second Vespers is drawn in the description of Pentecost, Trinity, Saints Peter and Paul, Assumption, and All Saints: the pope *facit* solemn first Vespers; and second Vespers he *consuevit audire.*[102] A similar situation is found on the feast of the Circumcision. On both the eve and the day, the pontiff *consuevit exire ad vesperas,* but the ceremonial records that although the pope attended second Vespers *nihil dicit, ymo capellani capelle totum faciunt.*[103]

On Corpus Christi and the Annunciation, both first and second Vespers were celebrated, though the ceremonial draws no distinction between the two services. We may conclude from the above evidence that papal attendance was expected at both offices, but the Holy Father was bound to officiate solely at the vigil service.[104] The feast of the Baptist is not comparable to any of the solemn feasts. It lacks a second Vespers, and the pope was held only to hear the vigil office.[105] On the feasts of Saint Stephen and John the Evangelist, Vespers was celebrated, but the pontiff was not obliged to attend.[106] This presents the interesting situation suggested by Conzié, namely, that the papal singers often performed Vespers in the presence of neither the Holy Father nor any officiating prelate.

It is again to the document of Conzié that we must turn for a more detailed account of the Vespers service. Although the descriptions in his ceremonial are less universal in their tone, they do provide an indication of the latitude allowed in the papal office.

In the year 1406, Benedict XIII is reported to have attended first and second Vespers on only a few feasts: Annunciation, Ascension, Pentecost, Corpus Christi, and Christmas. In each case, the vigil service was the more solemn of the two. The Curia was present for first Vespers on the Annunciation and the cardinals assisted the pontiff. The compiler of the ceremonial only notes that at the office performed the following day the singers began the hour.[107] At first Vespers of Ascension, the Supreme Pontiff intoned the hour, the hymn, the antiphon at the Magnificat, said the prayer, and gave the blessing. The following day, Benedict began the hour, said the prayer and the blessing, but performed only the censing at the *Magnificat.*

A sharper distinction between the solemn first Vespers and the second Vespers, where the singers had a greater role, is made in Conzié's description of Pentecost. On the eve of the great feast, the cardinals, prelates, and others gathered at the bishop's residence in Savona where Benedict was lodged. Then, led by the pontiff, all proceeded to the cathedral where the reverence was made by the members of the Sacred College. Here the pope intoned Vespers and the first antiphon, the cardinals the remaining antiphons according to their rank and title. The hymn, *Veni creator,* was intoned by the pontiff who, kneeling, prostrated himself at the cathedra (faldstool) while the *cantores* sang the first verse. He then gave the incipit for the antiphon *ad Magnificat,* incensed, said the prayer, and gave the blessing at the end. The following day, after Matins, Terce, and Mass, all gathered in the episcopal palace where an altar was prepared in the *tinellum* or dining hall. Here Benedict began second Vespers of Pentecost with the *Deus in adiutorium,* censed during the *Magnificat,* and said the prayer. Conzié informs us that the Holy Father *nihil aliud fecit.* It is likely that all the incipits were executed by the *cantores* under the direction of the *magister capelle.* Furthermore, at this office the *Hymnus fuit inchoatus per Magistrum Organorum.* Since the use of the organ to begin the Vespers hymn was deemed worthy of mention in this one instance, this performance of the *Veni creator* must have been somewhat out of the ordinary. The usual method of execution may have been the one employed the previous evening, namely, the incipit done by the voice.[108]

The heavy reliance on the *cantores* for the celebration of Vespers, especially those of the nonsolemn variety, and the documented use of the organ implies that such liturgical ceremonies were among the most musically sophisticated displays witnessed by popes in their chapel. Benedict's dependency on the singers was so complete that without their presence, papal Vespers could not have been held. Such was the case on 28 June 1406. After a long and particularly arduous journey from Savona to Finale, the singers were so tired that many of them were absent on the Vigil of Saints Peter and Paul. Consequently, no service transpired.[109]

After Christmas 1406, Benedict XIII was often indisposed, probably due to illness, and he either did not function at ceremonies or did very little while attending them. After celebrating solemn Pontifical Mass in the monastery of Saint-Victor at Marseille on Saint Stephen's Day 1406, the pope attended Vespers in a small chapel in which he customarily heard Mass on nonsolemn days while he was at Marseille. Though four cardinals were present, one of the *capellani capelle* began Vespers and concluded it, probably by giving the blessing. Benedict did not even cense but, instead, deferred to the prior of the cardinal priests. The following day, the pontiff did not attend Vespers. On the Vigil of Circumcision, the pope heard the evening hours in the small chapel (*capella secreta*) and only gave the blessing. The entire service, including all the incipits and censing, was likely performed by the *capellani capelle*. On the day of the feast, nothing of Vespers was done except what was to be said by the singers on the other common, or regular, days.[110] Conzié implies here that on nonsolemn days, the *cantores* were, in fact, the principal officiants at Vespers.

The rubrics for Vespers performed during the Triduum furnish more information concerning the participation of the papal singers. Within the first year of the coronation of a new pope, the *mandatum,* that is the washing of the feet of 12 subdeacons or chaplains, was to take place after the Mass on Thursday afternoon. During the washing, Vespers was sung. The ceremonials indicate that the singers were to perform the hour alone. The *capellani pape,* that is, the upper-level chaplains, *legendo decunt etiam vesperos ante papam.*[111] In 1406, because of an error made by the *clerici cerimoniarum* (the successors to the *clerici capelle*), the singers began Vespers before Benedict divested himself of pontifical garb. Only after the pope returned to his residence from the cathedral, did he go to the *tinellum* where he washed the feet of 13 poor men. This appears to be an alternate form of the *mandatum* rite, one performed by Benedict because it was not his first pontifical year.[112] During this service, something of an unspecified nature was sung by the *cantores.* One ceremonial has the following rubric: *Cantores vero interim cantant que cantanda sunt.* It is likely that the *mandatum* antiphons, similar to those found in later books of Roman usage, were chanted at this point.[113]

On Good Friday, Vespers of the previous day is said *legendo.* The rubrics further specify that *Et tunc etiam cantores dicunt vesperos legendo.* The text was to be recited in a way that the pope and other prelates could hear and understand the words.[114] The day was so solemn that there was no music at this office. Yet it is of particular importance that the execution of the hour was still the primary concern of the papal singers.[115]

In sum, Vespers was the most important and frequently celebrated hour for the bishop of Rome. First Vespers was always more solemn: the pope and cardinals were active participants, and the subdeacon, the acolytes, and the other *capellani commensales* were expected to take part. The *cantores* were no doubt present and providing the bulk of the music. The higher clergy merely read the texts of the antiphons in a low voice while they were sung by the *capellani capelle*. Second Vespers, on the other hand, did not require the pontiff nor the other curial officials for its proper execution. Here the singers, under the direction of the *magister capelle*, surely provided many of the incipits. It was the service at which we can unequivocally admit the presence and participation of an organ. It also seems highly likely that these services furnished opportunities for polyphonic performance of the *Benedicamus domino* and other pieces such as the hymn and perhaps the psalms. And it is certain that there were other Vespers services celebrated on nonsolemn days solely by the *cantores* which the pontiff and members of the Sacred College did not attend, and for which there is no extant record. There, at Vespers on the most solemn days, those officials who had the least association with musical performance held the stage. Consequently, on feasts of lesser rank, the *cantores* had a greater role in the service. This leads to the apparently paradoxical conclusion that the less solemn days of the year were those most likely to have a greater number of chants sung only by the singers of the chapel, and probably also that polyphony may have more easily been introduced into the service on those feasts that were less rigidly controlled by ancient and solemn liturgical tradition.[116]

## Polyphony in the Chapel

If we can assume that polyphonic performance of the music of the Church was most likely to occur at those services which depended heavily on the papal singers for their execution—namely, at the Mass celebrated *coram papa* and at the hours of Vespers that were least solemn (second Vespers)—it remains for us to determine when during the Church year such a practice was most likely to occur. One ceremonial yields some information in this regard by way of proscriptions. It states: when dealing with the *Temporale,* the office is not to be discanted from Passion Sunday up until Easter (except for the Kyrie, Credo, Sanctus, and Agnus) save Holy Thursday, when the entire office is to be discanted.[117] Polyphonic mass ordinaries, therefore, could have been performed throughout the entire year. All other polyphony, both in the Mass and divine office, was prohibited during Passiontide. The exception would have been when the feast of the Annunciation, for example, fell during the period in question, since it was included in the *Sanctorale* and thus not subject to this interdiction. The rubric seems to have offered the singers of the pope fifty weeks of unrestricted polyphony per year.

Collections of polyphonic mass ordinaries do exist, but, except for a few hymns found almost exclusivey in Apt, ms. 16 bis and several settings of the *Benedicamus domino,* polyphonic music from the canonical hours is not to be found. One would expect to see preserved a manuscript containing two- or three-voice arrangements of texts used in the office of Holy Thursday for example. In the absence of such written settings, we must provisionally conclude that the bulk of whatever liturgical polyphony was performed at the canonical hours was improvised on plainchant and that this state of affairs was taken for granted by the compilers of the ceremonials.

**The Organ in the Chapel**

Closely linked to the aforementioned rubric pertaining to the discanting of pieces from the Mass and office is one from the same ceremonial which states that the organ was not to be played in the chapel on the *Temporale* feasts from Septuagesima up until Easter, save Holy Thursday.[118] Our knowledge of the use of the organ in the chapel of the pope is limited to this rubric and to the reference of Pentecost 1406 which reported that the master of the organ began the hymn at second Vespers. The organ was likely used in the papal chapel at nonsolemn Vespers throughout the year except for the penitential season that commenced with Septuagesima. Indeed the hymn was the class of chant that was most prone to receive an organ setting. It is also highly probable that the instrument was played during the *mandatum* service, which was either executed during or after Vespers of Holy Thursday.

The similarity in the rubrics for the use of the organ and for the singing of polyphony in the papal chapel in no way suggests the simultaneous use of voices and instruments. In fact, there is no evidence of any musical instrument being used to accompany a sacred text throughout the period of the Avignon papacy. The mode of performance for the Vespers hymn was more likely to be *alternatim,* with voices and organ executing alternate verses. With regard to the Mass, there is unfortunately a lack of specific information. However, it in no way rules out the possible use of the organ in chants such as the Sequence.

The interdiction on polyphony in the papal chapel during Passiontide has been dated 1398 and is, therefore, the earliest reference to the singing of polyphonic mass ordinaries in curial usage.[119] Since the ceremonials tend to be conservative, the rubric likely represents a practice already well established.

The admonition concerning the use of the organ, on the other hand, is believed to date from after the escape of Benedict from the Palace of the Popes; consequently, it is impossible for us to determine whether or not an organ was ever employed in the liturgical services at Avignon. Furthermore, the first reference to a chaplain hired specifically to play the instrument occurs in 1405, when Raymundus Arnulphi took the oath as *magister organorum*. [120] From 1413 until 1416 the Dominican Johannes Fabri seems to have been the papal organist, though no specific reference to him playing the instrument has been found. [121] In 1413 he was responsible for transporting an organ from Peñíscola to Tortosa and back. Similar entries in the papal accounts for 1414 and 1415, if anything, certainly testify to the portability of the organ. On 17 September 1415, Franciscus de Linares was paid 110 Barcelonian solidi *pro reparatione organorum capellae domini papae*. [122] The organ in question may not be the same as the portative organ cared for by Johannes Fabri, but the notice does indicate that an instrument was still being used in the papal chapel.

By the late fifteenth century, the well-known prohibition on the use of the organ in the private papal chapel seems to have developed. Though there is no evidence of such an instrument in the Sistine Chapel, there are, however, references to the organ in papal liturgical services held at Saint Peter's and at other Roman churches. [123] Such an interdiction in the private chapel was probably part of the tradition established earlier at Avignon and at other papal residences as well. The distinction that needs to be made is one of function. While in Avignon and elsewhere, the popes employed two types of chapels: small private oratories and large chapels. The large structures, such as the Chapel of Saint John and the Great Chapel of Saint Peter were not papal chapels in the strict sense of the word, but they actually functioned as substitute stational churches. It was in these places that the bishop of Rome either celebrated or attended the services on the great feasts of the Church year. Moreover, when Pope Benedict XIII was bereft of his palace and its several chapels, the cathedral and monastic churches of the host city served as stational churches. [124] In addition, he often employed the *tinellum* of his residence as another vicarious stational church where Mass or Vespers was sung. It was in such a *tinellum* that Vespers of Pentecost was performed; and it was at this hour that the organ, doubtless of the portative variety, was played. Therefore, we may postulate that if an organ was ever employed during the papal liturgy at Avignon, it was likely in the Great Chapel of Saint Peter.

## Procession

Besides the Mass and the canonical hours, the ceremony that most necessitated the active participation of the *cantores* was the procession. The rubrics for several of these are preserved in the documents. On Palm Sunday, immediately after the junior cardinal priest blessed the palms and the Sovereign Pontiff distributed them to the members of the Curia, all the prelates and clerics were to go in procession to the door of the Great Chapel in the papal palace (to the door of the church when the pope was outside of Avignon). Two singers remaining inside the oratory commenced the hymn *Gloria laus* which, along with the antiphons, was sung under the direction of the master of the chapel. Because of

Plate 7. Door to the great chapel in the Palace of the Popes at Avignon. Mutilated trumeau figure is believed to be that of Saint Peter.

the participation of the *magister capelle* and the essential role played by two *cantores*, we can assume that the other chapel singers were important executants of the processional antiphons.[125]

Like rubrics are found for the feast of Purification. It is the singers who are given sole responsibility not only for the execution of the antiphon *Lumen ad revelationem gentium* but also for the performance of the other chants. The music in question was sung twice: the first time for the distribution of the candles to the members of the Sacred College and to curial officials; the second time the singers performed the designated antiphons while the prelates processed into the chapel from the parvis, after the pontiff had thrown small candles to the public gathered below the Indulgence Window.[126]

In addition to the papal processions that were part of an annual observance, there were occasional processions in which the singers participated. For example, each time the pontiff entered a city, he was received in procession. Though we have no information concerning the music performed, we do know that the popes were often, if not always, greeted by the sound of trumpets and other instruments.[127] In 1406 when Benedict entered Noves, Nice, Toulon, and Marseille the ceremony was noted by Conzié. While nothing specific is ever given concerning the singers, we might safely assume that when they were present, they were participants.

Pope Benedict took part in a procession with King Ferdinand of Aragon on the feast of Assumption 1414. The reason for such a display was to fulfill a request of the monarch. Ferdinand asked that a procession be held in order that he might see the processional ceremonies of the Roman Curia. The *capellani capelle pape* took part and, according to the compiler of the ceremonial, sang *Veni creator* and *Ave maris stella.*[128] It is probable that such hymns belonged to the repertory that the singers of the pontifical chapel usually chanted on such occasions. Although there is no direct evidence, it is possible that some verses of these hymns were performed in polyphony. We have already determined that the hymn was the piece most likely to receive a polyphonic setting. These two texts, in particular, are among those office hymns for which three-voice settings exist in the volume of polyphonic music, Apt, ms. 16 bis.[129]

## Papal Feasting

There is yet another occasion when the ceremonials note the presence of the papal singers: at the papal meal. Their function here is somewhat obscure. As we have already seen, by the early part of the fifteenth century, the *magister capelle* was instrumental in the proper observance of the rites carried out at the papal table. And although the *cantores* customarily were not present at such meals, the description of their office by Conzié does provide for individual attendance as substitutes for the *magister.*[130] However, there are certain pontifical feasts at which the *cantores* were either expected to be present or those at which their participation was requested by the pontiff.

In terms of the rubrics provided, the most rigorous of all papal meals was the dinner partaken after Vespers on Holy Thursday, the day commemorating the Last Supper. For this the Holy Father was required to be appropriately vested, as were the cardinals and the other curial prelates who shared the meal with the pontiff. At the conclusion of the dinner, grace was intoned, presumably by the master of the chapel. Part of the thanksgiving prayer included the recitation of the psalm *Miserere mei deus.* Though the ceremonials furnish no indication of musical participation by the singers, nevertheless all the *cantores* were to be nearby, a fact that one document particularly emphasized with the following rubric: *Memorandum est, quod omnes capellani commensales domini pape et*

*non commensales debent ista die comedere cum domino camerario splendide.*
While the singers may not have eaten in the same room as the pontiff, they were
no doubt available and in the palace.[131]

After grace was said, another ritual followed. It is known as the *collatio* or
the *potus in aula*. Spices, specifically pepper and cinnamon (*piper et
zizimberum*) were brought to the cardinals by the pantry workers. These spices
were then mixed with wine which was served to those present. The *potus in aula*
was done after the great meal of Holy Thursday but was prescribed for other
feasts as well. The ceremonial from the reign of Gregory XI requires that *collatio*
be held after solemn Vespers celebrated by the pope, especially on the eve of
Nativity, Pentecost, Saints Peter and Paul, Assumption, and All Saints.[132]

While the papal feast and the subsequent *collatio* is cited only a few times in
the preschismatic ceremonials, the compilers working during the time of
Benedict XIII frequently note such festive meals.[133] The curial prelates ate with
this pontiff whenever he created new cardinals.[134] On 11 June 1405 in the city of
Genoa, he consecrated 13 new bishops and 58 abbots; all partook in the papal
meal.[135] When Benedict met with Ferdinand of Aragon in 1414, besides the other
ceremonies that were recorded, the papal meal was shared.[136]

Furthermore, there is evidence that the singers sometimes partook in the
feasting. On the Saturday after Pentecost 1406, the pontiff, high curial officials,
and the ambassadors of the king of Cyprus held a great *prandium;* the *cantores*
were present as well.[137] On 1 July of that year there was an afternoon meal and
*collatio* with the ambassadors of Castile attended by *aliqui cantores*.[138] On both
the feast of Saints Peter and Paul and the feast of the Baptist, the *capellani capelle*
ate with the pope. On the Vigil of Christmas 1406, they participated in a splendid
meal and probably the *potus in aula,* though the Holy Father himself was not
present.[139] And on Epiphany the following year, the *capellani capelle* are
reported to have dined with the pontiff though they sat *in ultima mensa.*[140] They
also feasted after the Mass of Pentecost 1407.[141] Although it must be treated
carefully, the account of the ceremony following the Vigil Mass of Pentecost
1406 seems to imply that the chaplains of the papal chapel customarily partook
of the meal. The rubrics state that no one ate with the pontiff that day, *nec etiam
Capellani Cappellae.*[142] In any event, we can say with reasonable certainty that at
the *prandium* and the *collatio* of the great feasts of the year as well as occasions of
state, the singers were often present or available.

Diaries of the papal chapel singers compiled during the early sixteenth to
early seventeenth centuries frequently note the presence of the *cantores* at the
papal midday meal (*prandium*). It was after these dinners that the musician
guests were expected to repay their host by singing a *motetum coram papa.*[143] It
was probably at these times, or during the *potus in aula* held after Vespers, that
singers at the court of Avignon performed motets as well. Since the papal singers
were of mean status, and at best ranked *in ultima mensa,* it was not a question of
propriety that they be present. The likely purpose for their attendance was

musical. Their participation in state dinners, such as the two mentioned above, would have involved the singing of an appropriate motet.[144]

## Roman Tradition

According to all accounts, Benedict XIII was a conservative liturgist. When his chamberlain, François de Conzié, switched allegiance first to the Pisan pope in 1409, the household and chapel offices of the Aragonese pontiff were considered traditional enough to serve as a model. Conzié must have taken some of these Avignonese customs with him when he later swore fealty to Martin V. In addition to the rites collected by Conzié, many of the rituals practiced by Benedict were no doubt carried to Rome by the *clericus cerimoniarum* Matheus Petri. Matheus was one of the two clerks who prepared the rites and services for Benedict. He was employed by this pontiff from 1411 until 1423. After the death of the last pope of Avignon, Matheus went on to serve Eugene IV and Nicholas V until 1450.[145] Evidently he was successful in fulfilling the duties of his office, that is, preserving the ancient traditions of the Roman Curia.

While the practices of the papal chapel during the late fifteenth and early sixteenth centuries no doubt diverged to some extent from those of the early fifteenth century, the essentials of liturgical practice and tradition were the same. Though the types of pieces performed in the chapel and the styles of the music were quite different, the roots for the later practice existed well back into the fourteenth century. In this study of the papal liturgy, we have outlined only a few of the services and practices of the court of Rome and discussed those references that have had direct bearing on the performance of music at Avignon. When the ceremonials speak, the descriptions are often detailed and elaborate; but, so often on those subjects that most concern us, they are virtually silent. They do, however, offer the first references to the singing of polyphonic mass ordinaries and to the use of the organ in the chapel of the pope. Papal liturgy is one that permitted itself numerous options and yielded easily to impulse and chance. Avignon of the popes is long believed to have been an important musical center, and the papal chapel the prime source of liturgical polyphony. By examining these curial handbooks, we have been able to supply the setting and to suggest a liturgical framework for the music of the papal chapel at the end of the Middle Ages.

# 5

# The Apt Manuscript

## City of Apt

Fifty-three kilometers to the east of Avignon, high in the hills of the Luberon, lies the town of Apt. Today the center of an arrondissement in the department of Vaucluse, Apt is the seat of an archdiaconate within the archdiocese of Avignon.[1] In the fourteenth century, however, the city had its own bishop and cathedral situated at the hub of one of the several small Provençal dioceses. Though the administration of the see was dependent on the metropolitan of Aix, during the stay of the popes at Avignon there was also a marked reliance on the papal capital.

The chapter of the cathedral was founded in 991 and originally comprised 12 members. Not long after this date, it acquired numerous and significant sources of income. As a result, 13 beneficiaries were added to the core of canons. The chapter was considered to be the most distinguished group of clerics in the city, and some of its members came to be among the most powerful in Europe.[2] In 1334, for example, when he was named bishop of Cavaillon, Philippe de Cabassole held a canonicate at the cathedral of Apt. Pierre Ollier, *operarius* of the chapter, became an honorary chaplain of Gregory XI.[3] In the seventeenth century, when all the chaplains were obliged to attend the divine offices, there was knowledge of a long tradition of musical excellence at the cathedral. At that time (1638), the canons, as a body, had become ignorant of plainchant, and the other prebended clerics attached to the chapter were required to perform the music "as was done at Aix," since, they said, "at all times there have been famous musicians among the prebended who brought glory to the chapter of Apt."[4]

The provostry was the only dignity of the chapter, and was the greatest ecclesiastical honor to have been bestowed after the episcopacy.[5] As such, the title brought with it special privileges. For example, besides the bishop, it was the provost alone who was permitted to celebrate at the main altar; all canons and beneficed clerics were required to obey him. The office was often entrusted to men distinguished by merit of birth and deed. Among these were several notables. Durand André (ca. 1372) was said to be wise in the ways of medicine and long had been confessor to Blessed Delphine de Signe. When he died, in

Fig. 7.    Map of fourteenth-century area near Avignon, including
Apt, high in hills 53 kilometers to the east.

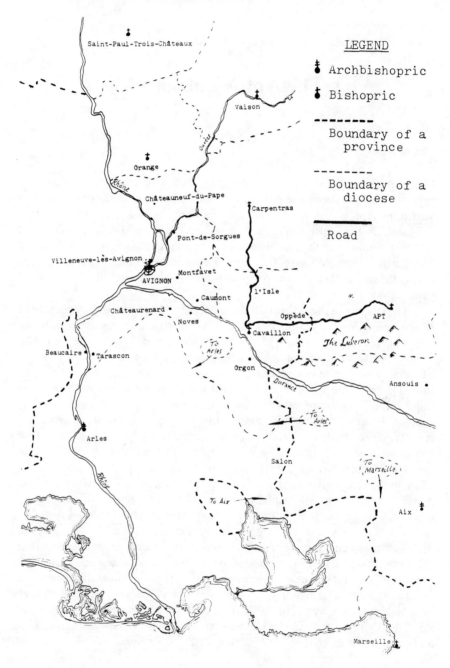

LEGEND

🜚  Archbishopric

🜚  Bishopric

-------  Boundary of a
           province

- - - - -  Boundary of a
           diocese

———  Road

1379, he was living at Rome in the court of Gregory XI. Guillaume Hortolan (ca. 1384-1389) was a supporter of Clement VII and served as a representative of the pontiff in France and elsewhere. He was rewarded in 1389 by being made patriarch of Jerusalem and is said to have died as bishop of Rodez. Raymond de Bretennes, listed as provost in 1400, was raised to the see of Lombez that same year. His successor was the *magister capelle pape,* Richardus de Bozonvilla.[6]

During the stay of the popes at Avignon, the city of Apt witnessed the great and near-great come and go. As with almost all late-medieval towns, it experienced its share of saints, both real and imagined. The hundred-year period of non-Italian pontiffs saw money and power channeled to Apt, and, consequently, the town held a modicum of cultural and political importance.

In 1385 Apt served as the meeting place for the Estates General of Provence. Twenty years earlier, a provincial council of the Church was convened there.[7] Shortly after the close of this council, Pope Urban V went to the city accompanied by four cardinals, among them the future Gregory XI. The accounts of the city yield little evidence of festivities, though the town treasurer spent 10 florins for a dais, a banner, and for certain decorations made to the house in which the Sovereign Pontiff was lodged.[8] Several other cardinals and numerous bishops are known to have passed through Apt during the second half of this century. Pierre Bertrand, cardinal bishop of Ostia, was sent to Rome in 1355 by Pope Innocent in order to officiate at the coronation of the Emperor Charles IV. Though Apt was not on the direct route from Avignon to Italy, this prelate did pass through the town on his return, 23 June 1355, and was received with great pomp.[9]

Secular princes managed to find their way to this small city as well.[10] After the solemnities of May 1382 that proclaimed Louis I of Anjou heir to the throne of Naples, the duke left Avignon for Carpentras; his wife, Marie de Blois, went north to Orange; and Amadeus of Savoy, the Green Count, traveled to Cavaillon, all of them to begin their ill-fated journey to Italy. On 13 June, the two princes arrived at Apt. Duke Louis, entitled as count of Provence and king of Sicily, entered in procession via the Porte de la Bouquerie. Young boys dressed in white greeted him shouting *Noël! Noël! Vive monseigneur de Calabre!*[11] On Monday, 29 January 1386, his son, Louis II, and Marie, his widow, as rulers of Provence and heads of the house of Anjou, once again directed their steps to this city in the Luberon. A second time young children met the entourage and, bearing the coat of arms of the royal visitor, they cried *Vive le Roy Loys!* A great procession of burghers, led by the bishop, was made on that day. On the next, in a cortege led by the bishop of Ventimiglia, the townsfolk paid homage to the Angevin prince and his mother. Duke Louis remained in the city until 21 July of that year. During the same period, Raymond, viscount of Turenne and nephew of the late Pope Gregory, also visited Apt.[12]

Devotion to one saintly couple did much to stimulate pilgrimages to Apt. Elzéar de Sabran, count of Ariano and lord of Ansouis (†1323), and his wife

Delphine de Signe (†1360), led lives of Christian charity, in continence and piety. Both Franciscan tertiaries, they were buried together at Apt whence their cult quickly spread. When Pope Urban visited in 1365, he knelt and prayed at their tomb. On the feast of Epiphany 1371, in the church of Saint-Didier of Avignon, the count was canonized.[13] When the saint's body was exhumed, 17 June 1373, singing and organ playing was said to have accompanied the solemnities. At the end of November of that year, James IV of Aragon, husband of Joanna of Naples, was in Avignon, but he quit the city before Christmas in order to visit Elzéar's relics at Apt.

Eight years after the death of Blessed Delphine, on 28 June 1368, the archbishop of Aix and the bishop of Vaison, as deputies of the pope, accompanied by the bishop of Apt, the chapter of the cathedral, the syndics, and many local notables, went to the church of the Franciscans to pay their respects at her tomb. They found many *ex voto* markers surrounding her sepulchre that had been placed as memorials to specific requests answered by God through her intercession.[14] On Sunday, 2 July, the contingent went to the cathedral where a Mass attended by 1,100 persons was solemnly sung. There they took testimony on the woman's sanctity. Among the evidence put forth was that offered by those present at her deathbed. Three young "ladies of quality" pensioned in the convent of Sainte-Catherine of Apt. declared that when the end arrived for the devout countess, a marvelous concert of all sorts of instruments was heard.[15] Such miraculous events were commonplace in the lives of the holy.

There were several other saints and feast days that enjoyed a particular devotion at Apt. Oldest among these were the cults of Saint Castor, Saint Auspice, and Saint Marcian.[16] Of a more recent date was the veneration of Saint Anne, mother of the Blessed Virgin. However, the most popular of holydays was that of Corpus Christi.

Corpus Christi was first celebrated at Liège in 1246 and proclaimed obligatory for the whole Church in 1264. The observance in France only became universal after the Council of Vienne in 1311 and from a decree renewing the devotion which was issued several years later by John XXII. The feast first began to be noted in Provençal calendars between 1316 and 1340. Be that as it may, the one notable exception to the gradual dissemination of this feast was the rapid acceptance of it at Apt: observance began here in 1277.[17] A missal copied at Aix in 1423 by Jacobus Murri, a cleric beneficed at the cathedral of Saint-Sauveur, illustrates the day with a depiction of the Corpus Christi procession, by that time, a well established practice in parts of Provence.[18] Beginning in the fifteenth century, the feast of the Eucharist was the occasion for adding representational figures, both biblical and historical, to these springtime parades. The first dramatic scenes that accompanied processions at Apt, however, reputedly date from the episcopacy of Bertrand de Meissenier (1348-1385). Documentary evidence from as early as the 1360s indicates that the cortege was likely accompanied by musicians, many of whom were brought into Apt from the surrounding region.[19]

Another popular devotion of Apt was one accorded Saint Anne. Local tradition had long located her tomb in the crypt of the cathedral, but her feast and office were not adopted before the first quarter of the fourteenth century.[20] The Roman pope, Urban VI, extended her cult to the whole Church in 1382 on the occasion of the marriage of Richard II of England to Anne of Bohemia.[21] On 17 April 1404 at Saint-Victor of Marseille, Benedict XIII presented a bull to Jean Fileti, nephew of Cardinal Jean La Grange and bishop of Apt, approving the veneration of her relics there.[22] The treasury of the cathedral held numerous ivory boxes that were donated in recognition of Christ's grandmother by the noble ladies and lords of Provence. The basilica also boasted relics such as the veil of Anne (in reality, an Arab standard) and a glass bottle containing some of the holy woman's perspiration.[23]

### Apt, ms. 16 bis

There is a rich treasure of musical and liturgical manuscripts at Apt which has come down to us today.[24] Some of the documents are clearly Aptensian, while others are of a more general nature.[25] More than 80 years ago, Amédée Gastoué discovered the two manuscripts that concern us here, the two which contain polyphonic works: Apt, ms. 9 and Apt, ms. 16 bis. Though it is generally assumed that the documents have always been housed with the goods of the chapter of the cathedral of Apt, Gastoué suggested the possibility that the manuscripts were brought from neighboring churches to the cathedral during the French Revolution. In fact, an inventory of the treasure made 26 October 1790 indicates that no such volumes were at that time in the possession of the chapter. However, this list contains only a few books, probably all in use at the time, and does not compare in any realistic way with the full catalogue of manuscripts compiled by Sautel in 1919.[26] At the outset of this study, therefore, we shall assume that both manuscripts have been in the treasury immemorially.

The more important of the two volumes is Apt, ms. 16 bis, a collection of polyphonic mass ordinaries, hymns, and motets. It has undergone several detailed catalogue descriptions, and all of the pieces have been published in modern editions.[27] Therefore, only three aspects of the manuscript which have not received sufficient attention will be discussed here: 1) the foliation numbers found on three of the gatherings; 2) the paper of the last two gatherings; and 3) the origins of the manuscript.

As bound today, Apt, ms. 16 bis consists of six irregular gatherings; the first four (I-IV) are of parchment, and the last two (V-VI) of paper. According to Gastoué, when he found the manuscript in 1899, it had been unbound for some time, the gatherings preserved in a disordered arrangement, only loosely held together by several very old pieces of string. The collection was subsequently rebound and covered, and afterwards a modern foliation was given to the document by the then archpriest of Apt, Paul de Terris. Unfortunately, the third and fourth fascicles were reversed in order either by the binder or in the process of binding, hence the present state of the document corresponds only partially to the nineteenth-century arrangement: I, II, IV, III, V, VI.[28]

While there is much blotting of the red ink that was used, there is no blotting from the first recto folio of gathering II (fol. 9) onto the last verso page of gathering I (fol. 8v.). This leads us to suspect that gatherings I and II were probably not always bound together in that sequence. There are additional indications that the present position of each bifolio with respect to adjacent bifolios was slightly different at one time. For example, the blotting of the red ink from folio 9v. to folio 10 does not align exactly. From these clues we can assume that ms. 16 bis was once a collection of loose gatherings and unbound folios.[29]

The first two quires (I, II) each consist of four folded sheets, and the third (IV) is a gathering of eight bifoliate leaves. The fourth fascicle (III) is made up of two bifolios plus a single sheet attached to the last folio by means of a parchment strip. The fifth section (V) is one folded paper sheet. For the last gathering, there are three paper sheets, folded in half, and one small piece of paper glued between its second and third leaves. The nineteenth-century arrangement with the modern foliation is illustrated in figure 8.

The original first three gatherings (I, II, IV) form one distinct group. Within this group, gatherings I and IV are most closely related. The parchment of II has been described as white and thin, while that of I and IV is thicker in texture and somewhat more yellow in color.[30] The latter two gatherings were formed from sheets approximately 270 mm in height (264.5 mm-270.5 mm). They were originally ruled with six staves arranged in double columns, followed by three systems extending completely across the page. This arrangement reflects the old-style layout prevalent in manuscripts dating from the first half of the century. The systems are crimson in color, uniformly 14.5 mm high. The original double-column format was maintained only for the first piece (Apt 1), a Kyrie copied on folios 1-2. On all the other folios in I and IV, the left- and right-hand portions of the first six systems have been more-or-less carefully joined with an ink similar in color to that used in making the staves of II (see fig. 9).

Gathering II has been formed from sheets that were cut to approximately 289.0 mm in height. The staff lines, nine per page, extend unbroken from left to right. Made with an ink slightly more orange in color than that used in making the staves of I and IV, they are of a height uniformly 15.5 mm. It appears as if the layout of this gathering, that is, the size and spacing of systems, was based on that of I and IV (see fig. 10). However, II was probably part of a collection whose folios were cut at a height greater than that of I and IV. In order to have some uniformity in size, parchment strips were glued to the bottom of the bifolios that make up I and IV, giving them a present length of approximately 285.0 mm. (see

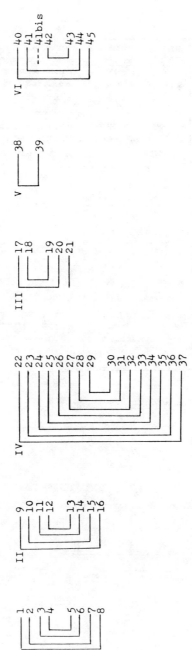

Fig. 8.  Apt, ms. 16 bis, the nineteenth-century arrangement with the modern foliation.

Fig. 9.

fol. 1v.                          fol. 8

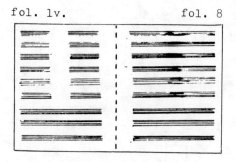

Fig. 10.

fol. 9v.                          fol. 16

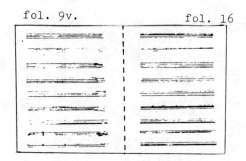

Fig. 11.   Gathering I and IV (top) and Gathering II (bottom).

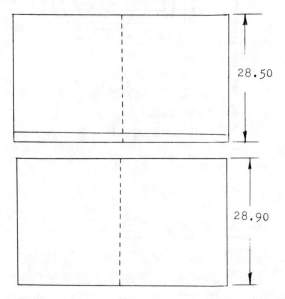

28.50

28.90

fig. 11). Evidently it was not considered feasible to trim the larger gatherings to the smaller dimensions of I and IV, most likely because in so doing, some notes would have been lost.

## Foliation of Gatherings I, and IV

Gatherings I and IV also contain some conflicting medieval foliations which, if systematically classified and arranged, offer clues to the order in which the pieces were entered into the manuscript. These two gatherings began as a stack of unruled and unlined parchment. The scribe responsible for the staves lined the paper and, after four sheets were completed, folded each quaternion (four sheets) into a quire. At least three quires were available to subsequent scribes. One of the quires was simply ruled (Q1), while two others were ruled, then numbered in the same ink that was used for the systems (Q2 and Q3). The numerals *i, ii, iii, iiii* were placed in the upper right recto of each folio in question. Presumably all three quires, Q1, Q2, and Q3 were prepared at the same time.[31]

The first piece to be copied was a Kyrie, Apt 1. It was entered into the unnumbered Q1, now folios 1-2 of gathering I. The note and text hand, ostensibly belonging to the same person, is called scribe A.[32] The note hand is small and fine, and it exhibits clefs whose parallel arms slant downward. The text is almost cursive; it is neither a bookhand nor notarial, but is clearly legible and seems almost Italianate. Scribe A entered no further works.

Sometime later, the quires passed into the hands of two other copyists, scribes B and C. B is fussy and careful. He makes his clefs very square, with the wide arms extending parallel: ⸙. The text hand is angular, fractured at the ends, with an occasional finishing hair line. Scribe C is recognizable immediately because the lower arm of his clef tends to slant downward at a much greater angle than the upper: ⸙. His text hand is generally much sloppier and seemingly hurried. It tends towards a *littera textualis* and lacks most of the formal qualities of B's *littera quadrata*. The minims of his letters often terminate in thick serifs. B appears to be more knowledgeable about manuscripts and might have been older than C, since he had already devised his own particular method for entering pieces into quires.

Scribe B's method of copying was unlike what one would first imagine, though it is totally logical. Pieces were not entered into a quire in an order corresponding to the consecutive numbering of the folios. But instead, the manuscript was conceived two bifolios at a time. The works were entered on the first verso and the following recto (see fig. 12, 1a), then on the conjugate folios: that is, the verso of the third folio and the recto of the last folio (1b). The scribe always began a work of some length on a verso-recto face pair. By leaving the innermost and outermost faces of the quire blank, he permitted the addition of an undetermined number of new surfaces, each blank folio providing two verso-recto face pairs (2a, 2b and 3a, 3b of fig. 13). Once the innermost recto is begun, the manuscript cannot be conveniently expanded. The solitary first recto and last verso pages are reserved for short pieces such as Kyries and motets.

Fig. 12.

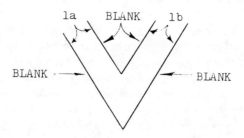

Fig. 13.

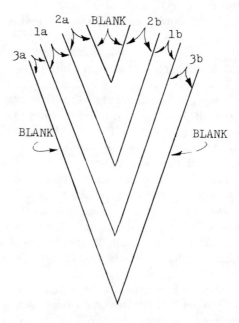

Among the first works to be added under scribe B's direction were those placed in Q2 (quire 2). Bifolios *i* and *ii* were removed, and they were given to yet another scribe whom we will call E. With a fine and angular note hand, E began to copy Apt 37 (25v.-26). Stäblein-Harder has pointed out that this scribe has a distinctive way of making his breves ⊨ and semibreves◆. The former is characteristic of the type used in the manuscripts Barcelona B and Bologna Q15 as well as later manuscripts.[33] The semibreves are typical of those found in examples of Italian notation ca. 1400 and after. Part of the *Amen* of Apt 37 was completed by scribe C (fig. 14).

Fig. 14.

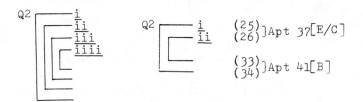

At approximately the same time this piece was being copied, scribe B transcribed the second part of Apt 41 (33v.-34). The two remaining bifolios were taken from Q2 (*iii* and *iiii*) but were jumbled in the process. Consequently, they appear out of order in the *i-iiii* sequence (see fig. 15). Scribe E began to copy Apt 39 onto the verso-recto face pair of these bifolios (27v.-28), while B completed the first part of Apt 41 (32v.-33). B then went on to add Apt 38 on a blank face pair (26v.-27). Scribe E needed more parchment as he continued to copy Apt 39, so he withdrew an unnumbered bifolio from another quire, possibly the innermost bifolio from Q1. It then became the innermost bifolio of Q2. He continued Apt 39 from folio 28v. to the new bifolio, 29-30v. (see fig. 16).

Fig. 15.

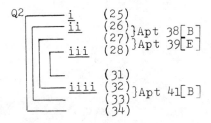

Fig. 16.

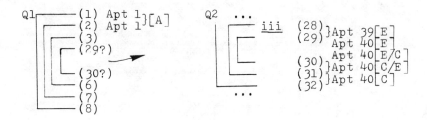

Not long after these pieces were entered, another work was begun by scribe E in conjunction with C, Apt 40. While E placed the text and the notes on the first page (29v.), C copied the end of the work (31v.-32). E continued to add the text and completed folio 30 and the first three lines of folios 30v. and 31. The music was then entered by C on all of the pages in question (30-31), and he finished texting the last six systems on folios 30v. and 31.[34]

A folio was removed from Q3 to wrap around the quinternion, thereby acting as a cover sheet, either to protect the gathering or to provide more writing surfaces (see fig. 17). The work was rubricated, and the composers' names were added. A title was given to Apt 40 ("Bonbarde"), and the fascicle was foliated in black ink, I-XI, in the upper right recto.[35] All these additions plus numerous corrections were made by scribe C (see fig. 17 and plate 8).

Fig. 17.

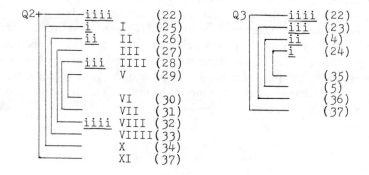

Plate 8.    Apt, ms. 16 bis: folio 28. Two medieval foliation numbers have been placed in the upper right recto of this folio: IIII (in black) and *iii* (in red).

Both B and C, working together, came upon another body of works. For these, they used Q3. Before beginning, they removed the cover sheet from Q2 and placed it back in its original position as bifolio *iiii* of Q3. On bifolios *iii* and *iiii* of Q3 both scribes proceeded to work, probably simultaneously. B copied the first part of Apt 34 (22-23), while C worked on the conjugate folios, copying Apt 44 (36v.-37v.). Then C went back to complete the unfinished work on Apt 34 (23v.) shown in fig. 18.

Fig. 18.

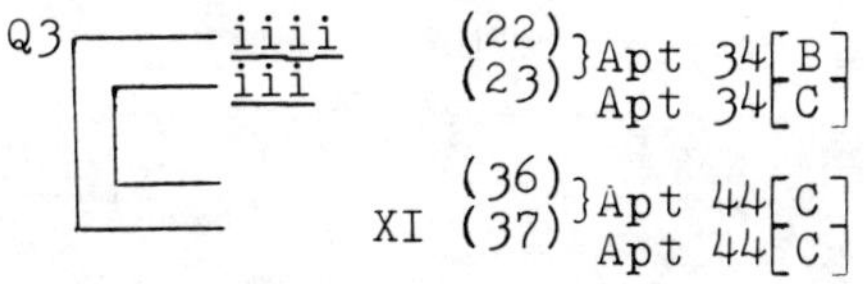

After this was done, C, working alone, proceeded to copy several more pieces, presumably drawn from the same group of sources. He took bifolios *i* and *ii* and used them to copy Apt 4 (4), Apt 5 (4v.), and Apt 35 (24). The bifolio pair *iii-iiii* was then placed around *i-ii*. One more piece was to be copied. But instead of writing on folio 24v. and continuing across to its conjugate folio (35), the compiler inserted the quinternion Q2 into the quaternion Q3, and he afforded himself the opening blank recto of Q2 on which to copy. Scribe C then transcribed Apt 36 (24v.-25) (see fig. 19).

Fig. 19.

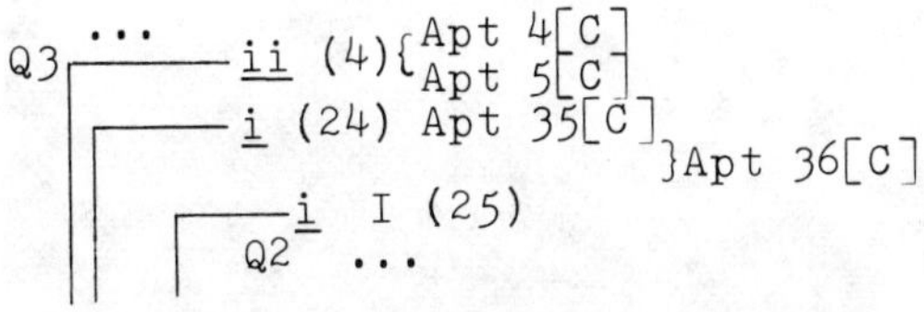

Presumably about this same time, a few pieces were added to Q1, then a ternion. Apt 2 was begun by scribe B (2v.-3, the first three systems); scribe C completed this work (3, the last six systems) and also added Apt 3 (3v.). C might then have gone on to copy Apt 8 (7v.-8), a Gloria labeled "chassa."[36] This scribe came upon a rather extensive piece for which he needed more parchment. Consequently, he extracted bifolio *ii* of Q3 which at that time had been part of the Q2-Q3 complex, and he inserted it into the ternion Q1.[37] C copied Apt 7 onto the resulting verso-recto face pair and onto the folios that follow (5v.-7). Last, two short pieces were added in the remaining space: Apt 6 (5), and Apt 9 (8v.)[38] (see fig. 20).

Fig. 20.

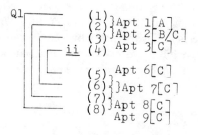

Plate 9.

About the same time that Q3 was being filled, scribe C was progressing with his own quire which has come down as gathering II. No other scribe worked on this portion of the manuscript. There is indication that C might have used B's method for entering works into a quire—that is, copying on verso-recto face pairs—but, apparently, he was far from mastering the technique. This gathering lacks the conflicting systems of foliation, and therefore the conclusions to be reached concerning the order of entry of the pieces are more conjectural.[39]

*Gathering II*

The first pieces to be set down were probably Apt 11 (9v.) and Apt 12 (10-11). Their appearance may date from the time that scribe E was at work. Contemporaneous with these entries was the inclusion of the hymns copied on the conjugate folios (15v.-16), Apt 21, Apt 22, Apt 23, and Apt 24. The hymns Apt 25 and Apt 26 (16v.) were probably added later but at the same time that the hymns Apt 17, Apt 18, and Apt 19 were included. Scribe C then copied the motet by Philippe de Vitry, Apt 16 (13v.-14).

It was most likely during the period that Apt 6 and Apt 9 were being copied into gathering I that C entered several more works into gathering II. First he transcribed the Sanctus and Agnus pair, Apt 13 and Apt 14 (11-12); then he probably copied Apt 10 (9). The last work to be entered was Apt 15 (12v.-13). This is in keeping with the rule that the verso-recto face pair of the innermost bifolio are among the last folios to be filled. However, it appears as though C ran out of available space at this point, since the work stands incomplete in this manuscript. While Stäblein-Harder believes that this situation was the intent of the scribe, it seems more than likely that the conclusion of this piece was copied onto a loose sheet of parchment or paper, inserted, though never glued into the gathering.[40] The hypothetical folio "12 bis" was subsequently lost. When this gathering was nearly completed, one more hymn was added, Apt 20 (15), probably as an afterthought. It may represent an original composition by scribe C who might not have had an exemplar from which to work. It is sloppily written and contains numerous errors.

The final entry into the amalgamation of Q2 and Q3 which came to be gathering IV was the pair Apt 42 and Apt 43. Both scribes B and C combined to copy these works (34v.-36). At this late stage in the compilation of the gathering, there was little remaining space.

*Gathering III*

Virtually all of the fourth gathering (III) is the product of a scribe called D. The parchment used here is very thick and rough, there are eight instead of nine systems per page, and the fascicle bears almost no relationship to the first portion of the manuscript (gatherings I, II, and IV). There is at least one leaf missing from the center of the gathering, since Apt 29 and Apt 30 (18v.-19) are incomplete. The first of the two works lacks the contratenor and the end of the tenor; the second of the two is without the beginning of its cantus I and much of the tenor. This missing material may have been copied onto a loose leaf, possibly the conjugate folio of 21-21v. This last sheet, glued onto the outer bifolio by means of a parchment strip, might have been attached by scribe C. There is no doubt that this gathering was in the possession of C, for one finds his typical square custodes

♮ on the strip, whereas those characteristic of D are lozenge-shaped ♦ . It appears as though D never placed custodes on folio 21v. Scribe D transcribed several motets at the end of the fascicle, Apt 31, Apt 32, Apt 33 (20v.-21v.). The last of these folios is much worn on its verso and therefore must have been either the first or last exterior page of a collection for some time. The rubrics of gathering III are sloppily done in a thick, bright-red ink. On the top of folios 17v. and 18, the attribution "loÿs" appears twice. However, next to these, two letters have been obliterated. The second is clearly the letter "ÿ" with a curlicue drawn above it. The first letter appears to be an "a." For what reason the attribution "loÿs aÿ" was reduced to "loÿs" is unknown.

### The Paper Gatherings V and VI

Gathering III is closely related to the final two fascicles of Apt, ms. 16 bis, the paper gatherings V and VI. Gathering V is a bifolio comprising folios 38-39; VI is a ternion (40-45) with the insertion of folio 41 bis (see fig. 21). The paper of the first of the two is extremely coarse and brittle. The color is quite dark and appears almost amber. The laid lines, running vertically, are irregular in shape, but evenly spaced, 20 lines per 40 mm. The chain lines are difficult to see and are only clearly visible at the edge of folio 39. They are unevenly spaced, approximately 40 to 49 mm apart, with one of them at an angle, indicating that an end may have broken off from the supporting frame.

Fig. 21.

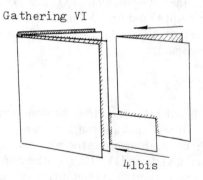

Gathering VI

41bis

A watermark, heretofore undiscovered, in the form of a dragon, appears in the center of the sheet, indicating that the paper was in large format (approximately 415-445 mm × 600-615 mm).[41] Unfortunately, the watermark cannot be traced completely since some of it lies in the fold. The original sheet of paper was folded twice and reduced to two bifolios of quarto size (see fig. 22).

Fig. 22.

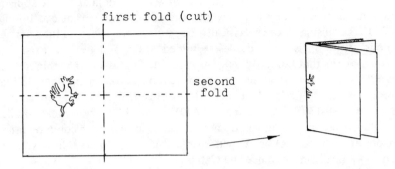

The mark itself appears to have broken off from the chain support that ran through it, and it has shifted approximately 40° so that the head of the dragon is raised (fig. 23). There are several extraneous lines appearing in our mark that are most likely bits of wire that have fallen from this central chain, thus explaining the change in position. According to Briquet, the paper bearing this mark is Italian and was in use from 1359 until the end of the century.[42] Out of 194 different specimens that he found, only 19 "dragons" were duplicates. Therefore, at least 175 types were in existence during a period covering 167 years.

Fig. 23.    Apt, ms. 16 bis: 38v.-39 (reduced).

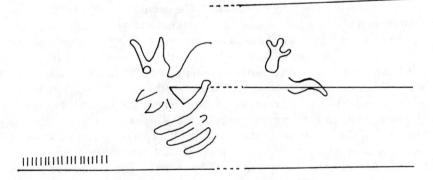

The three-toed variety of dragon, to which ours belongs, predominates in the area between Cremona, Verona, Ferrara, and Bologna. But it appears throughout northern Italy and beyond, though it is somewhat exceptional outside the peninsula. More specifically, our watermark relates to the group of "dragons" with finely formed toes, rounded jowls, and pointed ears. The published marks that fall into this group are listed in table 1. The thin muzzle allies our watermark most closely to no. 8 which appears on a paper dated 1392 at Ferrara. Less strongly related, but nevertheless close to the Apt "dragon" is no. 7, found from 1390-1395.[43] A search of the ADV and BMA did not reveal a similar mark. Papers bearing "dragons" do not appear to have been in common use in the Comtat Venaissin. Other papers displaying similar marks, however, are found sporadically in Provence and Catalonia.

Though dating by use of watermarks is approximate at best, it can provide some idea when this bifolio (gathering V, 38-39v.) was most likely copied. Using Briquet's method for determining a range of dates, that is, based on the 90 percent chance of a given paper having a duration of use extending 30 years ($\pm$15 years from the date found on the paper), we can say that the papers bearing the marks nos. 7 and 8 were likely in use during the periods 1377-1407 and 1380-1405, respectively.[44] If we make similar claims for the bifolio in question, it is possible that this portion of the Apt manuscript, if copied in Italy, dates from the earlier part of this range; if copied in Provence or Catalonia, it was likely done during the beginning of the fifteenth century.

Apt 45, a two-voice Credo and the only work to have been copied on this bifolio, is somewhat problematic. The issue has been discussed by Stäblein-Harder and need not be fully stated here.[45] The question involves the degree of completeness of the piece. There is a possibility that, as copied in the manuscript, Apt 45 represents only two-thirds of the total work. Either an upper voice or inner voice might be missing. Stäblein-Harder believes that because of the way in which this Credo was copied into the manuscript, no other part was meant to be added. While this may be the case, the discovery of the watermark determines the bifolio as one cut from a sheet of paper in large format and implies the existence of another bifolio cut from the same sheet. This could indicate that the hypothetical third voice was written out simultaneously by another scribe; it then may have been lent out for the purposes of performance, or simply lost before it was included in Apt, ms. 16 bis by scribe C. The strongest argument against this would be the hypothetical separation of the parts and their curious disposition on the two folios.

The last fascicle, gathering VI, essentially consists of three folios folded at the center. The paper, again coarse, is both lighter in color and more flexible to the touch than that used in gathering V. The laid lines run horizontally with 20 per approximately 32 mm. They alternate in shape, thick/thin, and are fairly regular in their spacing. The chain lines are at various angles to one another but

## Table 1. The Dragon Watermark

| No. | Date | Place | Bibliography |
|---|---|---|---|
| 1 | 1381<br>1384<br>1385<br>1390-92<br>1391 | Lucca<br>Udine<br>Paris<br>Venice<br>Voorne (Holland) | Briquet, vol. 1, no. 2630 |
| 2 | 1385 | Fabriano | Zonghi, no. 1032 |
| 3 | 1385/1400<br>1386 | Pljevlja (Yugo.)<br>Holland | Mošin, vol. 1, no. 1072 |
| 4 | 1388 | Split (Yugo.) | Mošin, vol. 1, no. 1056 |
| 5 } 6 | 1390 | Fabriano | Zonghi, nos. 1033, 1034 |
| 7 | 1390<br>1391<br>1391<br>1392<br>1392-93<br>1395 | Bologna<br>Venice<br>Reggio d'Emilia<br>Hamburg<br>Lucca<br>Palermo | Mošin, vol. 1, no. 1064 |
| 8 | 1392 | Ferrara | Briquet, vol. 1, no. 2660 |
| 9 | 1391<br>1390/1400 | Voorne<br>Dečani (Yugo.) | Mošin, vol. 1, 1065 |
| 10 } 11 | 1390/1400<br>1399 | Beograd (Yugo.)<br>Munich | Mošin, vol. 1, nos. 1068, 1069 |
| 12 | 1397 | Ferrara | Briquet, vol. 1, 2635 |
| 13 | 14th c./1410 | Dečani | Mošin, vol. 1, 1062 |
| 14 | 1403 | Vic (Spain) | Valls i Subirà, no. 1513 |
| 15 | 1404 | Ferrara | Briquet, vol. 1, no. 2661 |
| 16 | 1402-08<br>1403<br>1407-10<br>1410 | Udine<br>Calais<br>Provence<br>Marseille | Briquet, vol. 1, no. 2638 |
| 17 | 1406<br>1415 | Valencia<br>Barcelona | Bofarull y Sans, no. 733 |
| 18 } 19 | 1419 | Fabriano | Zonghi, nos. 1035, 1036 |
| 20 | 1412 | Fabriano | Zonghi, no. 1038 |
| 21 | 1414 | Fabriano | Zonghi, no. 1037 |
| 22 | 1415 | Ferrara | Briquet, vol. 1, no. 2639 |

are generally 40 to 52 mm apart. The attachments of the chains to the wooden support ribs are visible. The width of the entire sheet is approximately 420 mm. The height of the sheet fluctuates from 287.5 to 290 mm. There was more of the same paper available to the scribe because the paper fragment, folio 41 bis, was cut from a sheet of the same type. Perhaps the gathering was originally a quaternion (see fig. 24).

Fig. 24.

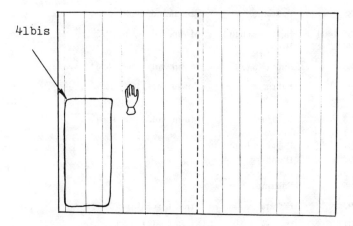

The watermark in the form of a hand (sometimes classified as a glove) appears upright in the center of folios 40-42. The hand appears between the chain supports as shown in figure 25 (drawn to scale) and plate 10 (enlarged).

Fig. 25.

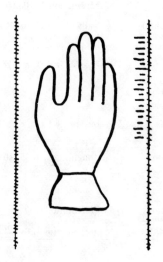

Plate 10.

The mark is very common and, according to Briquet, was spread over a wide geographical area.[46] Like the "dragon" paper, the "hand" is also of Italian origin, though probably originating in Piedmont. However, unlike the "dragon," the mark is very common in Provence. It has been thus noted by Briquet and many times by the archivist Hyacinthe Chobaut.[47] He included samples of this mark in his great compilation of Provençal watermarks housed in the BMA. In addition, a number of "hands" appear in paper used for the notarial acts of the city and chapter of Apt. Table 2 is a compilation of similar watermarks.

Our mark most closely relates to the more finely formed hands with large thumbs. All of these forms have a cuff, almost trapezoidal in shape, with a straight base. More specifically, the paper from gathering VI of Apt, ms. 16 bis bears chainlines exhibiting an alternating pattern (thick/thin) and is thus allied most closely to mark no. 6. This paper appears in notarial documents written at Apt between 1397 and 1410. It is impossible to tell exactly when this sheet was added to the document.

Again using Briquet's method for dating watermarks, one may say that there is a 90 percent chance that the paper of watermark no. 6 was used from 1395 until 1412. If gathering VI of Apt, ms. 16 bis was copied at Apt or in Provence, it is

# Table 2.  The Hand Watermark

| No. | Date | Place | Bibliography |
|---|---|---|---|
| 1 | 1361-68 | Apt | ADV, G II 57: *Actes notaires pour le chapitre d'Apt.* |
| 2 | 1389 | Pinerolo | Mošin, vol. 2, no. 4477 |
| 3 | 1389 | Pinerolo | Mošin, vol. 2, no. 4478<br>Briquet, vol. 3, no. 11080 |
| 4 | 1391-98 | Olot (Spain) | Valls i Subrà, vol. 1, no. 1648 |
| 5 | 1395 | Gruyère | Mošin, vol. 2, no. 4479 |
| 6 }<br>7 } | 1397/1410 | Apt | ADV, Geoffroy 1: *Brèves de Louis de Rocha.* |
| 8 | | | |
| 9 | 1390/1429<br>1399/1419<br>1400 | Lautrec<br>Muret<br>Aix | Mošin, vol. 2, no. 4480<br>Briquet, vol. 3, no. 11081 |
| 10 | 1401-02 | Apt | ADV, Pondicq 29: *Brevès de Rostaing Bonnet.* |
| 11 | ca. 1403 | Apt | ADV, Pondicq 58: *Brèves de Louis de Rocha.* |
| 12 }<br>13 }<br>14 | 1404 | Avignon | ADV, G I 119: *Comptes de l'évêque.* |
| 15 }<br>16 } | 1404-06 | Avignon | ADV, C 143: *Compte de Bertrand Gautier.* |
| 17 | 1405 | l'Isle | BMA, ms. 5910, Fonds Chobaut, 518. |
| 18 | 1405 | Apt | ADV, G II 84: *Chapitre d'Apt.* |
| 19 | 1405 | Apt | ADV, Pondicq 47: *Brèves de Bertrand Bellon.* |
| 19 }<br>20 } | 1405-06 | Apt | ADV, Pondicq 100: *Brèves de Colin Brisson.* |
| 21 }<br>22 } | 1405-06 | Avignon | ADV, C 144: *Compte de Bertrand Gautier.* |
| 23 | 1406-11 | Avignon | ADV, G I 721: *Notes brèves de Pierre Garneret.* |
| 24 | 1406-26 | Apt | ADV, Pondicq 170: *Brèves d'Elzéar Ricard.* |
| 25 | 1407 | Avignon | ADV, G I 722: *Fragment des notes du chapitre métropolitain.* |
| 26 | 1408 | Perpignan | Briquet, vol. 3, 11082 |

Table 2.   The Hand Watermark

| No. | Date | Place | Bibliography |
|-----|------|-------|--------------|
| 27 | 1409 | l'Isle | Chobaut, 521. |
| 28 | 1411-15 | Apt | ADV, G II 58bis: *Actes du chapitre. Colin Brisson.* |
| 29 | 1412 | l'Isle | Chobaut, 523. |
| 30 | 1415 | Carpentras | Chobaut, 375. |
| 31 | 1417 | Carpentras | Chobaut, 378. |
| 32 | 1419 | Oppède | Chobaut, 636. |
| 33 | 1420 | l'Isle | Chobaut, 525. |
| 34⎫<br>35⎭ | 1427 | Avignon | ADV, G I 119: *Comptes de l'évêque.* |
| 36 | 1429 | Avignon | ADV, G II 59: *Actes pour la préchantrerie.* |
| 37 | 1432 | Lyon | Briquet, vol. 3, no. 11084 |

possible that a similar range could be applied. It must be emphasized that such dating methods, though helpful, are not precise when working with identical marks and much less so when treating watermarks that are only similar.[48] However if we use these methods to suggest a range of dates for the paper used in the manuscript, we might say that fascicles V and VI were most likely compiled between 1377 (the early date for the "dragon") and 1412 (the late date for the "hand"). If one uses the narrowest range of dates, the time frame of 1395-1405 is reached.

Scribe D copied gathering V. It is highly probable that he also executed gathering VI though this is not as certain. Stäblein-Harder attributes folios 40-42v. to a scribe whom she calls G and holds another, called H, responsible for entering two lines of 42 v. through folio 45. She admits that G and H are quite similar to each other as well as to D.[49] I am inclined to attribute folios 40-42v. to a scribe whom I prefer to call $D_1$ and the remainder of the gathering to scribe $D_2$. The latter seems to be identical to the former though he might have sharpened his pen during the copying. Both $D_1$ and $D_2$ are so similar to the scribe responsible for gatherings III and V that all three could be the same hand. Gathering III, however, was compiled earlier than gatherings V and VI and, unlike the two paper fascicles, was rubricated and shows evidence of once being in the possession of C.

## The Relationship to Apt, ms. 9

There is no doubt that portions of Apt, ms. 16 bis were copied either at Apt or by someone who was closely associated with the city. This assertion is based on evidence found in the other manuscript of the treasure that contains a polyphonic work, Apt, ms. 9.

The volume dates from the thirteenth century for the most part but contains later additions.[50] They include several monophonic hymns, a calendar of the church of Apt, and a life of Saint Castor. On the verso of folio 5 a three-part setting of the hymn to Saint Anne, *Orbis exultens*, was begun. Except for the text and for a few variants, this work is identical to the setting of *Iste Confessor* found in Apt, ms. 16 bis (Apt 24).

The scribe who notated and texted folios 5v.-8 of Apt, ms. 9 does not appear to have worked on the collection of mass movements. However, on folio 5v. the word *tenor* is written twice, and on folio 6 the remaining two voices are each twice designated *viii* and *v*; all this was done in reddish-orange ink. Apt, ms. 9 and Apt, ms. 16 bis are the only manuscripts that exhibit this curious manner of labeling the upper voices.[51] It is likely, therefore, that the hymn to Saint Anne was written around the time that Apt 24, Apt 40, and Apt 41 were written and rubricated.

Given the special veneration Saint Anne received in the city of Apt and the Aptensian origins of ms. 9, it is clear that ms. 16 bis was associated with the city of Apt during the period in which scribe C was at work. It has been shown that C either owned or had custody of gatherings I, II, IV, and III, and that he worked at a time either contemporaneous with or subsequent to the time that the scribal complex D was operating. We can state with reasonable certainty, therefore, that C possessed fascicles V and VI as well. He seems to have been the last copyist to have entered a work in Apt, ms. 16 bis. During his career he had access to many polyphonic mass movements, some widely disseminated, and others not.

The Apt manuscript (16 bis), long considered to have originated in Avignon, is thought to contain the repertory of the papal chapel. From the above historical survey of fourteenth-century Apt, many possible sources for ms. 16 bis are clearly evident ranging from the singers of the princely chapels to itinerant musicians. Given the nature of the manuscript, it seems reasonable to suppose that the collection drew upon the holdings of some ecclesiastical institution or of individual churchmen. A cleric who may well have had a hand in the compilation of Apt, ms. 16 bis is the papal singer and *magister capelle*, Richardus de Bozonvilla. Richardus served as a singer in the pontifical chapel during the last quarter of the fourteenth century and held the title of *magister* from 1395 until his death in January of 1405.[52] He was provost of the cathedral of Apt where he presided at the chapter meetings sporadically from June 1400 until early March 1403. Two days after the last appearance of Richardus's name in the records of Apt, Pope Benedict XIII escaped from the Palace of the Popes to begin his journey through Provence and northern Italy. The *magister* and provost reappeared in August 1403 with the papal entourage at Pont-de-Sorgues.[53] In all likelihood, Richardus never returned to Apt.

Some of the material in Apt, ms. 16 bis might have been copied by scribe C in the city of Apt. If Richardus de Bozonvilla is indeed the link between the collection of mass movements and the city, then he might possibly be identical to scribe C.[54] The final version of 16 bis would have to have been completed by mid-1403 if Richardus, in fact, left the manuscript there. If the papal *magister capelle* were the last individual to have custody of the manuscript before it became the property of the chapter, the document would have had to have entered into the possession of the cathedral of Apt ca. 1405.

It is instructive to examine the repertory of Apt, ms. 16 bis in light of the above research. Gathering III was compiled at a time when the music preserved in the Ivrea manuscript was readily available and no doubt popular.[55] The pieces in Q3 (including Apt 4 and Apt 5) and in gathering VI are found in the Spanish manuscripts Barcelona B, Barcelona C, and Gerona.[56] Gerona itself is very closely related to Barcelona C. While the variants between Apt and these sources are often significant enough to preclude any claim of a direct relationship, it does argue for the popularity of these works at a given time and place. Thus for many of its compositions Apt, ms. 16 bis draws upon a fund of widely disseminated material.

Some of the pieces in ms. 16 bis are, however, unique. The collection of polyphonic settings of the office hymn is the first of its kind. All but two of the hymns are unique to this manuscript, and one of the two is the variant *Orbis exultens* from Apt, ms. 9. Significantly, the hymns have been entered in the collection to fill what would otherwise have been empty space; they were transcribed onto conjugate folios of gathering II. These hymns are particular to scribe C, a fact that further strengthens his link to ms. 9 and that marks these settings as extremely local phenomena. It is possible that the works are the first attempt to notate what until that time had existed only in an improvisatory tradition, possibly a *super librum* performance of polyphonic hymns. The hasty addition of *Veni creator* as an afterthought might very well represent an original composition by C, entered for the purpose of filling empty space.[57]

It is striking that only two Sanctus and one Agnus were copied into the manuscript and that movements based on the *Ite missa est* are totally lacking. The absence of Ites might merely be indicative of the dominance of Roman practice at this time, since the Ite, as we have seen from ceremonials, was always monophonic. However, the lack of polyphonic Ites might also reflect a particularly papal bias. The paucity of Sanctus and Agnus movements, on the other hand, presents a more intriguing problem. Since the scribes of Apt, ms. 16 bis, particularly B, seem to have conceived each gathering as a collection of similar works, or they at least strove to place movements in some kind of order (Kyrie-Gloria, Gloria-Credo), it is possible that a fascicle of Sanctus and Agnus (and perhaps even Ites) belonging to scribe B has been lost. Those Sanctus and

Fig. 26. The Approximate Order of Entry of Pieces into Apt, ms. 16 bis

| NO. | TYPE | (TITLE) | COMPOSER | SCRB. | GTHRG. | FOLIO | CONC. | COMMENTARY |
|---|---|---|---|---|---|---|---|---|
| 1 | Kyrie | (rex angelorum) | - | A | I | 1-2 | Iv 68 | |
| 27 | Sanctus | | | | | | | Apt modeled on Iv 52 Credo. |
| 28 | Gloria | (Baralipton/ Bararipton) | Loys | D | III | 17v-18 | Iv 52 | |
| 29 | Gloria | | Baralipton/ Bararipton ? | D | III | 18v | Iv 61 | Apt incomplete. |
| 30 | Credo | (Colla jugo) | Orles | D | III | 19-20 | Iv 26 | Apt incomplete. |
| 31 | Motet | | [de Vitry] | D | III | 20v | Iv 55 | And many others. See Ernest Sanders, "Philippe de Vitry," Grove 6, vol. 20, p. 27. |
| 32 | Motet | (Dantur officia) | - | D | III | 21 | Iv 29 | |
| 33 | Motet | (Imperatrix regina) | - | D | III | 21v | Iv 8 | Iv 8; Strasbourg, Bibl. mun., 222 C.22 (hereafter cited as Str). |
| 37 | Gloria | | Susay | E/C | IV | 25v | - | Attributed to Johannes Suzoy/ Susay active at the beginning of the 15th c. |
| 41 | Credo | | Jacobus Murrin | B | IV | 32v-34 | - | Possibly by Jacobus Murri, a cleric beneficed at the cathedral of Aix in 1423. |
| 39 | Credo | | [Baude Cordier] | E | IV | 27v-29 | - | Cordier was evidently employed by the duke of Burgundy. He may have died in 1397 or 1398. |
| 38 | Gloria | | | B | IV | 26v-27 | BL | |
| 40 | Credo | (Bonbarde) | [Prunet/Perneth] | E/C | IV | 29v-32 | - | Str; Brussels, Bibl. du Conservatoire; Padua, Bibl. univ., 684; Grottaferrata, Bibl. dell'Affarcia. |
| 45 | Credo | | | $D_1$ | V | 38-39 | - | Possibly incomplete. |
| 11 | Kyrie | | defronciaco | C | III | 9v | - | |
| 12 | Gloria | | Depansis | C | III | 10-11 | Iv 30 | |
| 21 | Hymn | (Ave maris stella) | - | C | III | 15v | - | Purification/Assumption |
| 22 | Hymn | (Jesu coronum virginum) | - | C | III | 15v | - | Common of Virgins |
| 23 | Hymn | (Deus tuorum) | - | C | II | 15v-16 | - | Common of Martyrs |
| 24 | Hymn | (Iste confessor) | - | C | II | 16 | - | Common of Confessors / Apt, Basilique Saint-Anne, Trésor 9; Paris, Bibl. ars., 196. Variants. |
| 46 | Credo | ([de rege]) | Sertis [Sortes] | $D_1$ | VI | 40-41 | - | Iv 60; Barcelona C; Toulouse, Bibl. mun., 94; Serrant, Château, ms. of the duchess of Trémoïlle; Leiden, Universiteitsbibliotheek, 251%, Rochester NY, Sibley Mus. Lib. Fleicher Frags., 44 / Possibly by Steve de Sort who served the kings of Aragon as singer and organist, Sep. 1394 /95, 1398-1405. |

| No. | Genre (text) | Composer | D | Sect. | Fols. | V | Remarks |
|---|---|---|---|---|---|---|---|
| 47 | Credo | Pellisson | D₁ | VI | 41v-42 | | Barcelona C. Pellisson sang in the papal chapel from 1391 until at least 1396 and in 1403-04. He died before November 1406. |
| 48 | Credo | - | D₁/D₂ | VI | 42v-45 | | Tournai, Bibl. de la Cathédrale, Voisin IV; Madrid, Bibl. nac. Va. 21-8. |
| 34 | Gloria (splendor patris) | [p.] tailhandier | | IV | 22-23v | B/C | Barcelona B; Barcelona C; Str. |
| 44 | Credo | - | | IV | 36v-37v | C | Barcelona B; Gerona; Str. Pierre Tailhandier, composer and theorist, fl. ca. 1390. |
| 4 | Kyrie | - | | I | 4 | C | Gerona. The second Kyrie of Apt 4 is in Gerona. |
| 5 | Kyrie | Chipre | | I | 5 | C | Gerona; Iv 49. |
| 35 | Kyrie | [Johannes Graneti]C | | IV | 24 | C | Barcelona B; Paris, Bibl. Sainte-Geneviève, 1257; Rome, Vat. Urb. lat., 1419. |
| 36 | Gloria | [peliso] | | IV | 24v-25 | C | Barcelona C; Str. See Apt no. 47 above. |
| 42 | Credo | Tapissier | | IV | 34v-36 | B/C | BL — Jean de Noyers, called Tapissier, was employed by the dukes of Burgundy. He died before 1410. |
| 43 | Sanctus | Tapissier | | IV | 36 | C | - |
| 2 | Kyrie (humano generi) | - | | I | 2v-3 | B/C | - |
| 3 | Kyrie (chassa) | - | | I | 3v | | - |
| 8 | Gloria | - | | I | 7v-8 | C | - |
| 7 | Gloria (qui sonitu melodie) | - | | I | 5v-7 | C | Iv 50; Str; Padua, Bibl. univ., 684; Rochester NY, Sibley Mus. Lib.; Fleicher Frags.; Nürnberg, Stadtbibl. III, 25.5. |
| 6 | Kyrie (o sacra virgo) | Perrinet | | I | 5 | C | - |
| 9 | Kyrie | - | | I | 8v | C | - |
| 17 | Hymn (Xriste redemptor omnium) | - | | III | 14v | C | All Saints' Day |
| 18 | Hymn (Conditor alme siderum) | - | | III | 14v | C | Advent |
| 19 | Hymn (Sanctorum meritis) | - | | III | 15 | C | Common of Several Martyrs |
| 25 | Hymn (Jhesu nostra redemptio) | - | | III | 16v | C | Ascension |
| 26 | Hymn (Ut queant lapsis) | - | | III | 16v | C | St. John the Baptist |
| 16 | Motet (Impudenter) | [de Vitry] | | III | 13v-14 | C | Iv 6; Str; and many others. See Sanders. |
| 13 | Sanctus | Fleurie | | II | 11-11v | C | No Benedictus copied. |
| 14 | Agnus | - | | II | 12 | C | - |
| 10 | Kyrie | Guymont | | II | 9 | C | - |
| 15 | Sanctus | - | | II | 12v-13 | C | Incomplete and with errors. |
| 20 | Hymn (Veni creator) | - | | II | 15 | C | Errors. |

Agnus that do remain in the present collection were among the last works to have been entered into their respective portions of the manuscript. This may reflect a lack of interest in collecting such movements, but more likely it indicates that the Sanctus and Agnus, being shorter than Glorias and Credos, were able to fit more easily in remaining space and thus were saved until last.[58] Another possible explanation for the dearth of these later movements is that they were improvised or adapted from other movements, as Sanctus Apt 17 was from Credo Ivrea 52. The tripartite Agnus could have been performed extemporaneously from one of the numerous Kyries included in this collection. Any further speculation, however, must await a study of all the sources.

The preceding discussion of Apt, ms. 16 bis has provided a notion of how a collection of polyphonic mass music was compiled in the late Middle Ages. By often focusing on minute physical detail, the study has revealed much concerning not only the date and provenance of the manuscript but also the order of entry of the pieces. The positioning of certain compositions within the manuscript may not be so much a reflection of their place or their importance in the liturgy as it is a result of the limited space available to the copyists. Moreover in this collection, each gathering was conceived as a self-contained unit that could be disassociated and removed from its companions for the purposes of loan or of copying. Portions of the document appear to have been compiled by earlier scribes who may have either loaned, given, or bequeathed their fascicles to later copyists. Furthermore, there are several gatherings that were worked on by a number of men simultaneously, though portions appear to have been in the possession of one scribe. While there is a sense of logic and uniformity evident in certain fascicles, it is obvious that this manuscript was never copied wholesale from a pre-existing exemplar; it was pieced together from a number of different sources at various times. Nor was there ever any question that this document might have served as a presentation copy; instead, as the physical evidence shows, it was a practical performing source into which numerous corrections were inserted. Finally, comparison with Apt, ms. 9 reveals a direct relationship between ms. 16 bis and the city of Apt in addition to its mere presence there. The document no doubt belonged to a cleric or to an ecclesiastical institution and may even contain a portion of the polyphonic repertory that was sung in the papal chapel at Avignon.[59] If it can indeed be said that portions of ms. 16 bis emanated from the *capella pape,* then the person most likely responsible for transporting the document to Apt as well as for transcribing many of the works therein is the man who served as the *magister capelle pape* from 1395-1405, Richardus de Bozonvilla.

# 6

# Conclusions

The papacy of the fourteenth century was a French institution. It was run by Frenchmen from a fortress-like palace situated in Provence, under the protection of the French crown. The prolonged absence of the Court of Rome from the Italian peninsula brought a change in some of the Roman traditions.

The *Schola cantorum,* which had been providing the more sophisticated music for many of the papal ceremonies at the beginning of the thirteenth century, had been replaced by a group of *capellani commensales* whenever the pope resided outside of Rome. But as the commensal chaplains came to be employed in other functions which took them away from the Curia, their role as executants of liturgical music waned. By the election of Benedict XII, this group of chaplains no longer fulfilled its musical tasks. To remedy the situation, the pontiff instituted a college of *capellani capelle* in 1334 expressly for the purpose of singing Mass and the canonical hours (Matins and particularly Vespers).

Clement VI, who had been an influential figure at the French royal court, imitated what was possibly the practice in Paris by filling his chapel with men from northern France and the Low Countries. This began a papal tradition that continued well into the sixteenth century. These northern clerics were educated and skilled executants of the liturgy who supplemented their chaplain's wage with stipends from varying numbers of ecclesiastical benefices, as well as from funds obtained through minor curial offices such as *scriptor.*

The fame of the college of papal servers, and indeed of all *capellani* who executed the divine office in the chapels of prelates at Avignon, became so widespread that by the last quarter of the fourteenth century these clerics were being actively recruited to staff the *capelle* of secular authorities. Individuals sometimes passed from patron to patron, often employed by family members of past, present, and future popes, a situation not unlike that found in the princely houses of Europe. And during the last decade of that century, there were composers of secular as well as sacred polyphony numbered among the singers of the *capella pape.*

In the first years of the fifteenth century, the peripatetic Aragonese pope, Benedict XIII, retained an organist for his chapel and might possibly have employed choirboys. While direct patronage of secular players and boy singers was apparently forbidden to the bishops of Rome, such was not the cased for the cardinals. There is, evidence showing that Gregory XI supported choirboys and that Benedict XIII served as patron to a harpist (Jacob de Senleches) before either of them had received the nod from the conclave.

The Supreme Pontiffs were always meticulous in avoiding any direct associations with purely secular entertainments, and they are often seen as defenders of a clergy devoid of worldiness. When the popes did encourage the performance of minstrels by granting them a small sum from the cameral treasure, it was solely to those musicians who either were attached to the households of visiting potentates or were employed by municipalities. This attitude no doubt shows only the public facade of the papacy. Even in pastoral prohibitions against mixing sacred and secular, by and large, the papal admonitions are concerned with public buffoonery and with those exhibitions that may have been witnessed by outsiders. Much of the activity of the chapel members, however, lies hidden, obscured by time and shrouded by the paucity of documentation.

The man who was listed first among the *capellani capelle* held the office of master of the papal chapel. He had two distinct functions; the first was as an administrator. The *magister* acted as paymaster to the chaplains and was responsible for the purchase and care of the vestments, linens, votive objects, and books used in the chapel. He likewise was liable for packing and transporting these items whenever the pontiff travelled. The second function of the *magister* was one that filled liturgical need; he directed the singers in the execution of the offices by no doubt providing incipits or by determining which of the chaplains should intone the chants. He also must have had some say in how the music was performed.

On the great feasts of the year, when pope and Curia presided, the ceremonials lay out extensive rubrics that contain little or no mention of the singing chaplains. While they did participate at these celebrations, on the feasts of lesser rank and probably on ferial days the singers played a more active role in the liturgy, to the point of being the sole participants in the service. By the end of the fourteenth century, these chaplains of the pope were permitted to sing polyphonic mass ordinaries throughout the entire Church year, though there was a restriction on other polyphonic music during Passiontide. It is highly likely that the singers performed works in polyphony, probably motets, after the papal meal at great celebrations. And there is a record of just such an occurrence in 1343.

There is one manuscript of polyphonic mass ordinaries, hymns, and motets long thought to have emanated from the pontifical chapel at Avignon: Apt, ms. 16 bis. The volume is a collection of self-contained fascicles, some closely related, others not. From the physical characteristics of the document one can clearly see that the collection was a practical manuscript. And from various foliation numbers placed on the pages, we have determined that Apt, ms. 16 bis was copied by several scribes, some of whom were working simultaneously. Much of the document was conceived two bifolios at a time and subsequently expanded to quaternions. The paper used in the last two gatherings might be dated as in common use ca. 1400. And the concordance of one of the hymns with another copied into Apt, ms. 9 indicates that the collection of mass settings has been associated with the city of Apt or with a cleric who had significant business there soon after the fascicles were compiled.

While there is no evidence of polyphonic collections either in the library of the popes or among the small number of chapel books listed in the inventories, Apt, ms. 16 bis might indeed contain some of the polyphonic mass movements and hymns performed in the pontifical chapel and some of the motets that were sung for the popes and cardinals. If there is a link between the *capella pape* and the manuscript, the most probable candidate is the papal *magister capelle* and provost of the cathedral of Apt, Richardus de Bozonvilla.

Avignon was for a brief moment the center of the Western world. It was here that the bishop of Rome lived as a "sinner among sinners." He and members of his Curia built palaces both within and without its walls bringing a great number of ambitious and talented clerics to Avignon to seek patrons. In many ways the city was the mid-point between Paris and Rome. It was here where secular met sacred; it was here where poets, scholars, and artist worked, and exchanged ideas. And it was here where, for almost a century, the musical art took root and flourished at the close of the Middle Ages.

# Notes

**Chapter 1**

1.  Robert Brentano, *Rome Before Avignon* (New York: Basic Books, 1974), pp. 16-17.

2.  Guillaume Mollat, *The Popes at Avignon, 1305-1378,* Janet Love, trans. (London: Thomas Nelson and Sons, 1963), pp. xiii-xiv (hereafter cited as Mollat).

3.  Elliott L. Binns, *The History of the Decline and Fall of the Medieval Papacy* (Hamden, CT: Archon Books, 1967), p. 104. This saying was originally used by Herodian in reference to the emperor: Where the emperor is, there is Rome. It was adapted by the fourteenth-century defenders of the Avignon papacy.

4.  Brentano, *Rome,* pp. 55, 85.

5.  Archives départementales de Vaucluse (hereafter cited as ADV), 25 J, Archevêché d'Avignon: fol. 32v. This document, essentially a ceremonial compiled ca. 1360, comes from the former cathedral of Vaison. "Item corrigantur servitores cantantes, aut corizantes et alios insolentes correxerint et si se non indispensabiliter de palatio removeantur." Marc Dykmans, "Les pouvoirs des cardinaux pendant la vacance du saint siège d'après un nouveau manuscrit de Jacques Stefaneschi," *Archivio della Societa Romana di storia patria* 104 (1981): 119-45.

6.  Emil Friedberg, *Corpus iuris canonici,* part 2, *Decretalium collectiones* (Leipzig: 1928), col. 1019 (hereafter cited as *Corpus iuris canonici*). André Pons, *Droit ecclésiastique et musique sacrée,* vol. 3 (St. Maurice, Switzerland: Editions de l'Oeuvre Saint-Augustin, 1960), p. 48 (hereafter cited as Pons). Also see *Liber Sextus decretalium d. Bonifacii papae VIII. Clementis papae V. Constitutiones, extravagantes tum viginti d. Ioannis papae XXII. tum communes.* (Venice: 1615), p. 287-88. Liber tertius, Titulus I, cap. I. "Clerici, qui, clericalis ordinis dignitati non modicum detrahentes, se ioculatores seu goliardos faciunt aut bufones, si per annum artem illam ignominiosam exercuerint, ipso iure, si autem tempore breviori, et tertio moniti non resipuerint, careant omni privilegio clericali."

7.  R. F. McNamara, "Stational Church," *New Catholic Encyclopedia* (hereafter cited as *NCE*), vol. 13, pp. 662-64.

8.  This is discussed in the following chapter.

9.  Mollat: 3-4, fn.

10. Mollat: 6.

11. Joseph Girard, *Evocation du vieil Avignon* (Paris: Les Editions du Minuit, 1958), p. 36 (hereafter cited as Girard).

12. Mollat: xix-xx.

13.    Philip E. Burnham, Jr., "Cultural Life at Papal Avignon, 1309-1376" (Ph.D. diss., Tufts University, 1972), p. 55 (hereafter cited as Burnham).

14.    Bernhard Schimmelpfennig, *Die Zermonienbücher der römischen Kirche im Mittelalter,* Bibliothek des Deutschen historischen Instituts in Rom, vol. 40 (Tübingen: 1973), pp. 170ff., 180ff. (hereafter cited as *ZKM*).

15.    *Corpus iuris canonici:* 1173. Pons: 66-67. *Clementinae constitutiones,* Liber tertius, Titulus XIV, cap. I. "Gravi nimirum turbatione movemur, quod ex nonnullorum rectorum negligentia, quae, dum spem impunitatis permittit, multam nutrire pestilentiam consuevit in subditis, plerique ecclesiarum ministri, modestia ordinis clericalis abiecta, dum offerre Deo sacrificium laudis, fructum labiorum suorum, in puritate conscientiae et animi devotione deberent, horas canonicas dicere seu psallere transcurrendo, syncopando, extranea quidem et plerumque vana, profana et inhonesta intermiscendo colloquia, tarde ad chorum conveniendo, seu ecclesiam ipsam absque rationabili causa ante finem officii exeundo frequenter, aves interdum portando, seu faciendo portari, canesque secum ducendo venaticos, ac, quasi nihil praetendentes de clericali militia, in corona, vestibus et tonsura divina etiam celebrare aut eis interesse nimis indevote praesumunt."

16.    *Corpus iuris canonici:* 1173. *Clementinae constitutiones,* Liber tertius, Titulus XIV, cap. II. "Dignum prorsus et congruum arbitrantes, quod clerici tam religiosi quam alii cardinalium sacrosanctae Romanae ecclesiae ac quorumcunque pontificum gratiam et communionem apostolicae sedis habentium commensales domestici, se possint ipsis in divinis officiis coaptare, ut illud, quod iidem cardinales, seu pontifices dicent officium, licite dicere valeant, nec ad dicendum aliquod aliud teneantur, sacri approbatione concilii indulgemus."

17.    Mollat: 6, 9-11.

18.    Mollat: 11-12, fn.

19.    Burnham: 59.

20.    Girard: 95-96.

21.    *ZKM:* 166. It is certain that he preached from here at least once, for the canonization of Louis of Toulouse, 6 April 1317. Girard: 96.

22.    L.-H. Labande, *Le Palais des Papes,* vol. 1 (Marseille: F. Detaille, 1925), p. 39 (hereafter cited as Labande).

23.    Labande: 47. Burnham: 59, 61.

24.    Labande: 38.

25.    K. H. Schäfer, ed. *Die Ausgaben der apostolischen Kammer unter Johann XXII., nebst den Jahresbilanzen von 1316-1375,* Vatikanische Quellen zur Geschichte des päpstlichen Hof- und Finanzverwaltung 1316-1378, vol. 2 (Paderborn: 1912), pp. 277, 310, 674, 683, 695, 787, 793, 794, 801, 802. Girard: 51. John must also have participated at liturgies celebrated in these churches. As a passage written in 1317 and included in a ceremonial indicates: "Et etiam si placet, commitit quod celebret episcopus seu presbiter cardinalis in ecclesia cathedrali civitatis, vel alibi sicut placet . . ." Marc Dykmans, *Le cérémonial papal de la fin du moyen âge à la Renaissance,* vol. 2, *De Rome en Avignon ou le cérémonial de Jacques Stefaneschi.* (Brussels: Institut historique belge de Rome, 1981), p. 411.

26.    Mollat: 14. Louis Caillet, *La papauté d'Avignon et l'eglise de France.* (Paris: Presses universitaires de France, 1975).

27.    John Edgar Weakland, "The Pontificate of Pope John XXII: Problems of Church Reform and Centralization" (Ph.D. diss., Case Western Reserve, 1966), p. 261. Pope John is credited

with being either the author or editor of 27 hymns or prayers. U. Chevalier, *Repertorium hymnologicum*, 6 vols. (Louvain and Brussels: 1892-1920), nos. 1761, 2663, 3616, 3983, 6093, 8483, 8521, 9578, 12022, 14725, 14726, 18190, 20788, 22655, 23597, 23749, 24444, 27686, 28563, 29562, 29678, 33171, 33769; *2322, 7807, 14081, 26661.

28.    Mollat: 14. August Coulon, ed.,    *Jean XXII (1316-1334). Lettres secrètes et curiales relatives à la France*, vol. 1 (Paris: 1906), p. 435, no. 513 (21 March 1318); pp. 903-4, no. 1051 (26 May 1320).

29.    "Dat vivendi normam in minoribus major regulata modesta ne vel illos circa quedam familiarium sinat affluere ... qua cavetur ne cardinales plus quam XX domicellos habeant nec robas donent familiaribus pape et nisi X ac X capellanos nec vadant ad campos ducant...." Cited in Weakland, "The Pontificate of Pope John XXII," p. 42 fn.

30.    Mollat: 15-18.

31.    Gustav Fellerer, "La *Constitutio docta Sanctorum patrum* di Giovanni XXII e la musica nuova del suo tempo," in *L'Ars nova italiana del trecento* (Certaldo: 1959), pp. 10, 13. Pons: 70. Karl Gustav Fellerer, "Zur Constitutio *Docta SS. patrum,*" in *Speculum musicae artis* (Munich: 1970), pp. 126-29. For two English translations of the bull, see the following: H. E. Wooldridge, *Oxford History of Music*, vol. 1, 2nd ed. (Oxford: 1929), p. 294 ff. Robert F. Hayburn, *Papal Legislation on Sacred Music* (Collegeville, MN: The Liturgical Press, 1979), pp. 20-22. For the full original text, see: *Extravagantes tum viginti d. Ioannis papae XXII.* (Venice: 1615), pp. 164-165. Liber tertius, Titulus I, cap. unicum. *Corpus iuris canonici:* 1255-57.

32.    Suspension of the cleric from his office for a period of eight days.

33.    Mollat: 26. For more information concerning his tenure as bishop of Pamiers see Emmanuel Le Roy Ladurie, *Montaillou: The Promised Land of Error*, Barbara Bray, trans. (New York: Vintage Books, 1979), especially pp. vii-xvii.

34.    Mollat: 27-32.

35.    See chap. 2, following.

36.    Mollat: 28-29, 33.

37.    Ludovico Muratori, *Antiquitates Italicae Medii Aevi*, vol. 3 (Milan: 1740), cols. 277-78. "Denanti a quesso Papa Benedetto venne uno Monaco de Santo Paulo de Roma (Frate Monozella avea nome) lo quale pe la morte de lo antecessore sio era eletto Abbate. Quesso era homo, lo quale se delettava de gire pe Roma la notte, facenno le mattiniate, sonnano lo Leguto, cha era bello sonatore e cantatore de ballate.... Quanno quesso fo eletto, denanti a la Santitate de Papa Benedetto disse: Santo Patre: io so' eletto da Santo Paolo de Roma. Hora lo Papa sao tutte le connitioni di chi li vao denanti. Disse: Sai cantare? Respuse lo eletto: Saccio. Lo Papa: Io dico, la Cantilena? Disse lo eletto: Le Canzoni saccio. Disse lo Papa. Sai sonare? Disse lo eletto: Saccio. Disse lo Papa: Io dico, se tu sai toccare li Organi e lo Leguto? Respuse quello: Troppo bene. Allhora mutao favella lo Papa e disse: E'convenevole cosa a lo Abbate de lo venerabele Monastero de Santo Paulo l'essere buffone? Va pe li fatti toi." Cited in Durnham: 391-392, fn. Translation of the dialogue based heavily on Burnham.

38.    Burnham: 55. See also F. Piola Caselli, *La costruzione del palazzo dei papi di Avignone (1316-1367)* (Milan, 1981).

39.    Labande: 52-53.

40.    Sylvain Gagnière, *The Palace of the Popes at Avignon*, 3rd edition ([Paris]: Caisse Nationale des Monuments Historiques, 1977), p. 50 (hereafter cited as Gagnière).

41.  Labande: 126, 53-54.

42.  Gagnière: 48-51.

43.  Labande: 55.

44.  Burnham: 70-71.

45.  Gagnière: 40-43.

46.  Labande: 60.

47.  Mollat: 34-35.

48.  At the time of their respective deaths, John XXII left 150,000 florins, Benedict XII 1,117,000 florins, and Clement VI 311,115 florins. Innocent VI fell into debt because of the burden of supporting wars in Italy. Urban V and Gregory XI, according to Mollat, "lived from hand to mouth." Mollat: 330.

49.  John E. Wrigley, "Studies in the Life of Pierre Roger (Clement VI) and of Related Writings of Petrarch" (Ph.D. diss., University of Pennsylvania, 1965), pp. 17, 25.

50.  Mollat: 37, fn. Wrigley, "Studies," pp. 31, 33-34.

51.  Wrigley, "Studies," pp. 53, 58, 60 fn.

52.  Paul Fournier, "Pierre Roger (Clément VI)," *Histoire littéraire de la France,* vol. 37 (Paris: 1938), p. 238.

53.  K. H. Schäfer, ed., *Die Ausgaben der apostolischen Kammer unter Benedikt XII., Klemens VI. und Innocenz VI. (1335-1362),* Vatikanische Quellen zur Geschichte des päpstlichen Hof- und Finanzverwaltung 1316-1378, vol. 3 (Paderborn: 1914), p. 197 (hereafter cited as Schäfer II).

54.  On 8 June 1344, the *magister hospitii* paid 300 florins to the *ystriones* of the duke of Normandy. Schäfer II: 262.

55.  Alfred Coville, "Philippe de Vitry," *Romania* 59 (1933): 524, 529. Ernest H. Sanders, "Philippe de Vitry," *The New Grove Dictionary of Music and Musicians* (hereafter cited as *Grove 6*), vol. 20, p. 22. Leo Schrade, ed., *The Motets of the Roman de Fauvel,* Polyphonic Music of the Fourteenth Century, vol. 1 (Monaco: [1956]), pp. 97-103 and *Commentary* to said volume, p. 37.

56.  K. H. Schäfer, ed., *Die Ausgaben der apostolischen Kammer unter den Papsten Urban V. und Gregor XI., (1362-1378),* Vatikanische Quellen zur Geschichte des päpstlichen Hof- und Finanzverwaltung 1316-1378, vol. 6 (Paderborn: 1937), p. 693 (18 July 1343), p. 699 (6 May 1344) (hereafter cited as Schäfer III).

57.  Conrad Eubel, *Hierarchia catholica medii aevi,* vol. 1 (Münster: 1898), p. 349.

58.  Ursmer Berlière, ed., *Suppliques de Clément VI (1342-1352),* Analecta Vaticano-Belgica, vol. 1 (Rome: Institut historique Belge de Rome, 1906), pp. 245-246, no. 971 (17 December 1345) in which Philippe is cited as *capellanus* of the pope and *consiliarius* of King Philip of France; p. 532, nos. 2042-2043 and fn. (6 August 1350) where he is called *capellanus;* p. 552, no. 2128 (3 January 1351) where he is called *electus Meldensis.* Idem, ed. *Lettres de Clément VI (1342-1352),* Analecta Vaticano-Belgica, vol. 6 (Rome: Institut historique Belge de Rome, 1924), p. 648, no. 1747 (17 December 1345). Coville, "Philippe de Vitry," p. 530 indicates that Philippe traveled to Villeneuve, where he resided from 30 September 1350 until some unknown date, at which time he returned to Paris. During the period September-October 1350, the Pope was

living in his palace at Villeneuve. Philippe was again in Villeneuve from ca. 23 December 1350 until February 1351. During this time he was consecrated bishop of Meaux.

59. "Petre Clemens, tam re quam nomine... Cephas es." "Est exorta radio spiritus Clemens sextus sanctus [sancti?] divinitus... Petrus primus, Petrum non desiris vices eius quia recte geris. Tu clemens es et Clemens dixeris... consoletur tristis Armenia et elatus succumbat Ismael et germinet Syria et depressus resurgat Israel..." Leo Schrade, *The Motets*, pp. 97-103.

60. Lawrence Gushee, "Jehan des Murs," *Grove 6*, vol. 9, pp. 587-88. Idem. "New Sources for the Biography of Johannes de Muris," *Journal of the American Musicological Society* 22 (1969): 8, 11-12, 19. Burnham: 374-78.

61. Gordon A. Anderson, "Leo Hebraeus," *Grove 6*, vol. 10, 669. Mollat: 39. Burnham: 374-78. Other members of Philippe's intellectual circle were Jehan de la Mote, who wrote the poem *O Victoriens* that quotes a motet by Philippe (*Cum status/Hugo/Magister*); Johannes de Aquiano dictus Sabaudia, a secretary working in the royal palace in 1350; Jehan Campions; and possibly Gilles li Muisis, who refers to Philippe, Jehan de la Mote, and Guillaume de Machaut in his poetry. He was also the author of a Latin poem of some length containing certain sections entitled, *De dominus papa Clemente sexto, De domino papa Benedicto,* and *De promotione magistri Petri Rogerii ad statum cardinalitatis.* Gilles is also the author of a poem entitled *Li estas des papes.* E. Pognon, "Du nouveau sur Philippe de Vitri et ses amis," *Humanisme et Renaissance* 6 (1938): 48-55. Idem, "Ballades mythologiques de Jean de le Mote, Philippe de Vitri, Jean Campion," *Humanisme et Renaissance* 5 (1936): 385-417. In *Histoire littéraire de la France,* vol. 36 (Paris: 1937): Antoine Thomas, "Jean de le Mote, trouvère," pp. 66-86; Alfred Coville, "Gilles li Muisis," pp. 250-324. Berlière, *Lettres,* p. 34, no. 104.

62. Ernest Hatch Wilkins, *Life of Petrarch* (Chicago: The University of Chicago Press, 1961), pp. 3, 8. Mechthild Caanitz, "Petrarca in der Geschichte der Musik" (Doctoral diss., Albert-Ludwigs-Universität, Freiburg-im-Breisgau, 1969), 13-18.

63. Ursmer Berlière, *Louis Sanctus de Beeringen* (Rome: 1905), p. 11-12. Caanitz, "Petrarca," pp. 9-13, 169-70.

64. Georges de Loÿe, "Réception du Pape Clément IV par les Cardinaux Hannibal Ceccano et Pedro Gomez à Gentilly et Montfavet 30 avril-1 mai 1343 (ou 1348)," *Actes du Congrès International Francesco Petrarca* (Avignon: Aubanel 1974), pp. 331-53. De Loÿe believes the earlier date, 1343, to be more likely. If this were 1348, it would have been in the midst of the ravages of the plague, a time when Clement is believed to have remained in the Palace of the Popes at Avignon. P. Pansier, *Les Palais cardinalices d'Avignon aux XIVme et XVme siècles,* vol. 1 (Avignon: J. Roumanille, 1925), pp. 18-22. Henry Bosco, "Sur un Diner offert au Pape Clément V, en 1303 par le Cardinal 'di Pelagrù'," *Annales d'Avignon* 2 (1913): 113-27.

65. "Fu guidato e rechato dagli schudieri ed achompagnato da chavalieri chogli stormenti de diverse maniere credo che'l suono degli stormenti mescholato choralegrarsi la gente risonasse insino a Vignone." De Loÿe, "Réception," p. 340.

66. "... vene chome il primo tramesso achompagnato chol mescholato romore de le genti e degli stormenti." De Loÿe, "Réception," p. 342.

67. "Vene la nona vivanda e per tramessa fu udito un chantare di cherici ma no veduti di boci d'ogni maniera grosse men grosse mezzane piciole et puerili chon una dolciezza soavisima che renderono cheta tuta la sala perche gli atenti orechi tuti feciono taciere le parlanti lingue per la soavita de la dolce melodia." De Loÿe, "Réception," p. 344

68.  See p. 121 of the present study.

69.  Burnham: 76-77.

70.  Burnham: 78-79. Labande: 126.

71.  Gagnière: 86-88.

72.  Burnham: 78. Labande: 126.

73.  Gagnière: 95.

74.  Gabriel Colombe, "Au Palais des Papes: La Chapelle Clémentine," *Mémoires de l'Académie de Vaucluse,* second series, 35 (1935): 82 (hereafter cited as Colombe).

75.  Gagnière: 96.

76.  Colombe: 87, 90, 93.

77.  Burnham: 185.

78.  Burnham: 187, 190.

79.  Colombe: 86, 98 fn. 35.

80.  Colombe: 81.

81.  Burnham: 182, 186-87, 207.

82.  Wrigley, "Studies," p. 83. This phrase is from Clement's Profession of Faith, made 5 December 1351. Mollat: 40.

83.  Mollat: 42, 44.

84.  Mollat: 45.

85.  Mollat: 46.

86.  Mollat: 49.

87.  Bernard Guillemain, *La Cour pontificale d'Avignon, 1309-1376* (Paris: Editions E. de Boccard, 1966), p. 370. Originally published as fascicle 201 of Bibliothèque des Ecoles Françaises d'Athènes et de Rome (hereafter cited as BEFAR), 1962 (hereafter cited as Guillemain).

88.  Mollat: 49-50.

89.  Mollat: 51. Guillemain: 447-48.

90.  Mollat: 51. Hélène Cingria, Philippe Barnicaud, and Bernard Tournois, *La Chartreuse du Val de Bénédiction, Villeneuve-lès-Avignon* ([Paris]: Caisse nationale des Monuments historiques et Sites, 1977).

91.  Mollat: 52-53.

92.  Mollat: 53.

93.  Guillemain: 370.

94.  Schäfer III: 9 (24 November 1362), 10 (13 December 1362).

95.  Gagnière: 107.

96.  The presence of a place called "Roma" within the papal palace at Avignon adds a new twist to the motto: *Ubi papa, ibi Roma.* This is particularly intriguing in light of the fact that the music

of Baude Cordier was reputedly known "as far as Rome." Craig Wright, *Music at the Court of Burgundy, 1364-1419* (Henryville, PA: Institute of Mediaeval Music, 1979), p. 132 fn. For a similar statement made earlier in the fourteenth century about Thomas de Duacho, see the discussion of the motet *Musicalis scientia* in Richard Hoppin and Suzanne Clercx, "Notes biographique sur quelques musiciens français du XIV$^e$ siècle," *Les colloques de Wégimont,* no. 2 (Paris: Société d'Edition "Les Belles Lettres," 1959), p. 65.

97.    "Et pro speciali dilectione septum pueros una cum magistro suo in scientia musicali peritissimo destinavit studio tolosano, qui in missa majori studii voce dulci harmonisarent, atque in aliis facultatibus proficerent et erudirentur." Etienne Baluze, *Vitae paparum avenionensium,* Guillaume Mollat, ed., vol. 1 (Paris: 1914), p. 416 (hereafter cited as Baluze). Mollat: 54.

98.    Schäfer III: 338; (25 April 1367) payment made to "... domino Johanni de Carmenhi, presbytero Atrebatensi, magistro Petro Forbissoni, Petro de Atrio, Guillelmo Dicren Cameracensis diocesis et Roberto de Capella ac Jacobo de Erin, clericis Atrebatensis diocesis, cantoribus missis ad medietatem expensarium pape apud Tholosam pro studendo, quia predictus thesaurarius solvit aliam medietatem, videlicet de 10 mensibus [December 1362] pro parte papam tangente 20 florinas." Also see Schäfer III: 318, 323, 363, 367. Note also that all the clerics involved originated from either the dioceses of Arras or Cambrai.

99.    Schäfer III: 341, (1362).

100.    Joseph-Hyacinthe Albanès, *Entrée solennelle du pape Urbain V à Marseille en 1365* (Marseille: 1865), pp. 28-30. "Item sian elegitz sers bons homes que provesiscan e provezir fassan que lings e barcas, o galoizas, si far si podra, fossan armadas aquel jorn, enramadas, enpennonadas, e si temps es, fossan en la plassa d'Areng en l'intrament del Papa, regatant per aqui e menant gran festa, tro qu'el Papa fos passat de la plaia, e pueis deian venir al port, e per aqui regatar e menar gran festa, an lors esturmens que aver porran, tro qu'el Papa sia jong al monestier, e pueis desarmon."

     "Item que nostre senhor lo Papa intri e intrar deia, an sa companhia, per lo portal de porta Gallega, tirant dreg camin ves la Trenitat, en local luec esser deia la badessa de sancta Clara an sas monegas, aqui cantants, e d'aqui non partan tro que nostre senhor lo Papa sia passat, e dada azellas la sieua benediction, e pueis tornon a lur monestier."

     "Item que nostre senhor lo Papa partent de la Trenitat vaga dreg camin per la carriera Franceza, e venga al canton de sant Tomas, on sian la badessa de sant Salvador an son covent, cantants, e resaupuda la benediction del Papa, tornon a lur monestier."

101.    Schäfer III: 99; (7 June 1365) "... de mandato pape domino Theodorico episcopo Wormaciensis pro ioculatoribus domini imperatoris pro dono speciali pro liberis eorum maritandis ... 100 florinas camere."

102.    Schäfer III: 205 (16 January).

103.    Mollat: 57-58. Johann Peter Kirsch, *Die Rückkehr der Päpste Urban V. und Gregor XI. von Avignon nach Rom, Auszüge aus den Kameralregistern des vatikanischen Archivs,* Quellen und Forschungen herausgegeben vor der Görresgesellschaft, vol. 6 (Paderborn: 1898), p. 102 (hereafter cited as Kirsch).

104.    Schäfer III: 85.

105.    Schäfer III: 223.

106.    Kirsch: 50 (31 July).

107.    Kirsch: 100.

108. Kirsch: 103.

109. Bibliothèque municipale d'Avignon (hereafter cited as BMA), ms. 2741, Recueil de pièces (*Manuscrit Bruneau,* 17th-18th-century, anonymous chronicle): fol. 119.

110. Mollat: 58.

111. Oskar Halecki, *Un Empereur de Byzance à Rome,* Rozprawy Historyczne, vol. 8 (Warsaw: 1930), pp. 190-99.

112. Mollat: 58.

113. Guillemain: 159, fn. 345.

114. Schäfer III: 358.

115. Schäfer III: 361 (26 February).

116. Schäfer III: 282 ( 5 November 1370) Colinus Chelhardi and Guillelmus Ulbi (Blanchi?); 365, 406, 412.

117. Schäfer III: 402.

118. Schäfer III: 363 (12 February 1371); 364, 394, 406, 473, 474, 476, 486.

119. Archivio Segreto Vaticano (hereafter cited as ASV), Coll. 457: fol. 21. I would like to thank Clara Kelly Marvin for her assistance in obtaining photocopies of several documents from the Archivio Segreto Vaticano.

120. Guillemain: 370.

121. Guillemain: 370.

122. Schäfer III: 424 (22 November-13 May 1373); 473-74, 475, 478, 538, 540, 542, 578, 657, 658 (20 September 1376). On 21 November 1352, Johannes de Seduno, *clericus* to the *capellani commensales,* was given charge of the expenses of the *capella secreta.* It is likely that the pope's small private chapels functioned as oratories where the *commensales* said low Masses. See Bernhard Schimmelpfennig, "Die Organization der päpstlichen Kapelle in Avignon," *Quellen und Forschungen aus italienischen Archiven and Bibliotheken* 50 (1971): 99; Franz Ehrle, *Historia bibliothecae romanorum pontificum tum Bonifatianae tum Avenionensis* (Rome: 1890), p. 730.

123. Ursula Günther, ed., *The Motets of the Manuscript Chantilly, musée condé, 564 (olim 1047) and Modena, Biblioteca estense,* α *M.5 24 (olim lat. 568),* Corpus Mensurabilis Musicae, vol. 39 ([Rome]: American Institute of Musicology, 1965), pp. xl-xlii.

*Triplum:* Pictagore per dogmata
fit virgo septenarius,
librat dies et climata,
quorum effectus varius,
et illa magna sidera:
Sic Iupiter primarius,

alter Mavortis opera
gessit, exinde tertius
nova dans mundo federa,
surgit ut Phebi radius
post dulcis ut Citerea,
quam sequitur Cilenius,

Cinthia reddit trophea.
Mirari Neptunum cogit
sorte sumpta cum Enea,
hic almus, qui modo cogit,
iam consummato spatio
capiet—quicumque legit

ut facta dicta ratio—
ubi caput fuit orbis.
Sedem firmabit Latio,
mentis ponet finem morbis,
nam tertia fert secula
auri, quae nectunt vincula.

*Motetus:* O terra sancta, suplica
summo pastori gentium
tuum adi Gregorium
et fletus tales explica:

Nunc, sancte pater, aspicis,
ecce conculcor misera,
Christus his lavit scelera
et fedor ab Arabicis.

Junge leones liliis
et rosas cum serpentibus;
indulge penitentibus.
Pacem dat pater filiis,

crucem in classe Syria.
Agar cognoscat aquilas,
Farfar delphini pinulas
et arma mittat Stiria.

*Tenor:* O rosa vernans caritatis.

124. Michael Grant, *Roman Myths* (New York: Charles Scribner's Sons, 1971), pp. 57-60, 95.

125. Grant, *Roman Myths,* pp. 65-67.

126. Grant, *Roman Myths,* pp. 109-10.

127. Grant, *Roman Myths,* p. 212.

128. *Aeneid,* 6. 792-94. As cited and interpreted by G. Karl Galinsky, *Aeneas, Sicily and Rome,* Princeton Monographs in Art and Archaeology, vol. 40 (Princeton, NJ: Princeton University Press, 1969), p. 228.

129. *Bulfinch's Mythology: The Greek and Roman Fables Illustrated* (New York: Viking Press, 1979), p. 305. Michael Stapleton, *A Dictionary of Greek and Roman Mythology* (London: Hamlyn, 1978), pp. 191-92, 212. Charleton T. Lewis and Charles Short, *A Latin Dictionary* (Oxford: Clarendon Press, 1879), p. 138.

130. Guillemain: 159, fn. 345.

131. Granger Ryan and Helmut Ripperger, trans., *The Golden Legend of Jacobus de Voragine* (New York: Arno Press, 1969), pp. 16-24. Donald Attwater, *The Penguin Dictionary of Saints* (Harmondsworth, England: 1965), pp. 250-51.

132. Lewis and Short, *A Latin Dictionary*, p. 148. James Parker, *A Glossary of Terms Used in Heraldry*, new edition (Rutland, VT: Charles E. Tuttle, 1970), pp. 213-17. A. C. Fox-Davies, *A Complete Guide to Heraldry*, rev. ed. (London: Thomas Nelson and Sons, 1969), p. 177.

133. S. Baiocchi, "Abbey of Farfa," *NCE*, vol. 5, p. 837.

134. Parker, *A Glossary*, pp. 207-8. Fox-Davies, *A Complete Guide*, pp. 190, 310.

135. Guillemain: 159, fn. 345.

136. Labande: cover illustration, and plate xiv. Gagnière: 68. Eric John, *The Popes* (New York: Hawthorn Books, 1964), inside back cover, front flyleaf; p. 274, illustration.

137. Frédéric Godefroy, *Dictionnaire de l'Ancienne Langue Française*, vol. 7 (Paris: 1938), p. 241.

138. Günther, *The Motets*, pp. xl-xli. Günther feels that the motet was written after Gregory began to plan his return to Rome. She has therefore dated the motet as having been written in early 1375. Because the text is a general call back to Rome and was written more as a tribute to the Roger family than anything else, I am content with ascribing the date 1371-1376 for the present.

139. Mollat: 62.

140. Kirsch: 216.

141. Kirsch: 219.

142. Kirsch: 222 and fn.

143. Girard: 49.

144. Girard: 50, 52. Mollat: 279-81.

145. Girard: 49. During the plague of 1348, 62,000 persons are said to have succumbed (at least according to a letter attributed to Petrarch's friend Louis Sanctus). J.-J. de Smet, ed., *Recueil des Chroniques de Flandre*, vol. 3 (Brussels: 1856), pp. 14-18. Mollat: 40 fn., 318.

146. I would like to thank Mme Anne-Marie Hayez for providing this information which she has culled from the archives of both Avignon and Rome.

147. Girard: 54.

148. P. Pansier, *Les palais cardinalices d'Avignon aux XIV^{me} et XV^{me} siècles*, 2 vols. (Avignon: J. Roumanille, 1926). Marc Dykmans, "Les palais cardinalices d'Avignon: un supplément du XIV^e siècle aux lists du Docteur Pansier." *Mélanges de l'Ecole français de Rome* 83 (1971): 389-438. Hervé Aliquot, "Les Livrées cardinalices de Villeneuve-lés-Avignon," (D.E.S. d'Histoire médiévale, Université d'Aix, 1976.) Idem, "Les livrées cardinalices de Villeneuve-lés-Avignon," in *Avignon: Genèse et débuts du Grand Schisme d'Occident*, Colloques internationaux du Centre national de la recherche scientifique, no. 586 (Paris: 1980), pp. 397-408.

149. Like the Sovereign Pontiffs, the cardinals not only maintained palaces but also varying numbers of chaplains to assist them in their own private devotions. During the pontificate of Urban V, nearly all the princes of the Church maintained sizeable chapels. Within the first months of this pope's reign alone, seven cardinals submitted supplications for their respective *magister capelle*. Raymond de Canilhac: Petrus Fabri; Elie de Saint-Yrieix: Garsius Sancii; Gilles Aycelin: Balduinus Heraudi; Hugues Roger: Amerus Alexandri; Andruin de Rocha: Jacobus dictus Ouyn; Hugues de Saint-Martial: Johannes de Novilla-supra-Saltam; Gil Albornoz: Bernardus de Luschis. This information has been obtained from the Traitment informatique des suppliques du Pape Urbain V (1362-1370), Palais des Papes, Avignon.

150.  Anne-marie Hayez, "L'érection de trois églises paroissiales avignonnaises en collégiales au XIV^e siècle," *Bulletin philologique et historique* (1979): 99-120.

151.  Girard: 52.

152.  Girard: 56.

153.  *Corpus iuris canonici:* 1173. *Clementinae constitutiones,* Liber tertius, Titulus XIV, cap. I. "Nonulli etiam tam clerici quam laici, praesertim in festorum certorum vigiliis, dum in ecclesiis deberent orationi insistere, non verentur in ipsis earumque coemeteriis choreas facere dissolutas, et interdum canere cantilenas, ac multas insolentias perpetrare, ex quibus ecclesiarum et coemeteriorum violationes, inhonesta, variaque delicta quandoque sequuntur, et ecclesiasticum plerumque perturbatur officium in divinae maiestatis offensam et adstantium scandalum populorum."

154.  Girard: 66, 311.

155.  Norbert Dufourcq, "Orgues comtadines et orgues provençales," *Mémoires de l'Académie de Vaucluse* 34 (1934): 99. Dufourcq, "Orgues comtadines et orgues provençales (supplément)," *Provence Historique* 5 (1955): 124.

156.  Karl Young, "Philippe de Mézières' Dramatic Office for the Presentation of the Virgin," *Publications of the Modern Language Association* 26 (1911): 181-234. Young, *The Drama of the Medieval Church,* vol. 2 (Oxford: 1933), pp. 225-45, 472-79. William L. Smoldon, *The Music of the Medieval Church Dramas* (London: Oxford University Press, 1980), pp. 250-52.

157.  Robert Brun, "Annales Avignonaises de 1382 à 1410: Extraites des Archives de Datini," *Mémoires de l'Institut Historique de Provence* 15 (1938): 35-36.

158.  Mollat: 315.

159.  William Braxton Ross Jr., "A Study of Latin Letters at the Court of Avignon in the Time of Clement V and John XXII, 1309-1334" (Ph.D. diss., University of Colorado, 1964).

160.  Anne McGee Morganstern, "Pierre Morel and Sculpture in Avignon During the Period of the Schism (1378-1417)" (Ph.D. diss., New York University, 1970), pp. 129-130, 141-46, 154-55. Gagnière: 43, 130 fn. 18. H. Chobaut, "Documents inédits sur les peintres et peintres-verriers d'Avignon, du Comtat et de la Provence occidentale de la fin du XIV^e au premier du XVI^e siècle," *Mémoires de l'Académie de Vaucluse* 4 (1939): 83-145. L.-H. Labande, "Les manuscrits de la Bibliothèque d'Avignon provenant de la librairie des papes du XIV^e siècle," extract from *Bulletin historique et philologique* (1894). Joseph Girard, "L'Exposition des manuscrits et miniatures du Musée Calvet (19 mars-1^er mai 1927)," *Mémoires de l'Académie de Vaucluse* 27 (1927): 35-47.

161.  V. Leroquais, *Les sacramentaires et les missels manuscrits des bibliothèques publiques de France,* vol. 2 (Paris: 1924), pp. 324-26.

162.  Jack Westrup, "Conducting," *Grove 6,* vol. 4, pp. 641-43; p. 642, plate 1. James W. McKinnon, "Representations of the Mass in the Medieval and Renaissance Art," *Journal of the American Musicological Society* 31 (1978): 33, figs. 4a, 4c. Figure 4a (New York, Morgan Library, ms. 800, fol. 40) by Nicolò da Bologna is stylistically close to the illustration in question.

163.  P. Pansier, "Annales avignonaises de 1370 à 1392, d'après le livre des mandats de la gabelle," *Annales d'Avignon* 3 (1914): 36-37.

164.  Pansier, "Annales," p. 71.

165.  Pansier, "Annales," p. 72.

166. Pansier, "Annales," p. 71.

167. Roger Ch. Logoz, *Clément VII (Robert de Genève)*, Mémoires et documents publiés par la Société d'histoire de la Suisse romande, 3rd series, vol. 10 (Lausanne: 1974), pp. 41-42 (hereafter cited as Logoz). Michel Hayez, "Avignon sans les papes (1367-1370, 1376-1379)," in *Avignon: Genèse et débuts du Grand Schisme d'Occident,* Colloques internationaux du Centre national de la recherche scientifique, no. 586 (Paris: 1980), p. 144.

168. Logoz: 63.

169. Logoz: 64, 71.

170. Logoz: 73.

171. Logoz: 4.

172. Logoz: 15.

173. Logoz: 130.

174. Michael Seidlmayer, *Die Anfänge des grossen abendländischen Schismas,* Spanische Forschungen der Görresgesellschaft, 2nd series, vol. 5 (Münster in Westfalen: 1940), pp. 309-10.

175. Logoz: 73.

176. Pansier, "Annales," p. 37.

177. Ursula Günther, "Zur Biographie einiger Komponisten der Ars subtilior," *Archiv für Musikwissenschaft* 21 (1964): 174. Antoni Rubio y Lluch, *Documents per l'historia de la cultura catalana mig-eval,* vol. 2 (Barcelona: 1921), p. 20.

178. See figure 5 of this book.

179. Baluze: 517-18. "Scripsit mirabiliter, dictavit notabiliter, et cantavit seu celebravit divina officia multum eleganter." Baluze, vol. 2: 908. "Peritus in multis idiomatibus, valde bene scribens, et vocem habens sonoram et magnam; erat valde eloquens et pulcherrime stature...."

180. Baluze, vol. 2: 908. "[Clemens] gentes armorum sustentans et cantores atque alios musicos." Noël Valois, *Le Grand Schisme d'Occident,* vol. 2 (Paris: 1901), p. 388, fn. (10 June 1383) 27 fl., 24 s. to three German *ioculatores;* (10 January 1386) 8 fl., 16 s. to *ioculatores* of the prince of Achaia, Amadeus VII of Savoy; (25 August 1386) 17 fl., 4 s. to Hermanus, *rex heraldoris sive ioculatori* of the duke of Brunswick; (25 August 1386) 8 fl., 16 s. to two *ioculatores* or *mimi* of Guillaume de Sanhes; (24 October 1390) 85 fl., 20 s. to four *ioculatores* of the count of Geneva, the pope's brother; (4 April 1393) 34 fl., 8 s. to four *ioculatores* of Duke Louis II of Anjou.

181. Willi Apel, ed., *French Secular Compositions of the Fourteenth Century,* vol. 1, Corpus Mensurabilis Musicae 53 ([Rome]: American Institute of Musicology, 1970), no. 21.

182. Apel, *French Secular Compositions,* no. 82.

183. Willi Apel, ed., *French Secular Compositions of the Fourteenth Century,* vol. 3 ([Rome]: 1972), no. 296.

> Inclite flos orti Gebenensis
> Cuius odor balsamis dulcior:
> Praestantibus roribus immensis
> Orbem reple ceteris altior!

Salveque, jocundare
Nec ad terram velis declinare
Propter paucum ventum. Nam dicitur:
"In adversis virtus perficitur."

Tibi favet ortus Hispanensis
Gallorumque virgultus carior,
Ortolanum producens extensis
Brachiis, qui viredis potior
Pro ruinis observare
Te satagit. Idcirco letare,
Nam te si quis turbat, evincitur,
In adversis virtus perficitur.

Pro te flores celaferus Encis
Fert. Namque iustis hic iustior
Veridicis. Certat pro te foncis
Quo favente quisque velocior.
Tuo ductus jubare
Se prosternet tuis pedibus. Quare
Si leteris sapit quod subditur
In adversis virtus perficitur.

184.  This is borne out in the clue provided in the last phrase of the ballade, "Therefore, if he knows the letters (in Latin, *litteras;* in French, *lettres*), he knows what is given below: In adversities...." "The letters" in a more specific sense means the Epistles.

185.  In spite of the reluctance of the Iberians to be swayed from official indifference, both Spanish cardinals, Martin de Salva and especially Pedro de Luna, worked hard to win support for the Clementine cause. Duke John of Gerona was also quite sympathetic to Avignon. Logoz: 157.

186.  Logoz: 3, 8.

187.  Valois, *La France,* vol. 2, pp. 34, 35, 37 fn.

188.  See the biographical index of this book, "Matheus de Sancto Johanne."

189.  John, *The Popes,* p. 278.

190.  Logoz: 172.

191.  Enrique Bayerri Bartomeu and Angel Eguíluz López de Murga, *Un Gran Aragonés (El papa Pedro de Luna)* (Barcelona: Porter Libros, 1973), pp. 3-26.

192.  J. P. Kirsch, "Pedro de Luna," *The Catholic Encyclopedia* (hereafter cited as *CE*), vol. 9, p. 431, Logoz: 157.

193.  It has been thought that Jacob's town of origin was Saint-Luc (near Evreux) and through various translations has become Senleches. However, this is probably not the case. Senleches or Salesches is a town in the diocese of Cambrai, deaconate of Haspra (département: Norde; canton: Quesnoy). *Pouillés de la province de Reims,* Recueil des historiens de la France, vol. 6 (Paris: 1907-1908), p. 294 B.

194.  Ursula Günther, "Jacob de Senleches," *Grove 6,* vol. 9, pp. 443-44.

195.  Kirsch, "Pedro de Luna," p. 431.

196.  Brun, "Annales," (1937): 14-17, 21-22.

197. Brun, "Annales," (1937: 38-39.

198. Kirsch, "Pedro de Luna," p. 432.

199. Jean Favier, *Les Finances pontificales à l'époque du Grand Schisme d'Occident 1378-1409*, fascicle 211 of BEFAR (Paris: 1966), p. 650.

200 Gagnière: 61. Kirsch, "Pedro de Luna," p. 432.

201. Brun, "Annales," (1937): 42.

202. Brun, "Annales," (1937): 43, fn.

203. Favier, *Les Finances*, p. 660.

204. Brun, "Annales," (1937): 45-46.

205. Brun, "Annales," (1937): 47. BMA, ms. 2741, Recueil de pièces (*Manuscrit Bruneau*), fol. 162v.

206. When the pope entered Nice, three *sonnors de trompe* preceded the cortege; they were paid three florins. Brun, "Annales," (1937): 48-52, 154.

207. John, *The Popes*, p. 280-81.

208. Kirsch, "Pedro de Luna," p. 443.

**Chapter 2**

1. "... reliquumque noctis spatium cum integri decantatione Psalterii ac innumera genuum inflexione excurrebat... intrinsecusque januis obseratis ac ministro soporato, ipse solitae institit psalmodiae in vicino oratorio. Rursus quodam die ibidem solus cum solo clerico sanctae psalmodiae insistebat..." J.-P. Migne, ed., *Wilbertus. Vita Leonis papae*, Patrologia Latina, vol. 153. (Paris: 1854), cols. 501 A-502 A.

2. "Datum XIX Kalend. Januarii [1026] per manus Bosonis episcopi S. Tiburtinae Ecclesiae et bibliothecarii S.A.S. interfui... Amasus [read: Amatus] episupus atque capellanus domini papae... " J.-P. Migne, ed., *Johannes XIX papa. Epistolae et diplomata*, Patrologia Latina, vol. 141. (Paris: 1853), col. 1135 A.

3. Bernhard Schimmelpfennig, *Die Zeremonienbücher der römischen Kurie im Mittelalter*, Bibliothek des Deutschen historischen Instituts in Rom, vol. 40 (Tübingen: 1973), pp. 6-16 (hereafter cited as *ZKM*).

4. Paul Fabre and L. Duchesne, eds., *Le liber censuum de l'église romaine*, vol. 6, 6, 2nd series of BEFAR (Rome: 1910), pp. 310-11. The former takes place at the basilica of St. Lawrence. "...et dominus papa cantat *Te Deum laudamus* cum cardinalibus in basilica et capellanis; primicerius cum scola extra basilicam sancti Silvestri stant, cantantes antiphonas de laudibus cum psalmis et Benedictus." The latter is celebrated at the Lateran basilica. "Capellani qui assistant ei [pape], iuvant eum in cantando...." Dykmans, *Le cérémonial papal de la fin du moyen age à la Renaisance*, vol. 2, *De Rome en Avignon ou le cérémonial de Jacques Stefaneschi*. (Brussels: Institut historique belge de Rome, 1981), p. 397.

5. Stephen J. P. van Dijk and Joan Hazelden Walker, *The Ordinal of the Papal Court from Innocent III to Boniface VIII and Related Documents*. Spicilegium Friburgense, vol. 22 (Fribourg, 1975) pp. 553, 555. Christmas vigil: "... vesperas in loco suo ornato. capellanis in habitu decenti cantantibus coram eo. Et si est Rome. pronunciat primicerius schole et secundum cantum schole si vero est alibi. pronunciat alius capellanus pape ebdomadarius... cantant capellani Laudes matutinales coram eo... [And after the Masses at dawn and of the day] redit lateranum, dicit vesperas suas in capella cum capellanis suis." Marc Dykmans, *Le*

*cérémonial papal de la fin du moyen âge à la Renaissance,* vol. 1, *Le cérémonial papal du XIII<sup>e</sup>* *siècle* (Brussels: Institut historique belge de Rome, 1977), p. 166. From the consecration of Gregory X (1271): "Et capellanus subdiaconus dicit letaniam cantando, aliis capellanis respondentibus." The rubrics are similar for the papal consecrations during the last two decades of the century as well as for the royal consecrations at which the pontiff presided. Dykmans, *De Rome en Avignon,* pp. 307, 317, and 450.

6.  J. Haller, "Zwei Aufzeichen über die Beamten der Curie," *Quellen und Forschungen aus italienischen Archiven und Bibliotheken* 1 (1898): 28. The *Schola cantorum* never left Rome. "De absentibus vero quibusdam, scilicet mapulariis, cantoribus, castellano abbacie ad pontem, hostariis ad Sancta Sanctorum, Grecis de Croca Ferrata, nichil ponitur hic, que sunt absentes et recipiunt [viandas, etc.] quando curia est Rome." See footnotes 4 and 5 and pp. 105-6, 115 of the present study.

7.  Bernard Guillemain, *La Cour pontificale d'Avignon, 1309-1376* (Paris: Editions E. de Boccard, 1966), p. 360 (hereafter cited as Guillemain). Originally published as fascicle 201 of BEFAR, 1962. Bernhard Schimmelpfennig, "Die Organisation der päpstlichen Kapelle in Avignon," *Quellen und Forschungen aus italienischen Archiven und Bibliotheken* 50 (1970): 80 and fnn. (hereafter cited as OPKA). Haller, "Zwei Aufzeichnungen," pp. 10-11. Late thirteenth-century document.

"De capellanis commensalibus

"Quilibet predictorum capellanorum consuevit habere duas vidandas in carnibus cum pictanciis et duas vidandas piscium et ovorum et unam annonam pro equo sine aplea et ferris, toto tempore excepto a kalendis maii usque ad festum Assumpcionis beate virginis, quia illo tempore dantur XL s. provenienses pro quolibet pro herba equorum, et XI candele in septimana pro cera et ensenium a coquina maiori, quando commedunt in aula. Consuevit eciam quilibet cappellanus recipere a camera in die coronacionis summi pontificis tantum duos malachinos pro presbiterio. In die Nativitatis Domini duos malachinos. In die Resurreccionis Domini duos malachinos, et valet quilibet malachinus VI turonensis grossos.

"Capellani vero predicti debent vacare circa officium divinum, iacere in capellania, ubi capellania assignatur eis, et surgere et dicere matutinum in aula vel capella ordinata de nocte, missam de mane et vesperas de sero in aula; portare crucem vicissim, quando dominus equitat et quando exit in ecclesia. Consueverunt associare camerarium, quando equitat, si requirantur, et facere ambaxiatas, quando imponuntur eis. Subdiaconus capellanus consuevit legere ad mensam, quando dominus commedit in aula. Subdiaconus eciam capellanus consuevit servire domino in missa, quando celebrat solemniter. Presbiter capellanus, quem dominus elegerit, consuevit habere librum paratum pro psalmis dicendis in vesperis, quando dominus exit ad vesperas in aula vel ecclesia, et parare librum cardinali servienti domino in vesperis pro oracione dicenda et in missa."

8.  This document dates from at time when the popes were outside of Rome since the service could take place either in a hall or in a church. The hall is probably a dining room that served as a makeshift chapel as we find in the ceremonial of Conzié 100 years later.

9.  This implies that the pope was not customarily at Matins.

10. Guillemain: 360.

11. Haller, "Zwei Aufzeichnungen," pp. 21-22.

"De clerico capelle

"Clericus capelle recipit unam viandam de carnibus et aliis et duos somerios et unum equum ad equitandum, quando dominus est in itinere, unum somerium scilicet pro capella et alium pro se.

"Ipse vero habet parare altare capellanorum pro missa et in vesperis, cum oportet, et assistere thesaurariis, quando dominus celebrat, et parare altare, quando pronunciantur prelati presentes in curia et quando ipsi prelati debent iurare seu palium debet tradi.

"De hostario capellanie

"Hostarius capellanie recipit unam vidandam de carnibus et aliis, unum somerium et unum equum ad equitandum, quando dominus est in itinere, VII candelas in septimana et pro matutinis XIII et pro festis duplicibus XXIIII candelas et unum torziolum de minoribus.

"Ipse vero debet custodire capellaniam et vocat capellanos ad matutinum et missas et vesperas et ministrat candelas et libros pro officiis."

12.  OPKA: 87. Bernard Guillemain, *Les recettes et les dépenses de la chambre apostolique pour la quatrième année du pontificate de Clement V (1308-1309)* (Rome: Ecole française de Rome, 1978). From p. 25, no. 232 *passim*. From p. 123, no. 1757 *passim* only one *clericus* is mentioned.

13.  OPKA: 88-89, and fn. Guillemain, *Les recettes,* pp. 52, 60, 65, 117; 45 and 71. Both Giffredus and Thomas are mentioned in the accounts during the year 1308/09.

14.  K. H. Schäfer, ed., *Die Ausgaben der apostolischen Kammer unter Johann XXII., nebst den Jahresbilanzen von 1316-1375,* Vatikanische Quellen zur Geschichte des päpstlichen Hof- und and Finanzverwaltung 1316-1378, vol. 2 (Paderborn: 1912-, pp. 568, 570 (hereafter cited as Schäfer I). Guillemain, *Les recettes,* pp. 40, 45, 52, 71, 80, 89, and 100.

15.  Schäfer I: 401, 408, 884-885. Guillemain: 362. OPKA: 89-90.

16.  Schäfer I: 563, 593, 597, 602; 427, 583. The wax castings called *agnus dei* were distributed the Saturday after Easter in the first year of a pontificate and then every seven years. For John XXII, this would have occurred in 1317, 1324, and 1331. Thomas was paid for the molds in 1322, 1325/26, and 1331/32. However, during the fourth year of the reign of Clement V (1308/09), the acolytes of the commensal chapel were reimbursed for having made the *agnus*. Guillemain, *Les recettes,* p. 80.

17.  OPKA: 89. Schimmelpfennig implies that the payment for the molds made in 1331/32 to a Thomas de Capella were not to Thomas de Eugubio, as Schäfer suggests, but instead to Thomas Galli. Schäfer I: 596. The appellation *cantor* shows that Thomas Galli was a singer. However, it might also indicate that his office included duties similar to those performed by a *cantor* in a cathedral church.

18.  See p. 8 of the present study.

19.  Schäfer I: 277, 674, 683, 695, 787, 793, 794, 801, 02. At Notre-Dame-des-Doms, Saint-Agricol, Notre-Dame-des-Miracles, and at the Dominican and Franciscan churches. On 22 January 1322, for example, the following six chaplains were paid for celebrating in the chapel of All Saints at the cathedral: Petrus de S. Vincentio, Guillelmus Rondelli, Alexander de Villa Dei, Guisbertus Carrerie, Geraldus Capucci, and Petrus.

20.  OPKA: 91.

21.  Oswald Holder-Egger, ed., "Cronicae S. Petri Erfordensis. Continuatio I," *Monumenta Erphesfurtensia, Scriptores Rerum Germanicum* (Hanover: 1899), p. 366. On the reforms of Benedict: "... Undecimo vult, quod omnes capellani sui horas canonicas dicant cum nota, et

quod omnes dormiant in uno dormitorio ac eciam comedant coram eo; quod dormitorium iam est in fieri pro eisdem; nec ipsi cappellani habebunt redditus alios quam victum mense papalis et vestitum. Et si aliqui cappellani aliquibus aliis indigent, possunt ab ipso domino papa requirere et non recipere aliunde." Also see Etienne Baluze, *Vitae paparum avinionensium,* Guillaume Mollat, ed., vol. 1 (Paris: 1914), p. 233.

22.  Baluze, *Vitae,* p. 230. "In domo seu hospitio suo XII capellanos absque rochetis habere voluit, qui decantabant cotidie horas diurnas pariter et nocturna."The rochet, a white linen garment, was reserved for use by important churchmen.

23.  K. H. Schäfer, ed., *Die Ausgaben der apostolischen Kammer unter Benedikt XII., Klemens VI. und Innocenz VI. (1335-1362),* Vatikanische Quellen zur Geschichte des päpstlichen Hof- und Finanzverwaltung 1316-1378, vol. 3 (Paderborn: 1914), p. 26 (hereafter cited as Schäfer II).

24.  OPKA: 92-93.

25.  See the biographical index for these two chaplains as well as for the other chaplains mentioned. It provides full bibliographies and much of the evidence for these conjectures and conclusions.

26.  For a description of the office of *scriptor* see Brigide Schwarz, *Die Organisation kurialer Schreiberkollegien von ihrer Entstehung bis zur Mitte des 15. Jahrhunderts,* Bibliothek des Deutschen historischen Instituts in Rom, vol. 37 (Tübingen, 1972). Also see Guillemain: 296-97. Though the term *scriptor* is often used, *scriptor litterarum apostolicarum* or *scriptor litterarum penitentiarum* is usually meant.

27.  OPKA: 92 and fn.

28.  Schäfer II: 44.

29.  OPKA: 93 and fn., Schäfer II: 60.

30.  Schäfer II: 77.

31.  Schäfer II: 94. The list of 1340 is followed by a payment made to the *clericus serviens in capella,* Cantonus Petri: 1) Petrus Sinterii, 2) Johannes de S. Quintino, 3) Johannes Bertrandi, 4) Privatus Pastorelli, 5) Stephanus de Utis, 6) Nicholaus Bertrandi, 7) Berengarius Ademarii, 8) Johannes de Tregos, 9) Guillelmus de Convenis, 10) Raimundus de Angladis, 11) Raimundus Servientis, 12) Raimundus Seguini, and 13) Johannes de Ayrolis (for 54 days). Schäfer II: 120.

32.  Schäfer II: 120, fn. and 140. For more information on the office of *magister capelle pape* see chap. 3, following.

33.  Schäfer II: 139.

34.  Schäfer II: 159, OPKA: 93.

35.  We may recall that Philippe de Vitry was a commensal chaplain of Clement VI.

36.  OPKA: 93-94. This notion is based on the wealth of documentary evidence of Pope John's financial support for the construction of new churches and chapels and for the celebration of Masses beyond the walls of the old episcopal palace. This idea fails to take into account the fact that the pontiff did indeed have the private episcopal chapels at his disposal as well as the former parish church of Saint-Etienne. Masses offered *pro papa* were probably done so as acts of propitiation for the spiritual and temporal welfare of the pope, not as Masses celebrated in place of the pontiff's own service. So it is entirely possible that the *capellani commensales* did fulfill some liturgical obligations even during the reign of John XXII.

37.    OPKA: 93.

38.    Schäfer II: 203.

39.    OPKA: 95. Gaufridus Isnardi, however, bore the title *capellanus intrinsecus* until his death, 26 July 1348.

40.    Schäfer II: 201.

41.    Schäfer II: 234. 1) P. Sainterii, 2) Privatus Pastorelli, 3) J. de Nobilaco, 4) Radulphus Ricardi, 5) G. de Flandria, 6) Matheus Valeta, 7) Raolinus Cossart, 8) Johannes de Sinemuro, 9) Johannes de Caunis, 10) Symon Mauricii, 11) Nicolaus de Noisiaco, 12) Johannes de Tregos (for 50 days).

42.    Schäfer II: 265. 1) P. Sainterii, 2) Johannes de Nobiliaco, 3) Privatus Pastorelli, 4) N. de Norsiaco, 5) Stephanus de Chaulageto, 6) Johannes Gervasii, 7) Guillelmus de Flandria, 8) Matheus de Valeta, 9) Raulinus Cossardi. At this time, Colinetus was still *clericus capelle*. The last time he appeared as papal familiar was 18 January 1345, though he might have retained his post until 1349. OPKA: 99.

43.    Schäfer II: 290.

44.    All information on the composition of the chapel not taken from payment lists and musicological sources has been deduced from published papal correspondence. For complete bibliographical information, see the biographical index of this book and search under the name of the chaplain in question.

45.    Schäfer II: 324.

46.    Guillemain: 363 and fn.

47.    By August 1349, Johannes Berghoen, nephew of the *magister capelle* Petrus Sinterii, took over the position of *clericus capelle* once held by Colinetus. During the same year, Johannes Valentis probably replaced Johannes Gervasii as *servitor*. Gervasii continued to be counted as a papal familiar until his death in 1352. It is difficult to define the duties of both the *clericus* and the *servitor* with any degree of precision. Johannes Berghoen, for example, was required to serve the *capella intrinseca* and its *capellani* by acting in the capacity of papal messenger and the like. Furthermore, by 1349, Johannes Valentis was listed as both *servitor* and *capellanus,* indicating a further loss of differentiation between the two posts. OPKA: 98.

48.    Schäfer II: 460.

49.    Schäfer II: 484.

50.    Northerners were included in the households and chapels of some Italian cardinals well before the pontificate of Clement. See Bernard Guillemain, *Histoire d'Avignon,* (Aix-en-Provence: Edisud, 1979), p. 253. For a specific case, see Dykmans, *De Rome en Avignon,* pp. 31-41. Guillemain suggests that Clement followed the precedent of the Italians.

51.    Schäfer II: 616, payment of March 1353. Documentation during this period is sketchy. On 6 August 1353, Johannes de Attrebato and Jacobus Comitis first appear in the supplications as *capellani capelle intrinsece.* Stephanus de Chaulageto was dead before 25 August 1353, and by 17 October 1354 he had been replaced as *magister* by Johannes Ademari. Besides Johannes Attrebato, there are no other *capellani* mentioned in the published papal correspondence of the period, although Jacobus Comitis, Johannes Clementis de Brullio, and Arnoldus Maseriis—all papal familiars—might have been serving as chaplains. The two *clerici* assigned to the *capella intrinseca* at this time were Alanus Avis and Bertrandus Majoris.

52.  OPKA: 98.

53.  Schäfer II: 625.

54.  Schäfer II: 653, 755. During the following year, two names reappear, but instead of receiving the designation "familiar," they are now specified as *capellani:* Johannes Clementis de Brullio and Arnaldus Maseriis. In 1359 Arnaldus is again present, this time accompanied by Petrus Saumati and Johannes Valentis. These last two remained in the chapel and appeared listed in the supplications of 1360 as *capellani capelle intrinsece* along with Johannes Attrebato. Sometime during this year, payment was made to eight chaplains and two clerks, one of whom was probably Alanus Avis.

55.  Nino Pirrotta, "Church Polyphony a propos of a New Fragment at Foligno," In *Studies in Music History: Essays for Oliver Strunk* (Princeton: Princeton University Press, 1968), p. 119 fn.

56.  Philippus Servonhi was functioning in the capacity of *clericus* from at least the end of October. He was no doubt brought in to fill the void left by the death of Bertrandus Majoris. By the end of Innocent's reign, Nicolaus de Bondevilla had joined as *capellanus.*

57.  The sources yield an abundance of information for the month of June 1363: Johannes Capel, Arnulphus Maseriis, and Egidius Quadrati are all listed as papal chaplains on 6 June; the 12th of the month saw Egidius Batelli, Guido de Naugro, and Johannes de Ulmo enter the chapel; and on 24 June the chaplain Marcial Cobrerii is mentioned in the documents. In August of 1363, Guido de Lange served as clerk of the chapel. During the spring of that year, Stephanus was still serving as *magister,* and in the fall, Walterus is again rferred to as *clericus.* Whether or not these men continued to serve in the chapel throughout the remainder of the year is not known. However, a payment made on 25 November indicates that eight chaplains were given wages for the two months in question, while certain others were paid for 48 days. Only one *clericus* served during this period. K. H. Schäfer, ed., *Die Ausgaben der apostolischen Kammer unter den Papsten Urban V. und Gregor XI., (1362-1378),* Vatikanische Quellen zur Geschichte des päpstlichen Hof- und Finanzverwaltung 1316-1378, vol. 6 (Paderborn: 1937), p. 72 (hereafter cited as Schäfer III).

58.  Schäfer III: 28. Philippus Servonhi, who several years earlier was employed as *clericus* of the chapel, became *capellanus et cantor capelle pape* in September 1364. Schäfer III: 29.

59.  Schäfer III: 112.

60.  Schäfer III: 30. The appelation *tenor capelle* seems a clear indication that part singing was practiced in the chapel of Hugues, brother of Clement VI.

61.  Schäfer III: 145. In three payments made from June to September, Johannes Johannis, apparently still a papal chaplain, is shown engaged in certain acts of charity made on the pope's behalf. Johannes de Ulmo became *magister capelle* in 1366, when he was joined in the chapel by Johannes de Rancovado, Johannes Petri, and a new chaplain and familiar, Ancelmus Martini.

62.  Guillaume Mollat, *The Popes at Avignon, 1305-1378,* trans. Janet Love (London: Thomas Nelson and Sons, 1963), pp. 57-58 (hereafter cited as Mollat). See p. 62 of the present study.

63.  Schäfer III: 182, 183, 242.

64.  Schäfer III: 32.

65.  Schäfer III: 34.

66. Johann Peter Kirsch, *Die Rückkehr der Päpste Urban V. und Gregor XI. von Avignon nach Rom, Auszüge aus den Kameralregistern des vatikanischen Archivs*, Quellen und Forschungen herausgegeben von der Görresgesellschaft, vol. 6 (Paderborn: 1898), pp. 69-70 (hereafter cited as Kirsch).

67. Kirsch: 136.

68. Schäfer III: 235. Guillelmus Bladeti became a chaplain on 24 December, 1369. Schäfer III: 36.

69. Mollat: 159-60.

70. Schäfer III: 367.

71. Schäfer III: 368.

72. Schäfer III: 368.

73. Schäfer III: 35, 145, 203, 375. OPKA: 105. Petrus was assigned to the *intrinseca* in 1369. Pontius was acting as *clericus capelle pape* from at least May 1367, though he served the *capella commensalis* in 1365. ASV, *Collectoria* 457: fol.21v. "Die xxiiii octobris. De mandato domini pape, dominus camerarius privavit et suspendit dominos clericos capelle, videlicet Petrum et Pontcium, de vadiis usque ad mandatum pape."

74. ASV, *Coll.* 457: f.21v. "Jo. Colini cantor fuit privatus de vadiis pro eo quia manus injecit in magistrum capelle."

75. Ursula Günther, "Zur Biographie einiger Komponisten der Ars subtilior," *Archiv für Musikwissenschaft* 21 (1964): 177, fn. (hereafter cited as Günther I).

76. Günther I: 177, fn.

77. Schäfer III: 476, 480.

78. Schäfer III: 477.

79. Guillemain: 493-96.

80. Schäfer III: 599.

81. The members of the chapel in 1374 no doubt included Johannes de Ulmo, Ancelmus Martini, Thomas Tauri, Johannes Lehoudain, Johannes Ruffi de Roquignies, and Johannes Volkardi. Two of the five chaplains receiving a partial wage at this time were Theobaldus Furnerii and Guido de Lange. Both had been absent from the chapel for a brief period. In 1375 Johannes de Ulmo continued to manage a chapel that consisted of Ancelmus Martini, Johannes Lehoudain, Johannes Ruffi de Roquignies, Theobaldus Furnerii, and probably also Philippus Servonhi and Thomas Tauri. By 15 May 1375, they were joined by Johannes Volkardi. During the first half of the following year, Ancelmus, Johannes Ruffi, and Theobaldus were in service as were no doubt Philippus and Johannes Volkardi. Johannes de Ulmo was dead by 23 May 1376 and his duties were assumed by Thomas Tauri before 12 June. Schäfer III: 656, 672.

82. Mollat: xiv-xv, 62.

83. Kirsch: 229. "Pro naulo 16 fardellorum et 8 famulorum capellanorum capelle dni nostri pape de Avinione usque Romam per supradictum Bernardum in recessu dicti dni nostri pape conductorum."

84. Günther I: 182 fn.

85.    See OPKA: 103-4 for a further discussion of the office of *subdiaconus*.

86.    Günther I: 182 fn. Cf. Schäfer III: 60, the payment of 215 unspecified florins.

87.    Günther I: 182, 183 fn.

88.    Günther I: 180.

89.    Günther I: 184.

90.    Günther I: 184.

91.    In the payments of 20 December 1384 and 11 February 1385 (due 1 October and 26 November 1384 respectively) the names of the same *capellani* are again given but in a different order. The former notice documents the addition of Johannes de Moleyo who stood in last place on the list and was only paid for seventeen days' service. By the time of the second payment, he had been replaced by Johannes Lenfant. The next record of payment for eight weeks service, due 22 January 1385, names the following: 1) Symon Aquetin, *magister,* 2) Matheus de Longarigua, 3) Ancelmus Martini, 4) Jacobus de Grivillari, 5) Thomas Multoris, 6) Richardus (II), 7) Henrietus [Poneti], 8) Johannes de Champienh, 9) Stephanus Turqueti, 10) Guillelmus de Ultraaquam, 11) Bertrandus [le Convoitie], 12) Jaquetus [Ringardi?], 13) Maheutus [de Sancto Johanne], 14) Johannes Lenfant. The clerks Pontius and Petrus were also paid. Günther I: 184, and fn.; 185, and doc. 2.

92.    Documentation concerning the composition of the papal chapel is scarce for the years between 1385 and 1393. Johannes Lenfant served as *capellanus* until at least 6 May 1385, the last known appearance of his name in the papal records. Thomas Multoris was referred to as chaplain in March 1387, and seems to have continued in papal service until at least 10 June 1388. The last reference to him, made 10 June 1390/93, designates him a papal familiar. Matheus de Sancto Johanne is named only one more time during the reign of Clement, appearing as chaplain and familiar in March 1386. The veteran *capellanus* Ancelmus Martini died as a familiar of the pope sometime before 11 September 1387. Matheus de Longariga served as *capellanus* in 1388 and is thus noted at the time of his death, which occurred before 14 May 1393. Finally, Henricus Poneti is noted as papal chaplain in 1388 and again in a citation dated 1 August 1390/93.

93.    Günther I: 182.

94.    Günther I: 187 fn.

95.    OPKA: 106.

96.    Günther I: 186-87.

97.    Günther draws this conclusion from the appearance of Richardus's name at the head of the list of chaplains. She is no doubt correct in light of what was to transpire. Günther I: 186-87.

98.    Günther I: 186-87, and doc. 3.

99.    Günther I: 187, fn.

100.    Enrique Bayerri Bartomeu and Angel Eguíluz López de Murga, *Un Gran Aragonés* (*El Papa Pedro de Luna*) (Barcelona: Porter Libros, 1973), pp. 25-26.

101.    Günther I: 187, and doc. 4. Franz X. Haberl, "Die römische *Schola cantorum* und die päpstlichen Kapellsänger bis zur Mitte des 16. Jahrhunderts," *Vierteljahrsschrift für Musikwissenschaft* 3 (1887): 213 (hereafter cited as Haberl).

102.  Günther 188, and doc. 4.

103.  Craig Wright, *Music at the Court of Burgundy, 1364-1419* (Henryville, PA: Institute of Mediaeval Music, 1979), p. 63. Vitrarii did not enter the ducal chapel. See the Biographical Index.

104.  Günther believed Johannes Regem to have been a substitute for Johannes Rogerii because the latter was only officially brought back into the chapel on 30 June 1396. However, a document whose exact date of compilation cannot be determined, but which was written between 22 October 1394 and 1 November 1395, calls him *capellanus capelle* [*pape*] *ac domini ducis Burgundie.* He might, in fact, have been serving in the papal chapel on an *ad hoc* basis, perhaps when the Duke of Burgundy was at Avignon. Johannes then might have been brought back into the papal "family," with all its attendant privileges, on 30 June 1396. See the biographical index.

105.  See the biographical index.

106.  Günther I: 188, and doc. 4.

107.  Günther I: 189.

108.  Günther I: 188.

109.  Günther I: 191.

110.  Günther I: 191-92. Franz Ehrle, ed., *Martin de Alpartils Chronica actitatorum temporibus domini Benedicti XIII,* Quellen und Forschungen herausgegeben von der Görresgesellschaft, vol. 12 (Paderborn: 1906), p. 60. In the list, Johannes de Boscho is classified as Aragonese. We believe the singer to have been from the North.

111.  Günther I: 192, and doc. 5.

112.  Günther I: 193.

113.  ASV, *Coll.* 457: fol. 257v.

114.  Günther I: 193.

115.  Ursula Günther, "Johannes de Janua," *Grove 6,* vol. 9, pp. 665-66.

116.  Günther I: 193-95. Ursula Günther, "Das Manuskript Modena, Biblioteca estense, $\alpha$.M.5,24 (*olim* lat. 568 = *Mod*)." *Musica Disciplina* 24 (1970): 42 (hereafter cited as Günther II).

117.  ASV, *Coll.* 457: fol. 181v. "Benedictus XIII recepit in capellanum sue capelle dominum Raymundum Arnulphi, presbyterum Lemovicensis diocesis, magistrum organorum ad vadia et stipendia unius alteriusque capellanorum ejusdem et juravit."

118.  OPKA: 106.

119.  Boys were employed in the Aragonese royal chapel from 1349. The duke of Berry is believed to have had choirboys in his chapel from at least 1370-1378. The first evidence of boy singers in the Sainte-Chapelle of the king of France dates from 1386. In spite of the well-documented outpouring of wealth to sustain a most splendid chapel, the dukes of Burgundy only began to maintain choirboys in 1406. The Roman popes briefly employed boys in the pontifical chapel after June 1425. We remind the reader that Pope Gregory XI did, in fact, have boy singers attached to his *capella* before his election. Higini Anglès, "Gacian Reyneau am Königshof zu Barcelona in der Zeit von 139.. bis 1429," *Studien zur Musikgeschichte, Festschrift für Guido Adler zum 75. Geburtstag* (Vienna: Universal-Edition, 1930), p. 67. *Anglès, Historia de la música medieval en Navarra* ([Pamplona]: 1970), pp. 255-256, 257. Ursula Günther, "Die

Musiker des Herzogs von Berry," *Musica Disciplina* 17 (1963): 80. Manfred Schuler, "Die Musik in Konstanz während des Konzils 1414-1418," *Acta musicologica* 38 (1966): 155. Idem, "Zur Geschichte der Kapelle Papst Martins V." *Archiv für Musikwissenschaft* 25 (1968): 31. Wright: 92. Haberl 220ff. Richard Jonathan Sherr, "The Papal Chapel ca. 1492-1513 and Its Polyphonic Sources" (Ph.D. diss., Princeton University, 1975), p. 79.

120.   OPKA: 106.

121.   Ludovico Muratori, ed., *Rerum italicarum Scriptores*, vol. 3, pt. 2 (Milan: 1734), col. 787 A (hereafter cited as *RIS*). "... quia Cantores propter pestilentiam et mortem unius ex eis erant dispersi et habere non poterant...."

122.   *RIS:* 787E. "... propter toedium multorum absentium Cantorum non fuerunt Vesperae Papales, nec aliae solemnitates servatae, quae illa die [vigil of Sts. Peter and Paul] fieri solent."

123.   Johannes de Cruce, Johannes Vinyas, and Ferricus Nusilleti were serving in the chapel during the month of June 1407, ASV, *Coll.* 457: fol.257v. By the late summer, Andreas de Choques appears to have replaced Johannes de Cruce. Gerardus Gerardi, who had been managing the *capella* for some time, is first referred to as *magister* in November of that year.

124.   Günther II: 43.

125.   *RIS:* 821 D; and J. B. Gattico, *Acta selecta caeremonialia sanctae romanae ecclesiae*, vol. 1 (Rome: 1753) as quoted in Günther I: 181 fn. The latter source differs from the former only in the addition of the sentence in brackets [ ].

"Item Summus Pontifex consuevit habere in sua Capella Cantores, et inter eos esse unus, qui vocatur Magister Capellae, ad cujus officium pertinet omnes alios dirigere, et gubernare, quatenus ad servitium dicte Capellae pertinet; qui in singulis diebus praesente, vel absente Domino nostro debent in Capella ad hoc ordinata missam alta voce dicere, et Vesperas cantare, ac etiam Matutinas, se, et quando pro solemnitate festi Dominus noster duxerit eis mandatum.
"Item dictorum Cantorum ultra dictum Magistrum videtur numerus XII. sufficere.
"Item ultra praedictos debent e Clerici, qui vacantur Clerici Capellae, seu Caeremoniarum, et sic in ipsa Capella sunt XV. Personae, qui quidem non consueverunt in Palatio Apostolico, nisi in certis solemnitatibus comedere; sed recipiunt certa stipendia in Libris Camereae contenta, et habent suas mansiones extra Palatium.
"[Item ultra dicta stipendia solet Summus Pontifex vestes omnibus annis dare eisdem.]
"Item inter istos sunt Presbyteri, qui debent alternis septimanis coram Domino nostro Missas dicere."

126.   Long before the period of the Avignon papacy, the commensal chapel had probably been expected to replace the *Schola cantorum* in some of the musical functions when pope and Curia were outside of Rome. See chap. 3, following.

127.   OPKA: 84.

128.   The injunction of 1334 that they receive the *victum mense papalis* supports the claim that Benedict at first sought only to reform the *commensales*. On 30 June 1360, it seems as though the chaplains were still living in a dormitory, as evidenced by the following notice: "... pro reparando unam sarralham et faciendo unam clavem in camera capellanorum dom. nostri pape, de mandato dom. Johannis magistri ejusdem capelle. V s." Anne-Marie Hayez, "Comptes du Palais sous Innocent VI (1352-1362) d'après le registre des Archives." Typescript transcription of documents from the Archivio segreto vaticano. ([Avignon]: [1982?]), p. 227.

129. Jean Favier, *Les Finances pontificales à l'époque du Grand Schisme d'Occident 1378-1409,* fascicle 211 of BEFAR (Paris: 1966), p. 258. Wright: viii. They were also able to supplement their income with earnings from other curial offices. For information concerning the status of two well-beneficed clerics see Jean Favier, "Le niveau de vie d'un collecteur et d'un sous-collecteur apostolique à la fin du XIV$^e$ siècle," *Annales du Midi 75* (1963): 31-48. The collector owned two viols and a lute; the subcollector possessed an *arpa sive guitera.*

130. This information plus much of the following table is based on Guillemain: 370-71.

131. Sherr, "The Papal Chapel." Haberl. Idem, *Wilhelm du Fay,* Bausteine für Musikgeschichte, vol. 1 (Leipzig: Breitkopf & Härtel, 1885).

## Chapter 3

1. Franz X. Haberl, "Die römische *Schola cantorum* and die päpstlichen Kapellsänger bis zur Mitte des 16. Jahrhunderts," *Vierteljahrsschrift für Musikwissenschaft* 3 (1887): 219. Georges Despy, "Note sur les offices de la curie d'Avignon: les fonctions du *magister capelle pape,"* *Bulletin de l'Institut historique belge de Rome* 28 (1953): 21-30. Bernard Guillemain, *La Court pontificale d'Avignon, 1309-1376* (Paris: Editions E. de Boccard, 1966), pp. 363, 366, fnn. Originally published as fascicle 201 of BEFAR, 1962. Ursula Günther, "Zur Biographie einiger Komponisten der Ars subtilior," *Archiv für Musikwissenschaft* 21 (1964): 181-182, fn. (hereafter cited as Günther I). Manfred Schuler, "Zur Geschichte der Kapelle Papst Martins V.," *Archiv für Musikwissenschaft* 25 (1968): 31-32. Bernhard Schimmelpfennig, "Die Organisation der päpstlichen Kapelle in Avignon," *Quellen und Forschungen aus italienischen Archiven und Bibliotheken* 50 (1971): 80-111 (hereafter cited as OPKA).

2. K. H. Schäfer, ed., *Die Ausgaben der apostolischen Kammer unter Benedikt XII., Klemens VI. und Innocenz VI. (1335-1362),* Vatikanische Quellen zur Geschichte des päpstlichen Hof- und Finanzverwaltung 1316-1378, vol. 3 (Paderborn: 1914), p. 44 (hereafter cited as Schäfer II). See the biographical index for complete bibliographies of individual personalities, especially regarding supplications and benefices.

3. Schäfer II: 140.

4. Schäfer II: 166.

5. Schäfer II: 120, fn.

6. Hermann Hoberg, *Die Inventare des päpstlichen Schatzes in Avignon, 1314-1376.* Studi e testi 111 (Vatican City: 1944), p. 103, fn. (hereafter cited as Hoberg).

7. Schäfer II: 204.

8. Schäfer II: 212.

9. Schäfer II: 213.

10. Schäfer II: 245, 302.

11. Schäfer II: 273, 274, 338.

12. Schäfer II: 302, 373, 401, 454.

13. Schäfer II: 252, 426, 434. Hoberg: 103.

14. Schäfer II: 273, 306, 338, 373, 401.

15. Schäfer II: 213.

16.   Schäfer II: 199.

17.   Schäfer II: 302.

18.   Schäfer II: 454. The payment was made on 24 May. The Curia was at Villeneuve from ca.2-
      ca.21 May. The feast of the Ascension was 6 May, Pentecost 16 May, Trinity 23 May.

19.   Schäfer II: 245.

20.   Schäfer II: 401.

21.   Schäfer II: 445.

22.   Hoberg: 153, 156. Schäfer II: 502-3.

23.   Schäfer II: 502-3.

24.   Schäfer: II: 548.

25.   Hoberg: 155, 319, 321, 322.

26.   Hoberg: 216-219.

27.   Franz Ehrle, *Historia bibliothecae romanorum pontificum tum Bonifatianae tum
      Avenionensis* (Rome: 1890), p. 221 (hereafter cited as Ehrle). Auguste Pelzer, *Addenda et
      emendanda ad Francisci Ehrle Historiae bibliothecae romanorum pontificum tum
      Bonifatianae tum Avenionensis* (Rome: 1947), p. 118. Today entry number 21 exists as BMA,
      ms. 203. See also: L.-H. Labande, "Les manuscrits de la Bibliothèque d'Avignon provenant
      de la librairie des papes du XIV$^e$ siècle," *Bulletin historique et philologique* (1894): 56-57.
      L.-H Labande, *Avignon,* vol. 1, Catalogue général des mss. des bibliothèques publiques de
      France, vol. 27. (Paris: 1894), pp. 111-14. M. Andrieu, *Le pontifical romain au moyen âge,*
      vol. 2, Studi e testi 87 (Rome: 1940), pp. 6-13. This manuscript contains extensive rubrics for
      the last three days of Holy Week. On fol. 22v., in the rites for the consecration of a priest,
      when the hands are anointed with oil, the celebrant says: "Consecrare et sanctificare...." A
      note inserted in the margin reads: "hic cantata *Veni creator spiritus.*" The manuscript is
      notated in full for the Mass of the Dedication of a Church, including the consecration of the
      altar stone, fols. 94v.-138v.

28.   Ehrle: 221-23.

29.   For the book lists of the popes of Avignon, see the following: Maurice Faucon, *La librairie
      des papes d'Avignon: sa formation, sa composition, ses catalogues (1316-1420),* fascicles 43
      and 50 of BEFAR (Paris: 1886-1887); Ehrle; Hoberg; Pelzer, *Addenda et emendanda;*
      Anneliese Maier, *Der letzte Katalog der päpstlichen Bibliothek von Avignon (1594)* (Rome:
      Edizioni di storia e letteratura, 1952). Maier, "Der Katalog der päpstlichen Bibliothek in
      Avignon vom Jahr 1411," *Archivum historiae pontificiae* 1 (1963): 97-177. Maier, "Die
      *Bibliotheca minor* Benedikts XIII. (Petrus' de Luna)," *Archivum historiae pontificiae* 3
      (1965): 139-91. Maier, "Ein Leihregister aus der Bibliothek des letzten Avignoner Papstes
      Benedikt XIII. (Petrus de Luna)," *Rivista di storia della Chiesa in Italia* 20 (1966): 309-27.
      Daniel Henry Williman, "The Books of the Avignonese Popes and Clergy: A Repertory and
      Edition of the Book-Notices in the Vatican Archives, 1287-1420" (Ph.D. diss., University of
      Toronto, 1973) (hereafter cited as Williman). Williman, *Records of the Papal Right of Spoil:
      1316-1412* (Paris: Editions du Centre national de la recherche scientifique, 1974)

30.   The devotion of Corpus Christi was encouraged by Pope Clement V in 1314. The feast of the
      Holy Trinity was universally instituted by Pope John XXII in 1334. Several new saints were
      added to the canon: Petrus de Murrone (1313), Louis of Toulouse (1317), Thomas de
      Cantalupe (1320), Thomas Aquinas (1323).

31.   *The Liber Usualis* (Tournai: Desclée, 1961), p. 1 (hereafter cited as *LU*).

32.   The same is probably the case with volumes 33 and 43. The former appears to begin with a collect from the Common of Saints, possibly the Mass for Two or More Martyrs; see *LU:* 1150. I have failed to identify the source of the password for the latter.

33.   Peter Jeffery, "Notre Dame Polyphony in the Library of Pope Boniface VIII," *Journal of the American Musicological Society* 32 (1979): 118-24. Williman is particularly helpful in understanding the nature of book collections. The volumes of Notre Dame polyphony studied by Jeffery probably found their way into the papal book treasure as spoils. It is not surprising that such volumes reached Italy when we consider the particularly French focus of the thirteenth-century papacy. See chap. 1 of this study. For evidence of books of polyphony in the possession of secular princes, see: María del Carmen Gómez Mùtane, *La mùsica en la casa real catalano-aragonesa durante los años 1336-1432,* vol. 1, *Historia y Documentos* (Barcelona: Antoni Bosch, [1977]), p. 198, doc. 223; p. 201, doc. 232; p. 204, doc. 432; p. 207, doc. 252; p. 208, doc. 441. Craig Wright, *Music at the Court of Burgundy 1364-1419* (Henryville, PA: Institute of Mediaeval Music, 1979), pp. 140-49 (hereafter cited as Wright). For evidence of manuscripts of polyphonic music in the possession of singers, see the following: Higini Angès, "Gacian Reyneau am Königshof zu Barcelona in der Zeit von 139. bis 1429," *Studien zur Musikgeschichte, Festschrift für Guido Adler zum 75. Geburtstag* (Vienna: Universal-Edition, 1930), pp. 69-70, and Wright: 74.

34.   Hoberg: 321-322.

35.   Schäfer II: 625-26.

36.   Schäfer II: 673.

37.   Schäfer II: 625-26. The *parcus cantorum* was the "pen" that surrounded the chapel singers. It was an enclosed area which, although level with the floor of the chapel, was probably situated just east of the *cancellus* not unlike the tribune of the later *capella Sistina.*

38.   Schäfer II: 673, 720.

39.   This is especially true in the case of Petrus Sinterii. See: Schäfer II: 159, 203, 234, 265, 390. His position on the lists, first among the *capellani,* agrees with the evidence found for other musical institutions, for example, *primicerius* (first on the wax-coated tablets) of the *Schola cantorum,* Haberl: 205-11; and *premier chapellain* of the Burgundian chapel, Wright: 74-77.

40.   K. H. Schäfer, ed., *Die Ausgaben der apostolichen Kammer unter Johann XXII., nebst den Jahresbilanzen von 1316-1375,* Vatikanische Quellen zur Geschichte des päpstlichen Hof- und Finanzverwaltung 1316-1378, vol. 2 (Paderborn: 1912), p. 29. H. Hoberg, ed., *Die Einnahmen der apostolichen Kammer unter Innocenz VI.,* vol. 1, *Die Einnahmen register des päpstlichen Thesaurars,* Vatikanische Quellen zur Geschichte des päpstlichen Hof- und Finanzverwaltung 1316-1378, vol. 7 (Paderborn: 1955), pp. 179-80.

41.   Schäfer II: 674-75. Hoberg: 360, 373, 389, 390, 392.

42.   K. H. Schäfer, ed., *Die Ausgaben der apostolischen Kammer unter den Papsten Urban V. und Gregor XI., (1362-1378),* Vatikanische Quellen zur Geschichte des päpstlichen Hof- und Finanzverwaltung 1316-1378, vol. 6 (Paderborn: 1937), p. 28 (hereafter cited as Schäfer III).

43.   Schäfer III: 112.

44.   Schäfer III: 156.

45.   Schäfer III: 182.

46.   Schäfer III: 183.

47.  Johann Peter Kirsch, *Die Ruckkehr der Päpste Urban V. und Gregor XI. von Avignon nach Rom, Auszüge aus den Kameralregistern des vatikanischen Archivs,* Quellen und Forschungen herausgegeben von der Görresgesellschaft, vol. 6 (Paderborn: 1898), pp. 12-13 (hereafter cited as Kirsch).

48.  Kirsch: 24, 45.

49.  Schäfer III: 242.

50.  Schäfer II: 625.

51.  Schäfer III: 243.

52.  Kirsch: 95-96.

53.  Kirsch: 143.

54.  Schäfer III: 367.

55.  Though the master of the chapel was usually responsible for the books of the chapel and for the transportation of the trappings of the chapel, sometimes the tasks were undertaken by others. For example, on 25 May 1369, Petrus de Arsenxis de Appamiis, the *socius* of the pope's *confessor,* Bishop Raimond Dacon of Fréjus, was paid for renting "15 asinorum, qui portaverunt res et libros capelle" from Montefiascone to Rome. Evidently, the amount of material needed for even a short vacation was quite substantial. Petrus was an Augustinian hermit. As *socius,* he was in charge of cleaning the chapel, reparations made on paraments, and transport of the chapel of Urban. His successor was Petrus Amelii de Brenac, also an Augustinian hermit, who helped perform much the same tasks when Gregory XI returned to Rome. The *confessor* and *socius* functioned much like the *magister* in this respect during the pontificates of Urban and Gregory. The *socius* later came to be called *sacrista.* The offices of *magister palatii, magister capelle,* and *sacrista* were united in the person of Bartholomaeus Antonii under the Roman Pope, Martin V, in 1418. Schäfer III: 248. OPKA: 100-2, 105. Haberl: 219.

56.  Williman: 623.

57.  Williman: abstract, 106-7.

58.  Hoberg: 472.

59.  Ehrle: 269-70. Williman: 631 ff.

60.  Frank Ll. Harrison, *Music in Medieval Britain,* 4th ed. (Buren, The Netherlands: Frits Knuf, 1980), pp. 77-81.

61.  Leslie A. St. L. Toke, "Little Office of Our Lady," *CE,* vol. 9, p. 294.

62.  Schäfer III: 488, 541, 603, 622, 623.

63.  Schäfer III: 672.

64.  Kirsch: 178, 181, 191.

65.  Williman: 668-69.

66.  Jean Favier, *Les Finances pontificules à l'époque du Grand Schisme d'Occident 1378-1409,* fascicle 211 of BEFAR (Paris: 1966), pp. 84-85.

67.  Günther I: 180.

68.  OPKA: 106.

69. Günther I: 187, fn.

70. Günther I: 186-187.

71. Günther I: 186.

72. Günther I: 187, fn.

73. Günther I: 188.

74. Günther I: 189. Schäfer II: 44.

75. Wright: 77.

76. Manfred Schuler. "Die Musik in Konstanz während des Konzils 1414-1418," *Analecta Musicologica* 38 (1966): 155.

77. Favier, *Les Finances,* p. 258. Wright: viii. With an écu equaling approximately 18 solidi, 6 denarii, or a total of 222 denarii, and the wage of a chaplain being about 80 denarii per day, 2,000 écus is the equivalent of 15 years, 2 months, and 14 days wages.

78. Frater Antonius, however, who served Benedict XII for 42 days in 1334/35, did eventually rise to the see of Lombez. At the cathedral of Apt, the office of provost is directly beneath that of bishop. Richardus also received remuneration for his duties as *scriptor.*

79. ADV, Apt, Etude Pondicq: ms. 100, fol. 120. "... Nicholas de Hubantus, litterarum apostolicarum scriptor, et Johannes Haubaut, canonicus Ebredunensis, exequitores et exequitorio nomini ultimi testamenti domini Ricardi de Bozonvilla quondam prepositi Aptensis ... dictum quondam dominum prepositum in suo ultimo testamento legasse ecclesie Aptensis pro anniversaria una, duobus aut pluribus, centum viginti quinque florinas currentes quas realiter deposuerunt de voluntate dominorum in facere anniversariam, tercia anniversaria cum vigiliis et nonam lectionibus mortuorum: unum, videlicet, 29 januarii, aliud 29 maii, aliud 29 septembris pro animabus dicti prepositi ... et benefactorum suorum executorum predictarum."

80. Professor Schimmelpfennig has informed me that the date of the document which bears Gerardus's name is 26 July 1429. Also see OPKA: 107, fn.

81. Despy, "Note sur les offices" has the most limited view of the *magister capelle pape,* and, unfortunately, has colored most of the scholarship including that of Guillemain. Schuler's "Die Musik in Konstanz" and "Zur Geschichte der Kapelle Papst Martins" deal with a later period in the history of the papal chapels, when indeed the office was held by men of higher standing, whence his conclusions. Nino Pirrotta, "Music and Cultural Tendencies in 15th-Century Italy," *Journal of the American Musicological Society* 19 (1966): 132-33, misconstrues the findings of Guillemain, which influences his conclusions about the *premier chapellain* of the dukes of Burgundy. Wright: 74-76 hints that the *premier chapellain* of the Burgundian chapel might have participated in the divine service, but he builds a case for the office being essentially nonmusical. The appelation *conseiller* as bestowed on Jacques de Templeuve ca.1425 might have been in recognition of his years of service in the ducal chapel rather than an indication of a clarification of his duties as *premier chapellain.* Wright: 76, fn. Even so, a direct correspondence may not necessarily exist between the chapel of the popes of Avignon and those of the dukes of Burgundy and pontiffs of Rome, nor between the leaders of said chapels.

82. Haberl and Günther I have argued for the musical functions of the post. David Fallows, in his review of Craig Wright. *Music at the Court of Burgundy, 1364-1419,* published in the *Journal of the American Musicological Society* 34 (1981): 550, argues for a more musical *premier*

*chapellain* at the court of Burgundy than does Wright. Michel de Fontaine, first chaplain of the French royal chapel in 1378, was responsible for copying at least some of the pieces of polyphonic music into the ms. Trémoïlle; see Wright: 148.

83.   Many of the singers of the papal chapel were able to sell their services at various secular courts. Johannes Cossardi was *precentor capelle* for Queen Eleanor of Aragon. Johannes Carnoten worked for the kings of France before his brief service to the pope. He went on to become *premier chapellain* of Duke Philip the Bold. See the biographical index.

84.   Wright: 74, fn.

85.   Bernhard Schimmelpfennig, *Die Zeremonienbücher der römischen Kurie im Mittelalter*, Bibliothek des Deutschen historischen Instituts in Rom, vol. 40 (Tübingen: 1973), pp. 126-31, 292-337 (hereafter cited as *ZKM*).

86.   *ZKM:* 298-300, XCVII. If there is a king present, he likewise was to receive a candle from the hand of the pope. This probably applied to other nobles as well. The ceremony took place in the south vestry of the papal palace while the curia was in Avignon.

87.   *LU:* 1357-58.

88.   *LU:* 1359-60.

89.   *ZKM:* 300-1. This is probably a variant of the antiphon *Juxta vestibulum et altare*. See *LU:* 523, 524. Karl Marbach, ed., *Carmina Scriptuarum* (Strasbourg: 1907), p. 360 gives the text as "Inter vestibulum, et altare plorabunt Sacerdotes ministri Domini, et dicent: Parce Domine, parce populo tuo: (et ne claudas ora canentium te, Domine.)" Joel 2:17, (Esther 13:17).

90.   The description of the ceremony as having taken place in a church indicates that the passage was written after Benedict XIII left Avignon and no longer could avail himself of the chapels of the papal palace.

91.   *LU:* 586, 590.

92.   *ZKM:* 312. *LU:* 884, 236.

93.   *LU:* 878.

94.   *ZKM:* 248, XLVII$_1$. Another oddity is that the Vespers hymn, *Veni creator spiritus,* is sung at Terce.

95.   *ZKM:* 259-60. *LU:* 523.

96.   *ZKM:* 239, XL[25]. "Post hec, cum dominus papa pervenerit ad sedem mense, completa benedictione mense subdiaconus dicit alta voce: *Iube, domine, benedicere.* Et recepta benedictione, vadit ad dextram partem pape in loco apto ad hoc. Et ibi sedens statim, postquam ministri ceperint fercula domino pape apponere, incipit legere vel legendam vel ystoriam vel omeliam diei illius vel festi vel aliud, si placuerit pape. Et debet legere distincte et tractim convenienter in modum lectionis nocturne. Et debet semper legere, dum pape est in mensa, excepto quando papa bibit. Potest etiam tunc durante prandio duas vel tres pausas facere congruentes. Et dominus papa consuevit semel vel bis de suis incisoriis ipsum subdiaconum exenniare."

97.   *ZKM:* 246, XLV. "... Et deinde subdiaconus incipit primam antiphonam coram eo et dominus papa reincipit dictam antiphonam."

98.   Stephen J. P. van Dijk and Joan Hazelden Walker, *The Ordinal of the Papal Court from Innocent III to Boniface VIII and Related Documents.* Spicilegium Friburgense, vol. 22

(Fribourg, 1975), pp. 550-51, 553. Marc Dykmans, *Le cérémonial papal de la fin du moyen âge à la Renaissance*, vol. 1, *Le cérémonial papal du XIII^e siècle* (Brussels: Institut historique belge de Rome, 1977), p. 99.

99. From the writings of Uguicio Borromeo de Vercelli: "Et notandum est etiam, quod subdiaconus, qui servivit una septimana de missa, in sequenti septimana debet servire de mitra...." *ZKM:* 239, XL$_{27}$.

100. By August 1397, Boniface IX, the Roman pope, had the abbot of Santa Maria de Rivaldis serving as his *magister*. Haberl: 219. By the late fourteenth century, the offices of *confessor* and *socius* (*sacrista*) at Avignon were held by bishops. OPKA: 101-2. The merger of the office of sacristan and *magister* under the Roman pope Martin V in 1418 without any doubt affected the status of the master of the chapel. Schuler, "Zur Geschichte der Kapelle Papst Martins," p. 31.

101. Richardus de Bozonvilla.

**Chapter 4**

1. This idea is explored at length in Johan Huizinga's classic, *The Waning of the Middle Ages* (New York: Doubleday, 1954).

2. Frank Ll. Harrison, "Music and Cult: The Functions of Music in Social and Religious Systems," in *Perspectives in Musicology* (New York: W. W. Norton, 1972), pp. 307-34. This article underscores the ceremonial as a document of potential use to musicologists.

3. Michel Andrieu, *Les Ordines romani du haut Moyen Age*, vol. 1 (Louvain: 1931), p. vii.

4. J. Baudet, "Cérémonial," *Dictionnaire d'archéologie chrétienne et de liturgie*, vol. 2, part 2 (Paris: 1910), col. 3296.

5. Marc Dykmans, *Le cérémonial papal de la fin du moyen âge à la Renaissance*, vol. 1, *Le cérémonial papal du XIII^e siècle* (Brussels: Institut historique belge de Rome, 1977), p. 7.

6. Andrieu, *Les Ordines*, p. 31.

7. Baudet, "Cérémonial," col. 3296.

8. Andrieu, *Les Ordines*, p. vi. S.J.P. van Dijk and Joan Hazelden Walker, *The Origins of the Modern Roman Liturgy* (Westminster, MD: 1960), pp. 67-75 (hereafter cited as *OMRL*).

9. *OMRL:* 81.

10. J.-P. Migne, ed., *Wilbertus, Vita S. Leonis papae*, Patrologia Latina, vol. 153 (Paris: 1854), col. 501 A-502 A.

11. *OMRL:* 81. Reinhard Elze, "Das *Sacrum Palatium Lateranense* im 10. und 11. Jahrhundert," *Studi Gregoriani* 4 (1952): 36. J.-P. Migne, ed., *Johannes XIII papa, Epistolae et decreta*, Patrologia Latina, vol. 135 (Paris: 1849), col. 982 B-C.

12. *OMRL:* 81. Elze, "Das *Sacrum Palatium*," p. 36. J.-P. Migne, ed., *Johannes XIX papa, Epistolae et diplomata*, Patrologia Latina, vol. 141 (Paris: 1853), col. 1135 A. Johannes Baptist Sägmüller, "Cardinal," *CE*, vol. 3, p. 335. In the eleventh century the bishop of Silva Candida was among the cardinal bishops. In the twelfth century, by then called Santa Rufina, this bishopric was united to that of Porto.

13. *OMRL:* 81.

14. *OMRL:* 74. Helmut Hucke, "Toward a New Historical View of Gregorian Chant," *Journal of the American Musicological Society* 33 (1980): 464-67.

15. *OMRL:* 84. Pierre Batiffol, *History of the Roman Breviary,* Atwell, M. Y. Baylay, trans. (London: Longmans, Green, and Co., 1912), p. 121.

16. Bernhard Schimmelpfennig, *Die Zeremonienbücher der römischen Kirche im Mittelalter,* Bibliothek des Deutschen historischen Instituts in Rom, vol. 40 (Tübingen: 1973), p. 4 (hereafter cited as *ZKM*).

17. Paul Fabre and L. Duchesne, eds., *Le Liber censuum de l'église romaine,* BEFAR, 2nd series, vol. 6, 6 (Rome: 1910), vol. 2, p. 144, col. 1, lines 5-7.

18. Fabre and Duchesne, *Le Liber,* p. 151, fn. 1.

19. *ZKM:* 16. Philippe Lauer, in citing a letter of Pope John XV (985-996), notes that the terms *Palatium Lateranense* and *Ecclesia romana* were used synonymously. *Le Palais de Latran* (Paris: 1911), p. 144.

20. Etienne Baluze, *Vitae paparum avinionensium,* Guillaume Mollat, ed., vol. 1 (Paris: 1914), pp. 230, 233.

21. Dykmans, *Le cérémonial,* p. 8.

22. *OMRL:* 11. Stephen J. P. van Dijk and Joan Hazelden Walker, *The Ordinal of the Papal Court from Innocent III to Boniface VIII and Related Documents.* Spicilegium Friburgense, vol. 22 (Fribourg, 1975).

23. S. J. P. van Dijk, "Medieval Terminology and Methods of Psalm Singing." *Musica Disciplina* 6 (1952): 16. S. A. van Dijk, "Historical Liturgy and Liturgical History," *Dominican Studies* 2 (1949): 180. *OMRL:* 25.

24. S. J. P. van Dijk, *Sources of the Modern Roman Liturgy,* vol. 1 (Leiden: E. J. Brill, 1963), p. 41.

25. Van Dijk, *Sources,* p. 41. *OMRL:* 294. It was probably at Assisi's cathedral where Francis first encountered Roman practice, it having been adopted by the canons.

26. E. Martene, *Thesaurus novus anecdotorum,* vol. 4 (Paris: 1717), cols. 557 E-558 C.

27. *ZKM:* 139.

28. Michael Ott, "Giacomo Gaetani Stefaneschi," *CE,* vol. 14, p. 284.

29. *ZKM:* 40-62; Edition, *ZKM:* 148-224.

30. *ZKM:* 62-100; Edition, J.-P. Migne, ed., *Ordo romanus XIV,* Patrologia Latina, vol. 78 (Paris: 1862), cols. 1121 D-1274 B.

31. *ZKM:* 107-17. Edition, J.-P. Migne, ed., *Ordo romanus XV,* Patrologia Latina, vol. 78 (Paris: 1862), cols. 1273 D-1368 B.

32. *ZKM:* 101-6. Edition, *ZKM:* 245-91.

33. *ZKM:* 120-126. Edition, Ludovico Muratori, ed., *Rerum italicarum scriptores,* vol. 3, pt. 2 (Milan: 1734), cols. 777-808 (hereafter cited as *RIS*).

34. *ZKM:* 126-31. Edition, *ZKM:* 292-337.

35. The most striking example recorded in the ceremonials notes the singing of the *Gloria in excelsis Deo* by the celebrants on All Souls' Day during the *missa pro defunctis. RIS:* 793 E.

36.    Van Dijk, *Sources,* p. 60.

37.    *ZKM:* 242, XLIII$_4$; 315-16, CXXV$_{2-3}$; 330-31, CXXX$_2$ *RIS:* 792 A, 793 D.

38.    Josef A. Jungmann, *The Mass of the Roman Rite,* vol. 1 (New York: Benziger Brothers, 1951), pp. 228-29.

39.    *RIS:* 786 C, 787 E, 790 C.

40.    *ZKM:* 302, CI$_1$; 304, CVIII; 315, CXXV$_2$; 300, XCVIII$_2$; 301, C$_1$; 314, CXXIII$_1$; and fn. 39 above.

41.    *ZKM:* 330-31, CXXX$_2$.

42.    *RIS:* 787 A. See the biographical index, "Johannes Boulette."

43.    *ZKM:* 287-88, LXXIV$_1$.

44.    *ZKM:* 288, LXXIV$_{2-5}$. For a clarification and a discussion of the history of the various ranks of the cardinalate, see: Johannes Baptist Sägmüller, "Cardinal," *CE,* vol. 3, pp. 333-41.

45.    *ZKM:* 248-53, XLVII.

46.    *RIS:* 777 B-D, 778 D, 779 B, 780, 782 C, 783 D, 785 E, 798, 799 D-E, 802 D-E, 803 C, 803 E, 804 E. Cf. *Ordo romanus XIV:* 1222 C-1224 D; Richard Jonathan Sherr, "The Papal Chapel ca. 1492-1513 and Its Polyphonic Sources" (Ph.D. diss., Princeton University, 1975), pp. 90-91 (hereafter cited as Sherr).

47.    *ZKM:* 152, IV$_2$.

48.    The subdeacon also aided the Holy Father in the recitation of these three movements plus the Agnus. The cardinal bishop or priest who acted as the principal chaplain of the pope also approached and joined in saying the Agnus. *ZKM:* 253-254, XLVII; *Ordo romanus XIV:* 1174 C.

49.    At Avignon, the large oratories were the Chapels of Saint John and Saint Peter.

50.    *RIS:* 777 C-778 A.

51.    *RIS:* 785 C, 786 C.

52.    *RIS:* 782 D, 784 C.

53.    *RIS:* 781 B-C.

54.    *RIS:* See the biographical index, "Johannes Ruffi de Roquinies."

55.    *RIS:* 784 E-785 A.

56.    *ZKM:* 332, CXXXI.

57.    *RIS:* 787 C, Monday, 28 June 1406: before boarding the galley; 789 B, Monday, 19 July: before leaving Finale; 791 B, Thursday, 29 August: before leaving for Nice. The ceremonial does not specify whether or not these services were *cum nota.* The second of these three Masses was at the Dominican church and was probably sung.

58.    *ZKM:* 186, XVII, for King Edward I of England (1307); 282, LXIX, mass for the dead said *coram papa;* 288-89, LXXV, for King Edward III of England (1377); 298, XCV, for deceased pontiffs (said each year, 314-15, CXXIV); *RIS:* 790 E, funeral procession for the Cardinal of Pamplona (1406); 791 A, exequies for the same cardinal (1406); 800 A, Mass for deceased pontiffs; 802 B, Requiem for the King of Castile (1407); 802 C, Requiem for the Queen of Aragon (1407).

59. *RIS:* 799 B.

60. *RIS:* 787 E, 790 C.

61. *RIS:* 792 A. There is some indication that Mass may have been customarily said in front of the pope on ferial days; *Ordo romanus XIV:* 1251. Dykmans, *De Rome en Avignon,* p. 468.

62. *RIS:* 778 A-B, 786 C, 799 B, 801 E, 802 B, 803 D; 785 C, 788 A, 790 C, 792 A, 792 B, 793 D, 797 B, 800 A, 805 A.

63. *RIS:* 778 A.

64. *RIS:* 781 B, 782 D.

65. *RIS:* 822 A.

66. *ZKM:* 263, LIV$_8$; 274, LXIV$_{18}$; 307, CXI$_8$; 309, CXI$_{14}$, fn.; 308, CXI$_{17}$.

67. *ZKM:* 214, XXXIV$_4$; 276, LXVI$_3$.

68. *ZKM:* 278, LXVII$_{2-3}$; 282, LXVIII$_2$; 310, CXII$_5$. Vigil of Pentecost, 312, CXV$_2$.

69. *ZKM:* 279, LXVII$_4$; 282, LXVIII.

70. At second vespers of All Saints' Day, the singers responded *Requiescant in pace* in *alta voce* at the end of the prayer. *ZKM:* 314, CXXII$_3$.

71. *ZKM:* 278, LXVI$_{8-9}$. The office of *clericus capelle* was suppressed during the later years of Pope Gregory's reign. This is true for the commensal chaplains as well.

72. *ZKM:* 281, LXVIII$_1$.

73. *ZKM:* 311, CXIII$_8$; 312, CXVI$_7$.

74. *ZKM:* 315, CXXV$_1$.

75. *ZKM:* 285-86, LXXII$_{5-6}$.

76. *ZKM:* 295, LXXXIII$_4$. Lauds was done between the Masses of Midnight and Dawn.

77. *ZKM:* 305, CIX$_2$. This service no doubt immediately followed Matins.

78. *ZKM:* 280, LXVII$_9$; 282, LXVIII$_2$.

79. *ZKM:* 236, XL$_2$; 248, XLVII$_1$. During the twelfth century, an office was celebrated at the hour of Prime on Good Friday and Easter. Dykmans. *De Rome en Avignon,* pp. 386, 397.

80. *ZKM:* L$_9$; 300, XCVII$_{12}$.

81. *ZKM:* 304, CVI$_2$; 296, LXXXV$_2$.

82. *ZKM:* 198, XXVI$_2$.

83. *ZKM:* 154, VIa$_1$; 156, VIb$_1$; 160, VIII$_{11}$, 218-20, XXXVIIa$_{3-4}$; 222, XXXVIIIa$_2$; 316, CXXVI$_4$.

84. *ZKM:* 149, II$_2$; 263, LIV$_5$. The Mass of the Holy Chrism occurs within the first year after the election of a new pontiff. *Ordo romanus XV:* 1306 B.

85. *ZKM:* 214, XXXIV$_5$. After the popes left Avignon, the service was probably held in a church. 310, CXIII$_1$.

86. *ZKM:* 239, XL$_{24}$; 241, XLI$_{10}$.

87. *ZKM:* 156, VIa$_8$; 158, VIb$_{11}$; 160, VIII$_{11}$; 195, XXIV$_5$; 306, CXI$_2$; 309, CXII$_3$. Benedict might have once recited the hour in a sacristy. *RIS:* 780 A.

88. *ZKM:* 247, XLVI$_2$; 312, CXVI$_2$; 335, CXXXV$_3$.

89. *RIS:* 783 E. By *Versus* Conzié may mean either the short responsory or the versicle.

90. *ZKM:* 248, XLVI$_4$; 312, CXVI$_2$.

91. In 1406, Matins of Christmas was performed in Saint-Victor of Marseille, *RIS:* 798 A; *ZKM:* 256, XLIX$_{2-5}$; 285-86, LXXII; 294-95, LXXXII$_7$. Such may have been the case in 1343. De Loÿe, "Réception," p. 352.

92. *ZKM:* 305, CIX; 306, CX$_{12}$.

93. *RIS:* 778 C-D, 779 E; *ZKM:* 309, CXI$_{23}$; 310, CXII$_{11}$.

94. *RIS:* 783 C, 780 D; *ZKM:* 312, CXV$_5$; 335, CXXXV$_5$; 313, CXVIII$_2$; 313, CXX; 314, CXXII$_1$.

95. Matins may possibly have been performed within the octave as well. *ZKM:* 248, XLVI$_4$. Also see *Ordo romanus XV:* 1337-1338 C and Sherr: 89.

96. *ZKM:* 245, XLIV$_1$; Sherr: 90.

97. *ZKM:* 246-47, XLV$_{2-8}$; 248, XLVI$_4$.

98. Such was the case at Terce of Pentecost, and at Matins and Lauds of Christmas.

99. *RIS:* 797 E, 798 C. *ZKM:* 294, LXXXI; 296, LXXXVI.

100. *RIS:* 799 D. *ZKM:* 297, XCII; 298, XCVI$_2$.

101. *ZKM:* 302, CIII.

102. *ZKM:* 312, CXV$_4$; 312, CXVI$_6$; 335, CXXXV$_5$; 313, CXVII; on the day it is further specified as *cum nota,* 313, CXX; 313, CXXI$_3$.

103. *ZKM:* 297, XC; 297, XCII$_1$.

104. *ZKM:* 302, CIII$_1$; 302-3, CIV$_{1,4}$; 313, CXVIII$_{1,4}$.

105. *ZKM:* 313, CXIX.

106. *ZKM:* 297, LXXXVII$_5$; 297, LXXXVIII$_2$.

107. *RIS:* 777 A-C. "To begin the hour" means to intone the *Deus in adiutorium.*

108. *RIS:* 783 A-C; 784 A-B. Both may have been performed *alternatim.*

109. *RIS:* 787 E. "... propter toedium multorum absentium Cantorum non fuerunt Vesperae Papales, nec aliae solemnitates servatae, quae illa die fieri solent." Neither was Vespers held if there was an insufficient number of cardinals present, *RIS:* 793 C-D.

110. *RIS:* 798 E-799 C. "... nisi [Vesperae] solitae dici per Cantores diebus aliis communibus."

111. *ZKM:* 152, III$_{11}$; 265-66, LVI$_2$; 266, LVII$_3$. *Ordo romanus XV:* 1311 D-1312 A.

112. *RIS:* 778 D-779 A. *ZKM:* 306, CX$_{11}$.

113. Cf. *The Liber Usualis* (Tournai: Desclée, 1961), pp. 671-76.

114. *ZKM:* 284-85, LXXI$_5$; 275, LXIV$_{22}$. *RIS:* 779 E, Conzié only specifies that in 1406 Benedict heard Vespers.

115. Vespers was performed after the Easter Vigil, on Easter day, probably on the Monday, Tuesday, and Saturday that followed. *ZKM:* 310, CXII$_{10}$; 311, CXIII$_7$; *RIS:* 802 E. *ZKM:*

374; 334, CXXXIV₇. The hours of Matins and Vespers may have been celebrated throughout the entire octave, though solely by the singers, 248, XLVI₄.

116. This is in agreement with the second law of comparative liturgy propounded by Anton Baumstark: "... les états anciens se maintiennent avec plus de ténacité dans les temps les plus sacrés de l'année liturgique." *Liturgie comparée,* 3rd edition (Chevetogne, Belgium: Editions de Chevetogne, 1953), p. 30. As it applies to musical practice, we see it manifested in the forms of chants, for example, vestigial verses (Communion of the Requiem Mass, tracts), processional antiphons (entry and communion of Holy Thursday), readings and responds (lections and canticles for the Paschal vigil, Ember Saturday), etc., which ordinarily have fallen away. This principle may be applied to the manner of execution of these chants as well, that is, as regards not only personnel but also likelihood and style of polyphonic settings. We might here propose a musicological corollary to the above law: New treatments of liturgical music make their first incursions during times of least solemnity and on feasts most recently added. In the papal chapel at Avignon, experimental treatments of liturgical music must have been performed on ferial days and lesser feasts, when the singers celebrated their own private service and for which we have no description in the *Ordo romanus.* Cf. Sherr: 92, 101. The feasts of Trinity and Corpus Christi might have been those of the *Temporale* that were most susceptible to innovation since they were recent additions to the calendar.

117. *ZKM:* 302, CII₁. "Sciendum quod a dominica in passione inclusive usque ad pascha, quando agitur de tempore, non discantatur officium preter *Kirie, Credo, Sanctus* et *Agnus,* excepto die Iovis cene, in quo totum officium discantatur." According to the ceremonials of the Roman Curia, the *Ite missa est* was to be sung by one man: the cleric who functioned in the office of deacon. The response, *Deo gratias,* was choral. The Ite could only have been monophonic during a solemn pontifical Mass or during a *missa coram papa.* Extant polyphonic settings of the Ite may reflect a usage which is not in agreement with that of the Roman Curia or may have been sung at private liturgies, especially at Masses celebrated by the singers without the presence of the pontiff. *ZKM:* 151, III₁₁; 229, XXXVIIIb₂₀; 251, XLVII₃₂; 255, XLVIII₁₆; 265, LVI₂; 280, LXVII₁₀; 282, LXVIII₂; 310, CXII₁₀. One early ceremonial assigns the Ite to the celebrant. *ZKM:* 240, XLI₁₀.

118. *ZKM:* 301, XCIX. "Sciendum est, quod a dominica in septuagesima inclusive usque ad pascha, quando agitur de tempore, non debent pulsare organa in capella pape, die Iovis in cena domini excepto."

119. *ZKM:* 128. Cf. Sherr: 97-98.

120. See the biographical index, "Raymundus Arnulphi."

121. See the biographical index, "Johannes Fabri."

122. Konrad Eubel, "Aus den Ausgabüchern der Schismapäpste Klemens VII. und Benedikt XIII.," *Römische Quartalschrift für Altertumskunde und für Kirchengeschichte* 18 (1904): 339-40.

123. Sherr: 79, 116.

124. *ZKM:* 36-38. Bernhard Schimmelpfennig, "Die Funktion des Papstpalastes und der kurial Gesellschaft im päpstlichen Zeremoniell vor und während des grossen Schismas," in *Avignon: Genèse et débuts du Grand Schisme d'Occident,* Colloques internationaux du Centre national de la recherche scientifique, no. 586 (Paris: 1980), pp. 317-28. His personal liturgy was carried out in the smaller *capelle secrete* such as the Chapel of Saint-Michel. For the first four Sundays of Lent 1406, Conzié records that the pontiff once again made the stations. *RIS:* 777 C-D.

125. *ZKM:* 262, LIII$_3$; 304, CVI$_1$; 332, CXXII.

126. *ZKM:* 258, L; 299, XCVII$_8$. Also see *RIS:* 800 B.

127. See chap. 1 of the present study, *passim.*

128. *ZKM:* 330, CXXIX$_2$.

129. For more information on processions see: Marc Dykmans, "D'Avignon à Rome: Martin V et le cortège apostolique," *Bulletin de l'Institut historique belge* (1968): 203-309, especially 292-93. *ZKM:* 338-49, especially paragraph 43. *RIS:* 808 C-810 C.

130. See pp. 72, 98-99 of the present study.

131. *RIS:* 802 E, 814 D. *ZKM:* 152, III$_{13}$; 267-270, LVIII-LXIII.

132. *ZKM:* 246, XLIV$_2$. Also see de Loÿe, "Réception," p. 346.

133. It was done on Laetare Sunday after the procession with the golden rose. *ZKM:* 261, LII$_6$.

134. *ZKM:* 323, CXXVII$_{8-9}$.

135. *ZKM:* 329-30, CXXVII$_{34}$. This occasion may have necessitated the hiring of additional singers.

136. *ZKM:* 330, CXXIX$_4$.

137. *RIS:* 785 A.

138. *RIS:* 788 B-C.

139. *RIS:* 786 C, 788 A, 797 E.

140. *RIS:* 799 E.

141. *RIS:* 805 A.

142. *RIS:* 783 A.

143. Anthony M. Cummings, "Toward an Interpretation of the Sixteenth-Century Motet," *Journal of the American Musicological Society* 34 (1981): 45-46, fnn. Sherr: 117-19.

144. It is worth noting that the account of the dinner given for Clement VI in 1343 claims that the clerics sang after the meal (ninth course) was finished.

145. See the biographical index, "Matheus Petri." See also the biographies "Jacobus Raymundi" and "Robertus Creque."

## Chapter 5

1. Joseph Sautel, "Apt," *Dictionnaire d'histoire et de géographie ecclésiastique,* vol. 3 (Paris: 1924), col. 1086.

2. Fernand Sauve, *Histoire d'Apt* (1903; reprint ed., Rognes: Editions Provence, [1980]), p. 66 (hereafter cited as Sauve).

3. BMA, ms. 1780: "Histoire ecclésiastique de la ville et du diocèse d'Apt par M. d[e] R[emerville] S[aint]-Q[uentin]," copy of Edouard Cartier (Apt: 1844), p. 425 (hereafter cited as Remerville). This pope had a hand in the internal affairs of the chapter. Discipline had fallen into such disrepair that, in 1372, he sent Jean Sabathery to reform the institution. Sauve: 66.

4.  BMA, ms. 1781: "Fragmens de l'histoire d'Apt pouvant servir de supplément à l'histoire civile et religieuse de la ville d'Apt de M. de Remerville," copy of Edouard Cartier ([n.p.]: 1871), p. 24. " . . . Les chanoines qui ont d'ordinaire été ignorans au chant, non contens d'avoir volu obliger les prébendés au plain-chant ont encore voulu per une témérité extraordinaire les obliger à la musique comme à Aix, parceque de tout temps il y a eu des prébendés fameux musiciens qui ont fait la gloire du chaptre d'Apt, ci-cause de cette bonté des prébendés qui ne sont jamais épargnées pour le servire et la gloire Dieu, les chanoines en ont voulu faire un[e] obligation, comme appert par leur demande de 1638."

5.  Remerville: 425.

6.  Remerville: 425-26.

7.  Sauve: 86. E.-V. Rose, *Etudes historiques et religieuses sur le XIVᵉ siècle, ou Tableau de l'Eglise d'Apt sous la cour papale d'Avignon* (Avignon: Aubanel, 1842), pp. 526-29 (hereafter cited as Rose).

8.  The Holy Father arrived in October 1365 and was probably accompanied by his usual entourage, including the *cantores*. Urban resided either in the house of Raybaud Beisson or with Jehan de Laudun. Remerville: 322-23. For conflicting evidence see: Bibliothèque municipale de Carpentras (hereafter cited as BMC), ms. 1958, *Histoire d'Apt* by Abbé Boze (Apt: Trémollière, 1813) with critical remarks added by Abbé Giffon, p. 206. Much of the documentation for the fourteenth century has been either lost or destroyed, and what has been preserved has often come down in seventeenth-, eighteenth-, and nineteenth-century histories, some of which exaggerate and others of which do worse. For a discussion of the problem and the relative merits of the sources, see: Sauve; J. de Font-Réaulx, "Les Sources de l'histoire d'Apt," *Provence historique* 18 (1968): 329-35; Augustin Roux, *La cathédrale d'Apt d'après des documents inédits* (Apt: Reboulin, 1949); ADV, Usuel 26, Michel Hayez, "Notaires d'Apt, Etude Pondicq," typescript catalogue and analysis of existing records. Avignon: September 1969-May 1970.

9.  Rose: 267, 528-29.

10. The king of Provence either went or was supposed to go to Apt in 1373 since they prepared a bed for him and made other necessary arrangements. BMC, ms. 1958, p. 207: "A xxviii de Jenoyer (1377) . . . Item que paguat als menestries de Mossen lo Senescal cant venc de Lombardia . . . s. viiii." The entries of all these nobles were surely the occasions for public display.

11. Rose: 499.

12. BMC, ms. 1668, *Recueil formé par abbé Rose,* fols. 24, 40-43, 45. Rose: 537-539. Sauve: 87.

13. Rose: 389-91. Rose claimed that trumpets and other instruments accompanied the papal procession to the church. After the bull of canonization was read, church bells were sounded and an organ was played. Rose's accuracy is questionable, however.

14. BMC, ms. 1958, pp. 212-15.

15. Remerville: 309-10.

16. BMC, ms. 1654, *Recueil concernant l'histoire religieuse d'Apt, formé par Grossi, prieur de Lioux,* fols. 153v.-154: (1375) "Item a xxiiii de setembre pausa aver pagat a Antoni Faraut per la festa que fes quant acompanhet la prosesion de sant Castre . . . s. ii, d. viii. Item a vi d'octobre a Guilhem Giraut, caratier, per la corda de lautes que fes far ad Avinhon que peza iii quintals. (Costa lo quintal iii flor) . . . flor x. Item a Juan Simonnet an sos companhons per la

festa que feron a sant Alzias ... s. viii. ... (x octobre) Item a Sauveta del Sanze per ii libras emieia de siera que si gastet cant acompanheron lo cap de sant Elzias lo jort de sant Hospici ... s. vi, d. viii." Nothing in the documents stipulates that Juan Simonnet or Antoni Faraut were musicians. Jehan Simoneau and his companions were also paid in 1373 at the exhumation performed "per la festa che feroun a Sant Aulzias." Rose: 647. BMC, ms. 1651, *Recueil intitulé: "Notes de M. l'abbé Giffon sur l'histoire religieuse d'Apt, colligés et mises en ordre par M. l'abbé Rose,"* 1841, fol. 232.

17.  Joseph Billioud, "Les manuscrits liturgiques provençaux du XIVe siècle," *Mémoires de l'Institut historique de Provence* 1 (1924): 61-65.

18.  Barbier de Montault, "La procession de la Fête-Dieu d'après les miniatures du XVe siècle," *Le manuscrit* 2 (1895): 66. Jacobus Murri is mentioned on 20 October 1419 in the will of Nicolaus Dominici, provost at the cathedral of Aix. Jacobus owned a house next to that of Nicolaus Archives des Bouches-du-Rhône, 2G, 320(2016).

19.  Rose: 275, 280. BMC, ms. 1654, fol. 146: (1367) "A xviii de Jun a pagat le ditcg Gili (Durant) als menestriers de Mosen Guiran que serviron a la festa de Dieu ... tres flor." fol. 148v.: (1370) "Item a xii de Jun an pagat per la festa de Dieu per los menestriers e per far las testieras del Apostols [heads of the apostles] e dels autre usasis e per la siera que cremeron de iiii tortias que cremeron a la festa de Dieu ... iiii. flor. iiii. s. iii. d. ... Mais, an pagat als menestriers de Buols [Buoux] per la festa de Dieu ... i. flor." fol. 149v.: (1372) " ... lo segon jorn de Jun ... Item pausa aver pagat al maistre +de la horgenas que menet la gitara la festa de Dieu ... v. s. Item pauza aver donat als Patriarcas que despendesan ... v. s. Item pauza aver pagat als menestriers de Setron [Sisteron?] ... i. flor. Item pauza aver pagat al trompaire de Viens ... viii. s. etc." fol. 150v.: (1373) " ... xxii del mes de Jun ... Item pauza aver paguat per despenssas fachas per la festa de Dieu que si feron de cavals fusts [wooden horses] e de formas d'enfants per honor de la dicha festa per menestriers e per despensas dels personats livras huech den. quatre ... f. x. d. iiii. ... viii de Jun venderon Raibaud Pitrolh e Raimon Fabre sindegues de la sivtat d'At [Apt] l'en pozision dels logadiers etc. a Bertran Bellon es a Peire de Setron etc. pauzan aver pagat per la festa de Dieu que pagueron per vi^{to} de pelon s. dos. ... Item a Ianequin menestrier per la dicha festa sonts hueg." fol. 156: (1377) "Item a xxix de May per la despensa del Camarlenc cant sa vec per far la cordi trompayres de Vyens que si vengron a la festa de Dieu ... i. flor. Item als menestriers de Manoasca [Manosque] per la dicha festa ... xxiiii. s. Item ad Anyqui que menet la vyolla a la dicha festa ... viii. s." Cf. BMC, ms. 1651, fols. 229v.-231v.

20.  Billioud, "Les manuscrits," p. 63.

21.  Jean Barroul, *Sainte-Anne d'Apt d'après une documentation nouvelle* (Apt: Reboulin, 1964), p. 7.

22.  BMC, ms. 1958, p. 270. BMC, ms. 1301; *Fonds Barjavel,* fol. 79. Remerville: 334.

23.  Arnaud d'Agnel, "Le Trésor de l'Eglise d'Apt," *Bulletin archéologique* (1904): 329-35. Roux, *La cathédrale,* p. 53. BMC, ms. 1652, *Recueil formé par abbé Rose,* fol. 122v.

24.  Joseph Sautel, "Catalogue descriptif des manuscrits liturgiques de l'église d'Apt," *Annales d'Avignon* 8 (1919): 53-111.

25.  Amédée Gastoué, *Inventaire des anciens manuscrits liturgiques conservés dans l'église d'Apt* (Avignon: Aubanel, 1900), p. 3.

26.  BMC, ms. 1652, fol. 119 bis. Sautel, "Catalogue."

27.  Sautel, "Catalogue," pp. 55-99; Alwin Elling, "Die Messen, Hymnen und Motetten der Handschrift von Apt." (Doctoral dissertation, Göttingen, 1924); Hanna Stäblein-Harder,

*Fourteenth-Century Mass Music in France,* Musicological Studies and Documents, vol. 7 ([Rome]: American Institute of Musicology, 1962) (herafter cited as Stäblein-Harder); *Repertoire international des sources musicales* (hereafter cited as *RISM*), vol. B IV$_2$, pp. 104-15. Editions: Amédée Gastoué, ed., *Le manuscrit de musique du trésor d'Apt* (Paris: E. Droz, 1936); Hanna Stäblein-Harder, ed., *Fourteenth-Century Mass Music in France,* Corpus Mensurabilis Musicae, vol. 28 ([Rome]: American Institute of Musicology, 1962); for additional information concerning editions see: *RISM* cited above and Ernest Sanders, "Philippe de Vitry," *Grove 6,* vol. 20, p. 27.

28.    Gastoué, *Le manuscrit,* p. ix, fn.

29.    This idea, along with many of the findings noted below, seem to substantiate the suppositions of Charles Hamm, "Manuscript Structure in the Dufay Era," *Acta Musicologica* 34 (1962): 166-84.

30.    Stäblein-Harder: 92.

31.    The foliation is only partially given by Stäblein-Harder: 9. It is possible that Q1 was also foliated but that the numerals have long since been trimmed off.

32.    Though many of the ideas proposed in the present study supersede those of Stäblein-Harder, the latter proved to be invaluable for providing a basis for this work. Furthermore, Stäblein-Harder discusses a number of topics, such as musical style and filiation of manuscripts, which will not be covered here.

33.    Barcelona, Biblioteca Orfeó Català, 2 and Bologna, Civico museo bibliografico musicale, Q15 (hereafter cited as BL).

34.    Where C is the notator and E is responsible for the text, Stäblein-Harder believes another scribe, called F, was operating. Stäblein-Harder: 94.

35.    This title may refer to the instrument of war known as the "bombarde à Aix." During the first decade of the fifteenth century, the city of Carpentras was known to have possessed one. In the spring of 1410, the syndics of Avignon requested it be brought to their city. At least three of these mortars arrived by 19 May. It took 36 horses to pull them. One was installed in the livrey of Thury, one in the livrey of Saint-Martial, and the third was positioned before the church of Saint-Pierre. On 23 May, the tour Philippe le Bel was fired upon using these weapons. Robert Brun, "Annales avignonaises de 1382 à 1410: Extraites des Archives de Datini," *Mémoires de l'Institut historique de Provence* 15 (1938): 189-90. Apt 40 is written for four voices, and the thicker texture might have been evocative of a canon blast. The bombardon is a bass shawm as well; therefore, it has also been suggested that the composer of this work (Perrinet, Perneth, or Prunet) may have been a shawm player, hence the title. Howard Mayer Brown, "Bombardon," *Grove 6,* vol. 3, p. 11. Gilbert Reaney, "Perrinet," *Grove 6,* vol. 14, p. 547.

36.    "Chassa" is Provençal for "chasser." It is possible that this word, written in brown script, was never meant to be considered a composer's name as has heretofore been assumed. Instead, it may have been a descriptive word used to designate the piece much as "Bonbarde" was used for Apt 40. It is possible that this two-voice work was in some way reminiscent of the secular *caccia.* Although the *caccia* is generally defined as a two-voice canon with an added instrumental tenor only 18 of 25 extant *caccie* fit this description. An early fourteenth-century treatise defines the form as a voice-exchange canon for 5 singers. This Gloria, Apt 8, while not able to be considered canonic, does rely most heavily on voice exchange. It is possible that this work represents an antiquated style of *caccia* which, by the mid-fourteenth century, was no longer employed in secular music. In any case, "chassa" should not be considered an

attribution. J. T. Avril, *Dictionnaire Provençal-Français* (Apt: Edouard Cartier, 1839); reprint 1970, p. 84. Kurt von Fischer, "Caccia," *Grove 6,* vol. 3, pp. 574-76.

37.   Folios 22-29 (Q2-Q3) then received the foliation ai, aii, aiii, [aiiii], av, avi, avii, avii[i] in brown ink, which was placed in the lower right-hand corner. This indicates that the gathering was the first in a series.

38.   Folios 1-4 then received the foliation i-iiii in black (or dark brown) ink, which was placed in the lower right-hand corner. Sometime afterwards, the designation bi, bii, biii, biiii was added, indicating that this gathering was the second in a series. See plate 8.

39.   Folios 9-12 bear the foliation ai, aii, aiii, aiii[i], similar to the other two gatherings. It was once the first gathering in a series.

40.   Stäblein-Harder: 70.

41.   Falconer Madan, *Books in Manuscript,* 2nd edition revised (London: Kegan, Paul, Trench, Trubner and Co., 1920), pp. 15-17.

42.   C. M. Briquet, *Les filigranes: Dictionnaire historique des marques du papier,* 2nd edition, reprint (New York: Hacker Art Books, 1966), vol. 1, pp. 190-91 (hereafter cited as Briquet).

43.   Both these marks are quite similar to one found on paper la used in the first five gatherings of the Reina codex (Paris, BN, ms. nouv. acq. fr. 6771). John Nádas, The *Codex Reina* Revisited. Paper read at the 48th Annual Meeting of the American Musicological Society, 4-7 November 1982, at the University of Michigan, Ann Arbor, Michigan. The author wishes to thank Professor Nádas for supplying reproductions of the watermark for comparison.

44.   Briquet, vol 1: xx-xxi.

45.   Stäblein-Harder: 81-82.

46.   Briquet, vol. 3: 562-64.

47.   BMA, ms. 5190, Fonds Chobaut, *Manuscrit Chobaut.*

48.   Allan H. Stevenson, "Briquet and the Future of Paper Studies," in *Briquet's Opuscula.* Monumenta Chartae Papyraceae historiam illustrantia, vol. 4 (Hilversum, Holland, 1955), pp. xl, xlii.

49.   Stäblein-Harder: 94.

50.   *RISM,* vol. B IV$_2$, p. 104.

51.   They appear on folios 31v. through 33v. of Apt, ms. 16 bis for the Credos Apt 40 and Apt 41. The numerals employed here are *viii* and *xii.* The numbers used in both manuscripts seem to indicate that the rubricator was considering the voices intervalically ([tenor], fifth, octave, twelfth.) Might this represent a primitive method of notating organ registration? Perhaps verses of the office hymn or passages of the Credo were performed by the organ.

52.   See the biographical index. It may not be coincidental that the dates of Richardus's tenure as *magister capelle pape* are identical to the narrow range of dates for the paper of gatherings V and VI proposed here.

53.   It is probable that Richardus joined up with the Curia during the intervening period, possibly when the pontiff was at Cavaillon in April 1403. Brun, "Annales," p. 45. The route from Apt to Avignon and Pont-de-Sorgues was via Cavaillon. Bernard Guillemain, *La Cour pontificale d'Avignon, 1309-1376* (Paris: Editions E. de Boccard, 1966), map 1.

54. This conforms to what we know about the duties and abilities of the *magister capelle pape*. Furthermore, the *premier chapellain* of the French royal chapel in 1378, Michel de Fontaine, was the scribe responsible for at least some of the copying of the Trémoïlle ms. See Craig Wright, *Music at the Court of Burgundy 1364-1419* (Henryville, PA: Institute of Mediaeval Music, 1979), p. 148.

55. David Fallows, "Sources," *Grove 6,* vol. 17, p. 663. Ivrea, Biblioteca capitolare, ms. 115 (CXV) (hereafter cited as Iv).

56. Barcelona, Biblioteca Central, 971 (olim 946), and Gerona, Archivo de la Catedral. See the table that follows.

57. During the late fifteenth and early sixteenth centuries, *Veni creator* was most often sung in an improvisatory style (*contrapuncto*). Richard Jonathan Sherr, "The Papal Chapel ca. 1492-1513 and Its Polyphonic Sources" (Ph.D. diss., Princeton University, 1975), p. 108. Tom Robert Ward, "The Polyphonic Office Hymn from the Late Fourteenth Century until the Early Sixteenth Century" (Ph.D. dissertation, University of Pittsburgh, 1969), pp. 10-14. Due to the abundance of ligatures found in the Tenor and Contratenor parts, Ward suggests that *Veni creator* may have received an instrumental performance.

58. In general, a greater number of Kyries, Glorias, and Credos are preserved in fourteenth- and early fifteenth-century manuscripts, *RISM*, vol. B IV$_2$, index.

59. Two works attributed to Pellisson (Apt 36 and 47) are directly traceable to the papal chapel. Pieces ascribed to Tapissier (Apt 42 and 43) and Cordier (Apt 38) might have been written for the duke of Burgundy; and at least one of the compositions (Apt 46) could be linked to the royal chapel of Aragon. The *capelle* of the last two Avignon pontiffs had close associations with both these princely houses.

# Appendix

# Biographical Index of
# Chaplains, Clerks, and Other Clerics
# Employed in the
# Papal Chapel at Avignon

Plate 11.   The Palace of the Popes

## Abbreviations

Papal documents published in the series Analecta Vaticano-Belgica. First series: Documents relatifs aux anciens diocèses de Cambrai, Liège, Thérouanne et Tournai. Brussels: 1908-1976.

AVB 1     *Suppliques de Clément VI (1342-1352),* Ursmer Berlière, ed., 1906.
AVB 4     *Lettres de Benoît XII (1334-1342),* Alphonse Fierens, ed., 1910.
AVB 5     *Suppliques d'Innocent VI (1352-1362),* Ursmer Berlière, ed., 1911.
AVB 6     *Lettres de Clément VI (1342-1352),* Vol. 1 (1342-1346). Philippe Van Isacker et Ursmer Berlière, eds., 1914.
AVB 7     *Suppliques d'Urbain V (1362-1370),* Alphonse Fierens, ed., 1924.
AVB 8     *Documents relatifs au Grand Schisme,* Vol. 1 *Suppliques de Clément VII (1378-1379),* Karl Hanquet, ed., 1924.
AVB 9     *Lettres d'Urbain V (1362-1370),* Vol. 1 (1362-1366). Alphonse Fierens et Camille Tihon, eds., 1928.
AVB 10    *Les Collectorie pontificales dans les anciens diocéses de Cambrai, Thérouanne et Tournai au XIV$^e$ siècle.* Ursmer Berlière, ed., 1929.
AVB 11    *Lettres de Grégoire XI (1371-1378),* Vol. 1, Camille Tihon, ed., 1958.
AVB 12    *Documents relatifs au Grand Schisme,* Vol. 1 *Letters de Clément VII (1378-1379).* Karl Hanquet et Ursmer Berlière, eds., 1930.
AVB 13    *Documents relatifs au Grand Schisme,* Vol. 3 *Suppliques et Lettres de Clément VII (1379-1394),* Hubert Nelis, ed., 1934.
AVB 14    *La Chambre Apostolique et les "Libri Annatarum" de Martin V (1417-1431),* François Baix, ed., 1960.
AVB 15    *Lettres d'Urbain V (1362-1370),* Vol. 2 (1366-1370). Camille Tihon, ed., 1932.
AVB 17    *Lettres d'Innocent VI (1352-1362),* Vol. 1 (1352-1355). Georges Despy, ed., 1953.
AVB 19    *Documents relatifs au Grand Schisme,* Vol. 5 *Lettres de Benoît XIII (1394-1422),* Vol. 2 (1395-1422), Marie-Jeanne Tits-Dieuaide, ed., 1960.
AVB 20    *Lettres de Grégoire XI (1371-1378),* Vol. 2, Camille Tihon, ed., 1961.
AVB 25    *Lettres de Grégoire XI (1371-1378),* Vol. 3, Camille Tihon, ed., 1964.
AVB 26    *Documents relatifs au Grand Schisme,* Vol. 6 *Suppliques de Benoît XIII (1394-1422),* Pervenche Briegleb et Arlette Laret-Kayser, eds., 1973.
AVB 27    *Documents relatifs au Grand Schisme,* Vol. 6 *Suppliques de Benoît XIII (1394-1422),* Pervenche Briegleb et Arlette Laret-Kayser, eds., 1973.
AVB 28    *Lettres de Grégoire XI (1371-1378),* Vol. 4, Camille Tihon, ed., 1974.
AVB 29    *Documents relatifs au Grand Schisme. Suppliques et Lettres d'Urbain VI (1378-1389) et de Boniface IX (1389-1394), Marguerite Gastout, ed., 1976.*

Documents published by Ecoles Françaises d'Athenès et de Rome. Paris: 1899-

*Lettres, Benoît XII,*
vol. 1    *Benoît XII (1334-1342). Lettres communes,* vol. 1. J.M. Vidal, ed., 1903.
vol. 2    *Benoît XII (1334-1342). Lettres communes,* vol. 2. J.M. Vidal, ed., 1906.
*Lettres, Clément VI,*
vol. 1    *Clément VI (1342-1352). Lettres closes, patentes et curiales se rapportant à la France.* E. Déprez, J. Glenisson, and G. Mollat, eds., 1910.
*Lettres, Urbain V,*
vol. 1    *Urbain V (1362-1370). Lettres communes.* M.-H. Laurent, ed., 1954-1958.
vol. 2    M.-H. Laurent, ed., 1964-1972.
vol. 3    Michel Hayez, ed., 1974, 1976.
vol. 4    Michel Hayez and Anne-Marie Hayez, eds., 1978.
vol. 5    Michel Hayez and Anne-Marie Hayez, eds., 1979.

vol. 6    Michel Hayez and Anne-Marie Hayez, eds., 1980.
vol. 7    Michel Hayez and Anne-Marie Hayez, eds., 1981.
vol. 8    Michel Hayez and Anne-Marie Hayez, eds., 1982.
vol. 9    Michel Hayez and Anne-Marie Hayez, eds., typescript.

Informatique    Traitment informatique des suppliques du Pape Urbain V (1362-1370). Work in progress undertaken by the Equipe de recherche (1057) associé du C.N.R.S., Palais des Papes, Avignon.

Other papal correspondence.

Gasparrini    *Le suppliche di Clemente VI: 1 (19 maggio 1342-28 maggio 1353).* T. Gasparrini Leporace, ed., 1948.

Accounts published in the series Vatikanische Quellen zur Geschichte des päpstlichen Hof- und Finanzverwaltung 1316-1378. Paderborn: 1912-1967.

Schäfer I    *Die Ausgaben der apostolischen Kammer unter Johann XXII.* K.H. Schäfer, ed., 1910.
Schäfer II    *Die Ausgaben der apostolischen Kammer unter Benedikt XII., Klemens VI. und Innocenz VI.* K.H. Schäfer, ed., 1914.
Schäfer III    *Die Ausgaben der apostolischen Kammer unter den Papsten Urban V. und Gregor XI.* K.H. Schäfer, ed., 1937.
Göller I    *Die Einnahmen der apostolischen Kammer unter Johann XXII.,* E. Göller, ed., 1910.
Göller II    *Die Einnahmen der apostolischen Kammer unter Benedikt XII.* E. Göller, ed., 1920.
Mohler    *Die Einnahmen der apostolischen Kammer unter Klemens VI.* L. Mohler, ed. 1931.
Hoberg I    *Die Einnahmen der apostolischen Kammer unter Innocenz VI.* H. Hoberg, ed., vol. 1, 1955.
Hoberg II    *Die Einnahmen der apostolischen Kammer unter Innocenz VI.* H. Hoberg, ed., vol. 2, 1967.

Other accounts and inventories.

Kirsch    *Die Ruckkehr der Päpst Urban V. und Gregor XI. von Avignon nach Rom, Auszüge aus den Kameralregistern des vatikanischen Archivs.* J.P. Kirsch, ed., 1898.
Ehrle    Franz Ehrle. *Historia Bibliothecae Romanorum Pontificum tum Bonifatianae tum Avenionensis,* 1890.
Williman    Daniel Henry Williman. "The Books of the Avignonese Popes and Clergy: A Repertory and Edition of the Book-Notices in the Vatican Archives, 1287-1420," 1973.
Hoberg    *Die Inventare des päpstlichen Schatzes in Avignon, 1314-1376,* 1944.

Other document sources.

*Pouillés*    Recueil des historiens de la France, 1904-1972.
*RG I*    *Repertorium Germanicum,* Vol. 1. E. Göller, ed., 1916.
*RG II*    *Repertorium Germanicum,* Vol. 2. G. Tellenbach, ed., 1933.
*RG III*    *Repertorium Germanicum,* Vol. 3. U. Kühne, ed., 1935.

General studies.

Eubel    Conrad Eubel. *Hierarchia catholica,* vol. 1, 1898.
Guillemain    Bernard Guillemain. *La cour pontificale d'Avignon (1309-1376),* 1962.
Mollat    Guillaume Mollat. *The Popes at Avignon 1305-1378,* 1963.
Seidlmayer    Michael Seidlmayer. *Die Anfänge des grossen abendländischen Schismas,* 1940.
Logoz    Roger Ch. Logoz. *Clément VII (Robert de Genève),* 1974.
Opitz    Gottfried Opitz. "Die Sekretärsexpedition unter Urban V. und Gregor XI.," 1944.

Favier        Jean Favier. *Les finance pontificales à l'époque du Grand Schisme d'Occident: 1378-1409,* 1966.
OPKA          Bernhard Schimmelpfennig. "Die Organisation der papstlichen Kapelle in Avignon," 1971.
ZKM           Bernhard Schimmelpfennig. *Die Zeremonienbücher des romischen Kurie im Mittelalter,* 1973.
OKS           Brigide Schwarz. *Die Organisation kurialer Schreiberkollegien von ihrer Entstehung bis zur Mitte des 15. Jahrhunderts,* 1972.

Archives and libraries.

ASV           Archivio segreto vaticano
ADV           Archives départmentales de Vaucluse
BMA           Bibliothèque municipale d'Avignon
BN, Coll. Bourg.   Paris, Bibliothèque National, Collection de Bourgogne.

Musicological sources.

Haberl        F.X. Haberl. "Die römische *schola cantorum* und die päpstlichen Kapellsänger bis zur Mitte des 16. Jahrhunderts," 1887.
Clercx        Suzanne Clercx. *Johannes Ciconia. Un musicien liégeois et son temps (vers 1335-1411),* 1960.
Günther I     Ursula Günther. "Zur Biographie einiger Komponisten der Ars subtilior," 1964.
Günther II    Ursula Günther. "Das Manuskript Modena, Biblioteca Estense, $\alpha$.M.5,24 (*olim* lat. 568 = *Mod*)," 1970.
Gómez Muntané  María del Carmen Gómez Muntané. *La música en la casa real catalano-aragonesa durante los años 1336-1432,* 1977.
Wright        Craig Wright. *Music at the Court of Burgundy, 1364-1419: A Documentary History,* 1979.

Music manuscripts.

Ao            Aosta, Biblioteca del Seminario, Codice senza segnatura
Apt           Apt, Basilique Sainte-Anne, Trésor, 16 bis
Barc. C       Barcelona, Biblioteca Central, 971 (olim 946)
BL            Bologna, Civico museo, Bibliografico musicale, Q 15
Ca6           Cambrai, Bibliothèque municipale, 6
Ca11          Cambrai, Bibliothèque municipale, 11
Ch            Chantilly, Musée Condé, 1047
Mod           Modena, Biblioteca Estense, $\alpha$.M.5,24
Mü 3232a      Munich, Bayerische Staatsbibliothek, Mus. ms., 3232a
Str           Strasbourg, Bibliothèque municipale, 222 C.22
Tr 93         Trent, Codex 93

## Members of the Chapel

ALANUS Avis dictus Vogel
  —Vogel, see Alanus Avis
ANCELINUS, see ANCELMUS
ANCELMUS Alandelonyer, see Ancelmus
Landeluy
  —Fabri, see Ancelmus Martini

—Landeluy
—Martini alias Calligarii
—Vlandelinc, see Ancelmus Landluy
ANDREAS de Choques
—de Mauro, see DROYNUS
—de Tho, see Andreas de Choques
ANDRIEU du Mor, see DROYNUS
ANEQUINUS Fabri, see Johannes Fabri
ANSELMUS, see ANCELMUS
ANTONIUS
ARNULPHUS de Maseriis
ASPROYS, see Johannes Symonis

BALDUINUS Piercoul
BARDARIAS, see Petrus Sinterii
BARDONERI, see Petrus Sinterii
BERENGARIUS Ademarii
BERNARDUS Ademarii
—Gralheri
BERTRANDUS le Connoitie
—le Convoitie, see Bertrandus le
    Connoitie
—Majoris alias Jaqueti
BETHUNA, see Guillelmus de Flandria
BONEDOMINE, see Johannes de Ayras

CALLIGARII, see Ancelmus Martini
CANTONUS Petri
COLETA
COLINETUS Martini
COUMPANUS de Cambello

DIONYSIUS Fabri
DROYNUS

EGIDIUS Bacelli, see Egidius Batelli
—Batelli
—Quadrati

FERICUS Musilen, see Ferricus Nusilleti
FERRICUS Nusilleti
FRANCISCUS
—de Goano

GERARDUS Gerardi
GIRARDUS, see GERARDUS
GUIDO de Lange
—de Naugro
GUILLELMUS Bladeti
—de Convenis
—Epi
—Fabri
—de Flandria alias Bethuna
—Lupi
—Mantolerii, see Guillelmus Motonerii

—Montolerii, see Guillelmus Motonerii
—Motonerii
—Rastelerii
—de Ultraaquam
—Villart de Blano
GUILLERMUS, see GUILLELMUS

HANETUS, see Johannes Hanini
HASPROIS, see Johannes Symonis
HAUCOURT, see Johannes de Altacuria
HENRICUS Busuardi, see Henricus Pousardi
—Ponel, see Henricus Poneti
—Ponet, see Henricus Poneti
—Poneti de Bossuto
—Pousardi
—Povel, see Henricus Poneti
—Pusuardi, see Henricus Pousardi
—Schonherze, see Henricus Scoenheze
—Scoenheze
—Stokouze, see Henricus Scoenheze
HENRIETUS (I), see Henricus Poneti
—(II), see Henricus Scoenheze

INGUERANNUS Benedicti

JACOBUS Brisart
—Comitis
—Griseovillari
—Griviller, see Jacobus de Griseovillari
—de Macas, see Jacobus de Massas
—de Massas
—de Massis, see Jacobus de Massas
—de Pratis
—de Prato, see Jacobus de Pratis
—Raymundi
—Ringardi
JAQUETI, see Bertrandus Majoris
JAQUETUS (I), see Jacobus Ringardi
—(II), see Jacobus Brisart
JOHANNES Ademari
—de Altacuria
—Ancelli
—Aneti, see Johannes Hanini
—de Athies
—de Attigniaco, see Johannes Petri
—de Attrebato, see Johannes de Ayras
—de Ayras alias Bonedomine
—de Ayrolis
—Berghoen
—Bertrandi de Hoyo
—de Bosco alias Peliçon
—Boulette
—de Bralli

—Broulete, see Johannes Boulette
—Burec
—lou Camus, see Johannes de Caunis
—Capel
—de Carnoten
—de Caunis
—de Champieng
—Clementis de Brolio, see Johannes
    Clementis de Brullio
—Clementis de Brullio
—Colini
—Cossardi
—de Cregrossio, see Johannes de
    Tregrossio
—de Cruce
—Daties, see Johannes Athies
—Desrame
—Durandi
—Fabri
—Fillon, see Johannes Carnoten
—Foliomeri
—Franciscus, see FRANCISCUS
—Frelvit, see Johannes Srelvit
—Gervasii alias le Picart
—Girardi Lathomi
—Godini
—Gonterii
—Hanini
—Haucour, see Johannes de Altacuria
—de Heys de Rancovado
—Houdain, see Johannes Lehoudain
—de Hyera, see Johannes de Ayras
—Johannis
—Lathomi, see Johannes Girardi
    Lathomi
—Lavanta, see Johannes de Venda
—Lehoudain
—Lenfant
—de Lovanis
—de Manso
—de Moley, see Johannes de Moleyo
—de Moleyo
—du Moloy, see Johannes de Moleyo
—Monterii
—Noalhaco
—Nobilihaco, see Johannes de Noalhaco
—Petri de Attigniaco
—Possardi, see Johannes Cossardi
—Ranconado, see Johannes de Heys de
    Rancovado
—Rauwes, see Johannes de Heys de
    Rancovado
—Rogerii alias de Watignies

—Roqueni, see Johannes Ruffi de Roquignies
—Ruffi de Roquignies
—de Sancto Quintino
—de Sinemuro
—Srelvit
—Symonis alias Hasprois
—de Tregros, see Johannes de Tregrossio
—de Tregrossio
—de Ulmo
—Valentis
—Verrerii, see Johannes Vitrarii
—de Vellery, see Johannes Vitrarii
—de Venda
—de Veredy, see Johannes Vitrarii
—Vinhas, see Johannes Vinyas
—Vinyas
—Vitrarii
—Vitrassi, see Johannes Vitrarii
—Volcarde, see Johannes Volkardi
—Volkardi dictus Ymmesoens

LAURENCIUS de Abbatisvilla
—de Allunsville, see Laurencius de
    Abbatisvilla

MARCIAL Cobrerii
MARTINUS de Prato
MATHEUS de Barbino
—de Longariga
—Petri
—de Sancto Johanne
—Valeta dictus Volta

NICOLAUS Benedicti
—Bernardi
—Bertrandi
—de Bondevilla alias de Spedona
—de Boudevilla, see Nicolaus de
    Bondevilla
—Martini, see Colinetus Martini
—de Nasiaco
—de Noisiaco, see Nicolaus de Nasiaco
—de Norsiaco, see Nicolaus de Nasiaco
—Raimundi
—de Spedona, see Nicolaus de
    Bondevilla
—Vacherii

PASCASIUS de Briella
PELIÇON, see Johannes de Bosco
PETRUS Baniardi
—Bataille
—Bomarc, see Petrus Baniardi
—Capucii

—de Ghiermegny, see Petrus de Guermini
—Godescalc, see Petrus Godescaut
—Godescaut
—de Guermini
—de Moncolo, see Petrus de
    Moncoulon
—de Moncoulon
—Montagut, see Petrus Saumati
—de Monteacuto, see Petrus Saumati
—de Montecolono, see Petrus de
    Moncoulon
—Rosseleti
—Rousseleti, see Petrus Rosseleti
—Salteti de Mimatis
—Santerii, see Petrus Sinterii
—Saumati alias de Monteacuto
—Sellerii
—Senterii, see Petrus Sinterii
—Sinterii alias Bardoneri (Bardarias)
—Solerii, see Petrus Sellerii
PHILIPPUS Roberti
—Sernain, see Philippus Servonhi
—Servani, see Philippus Servonhi
—Servoinh, see Philippus Servonhi
—Servonhi
Le PICART, see Johannes Gervasii
PONTIUS de Curte
PRIVATUS Pastorelli

RADULPHUS
—Cossardi
—Ricardi
—Tafardi, see Radulphus Cossardi
RAIMUNDUS de Anglade
—Arnulphi
—Seguini
—Servientis
RAOLINUS Cossart, see Radulphus Cossardi
RAYMUNDUS, see RAIMUNDUS
RAYNAUDINUS, see REGINALDUS
REGINALDUS de Hos, see Reginaldus du
    Houx
—du Houx
RICHARDUS (I)
—(II), see Richardus de Bozonvilla
    de Bozonvilla
ROBERTUS
—Creque
—Moti, see Robertus Nyot
—Nyot
—Pisson

SIMON Acquetini, see Simon Haquetin
  —Chauvin
  —Hacquetyn, see Simon Haquetin
  —Haquetin
  —Lacqueti, see Simon Haquetin
  —Mauricii
STEPHANUS Borgonho, see Stephanus
      Vergonio
  —de Chaulageto
  —Turqueti
  —de Ucis
  —Vergonio
SYMON, see SIMON

TEODORICUS Candelerii
THEOBALDUS Furnerii
THOMAS la Caille (de Caille)
  —le Quaille, see Thomas la Caille
  —Milonis
  —Multoris
  —Tauri

VOGEL, see Alanus Avis
VOLTA, see Matheus Valeta

WALTERUS de Bastonia, see Walterus de
      Vastonia
  —de Vastonia
WATIGNIES, see Johannes Rogerii

YMMESOENS, see Johannes Volkardi


# Dioceses of Origin

AMIENS (5)
  Jacobus Griseovillari
  Johannes Boulette
  Johannes Srelvit
  Laurentius de Abbatisvilla
  Matheus de Barbino

ARRAS (6)
  Arnulphus de Maseriis
  Egidius Batelli
  Guillelmus de Flandria
  Guillelmus Rastelerii
  Jacobus Comitis
  Johannes de Ayras

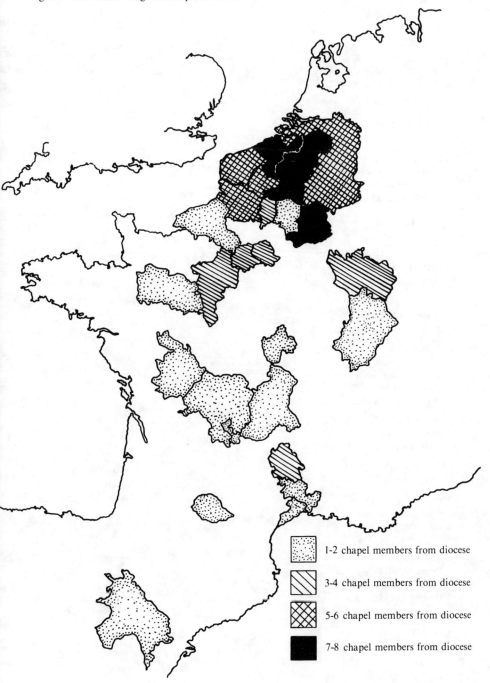

Fig. 27. Dioceses of origin of chapel members.

1-2 chapel members from diocese

3-4 chapel members from diocese

5-6 chapel members from diocese

7-8 chapel members from diocese

BESANÇON (1)
  Ferricus Nusilleti

CAMBRAI (8)
  Inguerannus Benedicti
  Jacobus Brisart
  Jacobus de Pratis (cl.)
  Johannes de Cruce
  Johannes Rogerii
  Johannes Symonis (?)
  Johannes Volkardi
  Petrus Sellerii

CHARTRES (3)
  Johannes Carnoten
  Johannes de Moleyo (mag.)
  Nicolaus de Bondevilla

CLERMONT (2)
  Petrus Saumati
  Stephanus Vergonio (mag.)

LAON (1)
  Johannes Ruffi

LE MANS (1)
  Theobaldus Furnerii

LIEGE (5)
  Alanus Avis
  Henricus Schoenheze
  Johannes Bertrandi
  Johannes Franciscus
  Walterus de Vastonia

LIMOGES (2)
  Johannes Ademari (mag.)
  Raymundus Arnulphi (mag. org.)

MAGUELONNE (1)
  Stephanus de Ucis

MEAUX (3)
  Johannes de Ulmo (mag.)
  Johannes Valentis
  Reginaldus du Houx

MENDE (4)
  Petrus Salteti (?) (cl.)
  Petrus Sinterii (mag.)
  Pontius de Curte (cl.)
  Privatus Pastorelli

NEVERS (1)
  Guillelmus Villart de Blano

NIMES (1)
  Marcial Cobrerii

NOYON (4)
Ancelmus Martini
Johannes de Altacuria
Johannes de Athies
Johannes de Sancto Quintino

PARIS (4)
Guido de Lange
Guillelmus Lupi
Johannes Desrame (?)
Simon Mauricii (?)

POITIERS (1)
Petrus Rosseletti

REIMS (7)
Colinetus Martini (cl.)
Guillelmus Fabri
Johannes Girardi Lathomi
Johannes de Heys de Rancovado
Johannes Lehoudain
Johannes Petri e Attignaco
Johannes Vitrarii

ROUEN (2)
Johannes Cossardi
Petrus Capucii

SARAGOSSA (1)
Jacobus de Macas

THEROUANNE (6)
Francisco de Goano
Johannes de Bralli
Johannes Capel
Johannes Hanini
Johannes Lenfant
Matheus de Sancto Johanne

TOUL (3)
Gerardus Gerardi (mag.)
Johannes Colini (?)
Richardus de Bozonvilla (?) (mag.)

TOULOUSE (1)
Johannes Johannis

TOURNAI (7)
Balduinus Piercoul
Johannes de Bosco
Johannes Clementis de Brullio
Johannes Fabri (cl.)
Johannes de Manso

Petrus de Guermini

TULLE (1)
Johannes de Noalhaco

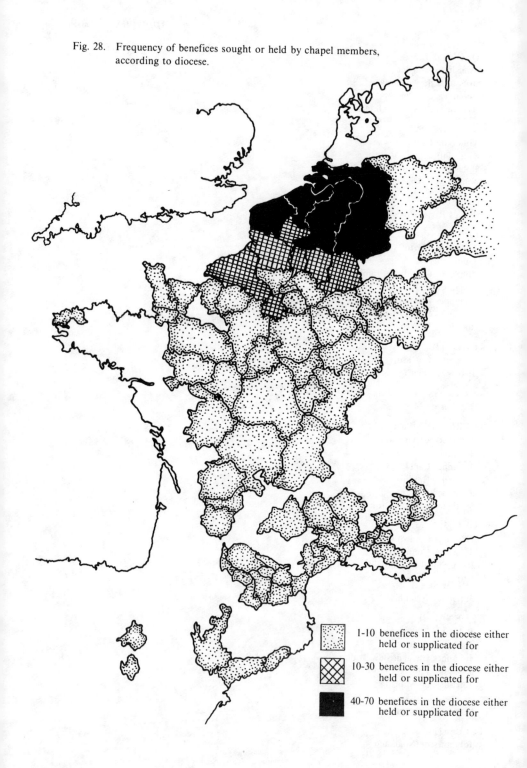

Fig. 28.  Frequency of benefices sought or held by chapel members,
according to diocese.

1-10 benefices in the diocese either
held or supplicated for

10-30 benefices in the diocese either
held or supplicated for

40-70 benefices in the diocese either
held or supplicated for

## Index of Benefices Held or Supplicated For

All benefices are chaplaincies, rectorates, or unspecified titles except where noted. (can.) = canonicate, (off.) = official title, (pars.) = parson, (treas.) = treasurer, (vic.) = vicar.

AGEN. *Le Mas d'Agenais:* Raimundus Seguini (?). *Castillonenès:* Raimundus Seguini (?). *Saint-Félix, Saint-Pierre-de-Romas, Auterive:* (decimator) Johannes Ademari.

AIX. (?) *Rocheurbarum* (can.) Johannes Johannis.

ALET. *Beaucaire:* Robertus Creque. *Esperaza:* Petrus Sellerii.

AMIENS. *Amiens:* Cathedral—(can.) Egidius Batelli, Johannes Boulette, Martinus de Prato. Saint-Nicolas-au-Cloître—(can.) Jacobus Griseovillari, (can.) Johannes Rogerii. Montières—Johannes Gervasii. *Corbie:* Petrus Saumati. *Erignies:* (pars.) Ancelmus Martini. *Le Crotoy:* Johannes Girardi Lathomi. *Roye:* (vic.) Jacobus Griseovillari.

ANGERS. *Angers:* Cathedral—(can.) Johannes Lenfant, (can.) Johannes Vitràrii. Saint-Laud—(cantor) Johannes Lenfant. Saint-Maurice—Thomas Milonis. *Morannes:* Philippus Servonhi. *Saint-Saturnin-sur-Loire:* Dionysius Fabri.

APT. *Apt:* (provost) Richardus de Bozonvilla.

ARRAS. *Arras:* Cathedral—(deacon) Thomas Multoris, (cantor) Stephanus Vergonio, (can.) Francisco de Goano,* (can.) Guillelmus de Flandria, (can.) Guillelmus Rastelerii, (can.) Jacobus Comitis, (can.) Johannes Symonis, (can.) Stephanus Vergonio, (can.) Thomas Multoris, (off.) Arnulphus de Maseriis, Egidius Batelli, Guillelmus Villart de Blano. *Aubigny:* Arnulphus de Maseriis. *Boyelles:* Johannes de Ayras. *Douai:* Saint-Amé—(can.) Ancelmus Landeluy, (can.) Guillelmus Rastelerii, (can.) Henricus Poneti, Arnulphus de Maseriis. Saint-Pierre—(can.) Robertus Creque. *Duisans:* Arnulphus de Maseriis. *Marck:* Johannes Gervasii. *Rouvroy:* Egidius Batelli. *Saint-Nicolas-sur-les-Fossés:* Johannes Symonis. *Saint-Vaast:* see CAMBRAI. *Vaudricourt:* Guillelmus Villart de Blano.

AUTUN. *Autun:* Cathedral—(can.) Guillelmus de Flandria, (can.) Guillelmus Villart de Blano. *Châtel-Censoir:* (can. and secular abbacy) Johannes de Cruce. *Létra:* (abbacy) Guillelmus de Flandria. *Millay:* Guillelmus de Flandria. *Montishélie:* Guillelmus Villart de Blano. *Saint-Aubin-en-Charollais:* Johannes Gonterii.

AUXERRE. *Auxerre:* Cathedral—(cantor) Nicholas de Bondevilla, (treas.) Simon Haquetin, Johannes Valentis.

AVIGNON. *Avignon:* Saint-Didier—(can.) Johannes de Cruce. *Villeneuve-lès-Avignon:* Notre-Dame—(deacon) Johannes Durandi, (can.) Guillelmus Lupi. Saint-André—(procurer) Guillelmus Lupi.

AVRANCHES. *Batilly:* Arnulphus de Maseriis.

BADAJOZ. *Badajoz:* Cathedral—(can.) Petrus Saumati.

BARCELONA. *Barcelona:* Cathedral—Johannes de Manso.

BAYEUX. *Bayeux:* Cathedral—(can.) Theobaldus Furnerii. *Douvres:* Manor of the Bishop—Philippus Servonhi.

BEAUVAIS. *Beauvais:* (subcollector) Johannes de Champieng. Cathedral—(can.) Alanus Avis, (can.) Johannes Fabri, (can.) Stephanus Turqueti, (can.) Thomas Tauri.

BEZIERS. *Les Aubertes:* Cantonus Petri.

CAMBRAI. *Cambrai:* Cathedral—(can.) Guillelmus de Ultraaquam, (can.) Henricus Poneti, (can.) Jacobus de Pratis, (can.) Johannes de Altacuria, (can.) Johannes Boulette, (can./off.) Johannes de Bralli, (can.) Johannes Carnoten, (can.) Johannes de Champleng, (can.) Johannes de Cruce, (can.) Johannes Ruffi, (can.) Johannes Symonis, (can.) Matheus de Longariga, (can.) Petrus Selerii, (can.) Philippus Servonhi, (can.) Richardus de Bozonvilla, (off./pars.) Francisco de Goano, (off.) Inguerannus Benedicti, (little vic.) Johannes Symonis, Johannes de Altacuria, Petrus Selerii, Philippus Servonhi, Robertus Creque. Sainte-Croix—(can.) Arnulphus Maseriis,

---

*Note: Francisco de Goano must read Franciscus de Goano throughout.

(can.) Jacobus Comitis, (can.) Johannes de Cruce. Saint-Géry—(scolastria) Johannes Vitrarii, (can.) Ancelmus Landeluy, (can.) Andreas de Choques, (can.) Egidius Quadrati, (can.) Henricus de Scoenheze, (can.) Inguerannus Benedicti, (can.) Johannes de Cruce, (can.) Johannes Lehoudain, (can.) Johannes de Ulmo, (can.) Johannes Vitrarii, (can.) Petrus Saumati, (can.) Petrus Sellerii, Egidius Batelli. Episcopal Chapel—Arnulphus Maseriis, Jacobus Comitis. *Antoing:* (treas.) Egidius Batelli, (can.) Egidius Batelli, (off.) Johannes de Bosco. *Antwerp:* (archdeac.) Jacobus de Pratis, (deac.) Johannes Volkardi, (can.) Johannes Volkardi, Johannes de Bralli. *Assche:* Philippus Servonhi. *Beaurevoir:* Johannes Vitrarii, Matheus de Sancto Johanne. *Beurele:* Jacobus de Griseovillari. *Brussels:* Petrus Saumati. *Cantimpré:* Johannes Boulette. *Enghien:* Johannes Rogerii. *Hal:* Petrus Saumati. *Haren:* Guillelmus Lupi. *Haute-Croix:* (pars.) Alanus Avis. *Herenthals:* Inguerannus Benedicti. *Le Câteau:* Saint-André—Guillelmus Lupi, Johannes de Cruce. *Le Toillon:* Inguerannus Benedicti. *Liessies:* Johannes Symonis. *Mons:* Saint-Germain—(can.) Guillelmus Lupi, (can.) Johannes de Bosco. *Nijlen:* Johannes Symonis. *Ogy:* Johannes de Bralli. *Paillencourt:* Matheus de Longariga. *Quievrain:* Henricus Poneti. *Renaix:* Saint-Hermès—(can.) Johannes Volkardi. *Rumst:* (pars.) Bertrandus Majoris. *Saint-Ghislain:* Johannes de Cruce, Petrus Guermini. *Saint-Vaast:* (or ARRAS?) Johannes de Altacuria, Johannes Boulette, Nicholas Vacherii, Petrus Sellerii. *Schellebelle:* Philippus Servonhi. *Soignies:* Saint-Vincent—(can.) Arnulphus Maseriis. Leprosarium—Philippus Servonhi. *Thun l'Evêque:* Petrus de Godescaut. *Valenciennes:* Francisco de Goano. *Wauthier-Braine:* (pars.) Ancelmus Martini.

CARCASSONNE. *Villemoustaussou:* (vic.) Johannes Vinyas.

CARPENTRAS. *Carpentras:* Cathedral—(precentor) Richardus de Bozonvilla, (can.) Richardus de Bozonvilla. *Corcolèze:* Bertrandus Majoris.

CAVAILLON. *Cavaillon:* Cathedral—(can.) Jacobus de Pratis.

CHALONS-SUR-MARNE. Bertrandus Majoris.

CHARTRES. *Chartres:* Cathedral—(cantor) Johannes de Moleyo, (can.) Richardus de Bozonvilla, Alanus Avis, Nicolas de Bondevilla. *Basochia:* Egidius Quadrati. *Poissy:* Johannes Valentis. *Villeneuve-en-Chevrie:* Petrus de Guermini.

CLERMONT. *Clermont:* Cathedral—(can.) Petrus Sinterii. *Saint-Genès*—(can.) Johannes de Ulmo. *Saint-Pierre*—(can.) Petrus Sinterii. *Cantal:* Petrus Sinterii. *Fontanges:* Johannes de Ayrolis.

COLOGNE. *Cologne:* Holy Apostles—(can.) Johannes Volkardi. *Aix-la-Chapelle:* St. Adalbert—(can.) Johannes Bertrandi. *Bonn:* (can.) Colinetus Martini.

COMPOSTELLA. *Compostella:* Cathedral—(can.) Johannes Bertrandi, (can.) Stephanus de Chaulageto.

COUTANCES. *Coutances:* Cathedral—(can.) Johannes Lehoudain. *Marigny:* Johannes de Venda.

EMBRUN. *Embrun:* Cathedral—(can.) Richardus de Bozonvilla. *Seyne:* Privatus Pastorelli.

EVREUX. *Evreux:* Cathedral—(can.) Andrieu du Mor, (can.) Johannes Franciscus. *Verneuil:* Guillelmus Lupi.

GAP. *Gap:* Cathedral—(can.) Johannes Godini.

LAON. *Laon:* Cathedral—(can.) Inguerannus Benedicti, (can.) Johannes de Altacuria, (can.) Johannes de Bralli, (can.) Johannes Clementis de Brullio, Johannes Rogerii, (can.) Matheus de Longariga, (can.) Matheus de Sancto Johanne, (off./pars.) Johannes Ruffi, Guillelmus Rastelerii. *Bernot:* Philippus Roberti. *Crécy-sur-Serre:* Radulphus Cossardi. *Guise:* Henricus Poneti. *Jouarre:* Johannes Girardi Lathomi. *Origny-Sainte-Benoîte:* Johannes Girardi Lathomi. *Puiseux:* Stephanus Vergonio. *Rozoy:* Saint-Laurent—(can.) Johannes de Altacuria, (can.) Johannes Symonis.

LAVAUR. *Lavaur:* Cathedral—(can.) Johannes Johannis.

LE MANS. *Le Mans:* Cathedral—(can.) Johannes de Bosco, (can.) Robertus Creque, (can.) Theobaldus Furnerii, Egidius Quadrati. *Souday:* Theobaldus Furnerii.

LERIDA. *Lerida:* Cathedral—(off./can.) Johannes Cossardi.

LIEGE. *Liège:* Cathedral of Saint-Jean—(can.) Guillelmus Lupi, (can.) Henricus Poneti, (can.) Henricus de Scoenheze, (can.) Jacobus Comitis, (can.) Johannes Gervasi, Walterus de Vastonia. Saint-Barthélemy—(can.) Henricus Poneti, (can.) Johannes Valentis. Sainte-Croix—(can.) Colinetus Martini, (can.) Johannes Ruffi. Saint-Denis—(cantor) Johannes Franciscus, (can.) Colinetus Martini, (can.) Gerardus Gerardi, (can.) Johannes Bertrandi, (can.) Simon Mauricii. Saint-Martin—(can.) Henricus Poneti. Saint-Paul—(can.) Bertrandus Majoris, (can.) Johannes de Ayras, (can.) Johannes Colini (?), (can.) Johannes Valentis, (can.) Richardus de Bozonvilla, (can.) Walterus de Vastonia. Saint-Pierre—(can.) Johannes Bertrandi, (can.) Johannes Clementis, (can.) Johannes Ruffi, (can.) Simon Mauricii. *Alken:* Johannes Valentis. *Avernas-le-Bauduin:* Johannes Ruffi. *Grave:* Johannes Rogerii. *Louvain:* Henricus Poneti. *Maastricht:* Saint-Servais—(can.) Alanus Avis, (off./can.) Henricus Poneti, (can.) Johannes de Venda (?), (can.) Johannes Volkardi, (can.) Petrus Baniardi, (can.) Walterus de Vastonia. Marian Church—(can.) Alanus Avis, (can.) Johannes de Venda. *Nivelle:* Sainte-Gertrude—(can.) Walterus de Vastonia. Saint-Sepulcre—Walterus de Vastonia. *Oerbecke:* Johannes Volkardi. *Tirlemont:* Saint-Germain—(cantor) Johannes Volkardi. *Tongres:* (can.) Johannes Franciscus (?). *Visé:* Walterus de Vastonia. *Walcourt:* Johannes Franciscus.

LISBON: *Sister:* Johannes Symonis.

LISIEUX. *Lisieux:* Cathedral—(can.) Johannes Franciscus, (can.) Guillelmus Lupi, (can.) Petrus Saumati. *Livarot:* Dionysius Fabri. *Quetteville:* Guillaume Lupi.

LODEVE. *Lodève:* Cathedral—(can.) Raimundus de Anglade. *Aurillac:* Petrus Salteti.

LOMBEZ. (Bishop) Antonius.

MAGUELONNE. *Castelnau-le-Lez:* Stephanus de Ucis. *Frontignan:* Stephanus de Ucis. *Poussan:* (vic.) Johannes de Tregrossio.

MAINZ. *Mainz:* St. Stephen—(can.) Walterus de Vastonia.

MEAUX. *Meaux:* Cathedral—(treas.) Johannes de Ulmo, (can.) Johannes Desrame (?), (can.) Johannes Girardi Lathomi, (can.) Johannes Valentis, (can.) Reginaldus du Houx. *Crécy:* Johannes de Ulmo. *Monteriaco:* Johannes de Ulmo.

MENDE. *Mende:* Cathedral—(can.) Pontius de Curte, Petrus Salteti. *Prinsujéols:* Gerardus Gerardi.

METZ. *Metz:* Cathedral—(can.) Franciscus de Goano, Johannes Colini (?). St. Peter—Franciscus de Goano.

MIREPOIX. *Antioque:* Raimundus Seguini.

NARBONNE. *Narbonne:* Saint-Hyppolite—Petrus Sinterii. *Caumonte:* Johannes de Ayras. *Cazillac:* Johannes de Ayras. *Durban:* Johannes Ademari. *Fontfroide:* Antonius, Guillelmus Motonerii. *Montgaillard:* Petrus Baniardi. *Vinassan:* Johannes Petri.

NEVERS. *Nevers:* Cathedral—(can.) Johannes de Bosco, Johannes Vitrarii.

NIMES. *Dourbies:* Stephanus de Ucis.

NOYON. *Noyon:* Cathedral—(cantor) Ancelmus Martini, (can.) Jacobus Brisart, (can./off.) Jacobus Griseovillari, (can.) Nicolaus Bondevilla, (can.) Philippus Servonhi, (can.) Simon Haquetin, Ancelmus Martini. *Brie:* Simon Haquetin. *Estacuria:* Petrus de Godescaut. *Jeancourt:* Petrus Bataille. *Marchellpot* (?): Simon Haquetin. *Nesle:* (can.) Jacobus Griseovillari, (can.) Johannes de Athies, (can.) Johannes Hanini, (can.) Petrus Saumati. *Prémony:* Johannes de Sancto Quintino. *Saint-Quentin:* Jacobus Brisart.

ORLEANS. *Orléans:* Saint-Aignan—(can.) Nicolaus de Bondevilla. Saint-Pierre-des-Filles—(can.) Nicolaus de Bondevilla. Saint-Laurent— Nicolaus de Bondevilla. Sigalonia: (provost) Nicolaus de Bondevilla.

PAMIERS. *Pamiers:* Beata Maria de Marcatuli—Nicolaus Vacherii.

PARIS. *Paris:* Cathedral—(can.) Johannes de Bosco, (can.) Johannes de Sinemuro, (can.) Petrus de Guermini, (can.) Philippus Roberti, Andreas de Choques, Guillelmus Lupi, Henricus de Scoenheze, Inguerannus Benedicti, Johannes Boulette, Johannes Fabri, Johannes Girardi Lathomi, Simon Mauricii. Le College des Bons-Enfants—Johannes Fabri. Saint-Eloi—Johannes Fabri. Saint-Germain-l'Auxerrois—(can.) Johannes Fabri, (can.) Philippus Servonhi, (can.) Simon Haquetin. Saint-Gervais—Johannes de Venda. Saint-Martin-des-Champeaux-en-Brie—(can.) Johannes de Ulmo, (can.) Nicolaus de Bondevilla, (can.) Theobaldus Furnerii, Johannes de Ulmo. Saint-Merri—(can.) Johannes Valentis. Sainte-Opportune—(treas.) Johannes Rogerii, (can.) Johannes de Altacuria, (can.) Johannes Franciscus. Saint-Pierre-de-Arsis—Johannes Fabri. *Saint-Denis:* Radulphus Cossardi.

PERIGUEUX. *Condat:* Raimundus Seguini. *Saint-Front:* (can.) Raimundus Seguini.

POITIERS. *Poitiers:* Cathedral—Dionysius Fabri.

REIMS. *Reims:* (collector) Johannes de Champieng. Cathedral—(can.) Egidius Quadrati, (can.) Johannes de Bosco, (can.) Johannes de Champieng, (can.) Johannes de Heys de Rancovado, (can.) Johannes Lehoudain, (can.) Johannes Rogerii, (can.) Petrus Saumati, Johannes Rogerii. Saint-Pierre-le-Vieux—Johannes Lehoudain. Saint-Rémy—Johannes Capel. Saint-Symphorien—(can.) Johannes Petri, (can.) Johannes Rogerii. *Ardeuil:* Johannes Lehoudain. *Brieulles-sur-Bar:* Johannes Vitrarii. *Duncherie:* Theobaldus Furnerii. *Montmarin:* Johannes Petri. *Mouzon:* Thomas la Caille. *Senuc:* Johannes de Cruce. *Suippes:* Johannes Ruffi.

RIEUX. *Puydaniel:* Johannes Durandi.

RODEZ. *Rodez:* Cathedral—(can.) Pontius de Curte. *Cassagnes/Bégones:* Stephanus Vergonio. *La Fouillade:* Stephanus de Chaulageto.

ROUEN. *Rouen:* Cathedral—(can.) Inguerannus Benedicti, Johannes de Altacuria, Johannes Franciscus. Saint-Amand—Johannes Boulette. *Anquetierville:* Guillelmus de Flandria. *Bourneville:* Henricus de Scoenheze, Inguerannus Benedicti. *Isneauville:* Andreas de Choques. *Le-Bec-Hellouin:* Guido de Lange (?), Guillelmus Lupi. *Montvilliers:* Matheus de Longariga, Philippus Servonhi. *Saint-Pierre-de-Montfort:* Guido de Lange (?), *Vesly* (?): Johannes Cossardi.

SAINT-PAPOUL. *Monferrand:* (vic.) Privatus Pastorelli. *Saint-Pons-de-Thomières:* Privatus Pastorelli.

SAINT-POL-DE-LEON. *Saint-Colomban:* Philippus Roberti.

SALAMANCA. *Cantalpiedra:* Johannes de Manso.

SARLAT. *Capdrot:* (archpriest) Johannes de Cruce.

SENLIS. *Senlis:* Cathedral—(can.) Johannes Valentis, (can.) Stephanus Turqueti.

SENS. *Sens:* Cathedral—(can.) Johannes Brali, (can.) Johannes de Sinemuro, (can.) Philippus Roberti, Martinus de Prato. *Bonchosiacum:* Philippus Roberti. *Ferrières-en-Gâtinais:* Johannes Rogerii. *Gumery:* Nicholaus de Bondevilla. *Pont-sur-Yonne:* Johannes Valentis. *Soucy:* Johannes Boulette.

SOISSONS. *Compiegne:* Saint-Maurice—(can.) Jacobus Griseovillari.

TARAZONA. *Tudela:* Marian church—(can.) Ancelmus Landeluy.

TARRAGONA. *Tarragona:* Cathedral—Johannes Cossardi. *Valles:* Philippus Servonhi.

THEROUANNE. *Thérouanne:* (subcollector) Johannes Capel, (pardoner) Coumpanus de Cambello. Cathedral—(treas.) Guillelmus Rastelerii, (treas.) Johannes Hanini, (can.) Ancelmus Landeluy, (can.) Johannes de Athies, (can.) Johannes de Bralli, (can.) Johannes Lenfant, (can.) Stephanus de Chaulageto. *Aire:* Saint-Pierre—(deacon) Jacobus Comitis, (deacon) Johannes Gervasii, (can.) Ancelmus Martini, (can.) Guillelmus Villart de Blano, (can.) Jacobus de Griseovillari, (can.) Johannes de Bralli, (can.) Laurencius de Abbatisvilla, (can.) Philippus Roberti, (can.) Stephanus Vergonio. *Cassel:* Marian church—(can.) Coumpanus de Cambello. Saint-Pierre—(can.) Guillelmus Rastelerii, (can.) Johannes Capel, (can.) Johannes Fabri, (can.)

Johannes Gervasii, (can.) Johannes Petri. *Coudekerque:* Franciscus de Goano. *Coupelle-Vieille:* Guillelmus Rastelerii. *Esen:* Johannes Ruffi. *Ferquen:* Johannes Capel. *Furnes:* Sainte-Walberge—(treas.) Guillelmus de Flandria, (can.) Ancelmus Martini, (can.) Jacobus Comitis, (can.) Johannes de Athies, (can.) Johannes Capel, (can.) Johannes Ruffi, (can.) Theobaldus Furnerii, (pars./off.) Thomas la Caille, Coumpanus de Cambello. *Ledringhem:* Coumpanus de Cambello. *le Maisnil:* Thomas Multoris. *Lillier:* Saint-Omer—(can.) Franciscus de Goano. *Marck:* Jacobus Comitis. *Saint-Omer:* Saint-Bertin—Johannes Capel. Saint Omer—(cantor) Johannes Capel, (can.) Gerardus Gerardi, (can.) Guillelmus de Flandria, (can.), Henricus Poneti, (can.) Johannes Capel, (can.) Johannes Hanini, (can.) Johannes de Ulmo, (can.) Radulphus Cossardi, (can.) Theobaldus Furnerii, (can.) Thomas Multoris, (vic.) Johannes Capel, Ancelmus Martini, Johannes Hanini. *Tatinghem:* Thomas Multoris. *Wardrecques:* Johannes Capel. *Wulveringhem:* Johannes Capel.

TOLEDO. *Toledo:* Cathedral—(can.) Johannes Ademari.

TOUL. *Toul:* Episcopal Palace—Richardus de Bozonvilla. *Saint-Dié:* (can.) Gerardus Gerardi, (can.) Richardus de Bozonvilla, (can.) Thomas la Caille, Gerardus Gerardi.

TOULOUSE. *Toulouse:* Cathedral—(can.) Alanus Avis, (can.) Petrus Baniardi. St.-Orens-de-Gameville. Johannes Johannis. *L'Isle-Jourdain:*(can.) Johannes Johannis.

TOURNAI. *Tournai:* Cathedral—(can.) Arnulphus de Maseriis, (can.) Egidius Batelli, (can.) Jacobus de Pratis, (can.) Johannes Ruffi, (can.) Petrus Baniardi, (can.) Petrus Bataille, (great vic.) Dionysius Fabri, Johannes Girardi Lathomi, Johannes Rogerii. Saint-Pierre—(can.) Simon Haquetin. *Ascq:* Johannes de Bosco. *Bruges:* Beghine—Petrus Bataille. Saint-Donatien—(can.) Egidius Batelli, (can.) Franciscus de Goano, (can.) Johannes de Ayras, (can.) Johannes de Bosco, (can.) Johannes Petri, (can.) Johannes Rogerii, (can.) Philippus Roberti, (can.) Theobaldus Furnerii, (can.) Thomas Multoris, Saint-Gilles—Petrus Bataille. Saint-Sauveur—Johannes Clementis de Brullio. *Carvin:* Dionysius Fabri, Johannes Clementis de Brullio. *Couckelaere:* Johannes de Bralli, Johannes Hanini. *Dottingnies:* Johannes Fabri. *Esquelmes:* Petrus Bataille. *Eyne:* Johannes Fabri. *Ghent:* Saint-Pierre—Petrus Saumati. *Lille:* Sainte-Marie-Madeleine—Johannes de Bosco (?). Saint-Pierre—(cantor) Johannes Clementis de Brullio, (scolastria) Johannes Clementis de Brullio, (can.) Ancelmus Landeluy, (can.) Guillelmus Villart de Blano, (can.) Henricus Poneti, (can.) Johannes de Bosco, (can.) Johannes Capel, (can.) Petrus Bataille, (can.) Stephanus Vergonio, (can.) Thomas Multoris, Balduinus Piercoul, Petrus Bataille, Simon Mauricii. *Ouckene:* Johannes Capel. *Ronque:* Johannes Fabri. *Saint-Amand-lès-Eaux:* Egidius Quadrati. *Saint-Eloi:* Balduinus Piercoul. *Seclin:* Saint-Piat—(can.) Arnulphus Maseriis, (can.) Dionysius Fabri, (can.) Guillelmus Rastelerii, (can.) Johannes de Altacuria, (can.) Johannes Clementis de Brullio, (can.) Johannes Gervasii, (can.) Matheus de Sancto Johanne, (can.) Thomas la Caille, (can.) Walterus de Vastonia. *Wahagnies:* Johannes Girardi Lathomi. *Wavrin:* Balduinus Piercoul.

TOURS. *Tours:* Saint-Martin—(can.) Philippus Servonhi, (can.) Richardus de Bozonvilla. *Château-Renalt:* Johannes Johannis.

TROYES. *Troyes:* Cathedral—(can.) Alanus Avis, (can.) Johannes de Champieng, (can.) Johannes de Heys de Rancovado. Saint-Etienne—(can.) Johannes de Heys de Rancovado.

UZES. *Domazan:* Guillelmus Rastelerii. *Navacelle:* Gerardus Gerardi. *Orsan:* Jacobus Comitis. *Valcrose:* Johannes Tregrossio. *Vallerauge:* Johannes de Sancto Quintino.

VERDUN. *Verdun:* Cathedral—(can.) Gerardus Gerardi, (can.) Jacobus Comitis.

VIVIERS. *Blachières:* Richardus de Bozonvilla. *Les Assions:* Raimundus de Anglade.

UNKNOWN. *Saint-Denis du Val*—Inguerannus Benedicti. Eyck: Marian church—Walterus de Vastonia.

---

Please see Addenda to Index of Benefices, p. 268

## Other Service

These higher ecclesiastics maintained certain clerics who, at some time during their careers, served in the papal chapel at Avignon.

The names of the clerics and the dates they were associated with the prelates are given. Where a relationship between patron and protégé has not clearly been established, the names are placed in

Some information has been taken from Guillemain and from Conrad Eubel, *Hierarchia catholica medii aevi*, vol. 1 (Münster: 1898) and vol. 2 (Münster: 1901). The citations are all drawn from volume 1 except where noted.

### Popes

Urban VI (Bartolomeo Prignano), 8/9 April 1378-†15 October 1389. Eubel: XXVII.
—Johannes Volkardi 1380-1381, *magister capelle*.
Martin V, 11 November 1417-20 February 1431. Eubel, vol. 2: I.
—Andreas de Mauro (?) 1417-1418, *capellanus*.
Eugene IV, 11 March 1431-†23 February 1447. Eubel, vol. 2: II.
—Matheus Petri 1431-1447, *clericus ceremoniarum*.
Nicholas V, 19 March 1447-†24 March 1355. Eubel, vol. 2: III.
—Matheus Petri 1447-1450, *clericus ceremoniarum*.

### Cardinals

Arnaud de Pellegrue, relative of Pope Clement V; cardinal deacon of s.Maria in porticu, 15 December 1305-†August 1331. Eubel: XX$_8$.
—Raimundus Seguini (?) 1316.
Gaucelme de Jean, nephew of Pope John XXII; cardinal bishop of Albano, 1330-†2 August 1348. Eubel: XXI$_3$.
—Johannes Gervasii 1338-1342.
Elie Talleyrand de Périgord, bishop of Auxerre; cardinal bishop of Albano, 4 November 1348-†17 January 1364. Eubel: XXI$_{27}$.
—Petrus de Guermini 1360-1364?
Gozzio Battaglia da Rimini, patriarch of Constantinople; cardinal priest of s.Prisca, 18 December 1338-†10 June 1348. Eubel: XXII$_1$.
—Cantonus Petri (?) 1343.
Bertrand de Déaux, archbishop of Evreux; cardinal bishop of Sabina, 4 November 1348-†21 October 1355. Eubel: XXII$_2$.
—Walterus de Vastonia 1353-1354.
Gui de Boulogne, uncle of Pope Clement VII, archbishop of Lyon; cardinal bishop of Porto, 1350-†25 November 1373. Eubel: XXIII$_2$.
—Thomas la Caille 1371.
Etienne Aubert, bishop of Clermont; cardinal priest of ss.Johannes et Paulus, 20 September 1342-13 February 1352. The future Pope Innocent VI. Eubel: XXIII$_5$.
—Jacobus Comitis 1350.
Hugues Roger, brother of Pope Clement VI, bishop of Tulle; cardinal priest of s.Laurentius in Damaso, 20 September 1342-†21 October 1363. Eubel: XXIII$_6$.
—Johannes Petri de Attigniaco 1362.
Guillaume de la Jugie, nephew of Pope Clement VI, cardinal deacon of s.Maria in Cosmedin, 20 September 1342-†28 April 1374. Eubel: XXIII$_{10}$.
—Philippus Servonhi for over 20 years.
—Johannes Bertrandi 1346.
—Guido de Lange (?) 1362.
—Johannes Petri de Attignaco 1367.

Pierre Roger de Belfort, nephew of Pope Clement VI; cardinal deacon of s.Maria nova, 28/29 May 1348-30 December 1370. The future Pope Gregory XI. Eubel: XXIII₁₃.
—Martinus de Prato (?) before 1371.
Gilles Rigaud, abbot of the Benedictine monastery of Saint-Denis; cardinal priest of s.Praxedis, 17 December 1350-†10 September 1353. Eubel: XXIII₂₂.
—Guillelmus Lupi 1353.
Jean Duèse de Caraman, nephew of Pope John XXII; cardinal deacon of s.Georgius ad velum aureum, 17 December 1350-†1 August 1361. Eubel: XXIII₂₅.
—Walterus de Vastonia 1357.
Audoin Aubert, nephew of Pope Innocent VI, bishop of Maguelonne; cardinal priest of ss.Johannes et Paulus, 15 February 1353-ca. 13 July 1361; cardinal bishop of Ostia until †10 May 1363. Eubel: XXIV₁.
—Guillelmus Lupi 1353-1355.
—Bertrandus Majoris 1361.
—Egidius Batelli 1362.
Elie de Saint-Yrieix, bishop of Uzès; cardinal priest of s.Stephanus in Coeliomonte, 23 December 1356-ca. 10 May 1363; cardinal bishop of Ostia until †10 May 1367. Eubel: XXIV₂.
—Johannes de Ulmo 1362.
—Johannes de Noalhaco 1363-1367.
Francesco degli Atti de Todi, bishop of Florence; cardinal priest of s.Marcus, 23 December 1356-ca.25 August 1361. Eubel: XXIV₃.
—Johannes Petri de Attigniaco 1361.
Pierre Monteruc, nephew of Pope Innocent VI, bishop of Pamplona; cardinal priest of s.Anastasia, 23 December 1356-†30 May 1385. Eubel: XXIV₄.
—Henricus de Scoenheze 1378.
Pierre la Forêt, archbishop of Rouen; cardinal priest of Basilica XII apostolorum, 23 December 1356-†7 June 1361. Eubel: XXIV₇.
—Johannes Capel 1360.
Jean de Blauzac, bishop of Nîmes; cardinal priest of s.Marcus, 17 September 1361-1372; cardinal bishop of Sabina until †8 July 1379. Eubel: XXIV₁₀.
—Johannes de Bosco 1364-1379.
—Henricus Poneti 1371.
—Richardus de Bozonvilla 1371-1379.
Gilles Aycelin de Montaigut, bishop of Thérouanne, chancellor of King Charles V of France; cardinal priest of s.Martinus in monte, 17 September 1361-26 July 1368; cardinal bishop of Frascati until †5 December 1378. Eubel: XXIV₁₁.
—Johannes Lathomi 1378.
Etienne Aubert, nephew of Pope Innocent VI, bishop of Carcassonne; cardinal deacon of s.Maria in Aquiro, 17 September 1361-22 September 1368; cardinal priest of s.Laurencius in Lucina until †29 September 1369. Eubel: XXIV₁₃.
—Theobaldus Furnerii 1364.
Guillaume Bragose, bishop of Vabres, cardinal deacon of s.Georgius ad velum auream, 17 September 1361-6 December 1362; cardinal priest of s.Laurentius in Lucina until †11 November 1367. Eubel: XXIV₁₄.
—Ancelmus Martini 1362.
Hugues de Saint Martial, cardinal deacon of s.Maria in porticu, 17 September 1361-†1403. Eubel: XXIV₁₅.
—Egidius Batelli 1391/93.
Anglic Grimoard, brother of Pope Urban V, bishop of Avignon; cardinal bishop of Albano 17 September 1367-†16 April 1388. Eubel: XXV₁.
—Johannes Volkardi 1368-1371.
—Jacobus de Griseovillari 1371.

Guillaume d'Aigrefeuille, (the younger), relative of Pope Clement VI; cardinal priest of s.Stephanus in Coeliomonte, 12 May 1367-†13 January 1401. Eubel: XXV₄.

—Thomas Multoris 1371-1376.

—Matheus de Longariga 1372.

—(Guillelmus Villart de Blano 1376.)

—Gerardus Gerardi 1394.

Simon Langham, archbishop of Canterbury; cardinal priest of s.Sixtus, 22 September 1368-August 1373. Eubel: XXV₇.

—Johannes Capel 1371, *magister capelle*.

Robert de Genève, bishop of Cambrai; cardinal priest of Basilica XII apostolorum, 30 May 1371-20 September 1378; The future Pope Clement VII. Eubel: XXVI₅.

—Philippus Roberti 1373.

—Thomas la Caille 1375.

Guillaume de Chanac, bishop of Mende; cardinal priest of s.Vitalis, 20 May 1371-†30 December 1383. Eubel: XXVI₆.

—Johannes Fabri before 1384.

Guillaume Noellet, cardinal deacon of s.Angelus, 30 May 1371-†4 July 1394. Eubel: XXVI₁₁.

—Jacobus de Griseovillari 1378, *magister capelle*.

Pedro de Luna, cardinal deacon of s.Maria in Cosmedin, 20 December 1375-28 September 1394. The future Pope Benedict XIII. Eubel: XXVI₂₁.

—Johannes Rogerii 1378.

—Ancelmus Landeluy 1378.

—Johannes Fabri 1378, 1392-1394.

Niccoló Brancaccio, bishop of Cosenza; cardinal priest of s.Maria trans Tiberim, 16 December 1378-1388; cardinal bishop of Albano until 29 June/3 July 1412. Eubel: XXX₂.

—Petrus Bataille 1391.

Pierre-Raymond de Barrier, bishop of Autun; cardinal priest of ss.Marcellinus et Petrus, 16 December 1378-†13 June 1383. Eubel: XXX₄.

—Johannes Hanini 1378.

Pierre de Cros, cousin of Pope Clement VI, archbishop of Arles; cardinal priest of ss.Nereus et Achilleus, 23 December 1383-†16 November 1388. Eubel: XXX₉.

—Johannes de Cruce 1388.

Jean de Brogni, bishop of Viviers; cardinal priest of s.Anastasia, 12 July 1385-1405. Eubel: XXX₂₄.

—Johannes de Cruce 1392.

Martin de Salva, bishop of Pamplona; cardinal priest of s.Laurencius in Lucina, 23 July 1390-†22 October 1403. Eubel: XXX₂₉.

—Johannes Boulette 1403.

Piero de Fonseca, cardinal deacon of s.Angelus, 14 December 1412-†21 August 1422. Eubel: XXXI₁₅.

—Jacobus Raymundi 1418.

**Bishops**

Guillaume de Mandagout, bishop of Uzès, 14 February 1318-†21 April 1344, Eubel: 540.

—Johannes de Sancto Quintino 1336.

Jean de Cojordan, bishop of Avignon, 10 May 1336-1349. Eubel: 126.

—Raimundus Servientis (?) 1337.

Pierre Roger, archbishop of Rouen, 14 December 1330; cardinal priest of ss.Nereus et Achilleus, 8 December 1338-7 May 1342. The future Pope Clement VI. Eubel: 447, XXII₃.

—Guillelmus de Flandria 1338.

Guy de Ventadour, bishop of Vabres, 17 February 1349-†before 17 October 1352. Eubel: 540.

—Guillelmus Lupi before 1352.

Jean d'Auxois, bishop of Auxerre, cardinal?-†10 January 1359. Eubel: 122.
—Egidius Quadrati 1357.
Andrea Avvocatti, bishop of Como, 27 February 1357-†before 9 March 1362. Eubel: 225.
—Johannes Capel 1358.
Philippe Cabassole, bishop of Cavaillon, 17 August 1334-18 August 1361; patriarch of Jerusalem until 22 September 1368. Eubel: 287, 185, XXV₆.
—Johannes Johannis 1360-1362.
Pierre d'Auxy, bishop of Tournai, 18 May 1379-†before 2 March 1388. Eubel: 517.
—(Nicholaus de Bondevilla before 1379, served several cardinals.)
Guillaume de Lestrange, bishop of Rouen, 22 December 1375-†March 1389. Eubel: 447.
—Johannes Franciscus 1378.
—Inguerannus Benedicti 1378.
Francesco Galli, bishop of Asti, 1381-†before 13 November 1408. Eubel: 115.
—Balduinus Piercoul 1406.
Jean de Boissy (?), bishop of Amiens, 29 March 1389-†4 September 1410. Eubel: 84.
—Johannes Hanini 1393.
Henri Bayler (?), bishop of Alet, 27 May 1390-†after April 1420. Eubel: 246.
—Petrus Sellerii 1393.

## Secular Authorities
The following secular authorities maintained clerics some of whom can also be found in the papal chapel of Avignon.
    Except for the ducal court of Burgundy and the royal court of Aragon, information concerning secular patronage is quite incomplete.

King Charles V of France (1364-1380).
—Johannes Carnoten before 1380.
—Johannes Symonis 1380.
King Charles VI of France (1380-1422).
—Johannes Carnoten before 1384.
—(Johannes Vitrarii 1406.)
Duke Philip the Bold of Burgundy (1363-1404).
—Johannes Carnoten 1369, 1374-1379 (sporadically), 1384-1399, first chaplain.
—Johannes Rogerii 1391-1392, 1394-1404.
—Johannes Vitrarii 1394.
—Stephanus Turqueti 1394-1400.
—Andrieu du Mor 1394-1404.
—Johannes Franciscus 1394-1404.
—Henricus de Scoenheze 1394-1404.
—Reginaldus du Houx 1395-1404.
—Johannes de Moleyo 1399, first chaplain; 1401-1404.
Duke John the Fearless of Burgundy (1404-1419).
—Johannes Franciscus 1404-1414.
—Andrieu du Mor 1404-1414.
—Johannes Vitrarii 1406.
Duke John of Berry (1360-1416).
—Johannes Rogerii 1403.
Duke Louis of Orléans (1392-1407).
—Matheus de Sancto Johanne (?) 1389.
Duke Louis of Guienne.
—Johannes Rogerii 1414-1415.
—Johannes Franciscus 1414-1415.

Please see Addenda to Other Service, p. 268.

Queen Joanna I of Naples (1343-1382).
—Matheus de Sancto Johanne (?) 1363.
Duke Louis I of Anjou (1360-1384).
—Johannes Lenfant 1377.
—Matheus de Sancto Johanne 1378.
Duke Louis II of Anjou (1384-1417).
King of Naples from 1389
—Johannes Symonis (?) 1390-1393.
—Johannes de Bosco (?) 1393.
King Peter IV of Aragon (1336-1387).
—Johannes Cossardi 1353.
—Robertus Nyot 1379-1380.
Queen Eleanor of Aragon (1349-1375).
—Johannes Cossardi 1354-1356, 1362.
Duke John of Gerona, heir to the throne; then King John I of Aragon (1387-1395).
—Johannes Fabri 1384-1385.
—Johannes Rogerii 1384-1385.
—Robertus Creque 1394.
King Alfonso V the Magnanimous of Aragon (1416-1458).
—Johannes Fabri (?) 1416, 1420, 1422.
King Ferdinand of Portugal (1367-1383).
—Johannes Symonis 1378.
—(Thomas Multoris 1380).
Guillaume Rolland, Lord Marshal of the Roman Curia (1354-1360).
—Dionysius Fabri 1359-1360.

# Biographies

## ALANUS AVIS dictus VOGEL
Cleric from the diocese of Liège, he received holy orders after being dispensed from the illegitimacy of birth. On 3 August 1354, this *clericus capelle intrinsece was required* to resign his chaplaincy at Saint-Piat of Chartres in order to receive the parsonage of Haute-Croix (in the diocese of Cambrai), however, he was allowed to retain his canonicate at the church of Notre-Dame of Beauvais. He requested a canonicate at Saint-Servais of Maastricht (Liège) on 18 April 1357. By 5 September 1360 when he asked for a canonicate at the altar of Our Lady in the cathedral of Troyes, he held the benefices at Maastricht and Haute-Croix, while continuing to serve as papal *clericus*. In August of the following year, we find the last reference to his papal service when he submitted a supplication for a canonicate at the cathedral of Toulouse belonging to Petrus Baniardi (q.v.). There is no indication that this benefice nor the one at Troyes was ever granted. Alanus passed into the Roman obedience, and under Boniface IX he was accorded the rights to a canonicate at the Marian church of Maastricht. He died on 2 October 1397.
(AVB 5: 216, no. 516; 348, no. 821; 626, no. 1535; 710, no. 1751. AVB 17: 273, no. 811. AVB 29: 484, no. 573. *RG* II: 43, 87.)

## ANCELMUS LANDELUY (LANDELUYC, ALANDELUYE, ALANDELONYER, VLANDELINC)
On 15 November 1378, as priest and chaplain of cardinal Pedro de Luna (the future Benedict XIII) he was granted a canonicate at Saint-Amé of Douai (Arras). This was immediately cancelled *quia defectum natalium*, probably illegitimacy, and he was given one at Saint-Géry of Cambrai instead. In 1391/92 he was provided a canonicate at the cathedral of Thérouanne. He appears as chaplain

on the first list compiled after the election of his former (?) patron. On 21 October 1394 he submitted a supplication on behalf of his familiar, Thomas Leonardi. Ancelmus is called chaplain on lists compiled at the end of December 1395 and in April 1396. On 24 May 1396 he gave up a canonicate at the Marian church of Tudela (Tarazona) to receive by *motu proprio*, a canonicate at Saint-Pierre of Lille (Tournai). The following spring, evidently still serving in the papal chapel, he was granted a dispensation in order to exchange an unspecified benefice. He again appears mong the papal chaplains when they were assembled at Pont-de-Sorgues on 9 August 1403. He seems to have discontinued papal service not long after this date.
(AVB 12: 31-32, no. 110. AVB 13: 745, no. 2238. AVB 19: 26-27, no. 58; 49, no. 126. AVB 26: 178, no. 680. Haberl: 213. Günther I: 187, 188, 192, doc. 4, doc. 5.)

ANCELMUS MARTINI alias CALLIGARII (FABRI)
First appearing in a rotulus as *cantor capelle* of Cardinal Guillaume Bragose, this deacon of Noyon requested a canonicate at the cathedral of Noyon on 19 November 1362. In January 1363 he was provided a canonicate at Saint-Pierre of Aire (Thérouanne). On 24 May 1366, as a priest, he was received into the papal chapel. A letter written to the chapter of Noyon by the chamberlain stated that Ancelmus was to receive his prebend in absentia because he was a papal chaplain from 24 June 1366. He made the journey to Rome with Urban, since on 5 November 1367, he and Johannes de Rancovado (q.v.) were paid at St. Peter's for renting two horses to aid in the transportation of the curia from Viterbo to Rome. In a supplication dated 13 September 1368, it states that this *capellanus capelle pape* served in the cathedral of Noyon *per duodecim annos in diurnus divinis*. At that time, the canonicate at Noyon was granted. He was allowed to keep his canonicate at Furnes (Thérouanne) but he had to give up the chaplaincy at Noyon. Only on 9 January 1371, though, does it appear that the benefice at Furnes was actually conferred. Six days following, he was received among the *cantores* of the newly elected Gregory XI. The cantorate of Noyon was bestowed on him by 8 January 1372, though he probably only officially began to hold the title on 5 October 1375. One month later he was forced to abandon his canonicate at Sainte-Walberge of Furnes. By 20 June of the following year, he was *scriptor*, held a semiprebend at the church of Saint-Omer, and was given the parsonage of Erignies (Amiens). He was listed among the chaplains paid on 19 September 1379. In May 1380 he possessed a parsonage of Wauthier-Braine (Cambrai), for which he gave up the canonicate of Noyon. He was named in the chapel records during fall of 1382 and again two years later. On 22 January 1385, he was paid his chaplain's wages. In October of that year, still listed as a papal *scriptor*, he resigned the cantorate of Noyon. He died before 11 September 1387 as a papal familiar. His service in the papal chapel, whether as *capellanus* or *scriptor*, seems to have been continuous from 1366.
(Schäfer III: 31, 368. AVB 7: 143, no. 480; 151, no. 503. AVB 11: 40, no. 49. AVB 13: 256, no. 1395; 412, no. 117; 412-413, no. 119; 561, no. 1041. AVB 15: 163-164, no. 2264, fn. AVB 20: 8-9, no. 1406, fn. AVB 25: 176, no. 3366; 206, no. 3428; 339, no. 3666; 540, no. 4056. Kirsch: 69-70. *Lettres, Urbain V*, vol. 1: 45, no. 981; vol. 7:8, no. 21185. Informatique: S03602316, fol. 227; S03700298, fol. 35v.; S03700528, fol. 59v. Günther I: 180, 182 fn., 184, 185. *OKS*: 64 fn.)

ANDREAS DE CHOQUES (THO)
On 26 August 1407, in a supplication requesting a canonicate at Saint-Géry of Cambrai, he was called familiar and *capellanus capelle*. The benefice was granted on 13 September. During this time, he held the rectorate at Isneauville (Rouen) and a perpetual chaplaincy at Notre-Dame of Paris.
(AVB 19: 206, no. 543. AVB 26: 809, no. 3647.)

ANTONIUS
*Frater* Antonius received payment for forty-two days of chapel service in 1335. He was among the first chaplains of Benedict XII. To understand certain hypotheses, a brief history of the Cistercian abbey of Fontfroide (Narbonne) is necessary. In 1311, Cardinal Arnaud Nouvel, abbot of Fontfroide, gave the abbacy to his nephew, Jacques Fournier. Jacques held the office for several

years. In the fall of 1333 and again in the late summer of 1334, an Antonius Germani, monk of Fontfroide, acted in several financial transactions for the Holy ee. By 1 February 1336, a *frater Antonius*, the fourth successor of Jacques Fournier, is listed as abbot of the monastery. On 23 March he was granted a plenary indulgence. On 2 April 1338 Guillelmus Mantolerii (q.v.), monk of Fontfroide, acted as procurer in the name of the abbot, *frater Antonius*. The monastery itself was held in *singularis dilectionis favore* by Benedict, and throughout the Avignon papacy it provided brothers, *fratres de bulla*, responsible for affixing the leaden seals to papal bulls. Keeping in mind the favored position of Fontfroide and the close association between the monastery and Benedict XII, it is possible that the same Antonius who briefly served the pope's chapel, might have come from this abbey. After his short stay in the curia, he might have been rewarded for his service to the pope by being appointed as abbot. The association of the two names linked to the papal chapel, namely, Guillelmus and Antonius, both monks, with the pope's most favored abbey leads us to the conclusion that the abbot and the chaplain were one and the same. Whether or not he can definitely be identified with Antonius Germani, the monk who had dealings with the Curia will probably never be determined. However, Antonius the abbot was promoted to the see of Lombez on 1 October 1341, which he held until his death, 7 September 1348.

(Schäfer II: 26. Göller I: 275, 599, 600. Göller II: 54, 127. *Lettres, Benoît XII*, vol. 1: 309, no. 3418. *Benoît XII (1334-1342). Lettres closes et patentes intéressant les pays autres que la France.* J.-M. Vidal and G. Mollat, eds. Paris, 1950: 585, nos. 1998-1999. Guillemain: 120, 320. Mollat: 26, 292. Jean Berthold Mahn, *Le Pape Benoît XII et les Cisterciens*, fascicle 295 of Bibliothèque de l'Ecole des Hautes-Etudes. Paris, 1949: 47. Williman: 450.)

## ARNULPHUS DE MASERIIS

Priest from the diocese of Arras, he held a benefice at the church of Duisans (Arras) when, on 8 January 1353 he asked for a canonicate at the cathedral of Tournai. There is no evidence that he was in any way associated with the chapel of Innocent VI. He does appear among the first supplicants along with Johannes de Attrebato (q.v.) and Jacobus Comitis (q.v.), and by 3 May 1354 he is called familiar of the pope. At that time, he is provided the canonicate at the church of Sainte-Croix (Cambrai) and the chaplaincy in the episcopal chapel of Cambrai given up by Jacobus Comitis. Besides the rectorate at Duisans, he was also expecting a prebend *in forma speciali* at the church of Saint-Amé of Douai. When he submitted a supplication requesting a canonicate at the collegial church of Saint-Vincent at Soignies (Cambrai) in August 1358, he was *capellanus capelle intrinsece*, and had added the chaplaincy of the leprosarium of Aubigny (Arras) to his growing list of benefices. Still papal chaplain in January 1359, his request for a benefice in the church of Saint-Etienne at Batilly (Avranches) was only granted when he resigned the chaplaincy at Aubigny. In May 1363 he acted as official of the diocese of Arras and as procurer. On 6 June of that year it was mandated that Arnulphus de Maseriis, *capelle pape capellanus*, receive the fruits of his benefices *integre*. He died outside of the curia before 22 June 1375. The following day, a canonicate he held at Saint-Piat of Seclin was granted to Thomas La Caille (q.v.).

(AVB 5: 1, no. 1; 189, no. 457; 488, no. 1189; 516, no. 1216; 543, no. 1329. AVB 9: 326, no. 786; 326, no. 787; 336, no. 809. AVB 17: 242, no. 716; 243, no. 717. AVB 25: 115, no. 3243; 116, no. 3244; 294, no. 3570. *Lettres, Urbain V*, vol. 1: 240, no. 2372; 240-241, no. 2373; vol. 2: 6, no. 4986.)

## BALDUINUS PIERCOUL

In February 1406, this priest from the diocese of Tournai submitted two supplications requesting a benefice at Saint-Pierre of Lille (Tournai). Although he was allowed to hold a chaplaincy in the hospital of Saint-Eloi (Tournai), he was told to surrender the rectorate of the church of Saint-Martin in the town of Wavrin. On 10 September of the same year, he submitted another supplication for the Lille benefice. In this document he states that *ante substractionem*, he served *per multa tempora* as cleric or *servitor* of the sacristan of the chapel. But by this time, he was in the service of the bishop of Asti, Francesco Galli. In the document granting the benefice (a chaplaincy) also bearing a 10 September date, Balduinus is called *servitor in capella pape et servitor Francisci* and rector of Warneton, not Wavrin. This may be a question of a less-than-careful scribe. (AVB 19: 195-196, no. 512. AVB 26: 778, no. 3551; 783, no. 3571; 793, no. 3604.)

BERENGARIUS DEMARII (=BERNARDUS ADEMARII? q.v.)
He received payment as chaplain of Benedict XII in 1337, 1339, and 1340.
(Schäfer II: 60, 94, 120.)

BERNARDUS ADEMARII (=BERENGARIUS ADEMARII? q.v.)
He was paid as chaplain of Benedict XII in 1336. He might have been the Bernardus Ademarii, a Cluniac monk from Solesmes (Limoges), who acted as procurer for the abbot on 29 September 1336.
(Schäfer II: 44. Göller II: 58.)

BERNARDUS GRALHERI
Although only the name Bernardus is recorded, this chaplain probably served in the reassembled chapel of Benedict XIII at Pont-de-Sorgues as recorded in the list of 9 August 1403. His full name is given with those of the chaplains who served for the two months previous to 8 November 1404. Nothing more is known about him.
(Günther I: 192, 193, doc. 5.)

BERTRANDUS LE CONNOITIE (CONVOITIE?)
He is cited among the members of the papal chapel on 30 October and 20 December 1382. He is probably identical to the Bertrandus who is listed as having been paid for service as chaplain up to 22 January 1385 and who is named in the payment of 30 October 1393.
(Günther I: 180, 185, 186-187, doc. 2.)

BERTRANDUS MAJORIS alias JAQUETI
*Clericus capelle intrinsece* on August 1354, he was granted the parsonage of Rumst (Cambrai). At that time, he held a benefice for poor clerics under the jurisdiction of the bishop of Châlons-sur-Marne. By November 1357 he added the title canon of Saint-Paul of Liège and submitted a supplication for a benefice at the rural church of Corcoleze (Carpentras). On 1 August 1361 his name appears in a supplication as clerk of the chapel, cameral familiar, and commensal of the nephew of Innocent VI, Audoin Aubert, the cardinal of Maguelonne (consecrated somewhat after 13 July 1361). In this document, the cardinal sought the canonicate at Liège and the parsonage at Rumst left vacant by the death of Bertrandus, whom he had held in his home and whose medical expenses he had incurred for four years.
(AVB 5: 216, no. 517; 414, no. 994; 705, nos. 1736-1737. AVB 17: 274, no. 812. Eubel: 19.)

CANTONUS PETRI
He was cited as clerk of the chapel of Benedict XII in two notices from 29 June and 24 August 1336, and in the accounts for the years 1337 and 1340. On 6 July 1338, he was required to reside in the place of his benefice, Saint-Nazaire of Les Aubertes (Béziers). He might have passed into the service of Cardinal Gozzio Battaglia da Rimini as chaplain, familiar, and commensal where a Sanctius Petri (Cantonus=Çantonus?) was cited in 1343.
(Schäfer II: 60, 120. *Lettres, Benoît XII*, vol. 2: 19, no. 5403. OPKA: 93 and fn. Gasparrini: 167, no. 393; 241.)

COLETA
This is no doubt an alias. He was listed among the first chaplains of Benedict XII.
(Schäfer II: 26.) COLINETUS (NICOLAUS) MARTINI

From the diocese of Reims, this clerk of the papal chapel was the son of Johannes Martini de Thudinio (Thuin) and his wife Ozilla, and the brother of Johannes. The first reference to Colinetus dates from 21 May 1342, when as *clericus capelle* he sought and was granted a canonicate in the church of Saint-Denis at Liège. On 3 August 1342, he is first noted as receiving payment for his papal service. Again, on 11 October of that same year, he was granted another canonicate in the city of Liège, this time at Sainte-Croix. Although in February 1343 he was given permission to receive his prebend at Saint-Denis without residence, in April of the following year he wrote to the pope asking him to intercede in the matter of receiving his prebends at Liège. At that time, the canons of said churches informed him that if he had not made at least his *primam residentiam personalem* within two years, he would be deprived of at least some portion of his prebend. Colinetus, still *clericus* and familiar, asked the pope for a dispensation *ut quod nullo unquam tempore ad personalem residentiam predictam faciendam in ipsis ecclesiis vel earum altera teneatur.* On 5 March 1343, called canon of Saint-Denis, Sainte-Croix, and Bonn (Cologne), he requested the promotion to Holy Orders. He was paid for papal service during the year 1343/44 and again on 5 June 1344. He continued as a papal familiar at least until 18 January 1345. Several times he submitted requests on behalf of members of his family.

(Schäfer II: 203, 234, 265, AVB 1: 2, no. 6; 2, no. 7; 53, no. 247; 58, no. 275; 68, nos. 325-326; 165, no. 700; 192, no. 787. AVB 6: 2, no. 5; 176, no. 547; 250, no. 765. AVB 7: 148, no. 492.)

## COUMPANUS DE CAMBELLO

Among the first chaplains of 1335, there is no other precise information on this chaplain. However, because of the rarity of his name, we suggest that he be identified with the Campannus de Cambello (Combello) who gave up the rectorate of the church at Ledringhem (Thérouanne) and exchanged a benefice at Saint-Walburge of Furnes (Thérouanne) for the office of pardoner of the diocese of Thérouanne on 16 March 1354. He held this post until at least 22 October 1367. He was also canon at the Marian church of Cassel (Thérouanne).

(Schäfer II: 26. AVB 5: 170, no. 419; 170-171, no. 420, fn. AVB 10: 162. AVB 17: 223, nos. 650-651; 338, no. 1002.)

## DIONYSIUS FABRI

He probably began curial service as chaplain of the Lord Marshal of the Roman curia in whose employ he was cited on 10 April 1359 and again on 23 May 1360. In order to receive a benefice at the church of Carvin (Tournai) that was left vacant at the death of Johannes Clementis de Brolio (q.v.), he gave up a benefice that he held in the parish church of Livarot (Lisieux). At that time, 13 February 1363, he also held benefices in the church of Saint-Saturnin-sur-Loire (Angers) and expected another in the cathedral of Poitiers. In a supplication made to Urban V two days later, Dionysius claimed that he had served in the apostolic palace for several years and that he continued in this service at that time. On 25 April 1363, he renounced the chaplaincy of the Twelve Apostles at Poitiers. Three days later he is documented as having resigned his benefice in Angers. On 14 March 1364, he was granted the canonicate at Saint-Piat of Seclin (Tournai) left vacant by the resignation of Walterus de Vastonia (q.v.). He was then called *capellanus capelle intrinsece.* Approximately one month later he requested the great vicariate at the major altar of the cathedral of Tournai. For this he abandoned the benefice at Carvin on 3 September 1367.

(AVB 5: 177, no. 435, fn.; 704, no. 1735, fn. AVB 7: 137, no. 463; 171-172, no. 563; 264, no. 783; 275, no. 820; 449, no. 1226; 458, no. 1245; 518, no. 1368. AVB 9: 192, no. 546; 233-234, no. 640; 469, no. 1102. AVB 10: 236, 243, 246, 250. AVB 15: 76-77, no. 2118, fn. Hoberg I: 277, 311. *Lettres, Urbain V*, vol. 1: 172, no. 1922; 192, no. 2049; vol. 3: 124, no. 9465; vol. 6: 86, no. 19053. Informatique: S03700037, fol. 6; S03700077, fol. 11; S03700782, fol. 94v.; S03801975, fol. 210v.; S03802167, fol. 226.)

## DROYNUS

He was paid for his service in the papal chapel on 30 October 1393. His name might more correctly read Androynus. If this is indeed the case, then he may be identical to the singer Andrieu du Mor. Andrieu was reported to have been a former chaplain of Clement VII when, on 2 November 1394, he was hired into the chapel of Duke Philip of Burgundy. He served until the interrment of the duke (June 1404) and then went to Evreux where he and Johannes Franciscus (q.v.) held canonicates. As chaplain of John, duke of Burgundy, he was probably summoned for service on special feasts. He may be the Andreas de Mauro who was a chaplain of Pope Martin V until August 1418. (Günther I: 186. Wright: 63, 85, 89, 221-230. Manfred Schuler, "Zur Geschichte der Kapelle Papst Martins V.," *Archiv für Musikwissenschaft* 25 (1968): 36.)

### EGIDIUS BATELLI (BACELLI)

He was a priest from the diocese of Arras. He held a benefice at the cathedral of Arras on 30 June 1353, when he submitted a request for a canonicate and the treasureship of the Marian church at Anthoing (Cambrai). He was granted a plenary indulgence on 29 April 1360. In April 1362 he acted in fiscal matters for the diocese of Reims, and later that year, on 28 November he was listed as chaplain of Cardinal Audoin Aubert of Ostia, the nephew of Innocent VI. At that time, he was a student in canon law, held a benefice in the parish church of Rouvroy (Arras), the aforementioned titles at Anthoing, and reserved a prebend in the church of Saint-Géry at Cambrai. Cardinal Audoin died on 10 May 1363, and not long after, on 12 June 1363, Egidius was admitted to the *capella intrinseca pape*. He was called *capellanus capelle* and bachelor *in decretis* when a canonicate at Saint-Donatien of Bruges (Tournai) was conferred upon him in June 1366. To receive this benefice, he was required to abandon his positions at Rouvroy, Anthoing, and Tournai. He had some difficulty in obtaining the canonicate at Bruges, and he might not have actually resigned all of his benefices. In September 1367, he reserved a canonicate at the cathedral of Tournai. When this reservation was confirmed, 5 January 1371, he held the treasurership at the church of Anthoing. On 19 June 1372 he was given a canonicate at the cathedral of Amiens. A document bearing the same date shows him to have resigned his canonicate at Saint-Donatien. However, a third reference of 19 June 1372 indicates that he was dead before this date. Later documents seem to indicate that he might still have been alive up until the early 1390s, or at least that another Egidius Batelli, one with similar benefices, might have existed (a nephew perhaps?). We find him resigning his canonicate at Tournai on 22 June 1384, and a notice of 19 June 1394 claims that he resigned his benefice at Saint-Donatien for the purposes of exchange. Records from the collectory of the diocese of Tournai indicate that he never was a legal canon of the cathedral and that he died before 1 May 1393 outside of the Curia, at which time he was familiar of Cardinal Hugues de Saint-Martial (cardinal from 17 September 1361-†1403). (Schäfer III: 28. AVB 5: 101, no. 264, fn.; 567-568, no. 1388, fn. AVB 7: 106, no. 380; 667-668, no. 1716; 670, no. 1720. AVB 9: 840-841, no. 1800. AVB 10: 249, 555, 556. AVB 11: 16-18, no. 16; 580, no. 1155; 785, no. 2495. ABV 15: 141-142, no. 2226; 376, no. 2628. AVB 17: 151, no. 433. AVB 20: 114-115, no. 1658; 115, no. 1659. *Lettres, Urbain V*, vol. 5: 87, no. 16355; vol. 7: 66, no. 21116; 404, no. 22512. Informatique: S03600421, fol. 47. Hoberg II: 89, no. 310.)

### EGIDIUS QUADRATI

He was priest and familiar of Cardinal Jean d'Auxois († 10 January 1359) on 20 June 1357, when he requested a benefice in the parish church of Saint-Amand-lès-Eaux (Tournai). At the time of the request, he already held the chaplaincy of Saint-Christophe in the cathedral of Le Mans and the rectorate of the parish church of *Basochia* (Chartres), either Bazoches-lès-Hautes or Bazoches-en-Dunois. On 25 April 1361, in submitting a request for the canonicate at the cathedral of Reims vacant by the death of Petrus Saumati (q.v.), he was called *capellanus capelle intrinsece*. At that time, he still held his benefice at Saint-Amand-lès-Eaux. Six months later, in October of that same year, he asked for the canonicate at the collegiate church of Saint-Géry (Cambrai), also once having belonged to Petrus Saumati. He continued to be listed as a chaplain of the papal chapel at least until 6 June 1363, when the pope mandated that, as papal familiar, he was required to remain with the curia, and therefore was allowed to receive his prebend in absentia. He died either before or during the year 1388/89, by which time he had already abandoned his benefice in Tournai. (AVB 5: 369, no. 876; 669, no. 1639; 731, no. 1810. AVB 9: 337, no. 812. AVB 10: 554. *Lettres, Urbain V*, vol. 2:6, no. 4985.)

## FERRICUS NUSILLETI (FERRITINUS, FERICUS MUSILEN)

He was a priest from the diocese of Besançon, received into the papal chapel on 15 June 1407. He was paid for his service in the city of Perpignan 1408/09.
(Günther II: 43. ASV, *Coll.* 457: fol. 257v.)

## FRANCISCUS

He was paid for his chapel service on 30 October 1393. Listed only as Franciscus, this might have been a reappearance of Franciscus de Goano (q.v.) who served the chapel of Clement VII earlier in his pontificate. But he is more likely Johannes Franciscus. In a rotulus submitted 27 November 1378, this cleric from the diocese of Liège was said to be *deserviens in capella* of Guillaume de Lestrange, archbishop of Rouen (†March 1389). At this time, Inguerannus Benedicti (q.v.) was also a member of the same chapel. Johannes requested a benefice at Liège and asked to be allowed to hold a chaplaincy at the Marian church of Walcourt (Liège). It is possible that the benefice received was the cantorate at Saint-Denis of Liège, a title he is said to have held by 1384. When he received a canonicate at Evreux on 20 April 1394, a perpetual chaplaincy at the cathedral of Rouen was given to Johannes de Altacuria (q.v.). On 2 November of that year, after the death of Pope Clement VII, Johannes Franciscus (Jehan François) was hired into the chapel of Duke Philip, and he joined the Burgundian court by 7 January of the following year. The Burgundian records cite him as a former chaplain of Pope Clement. By this time he had acquired a canonicate at Lisieux, and on 6 March 1400 he had resigned one at Sainte-Opportune of Paris. After his patron was buried in June of 1404, he retired to Evreux where he still held his canonicate. He possessed this benefice at least until May 1412. During the years 1414 and 1415 he was called upon to serve Duke Louis of Guienne. Wright has indentified him as the composer Jehan Franchois de Gembloux (Gemblaco). Papal documents do refer to a Johannes de Gemblaco, cleric from the diocese of Liège, who was seeking a canonicate at the Marian church of Tongres (Liège) in 1394, but this might be another individual. The works of the composer Johannes Franchois include two settings of the *Patrem*, two of the *Et in terra*, three rondeaux, all three-voice works, and the motet *Ave virgo* that appears in four- and five-voice arrangements. His works are found in Ao, BL, Ca 6, Ca ll, Mü 3232a, and Tr 93.
(Günther I: 186-187, doc. 3. AVB 8: 509, no. 1816. AVB 13: 783, no. 2480. AVB 26: 359, no. 1578. Wright: 63, 64, 67, 69-70, 85, 92, 169-171, 221-230. Craig Wright, "Johannes Franchois de Gemblaco," *Grove 6*, vol. 6, p. 774. James T. Igoe, "Johannes Franchois de Gembloux, " *Rivista Musicale Italiana* 4 (1970): 3-50.)

## FRANCISCUS DE GOANO

Franciscus first makes his appearance in the papal documents in late November 1362 when, as familiar of Cardinal Gilles Aycelin de Montaigut and canon of Saint-Pierre at Braque (Reims) this cleric from Thérouanne sought a canonicate at Saint-Pierre of Aire (Thérouanne). On 24 January 1371 he was given a canonicate at Saint-Pierre of Cassel (Thérouanne), at which time he already held one at Saint-Martin of Vieil-Hesdin (Thérouanne). By the beginning of December 1372, Franciscus was clerk to Gérard de Dainville, bishop of Cambrai. But three years later he was in the service of Cardinal Francesco Tebaldeschi. He then possessed benefices at Vieil-Hesdin and Coudekerque (Thérouanne) and asked again for a benefice at Cassel. Within several months, he had been advanced from subdeacon to priest, and on 13 April 1377 he received a canonicate at the cathedral of Metz as papal chaplain. Franciscus makes his appearance in numerous papal documents written during the month of November 1378. He held the canonicate at Metz and the rectorate of Coudekerque when a canonicate at Saint-Donatien of Bruges was conferred on him. He is also named in a rotulus of familiars of the late Pope Gregory, in which he claims to be a *capellanus capelle* of Clement VII. At that time he requested and was granted a benefice at the cathedral of Cambrai, for which he had to resign his rectorate at Coudekerque. The registers show that he was given a dispensation for a defect of birth on the same day that he probably was granted the rectorate of La Cauchie at Valenciennes (Cambrai). He is listed among the papal chaplains in a record of the payment made 19 September 1379. He no longer seemed to have been a member of the chapel in September 1386 when he exchanged his canonicate at Metz for one at Thérouanne. He was then chaplain of the altar of Saint John the Evangelist in the church of Saint Peter *ad Ymagines* at Metz, canon of the cathedral of Arras, rector at Valenciennes, and e probably maintained his position as rector of Coudekerque. It is possible that he was the Franciscus (q.v.) who was paid for service in the papal chapel on 30 October 1393. At the time of his death, which took place before 2 July 1404, there was still some knowledge of his papal service. On this date he was referred to as familiar and chaplain of Clement VII. After his death, a canonicate at Arras and benefice at Saint-Omer of Lillier (Thérouanne) became vacant.

(AVB 7: 46, no. 121. AVB 8: 5, no. 16; 23, no. 72; 57, no. 184, fn.; 682, no. 2492. AVB 10: 435-436. AVB 11: 121, no. 205. AVB 12: 5, no. 16; 13-14, no. 45; 22, no. 79; 123, no. 446. AVB 13: 586, no. 1191. AVB 20: 599, no. 2751, fn. AVB 25: 215-216, no. 3443 and fn.; 438-439, no. 3884. AVB 26: 733, no. 3379; 798, no. 3616. Günther I: 182 fn., 186-187, doc. 3. Informatique: S03602298, fol. 225v.) GERARDUS GERARDI (GIRARDUS GIRARDI, GARDI)

In a supplication dated 16 October 1394, Gerardus was said to be from Saint-Dié. At the time he was canon of Verdun, familiar of Cardinal Guillaume d'Aigrefeuille, held a canonicate and rectorate of Saint-Dié (Toul), and was seeking a canonicate at Saint-Omer (Thérouanne). On 29 September 1403, he was received into the papal chapel at Pont-de-Sorgues. He served in November 1404, according to records, and by 24 April 1405, after the death of Richardus de Bozonvilla (q.v.), he was *locum tenens magistri capelle*. He is listed in the accounts from the following 3 July. In September of the following year, he acted as procurer in an exchange between Petrus Sellerii (q.v.) and Nicolaus Vacherii (q.v.). On 26 November 1407 he was granted a canonicate at Saint-Denis of Liège. He was permitted to keep his canonicate at Saint-Dié and rectorates at Prinsujéols (Mende) and Navacelle (Uzès). Besides being *magister capelle*, he held the title of *scriptor*. He was serving as master of the chapel on 4 May 1408. Because he was *familiaris et capellanus Petri de Luna*, the Council of Pisa deprived him of his canonicate at Saint-Dié on 28 July 1413. Gerardus held the office of *magister capelle* for Benedict according to a document sent from Barcelona on 18 July 1416 by King Alfonso V of Aragon to the Council of Constance. Schimmelpfennig has discovered evidence of this chaplain which dates from July 1429.

(Günther I: 193, 194, 195. Günther II: 42, 43. AVB 19: 195, no. 509; 211, no. 557. AVB 26: 43-44, no. 122. ASV, *Coll.* 457: fol. 257v. OPKA: 107 fn. *RG* III: 336. Heinrich Finke, *Acta Concilii Constanciensis*, vol. 3. Münster in Westphalen, 1926, p. 578.)

## GUIDO DE LANGE

He was a member of the papal chapel when he left the Curia, presumably on business, on 5 November 1373 with Johannes Ruffi de Roquinies (q.v.) and Theobaldus Furnerii (q.v.). The date of their return was entered as 11 November. Guido is listed as being among the members of the chapel on 2 October 1374 and again on 30 October, when he and Theobaldus left the service of the chapel. No date for their return was ever entered, and we have no further information on Guido de Lange. He was the Parisian cleric who, as familiar and commensal f Cardinal Guillaume de la Jugie, reserved a benefice at the Benedictine monastery of Le-Bec-Hellouin (Rouen) on 20 November 1362. He was named rector of Saint-Pierre-de-Montfort (Rouen) on 9 November 1363. The document refers to him as *clericus capelle pape*.

(*Lettres, Urbain V*, vol. 1: 322-323, no. 2909; vol. 3, 48, no. 9062. Günther I:177, fn. Ursula Günther, "Johannes Vaillant." In *Speculum musicae artis: Festgabe für Heinrich Husmann zum 60. Geburtstag*. Munich: Wilhelm Fink, 1970, p. 174. Informatique: S03602342 fol. 229; S04000804, fol. 99.)

## GUIDO DE NAUGRO

He was admitted to the group of papal chaplains on 12 June 1363.
(Schäfer III: 28.)

## GUILLELMUS BLADETI

He was brought into the *capella intrinseca* on 24 December 1369.
(Schäfer III: 36.)

## GUILLELMUS DE CONVENIS

Guillelmus was chaplain of Benedict XII in 1335, 1336, 1337, 1339, 1340, and 1342.
(Schäfer II: 26, 44, 60, 94, 120, 159.) GUILLERMUS EPI

He was paid on 21 June 1405 in the city of Genoa for his service as *cantor*.
(Günther I: 194. Günther II: 42.)

## GUILLELMUS FABRI

This cleric from the diocese of Reims was sworn into the papal chapel on 11 June 1395 along with
Johannes Srelvit (q.v.). Nothing more is known about him.
(Günther I: 189, doc. 4.)

## GUILLELMUS DE FLANDRIA alias DE BETHUNA

Cleric from the diocese of Arras, he was a protégé of Cardinal Pierre Roger in 1338. At that time, he
received a benefice at Anquetierville (Rouen). When the cardinal became Pope Clement VI,
Guillelmus served him as chaplain. He was listed as such in a document dated 3 August 1342. Later
that month the office of *scriptor* was conferred on him. In November 1342, he had given up his
benefice in Rouen which was then bestowed on Fgidius Waguel, a *clericus commensalis*. He was
listed among the chaplains again on 28 October 1342, during the year 1343/44, and on 5 June 1344.
In September 1342, he was given a canonicate at the cathedral of Arras, at which time he was called
*scriptor et familiaris* of the pope. He is thus designated in a number of documents dating up until 8
October 1347. He sought a canonicate at Sainte-Walberge of Furnes (Thérouanne) on 9 June 1348,
and this, together with the treasurership of that church, was conferred on 29 May 1350. Continuing
to retain his position as *scriptor* and familiar of the pope, on 15 January 1352 he gave up a
canonicate at the cathedral of Autun, the abbacy of Saint-Etienne at Létra, and the rectorate of the
church at Millay (both Autun) in exchange for a canonicate at Saint-Omer of Saint-Omer
(Thérouanne). As late as 6 June 1353 he was listed as papal *scriptor* working in the diocese of Arras.
After his death, which took place outside of the Curia before 19 November 1355, all his titles
became vacant, including the title of *grossator litterarum*. In the margin of a volume of
supplications to Pope Clement VI, next to a request made by *scriptor* Johannes Courtois, appears
the witticism: "They promoted Courtois splendidly." The remark is signed: G. del Boy, G. de
Flandria, J. de Sinemuro (q.v.).
(Schäfer II: 203, 204, 234, 265. *Lettres, Benoît XII*, vol. 2: 40, o. 5577. *Lettres, Clément VI*, vol. 1:
191, no. 1117. AVB 1: 33, no. 162, fn.; 180, no. 747; 180, no. 748; 213, no. 856; 339, no. 1284; 362,
no. 1359; 515, no. 1980; 607, no. 2345. AVB 5: 317, no. 744; 318, no. 745; 318, no. 746; 321, no. 757;
484, no. 1179. AVB 6: 212, no. 655; 597, no. 1607; 612, no. 1647; 630, nos. 1711-1712. AVB 7: 310,
no. 914, fn.; AVB 10: 166, 174. AVB 17: 403, no. 1207; 403, no. 1208; 403, no. 1209; 406, no. 1217.
Mohler: 255. Hoberg II: 90, no. 315. *OKS*: 63 fn. 66. John E. Wrigley, "Studies in the Life of Pierre
Roger (Clement VI) and of Related Writings of Petrarch"(Ph.D. diss., University of Pennsylvania,
1965), pp. 72-73.

## GUILLELMUS LUPI

Cleric of Paris, he was chaplain of Guy de Ventadour, bishop of the Benedictine see of Vabres (†
before 17 October 1352) Guillelmus was chaplain at the altar of Saint-Jacques in the abbey of
Saint-André at le Câteau (Cambrai) and had a canonicate at Saint-Germain of Mons (Cambrai)
from 7 September 1349. On 18 January 1353, when he was granted a benefice at the Benedictine
monastery of Le-Bec-Hellouin (Rouen), he was chaplain and familiar of Cardinal Gilles Rigaud,
the abbot of the Benedictine abbey of Saint-Denis. At that time Guillelmus was rector of the parish
church of Saint-Laurent at Verneuil (Evreux), was expecting a prebend at the church of Notre-
Dame at Villeneuve-lès-Avignon, and held the benefices already mentioned. Cardinal Gilles

Rigaud died on 10 September of that year, and it was probably not long afterwards that Guillelmus entered the service of another cardinal, Audouin Aubert, the nephew of Pope Innocent VI. On 20 December 1353, he is called chaplain and familiar of Audouin in a supplication for a chaplaincy at Notre-Dame of Paris. Within the eleven months since the date of the last request, he seems to have exchanged most of his benefices, for at that time he only held benefices at the church of Saint-Laurent at Quetteville (Lisieux) and at the abbey of Saint-André. By 21 November 1355 he had been named *capellanus capelle intrinsece* of the pope and was in the process of obtaining a canonicate at Saint-Jean of Liège. He is noted again in papal service on 3 June 1356, when he was given an almuce as a member of the papal chapel. The prebend at Liège was bestowed on 1 May 1356. One year later, still a *capellanus* of the pope, in a request for a canonicate at the cathedral of Lisieux, we find that he had also augmented his list of benefices with the altar of Sainte-Elizabet at the parish church of Haren (Cambrai). He gave up his benefice at Saint-André in March 1358, and on 24 June 1359 the remainder of his acquisitions were relinquished, since a bit before this date he had become a member of the Carthusian order. By 8 November 1362, he was living at the monastery of Villeneuve-lès-Avignon. He was still alive in September 1374, when he acted as procurer in the Roman Curia for the Carthusians of Villeneuve.
(Schäfer II: 625. Schäfer III: 520. AVB 5: 14, no. 38; 136, no. 342; 149, no. 374, fn.; 319, no. 751; 358, no. 844; 448, no. 1083; 531-32, nos. 1301-1302. AVB 9: 9, no. 6. AVB 17: 24, no. 51. *Lettres, Urbain V*, vol. 1: 315, no. 2857.)

## GUILLELMUS MOTONERII (MANTOLERII, MONTELERII)
*Frater.* He was among the first chaplains of Benedict XII. He was paid for 53 days. He probably was from the monastery of Fontfroide (Narbonne) and was the Guillelmus Mantolerii, a Cistercian monk who acted as procurer on 2 April 1338 in the name of the abbot, *frater Anthonius* (q.v.). He again acted on behalf of the abbot of Fontfroide on 14 August 1347. Guillemain believes him to have been from a noble Avignonese family, though this seems unproven. (Schäfer II: 26. Göller II: 127. Mohler: 146. Guillemain: 363, and fn.)

## GUILLELMUS RASTELERII
From the city of Béthune in the diocese of Arras, Guillelmus is reported to have first entered the papal chapel on 9 August 1348. In June 1351, he requested a canonicate and the treasurership of the cathedral of Thérouanne which he declined when it became available. The following month he was provided canonicates at Saint-Pierre of Cassel (Thérouanne) and Saint-Pierre of Seclin (Tournai), although the latter should probably read Saint-Piat. At this time, he was rector of the parish church of Domazan (Uzès). From mid-1351 until 2 May 1352 he was called papal familiar, and documents from 9 May and 30 December 1353 call him chaplain of Pope Clement VI. On 8 April of the following year he exchanged his rectorate at Domazan for a canonicate at Saint-Amé of Douai (Arras) and for the parish church of Coupelle-Vieille (Thérouanne). At that time he also held a canonicate at the cathedral of Arras and chaplaincy at Laon.
(AVB 1: 563, no. 2174; 574, no. 2215; 578, no. 2229; 589, no. 2271; 616, no. 2378. AVB 5: 77, no. 204; 178, no. 437; AVB 10: 162-63. AVB 17: 201, no. 587; 230, no. 674-75.)

## GUILLELMUS DE ULTRAAQUAM
He first appears in the papal chapel as one of the chaplains paid during the fall of 1382. He is again named in a list of *capellani* who served during the two-month period ending 22 January 1385. In a document dated 14 May 1393, he is called a papal familiar. At that time, a canonicate at the cathedral of Cambrai, vacant through the death of Matheus de Longariga (q.v.), was bestowed on him. He was again paid for his service on 30 October 1393.
(AVB 13: 764, no. 2348. Günther I: 180, 185, 186-87, doc. 2, doc. 3.)

## GUILLELMUS VILLART DE BLANO
Priest from the diocese of Nevers, chaplain of the papal chapel, rector of he church at Vaudricourt (Arras), and holder of a chaplaincy in the cathedral of Arras, he asked for a canonicate at Saint-Pierre of Aire (Thérouanne), 19 August 1361. On 11 November 1362, still retaining all of the above

titles, he solicited for a canonicate at Saint-Pierre of Lille (Tournai). In June of the following year, no longer called papal chaplain, he gave up his benefices at Vaudricourt and at the cathedral of Arras in order to receive the canonicate at Lille. In a document of 10 June 1376, which confers a canonicate at the cathedral of Autun on him, Guillelmus is called chaplain of the chapel of Popes Innocent VI and Urban V and canon of Saint-Pierre of Lille and Saint-Pierre of Aire. This document was submitted on his behalf by Cardinal Guillaume d'Aigrefeuille though no relationship between the two is specified. In March 1384 he exchanged his canonicate at Lille for the rectorate of Montishélie (Autun). He is cited again, when he resigned his benefice at Aire, between 1388 and 1390.

(AVB 5: 710, no. 1752. AVB 7: 6, no. 8; 293, no. 865; 296, no. 873; 298, no. 881. AVB 9: 29-30, no. 50; 335, no. 805; 342, no. 821. AVB 10: 180, 457. AVB 13: 512, no. 736. AVB 25: 334-35, no. 3656. *Lettres, Urbain V*, vol. 1: 246, no. 2409; 371, no. 3336; 391, no. 3497. Informatique: S03602187, fol. 216v.; S03900601, fol. 71; S03901000, fol. 113.)

### HENRICUS PONETI DE BOSSUTO (HENRIETUS, PONEL, POVEL)

On 12 January 1371, a canonicate at Saint-Jean of Liège was conferred on this cleric when he was familiar and commensal of Cardinal Jean de Blauzac. By November 378, this subdeacon was prepared to resign the chaplaincy of Blessed Mary at Louvain (Liège) in order to receive a canonicate or other office at Saint-Servais of Maastricht (Liège). At the time, he retained his canonicate at Saint-Jean and was called papal familiar. Within the next week and a half, Henricus filed requests for his brother Nicolaus. On 12 February of the following year, called *orator* and subdeacon of the chapel, he requested a canonicate at Saint-Barthélemy of Liège that was granted on 3 March. The title of subdeacon without doubt refers to the station in holy orders and not to a particular chapel function. The name of this cleric appears in the list of *capellani* paid 19 September 1379. Still a papal familiar on 25 February 1381, a document informs us that he resigned a canonicate at Saint-Martin of Liège for one at Saint-Amé of Douai (Arras). Henricus again appears in the chapel registers from the fall of 1382, and, on January 1385, he is listed under the name Henrietus. On 8 January 1388, as papal familiar, canon of Saint-Jean at Liège, Saint-Amé at Douai, and rector of the parish church of Quiévrain (Cambrai), he was provided not only a canonicate at the cathedral of Cambrai, but also a rectorate at the church of Saints-Gervais-et-Protais of Guise (Laon). Three months later, a number of documents were filed in which Henricus was granted an indulgence, the rights to his prebends in absentia, and the privilege to celebrate the divine offices in places under papal interdict. Several documents from the following year emphasize the fact that this cleric was a canon of Cambrai. The name Henrietus is written in the payment lists of 30 October 1393, though this time it probably refers to Henricus Scoenheze (q.v.). In a supplication compiled soon after the consecration of Benedict XIII, Henricus is called *capellanus capelle* of Clement VII, canon of Cambrai, Saint-Pierre of Lille (Tournai), rector of Quiévrain, though deprived of Saint-Jean of Liège *per intrusum*. At the time, Henricus asked for a canonicate at Saint-Omer.

(AVB 8: 5-6, no. 18; 621, no. 2326; 633, no. 2355; 421, no. 1410. AVB 10: 368, 540. AVB 11: 82, no. 141. AVB 12: 27, no. 99; 199, no. 745. AVB 13: 433, no. 244; 624, no. 1447; 630, nos. 1488, 1489, 1491; 631, nos. 1492, 1493. AVB 26: 35, no. 99. Günther I: 180, 182 fn., 185, 186-87, doc. 2 and 3.)

### HENRICUS POUSARDI (PUSUARDI, BUSUARDI)

He was listed among the papal chaplains at least from 8 November 1404. Several times his name appears in the papal documents of 1405. On one occasion during this year, he accepted the wages on behalf of the *clerici* along with Jacobus de Macas (q.v.). He is again documented as a papal chaplain in the records of the wages paid at Perpignan, 1408/09.

(Günther I: 193, 194. Günther II: 42, 43.)

## HENRICUS DE SCOENHEZE (STOKOUZE, HENRIETUS, HENRI SCHOENHERZE, HENRY LE LIEGOIS, D'ESCOINHEZE, etc.)

This cleric from the diocese of Liège was familiar and clerk of the chapel of Cardinal Pierre de Monteruc († 30 May 1385) when he was given a canonicate at Saint-Jean of Liège. On the same day, 15 November 1378, a benefice under the jurisdiction of the chapter of the cathedral of Paris was conferred on him. He passed the examination for the office of *tabellionatus* (scribe) on 5 September 1382. By 8 April 1389 he had become chaplain of the papal chapel. In a document bearing this date, he reserved a rectorate at the parish church of Bourneville (Rouen) to be conferred after the death of Inguerannus Benedicti (q.v.). He is again called papal chaplain on 14 October 1392, when he was given this rectorate and a canonicate at Saint-Géry of Cambrai. He is listed as Henrietus in the payment to the chaplains made 30 October 1393. On 2 November 1394 he was hired by Duke Philip of Burgundy to serve as chaplain of his chapel. He was in service every year until the duke's death and internment in June 1404.

(AVB 8: 74, no. 250. AVB 10: 552, AVB 12: 47, no. 156; 48, no. 157. AVB 13: 465, no. 455; 649, no. 1616; 741, no. 2210; 741, no. 2212. Wright: 63, 221-30.)

## INGUERANNUS BENEDICTI (INGUERRAMUS)

On 30 June 1376, possessing chaplaincies at Le Toillon (Cambrai) and Herenthals (Cambrai), he asked for another unspecified benefice at Cambrai. This cleric from the diocese of Cambrai was a familiar and *deserviens in capella* of Cardinal Guillaume de Lestrange, archbishop of Rouen, on 27 November 1378. At that time, he requested an official title at the cathedral of Cambrai. He already possessed the chaplaincy at Le Toillon and had added the altar of Saint-Léonard at the cathedral of Paris and a certain other one at the cathedral of Rouen. The cardinal died in March 1389 and by 8 April 1389, Inguerannus had become a papal chaplain. At that time, Henricus Scoenheze (q.v.) reserved the rectorate at Bourneville (Rouen) that he was to receive after the death of Inguerannus. He also held a rectorate at Saint-Denis *du Val* and was cited as a papal familiar. On 22 April of that same year, as *capellanus capelle*, he received remission of annates to be paid on a benefice in the diocese of Cambrai. On 26 February of that following year we are told what that benefice was when he abandoned a canonicate at Saint-Géry while at that same time still holding a canonicate at Laon. On 14 October 1392 he gave up the benefice at Laon in order to get a canonicate at the cathedral of Cambrai. By 25 March 1393, Inguerannus Benedicti, papal familiar and chaplain, had died outside of the Curia. His canonicate at Cambrai was given to Johannes de Champigneyo (q.v.). No payment list seems to have survived from this time bearing the name of Inguerannus, and it is impossible to ascertain whether or not his service extended beyond the years in which he was cited, 1389 and 1393.

(AVB 8: 508, no. 1815. AVB 10: 540, 546, 553. AVB 13: 649, no. 1616; 671, no. 1760; 741, no. 2210; 760, no. 2327; AVB 25: 346, no. 3678.)

## JACOBUS BRISART

This chaplain was probably listed on 5 October 1395 under the name Jaquetus. On 13 October, he submitted a supplication requesting a canonicate at the cathedral of Noyon. In the document, he is called cleric of the diocese of Cambrai and *capellanus capelle*. At that time, he held a rectorate in the parish church of Saint-Rémy at Saint-Quentin *in Viromandia* (Noyon). He appears again (?) as Jaquetus in the list of those chaplains paid for service in the chapel up to 12 April 1396.

(AVB 26: 10, no. 12. Haberl: 213. Günther I: 187, 188, doc. 4.)

## JACOBUS COMITIS

From the diocese of Arras, he is named in a supplication dated 30 January 1350 as familiar, chaplain, and commensal of Cardinal Etienne Aubert (the future Innocent VI) when he requested a canonicate and deaconate of Saint-Pierre of Aire (Thérouanne). In a document of 11 January 1352, in which he exchanged the deaconate at Aire and a chaplaincy at Marck (Thérouanne) for a canonicate at Saint-Jean of Liège with Johannes Gervasii (q.v.), no indication of his association with the cardinal is given. Neither is any association made in two notices of 8 January 1353 wherein he resigns his canonicate in Liège for a canonicate at Sainte-Croix (Cambrai) and for a perpetual chaplaincy in the episcopal palace of Cambrai. One week later, however, in a request for a canonicate at Sainte-Walberge, he is called papal familiar. By August of that year, we see him as *capellanus capelle intrinsece* and *lector Biblie*, referring to the custom of having someone read passages from the Bible while the pope dined. At that time, Jacobus requested a benefice in the parish church of Orsan (Uzès). On 28 April 1354, as papal familiar, he was given a canonicate at the cathedral of Verdun, and several days later, he received one at the cathedral of Arras. At this time, his benefices at Sainte-Croix and in the episcopal palace of Cambrai were resigned and bestowed on Arnulphus de Maseriis (q.v.).

(AVB 1: 491, no. 1884; 607-8, no. 2346. AVB 5: 2, no. 4; 4-5, no. 11; 114, no. 293; 185, no. 450; 188-189, no. 456. AVB 17: 7-8, nos. 10-12; 13, no. 25; 164, no. 475; 238, no. 705; 242, no. 715; 242, no. 716; 242-43, no. 717.)

### JACOBUS DE GRISEOVILLARI (GRIVILLARI, GRIVILLER)

On 12 July 1366, when he was granted a canonicate at Saint-Pierre of Aire (Thérouanne), this deacon of the diocese of Amiens and vicar of Roye (Amiens) had to give up all claims to a canonicate at Saint-Nicolas-au-Cloître (Amiens). On 11 January 1371, he asked for a canonicate at the church of Nesle (Noyon). At that time he was chaplain of the Cardinal of Albano, the brother of Urban V, Anglic Grimoard. He held this canonicate and one at Saint-Maurice of Compiègne (Soissons) at the end of May of that same year, when he resigned the benefice at Aire. He served as *magister capelle* to Cardinal Guillaume Noellet according to a document dated 15 November 1378. He was then a rector at Beurele (Cambrai) and was also seeking a canonicate and some official title at the cathedral of Noyon. Less than a year later, on 19 September, he was listed among the chaplains of the papal chapel. He was given his wages for his service as chaplain on 30 October and 20 December 1382, and he was again noted as a chaplain who served Clement VII for the two months prior to 22 January 1385.

(AVB 7: 675, no. 1729. AVB 8: 77, no. 259. AVB 9: 844, no. 1810. AVB 11: 57-58, no. 83. AVB 20: 102, no. 1626; 102, no. 1627. Günther I: 180, 182 fn., 185, doc. 2. *Lettres, Urbain V*, vol. 5: 93, no. 16387.)

### JACOBUS DE MASSAS (MASSIS, MACAS)

This chaplain was from the diocese of Saragossa. He took the oath at Tarascon on 13 January 1404. Jacobus was paid for his services on 8 November and again on 24 April 1405 when he and Henricus Pousardi (q.v.) accepted payment for the *clerici*. He makes one last appearance, according to available information, in the records of the wages paid on 3 July 1405.

(Günther I: 193 and fn., 194. Günther II: 42. ASV, *Coll.* 457: fol. 257v.)

### JACOBUS DE PRATIS (PRATO)

Two documents, the first dated 13 October 1394, and the second 4 April 1399, provide this papal familiar and cleric from Cambrai with a benefice at the cathedral. By 13 October 1405, he was granted a canonicate at Tournai, already possessed one at Cambrai and Cavaillon, and held the archdeaconate of Antwerp. He was papal familiar, commensal, and *scriptor* at that time. His name appears in the lists of chapel members made on 8 November 1404, and on 24 April and 3 July 1405, probably as *clericus*, though this is not specified. He died of the plague in Genoa during the month of October 1405. His canonicate at Cambrai then went to Johannes Broulette (q.v.). Two documents refer to him as *clericus cerimoniarum*, and one names him familiar and *capellanus capelle* as well. A third source calls him *scriptor litterarum apostolicarum* and chaplain of the chapel.

(AVB 19: 99, no. 225; 187, no. 489; 188, no. 491. AVB 26: 23, no. 59; 504, no. 2387; 521, no. 2434; 719, no. 3339; 774-75, no. 3541. Günther I: 193. Günther II: 42. *ZKM*: 130-31.)

**JACOBUS RAYMUNDI**
He served as *clericus cerimoniarum* for Pope Benedict XIII from 1411 until 1417. In 1418, in the retinue of Cardinal Piero Fonseca, he transferred his allegiance to the Council of Constance. (*ZKM*: 99, 131, 331.)

**JACOBUS (JAQUETUS) RINGARDI**
Jacobus was paid for his service as chaplain on 30 October and 20 December 1382 and again on 26 March 1383. In this last notice he is called Jaquetus Ringardi. He probably should be identified with the Jaquetus (I) who was in the chapel in September 1379 and January 1385. (Günther I: 180, 182 fn., 184, 185, doc. 2.)

**JOHANNES ADEMARI**
He was paid for the expenses incurred in the papal chapel beginning 12 September 1353. He must have taken over the office of *magister capelle* not long after the death of his precedessor, Stephanus de Chaulageto (q.v.). His activities before this date are unknown. In 1355 he held the rectorate at Durban (Narbonne), and at some time held a canonicate and prebend at the cathedral of Toledo. On 21 November 1355, as master of the chapel and *grossator litterarum*, he asked to be given the office of *decimator* (in charge of receiving the tithe or *dîme*) for the churches of Saint-Félix, Saint-Pierre-de-Romas, and Auterive (all in Agen). On 30 May 1361, in a supplication for the office of *scriptor* of penitential letters that once belonged to Johannes Clementis de Brullio, we discover more about the *magister*. He came from the diocese of Limoges and was a student of civil law. By 24 July of that year he was dead, probably of the plague.
(Schäfer II: 548, 578, 625-26, 673, 674-75, 20. Hoberg: 155, 216 ff., 219, 319, 321, 322, 360, 373, 389, 390, 392. Ehrle: 221-23. Hoberg I: 179-80. AVB 5: 177, fn.; 320, no. 753; 684, no. 1676. *Lettres, Urbain V*, vol. 1: 153, no. 1804. Schäfer I: 29. *OKS*: 63 fn, 64. Informatique: S03601946, fol. 195.)

**JOHANNES DE ALTACURIA (HAUCOURT)**
A priest from the diocese of Noyon, on 8 January he resigned a perpetual chaplaincy at the altar of the Holy Trinity at the cathedral of Cambrai for the purpose of permutation. By 22 April 1393 he had entered the service of the papal chapel, though he might have already been a chaplain for some time. On that date, he was given a canonicate at Saint-Piat of Seclin (Tournai) vacant through the death of Simon le Corieur, a former chaplain at the Burgundian court. Johannes was paid with the other members of the papal chapel on 30 October 1393. On 20 April of the following year, called canon of Seclin and familiar and chaplain of the pope, he was provided with the perpetual chaplaincy of Saint-Paul at the cathedral of Rouen. He was included among the first of the chaplains of Benedict XIII according to the list of 5 October 1394. In a supplication written about one week later, he asked for a canonicate at either Cambrai or Laon. At the time, he possessed a rectorate at the parish church of Saint-Vaast (Cambrai) in addition to his chaplaincy at Rouen and canonicate at Seclin. About one week after this document was submitted, Johannes is seen requesting a benefice at Cambrai on behalf of another. His name appears in the records of the payment made to the papal chaplains for the two months service prior to 12 April 1396. He continued to serve in the chapel, and he is cited as a member on 19 September 1397. At that time, he resigned his benefice at Seclin in order to exchange it for a canonicate at Saint-Laurent of Rozoy (Laon). He seems to have also held a canonicate at Sainte-Opportune of Paris which he resigned on 8 April 1400. He is listed again among the members of the papal chapel regrouped at Pont-de-Sorgues on 11 August 1403. Three compositions attributed to him survive: two three-voice rondeaux and one three-voice virelai. His works are found in Ch and in O.
(Günther I: 186-88, 192, doc. 3-5. Haberl: 213. AVB 13: 751, no. 2270; 763, no. 2342; 783, no. 2480. AVB 19: 69, no. 163. AVB 26: 10, no. 15; 178, no. 681. Wright: 67. Ursula Günther, "Johannes Haucourt," *Grove 6*, vol. 8, p. 302.)

## JOHANNES ANCELLI
On 6 April 1342 this *capellanus capelle* was involved in a financial transaction. He is probably identical to one of the other Johannes who were active in 1342.
(Göller: 193.)

## JOHANNES DE ATHIES
A cleric from the diocese of Noyon, Johannes entered the chapel on 11 June 1348. On 12 December 1349 this *capellanus capelle* was provided a canonicate in the cathedral of Thérouanne. During his life, he held a canonicate at the Marian church of Nesle (Noyon) but exchanged it for an unspecified benefice. At his death, which occurred before 9 June 1356, he was a canon at the church of Sainte-Walberge at Furnes (Thérouanne).
(AVB 1: 484, no. 1860. AVB 5: 395, no. 947; 653, no. 1603. AVB: 10: 168, 170. Clercx: 14 fn.)

## JOHANNES DE AYRAS (ATTREBATO, HYERA) alias BONEDOMINEA
Johannes Hyera, of the diocese of Arras, is first recorded as having entered the papal chapel on 25 April 1348. It is probably this same person who is called familiar of the pope in January 1353, at which time he received a canonicate at Saint-Donatien of Bruges (Tournai) and already held a benefice at the church of Boyelles (Arras). On 6 August 1353, as chaplain of the *capella intrinseca*, Johannes asked for the combined benefice at Caumonte and Cazillac (Narbonne). In July 1354 he sought a canonicate at Saint-Paul of Liège, and in June of the following year he was granted the privilege of receiving his prebends in absentia, a right usually accorded clerics whose presence at the curia was required. He was given an almuce in June 1356 as one of the chaplains of the pope. He is again found in the papal supplications twice during the year 1360 when as *capellanus capelle* he requested benefices on the behalf of others. It is possible that he died during the early months of 1361, since the last recorded payment of his prebend at Bruges was made in 1360, the last year in which his name appears. He might be the Johannes de Attrebato who was in the French royal chapel in December 1362. This cleric reserved a benefice at Saint-Eloi of Paris for which he was made to abandon a chaplaincy at Poissy (Chartres).
(Schäfer II: 625. AVB 5: 613, no. 1498; 114-15, no. 295; 208, no. 498; 639, no. 1570. AVB 10: 263, 270, 280, 289, 308. AVB 17: 9, no. 15; 165, no. 477; 268, no. 793; 355, no. 1063: Clercx: 14 fn. Informatique: S03600696, fol. 78.)

## JOHANNES DE AYROLIS
He probably held the rectorate of the church of Fontanges (Clermont) in July of 1338. He is named among the chaplains of Benedict XII in 1339, 1340, and 1342.
(Schäfer II: 77, 94, 120, 159. *Lettres, Benoît XII*, vol. 2: 19, no. 5404.)

## JOHANNES BERGHOEN
Nephew of Petrus Sinterii (q.v.), he served the *capella intrinseca* and their *capellani* on 25 August 1349.
(OPKA: 98, fn.)

## JOHANNES BERTRANDI DE HOYO
He was a canon of Saint Adalbert at Aix-la-Chapelle on 6 June 1336, when he obtained a canonicate at Saint-Denis of Liège. He is listed as chaplain of the pope in 1336 and 1337. From a document dated 1 September 1338 we learn that he was allowed to receive the fruits of his benefice in absentia. He continued in papal service as chaplain in 1339, 1340, and 1342. On 30 October 1346 he was in the employ of the cardinal deacon Guillaume de la Jugie as his chaplain and familiar. By this time he had added a canonicate at Saint-Pierre of Liège to the one at Saint-Denis and had submitted a supplication for a canonicate at the cathedral of Compostella.
(Schäfer II: 44, 60, 94, 120, 159. *Benoît XII (1334-1342). Lettres closes et patentes intéressant les pays autres que la France*. J.-M. Vidal and G. Mollat, eds. Paris, 1950: 573, no. 1972. AVB 1: 284, no. 1094.)

JOHANNES DE BOSCO alias PELIÇON (PELISO, PELLISSON, PELLISSONUS)
This papal chaplain bears one of the most common names of all the curialists, and there may have been several persons by that name active in the Curia. He probably was the cleric from the diocese of Tournai who received the office of *tabellionatus* on 10 September 1365, being neither married nor in Holy Orders. On 11 January 1371, as familiar and *cubicularius* (chamber valet) to Cardinal Jean de Blauzac, this rector of the church of Ascq (Tournai) received a canonicate at Saint-Pierre of Lille (Tournai). Almost two years later, on 4 November 1372, while serving the cardinal in the same capacity, he asked that to his pair of benefices the canonicate of Saint-Denis at Passau in the cathedral of Paris be added. In January 1374, this request is reported as having been granted. On 15 November 1378, Johannes gave up a canonicate at Saint-Germain at Mons (Cambrai) and the chaplaincy at Ascq in order to acquire a canonicate at Saint-Donatien of Bruges (Tournai). At that time, he still was in the service of the cardinal and retained his benefice at Lille. Jean de Blauzac died 8 July 1379, and a rotulus of his familiars was drawn up on the following 11 August. Among those named were Johannes and Richardus de Bozonvilla (q.v.). For some reason Johannes was not able to receive the canonicate at Bruges, therefore he continued to hold those benefices that he was prepared to relinquish in 1378. In this document, we learn that he served the cardinal *per xv annos et amplius*, and that he desired a canonicate and official title at the Marian church of Anthoing (Cambrai). We know nothing of Johannes' whereabouts for the next decade. In 1389 he is reported to have received the chaplaincy of Saint-Maurice in the church of Sainte-Marie-Madeleine at Lille, but there seems to be some confusion in the documents with a Petrus de Bosco. He in fact did receive this benefice on 21 March 1391 for which he resigned the rectorate of Ascq. Günther states that Johannes began his service in the papal chapel in 1391 and received a "papal grant as musician" to Louis II, duke of Anjou, in 1393, though he must have received this title by 1390. Here we may be dealing with another personality. The papal chaplain might have been the *scriptor* Johannes de Bosco who served during the reign of Clement VII, though, again not enough information is given for us to know for certain. Complicating matters further was yet another Johannes de Bosco, cleric of Tournai and familiar of Cardinal Amédée de Saluces, who was actively seeking benefices from 1391 to 1393. In any event, our Johannes first appears in the extant records of the chapel on 30 October 1393. He remained in papal service after the election of Benedict and was thus cited on 5 October 1394. On the following 21 October, he submitted a request on behalf of another for a canonicate at Saint-Pierre of Lille. He continued to serve presumably until the next notice for chapel service which records the payment due 12 April 1396. This notice provides more information about our chaplain. After the appearance of the name Johannes de Bosco, we find what was presumed to have been another chaplain whose name was transcribed as "P. Feruit." The proper interpretation of the name of this so-called chaplain becomes clear when we consider the following information. Cited among the canons of the cathedral of Nevers during the year 1399 is one Johannes de Bosco alias Peliçon. The correct interpretation of the notice from 1396 is therefore, "Johannes de Bosco P. servit." The Johannes de Bosco who remained in the papal palace according to the list of October 1398, and who is said to be a Catalan is probably wrongly identified with our chaplain. Whether he served at Saint-Germain-l'Auxerrois (Paris) in 1400 as Wright claims is open to debate. However, when Benedict reassembled his chapel at Pont-de-Sorgues, Johannes was listed among its members. After that notice of 11 August 1403, we find one more, dating from 8 November 1404, which shows Johannes still serving in the chapel of the pope. He probably did not make the journey to Italy with the Curia. He died before 30 November 1406, at which time Robertus Creque (q.v.) requested a canonicate at Le Mans, left vacant by the death of Johannes. A benefice at Reims belonging to him also became vacant on that date. The works attributed to him under the name Bosquet and Boquet are found in Str, BL, and Em. They include a three-voice *Et in terra* and a four-voice *Patrem*. Under his pseudonym Peliso, Pellisson or Pellissonus, he is knows from an *Et in terra* and a *Patrem* found in Apt and in the Spanish source Barc. C. Both are three-voice. Though no hard evidence has ever been cited linking the composer Bosquet with the papal chaplain, if he is to be identified with the

papal chaplain, then it is not particularly surprising that both the composers Bosquet and Pellisson produced only mass movements. The long association that Johannes had with Richardus de Bozonvilla both as *cubicularii* of Cardinal Jean de Blauzac for at least eight years and as papal chaplains would have given Richardus a good opportunity to collect some compositions of his long-time associate in his personal collection.

(Günther I: 187 fn., 188, 190 fn., 192-193. AVB 8: 671, no. 2464; AVB 9: 725-26, no. 1598. AVB 10: 549, 564-65. AVB 11: 64, no. 97. AVB 12: 52, no. 171; 52, no. 172. AVB 20: 193, no. 1855; 466, no. 2446. AVB 26: 178, no. 683; 796, no. 3611. *Lettres, Urbain V*, vol. 4: 487, no. 15418. Haberl: 213. Wright: 67 fn. Ursula Günther, "Johannes de Bosco," *Grove 6*, vol. 9, p. 661. Gilbert Reaney, "Peliso," *Grove 6*, vol. 14, p. 342. *Pouillé*, vol. 4, *La Province de Sens*: 513. Logoz: 216 fn. Franz Ehrle, "Martin de Alpartils *Chronica actitatorum temporibus Domini Benedicti XIII*," *Quellen und Forschungen aus dem Gebiete der Geschichte*, 12 (1906): 60.)

## JOHANNES BOULETTE (BROULETE)

On 29 October 1394, this priest from the diocese of Amiens supplicated for a benefice either at the Benedictine monastery of Saint-Vaast (Cambrai) or at the Augustinian monastery of Sainte-Marie at Cantimpré (Cambrai). In a document dated 13 October 1403, as papal familiar and *capellanus* and as rector of Saint-Vaast, he sought a benefice under the jurisdiction of the bishop and chapter of the cathedral of Paris. A document dated one week later calls him familiar of Cardinal Martin de Salva (†22 October 1403). At that time, he officially received Saint-Vaast for which he was to give up the rectorate at Soucy (Sens) but continued to hold a benefice at the Benedictine convent of Saint-Amand (Rouen). The presence of this document may not reflect any change in status for Johannes as much as it may indicate a lag between the information on the supplication and the status of the supplicant at the time of conferral. Perhaps complicating matters somewhat is the supplication written between 16 and 23 October of that same year in which he is called chaplain and familiar of the late cardinal. Here he asks for a benefice at Amiens. It is possible that near the ultimate demise of the cardinal, Johannes entered the service of the pope. He might still have been formally a chaplain of the cardinal, though he was not in his service. In a document from 2 November, we find him abandoning Soucy. Johannes only officially became a member of the papal chapel on 7 December 1403 in the city of Tarascon, where the oath was administered. He received payment as such on 8 November 1404. On 2 November 1405, Johannes was given the canonicate and prebend that belonged to Jacobus de Prato (q.v.). For this he resigned Saint-Vaast then conferred on Nicolaus Vacherii (q.v.). Before or on 27 June 1406, in the city of Noli (Savona) Johannes died of the plague. He was still *capelle pape capellanus et pape continuus commensalis* when he died *in loco de Finario* (at the place down from Finale Ligure). His death struck fear into the other chapel singers, and they could not be gathered to perform the papal service.

(AVB 19: 108, no. 249, no. 308; 139, no. 339; 187, no. 488-89; 194, no. 508. AVB 26: 335, no. 1418: 584, no. 2761; 633, no. 2974; 719, no. 3339; 791, no. 3597. Günther I: 193. ASV, *Coll.* 457: f.257v. *Rerum italicarum scriptores*, 3, 2: 787 A.)

## JOHANNES DE BRALLI (BRAILLI, BRAILLIACO, BRALI, BRALHY)

Cleric from the diocese of Thérouanne, in 1338 he received a dispensation from the illegitimacy of birth. On 25 April 1348, he is said to have entered the papal chapel. Four months later, called *capellanus capelle* of the pope, a canonicate at the cathedral of Laon was conferred on him. In September, he received the canonicate at Sens left vacant by the death of Johannes de Sinemuro (q.v.). As papal familiar, he was provided a canonicate at he cathedral of Thérouanne on 12 June 1349, and he requested one at the cathedral of Cambrai on 9 September 1350. He exchanged the canonicate at Thérouanne for one at Saint-Pierre of Aire (Thérouanne) and for a chaplaincy in the castle of Couckelaere (Tournai) on 10 June 1351. The next month, Johannes resigned his benefice at Aire, then conferred on a Roger de Brali. He also gave up his chaplaincy in the Marian church of Antwerp (Cambrai), and in November, as papal familiar, he received the rectorate at Ogy (Cambrai). In 1374 Johannes acted as official of the diocese of Cambrai in one document and as an

executor during the year 1378. He was again acting as an official of the chapter of Cambrai in 1384, but was no longer alive in 1392.
(Clercx: 14 fn. AVB 1: 374, no. 1408; 377, no. 1414; 452, no. 1736; 539, no. 2073; 561, no. 2166; 566, no. 2184; 580 no. 2236; 580, no. 2237; 616, no. 2379; 653, no. 2509. AVB 8: 67, no. 222. AVB 10: 587. AVB 12: 138, no. 125. AVB 13: 513, 743. AVB 17: 40, no. 89; 394, no. 1183; AVB 20: 654, no. 2864. *Lettres, Benoît XII*, vol. 2: 74, no. 6018.)

## JOHANNES BUREC
He was paid for his service as *cantor* in Genoa on 21 June 1405.
(Günther I: 194. Günther II: 42.)

## JOHANNES CAPEL
After serving in the city of his birth, Saint-Omer, for approximately 15 years, he joined the curia. On 13 September 1358, having already obtained a vicariate at Saint-Omer of Saint-Omer (Thérouanne), he submitted a supplication requesting a benefice under the jurisdiction of the abbot of the monastery of Saint-Bertin at Saint-Omer. At that time, he was familiar of Andrea Avvocatti, bishop of Como, nephew of the late cardinal of Tournai, Andrea Ghini Malpigli de Florentia. The next reference to Johannes comes on 2 August 1360 when, as cleric, familiar, and commensal of Cardinal Pierre la Forêt, he asked for a benefice under the jurisdiction of the abbot of the monastery of Saint-Rémy, O.S.B., at Reims. The cardinal died on 7 June 1361, and four months later, on 8 October, Johannes was already in *cantorum capelle pape receptus* and was requesting the office of *scriptor litterarum apostolicarum*. By November 1362, Johannes had acquired a totally different array of benefices: a canonicate at Saint-Pierre of Lille (Tournai), the rectorate of the parish church of Ouckene (Tournai), and he requested a canonicate at Saint-Omer. At that time, he referred to himself as *devotus orator, presbiter*, and *capellanus capelle*. On 6 June 1363 as *scriptor*, familiar, and papal chaplain, he was accorded the privilege of not having to reside at the place of his benefices, but instead was granted his prebends in absentia. One year later he requested that the pope bestow an indulgence of 1 year and 40 days on those who are penitent, confess, and who visit the church of Ouckene dedicated to Saint-Martin (where he was rector) on the feasts of Christmas, Epiphany, Easter, Ascension, Pentecost, Trinity, Corpus Christi, St. John the Baptist, Sts. Peter and Paul, All Saints, St. Martin, the four principal feasts of the Virgin, and the octaves of said feasts. Johannes apparently worked as papal *scriptor* until 2 May 1370. A canonicate at Saint-Pierre of Cassel (Thérouanne) was conferred on him 12 January 1371, through the consideration of Cardinal Simon de Langham, O.S.B., archbishop of Canterbury († 22 July 1376). At this time he was called familiar and *magister capelle* to the cardinal. He continued to hold his canonicate at Saint-Omer but now possessed the rectorate of Wardrecques (Thérouanne) as well. In September of 1380, he asked for a canonicate at Sainte-Walberge of Furnes (Thérouanne) and, in November, received the *cantoria* of Saint-Omer which obligated him to resign the rectorate of Ferquen (Thérouanne). On 7 January 1384 he was admitted to the select group of *capellani honores* of the pope. He acted as papal subcollector in the diocese of Thérouanne from 11 April 1386 until his death which occurred before 18 November 1389. By this time he only retained his titles at Saint-Omer, a canonicate at Cassel, and a rectorate at the parish church of Wulveringhem (Thérouanne).
(AVB 5: 504, no. 1227; 611, no. 1491; 731, no. 1809. AVB 7: 6, no. 7; 408, no. 1143; 488, no. 1311. AVB 9: 29, no. 49; 337, no. 811; 422, no. 995. AVB 10: xvi-xvii, xxxviii, 404 fnn., 424, 431-36, 473, 485-86, 511, 529-31, 576, 581, 636, 653-54, 659-60, 693-95. AVB 11: 84, no. 144 and fn. AVB 13: 80, no. 498; 100, no. 632; no. 130, no. 808; 429, no. 223; 495, no. 636; 507, no. 709; 566, no. 1070; 664, no. 1713; 664-665, no. 1715; 665, no. 1717; 696, no. 1911. AVB 15: 327, no. 2539. *OKS*: 63, 64, 132. *Lettres, Urbain V*, vol. 1: 391, no. 3499; vol. 2: 6, no. 4984; vol. 3: 415, no. 11198; vol. 9. no. 25842. Informatique: S03602186, fol. 216.)

## JOHANNES CARNOTEN
He was admitted to the group of *cantores* on 3 January 1371. Nothing more is known about this chaplain's service with the pope. He was probably the singer Jean Fillon de Chartres (*Carnotensis*)

who had been a member of the chapels of King Charles V and Charles VI of France and, from at least 1369, the dukes of Burgundy. His service to the French royal family was said to have begun in 1359. According to information provided me by Professor Craig Wright, there is no extant record of Jean having been in the Burgundian chapel from 1370 until 1374 when his name once again appears. From 1384 until the spring of 1399 Jean served as first chaplain of the Burgundian chapel, a position roughly equivalent to that of the papal *magister capelle*. At the beginning of 1392 he was granted a canonicate at the cathedral of Cambrai. In this document he is called *Johannes Fillon alias de Carnoto*. He was still alive in 1402. (Schäfer III: 368. AVB 13: 720, no. 2067. Wright: 57, 59, 71 fn., 74, 76. BN, Coll. Bourg., vol. 23: 38, 90v.)

### JOHANNES DE CAUNIS (LOU CAUNIS, LOU CAMUS)
He served as chaplain of the pope in 1342 and during the year 1343/44. (Schäfer II: 203, 234.)

### JOHANNES DE CHAMPIENG (CHAMPIENH, CHAMPIGNEYO)
This chaplain entered the papal chapel on 17 September 1381 and is listed on 30 October and 20 December 1382. His service in the papal chapel extended at least until 22 January 1385. The identification of this chaplain with anyone by that name who appears in the curial letters will be tentative, pending the production of more specific information. Günther identified him with the priest, *doctor in decretis* and master of arts of the University of Paris, who was on the faculty of canon law at least from 18 October 1369. In 1376 he received a canonicate at Cambrai vacant through the death of a Nicolaus Sortes. By November 1378, at which time he requested a benefice at Laon, he possessed the *cantoria* of Cambrai, a canonicate at the Marian church of Nesle (Noyon), and the rectorate of Les-Trois-Pierres (Rouen). According to information provided in a document written in 1371, we know that Johannes was at that time *etiam etatis quinquaginta annorum vel circa*. This would have made him approximately sixty years of age at the time f his entry into the papal chapel. The other Johannes de Champigneyo named in the documents, and more probably the papal chaplain, first appears as subcollector of Beauvais on 1 June 1387. On 28 June 1388 as canon of Troyes, he was selected to be provisionary collector in the province of Reims for the apostolic camera. On 6 April 1389 the title was made permanent. On 25 March 1393 he received a canonicate and prebend at the cathedral of Cambrai that was left vacant through the death of Inguerannus Benedicti (q.v.). He served as collector until his death 25 February 1400. He was called *capellanus noster* at the time of his appointment, however, the appellation was possibly honorific and not indicative of any real chapel service. He also held a canonicate at Reims. (Günther I: 180, 182, 183 fn., 185, doc. 2. AVB 8: 114-15, no. 358; AVB 10: xiv, 441, and *passim*. AVB 11: 128-29, no. 250, fn. AVB 13: 312, no. 1735; 590, no. 1217; 637, no. 1531; 760, no. 2327. AVB 25: 244, no. 3490 and fn. Favier: 706.)

### JOHANNES CLEMENTIS DE BRULLIO (BROLIO, BRULLIS, BREUIL, BRULHIO)
On 24 June 1345 this cleric from the diocese of Tournai was among those listed on a supplication for the office of *tabellionatus*, scribe of contracts and testaments. On 24 July 1347 he was admitted to the group of *capellani*. One month later he is called papal familiar as he requests a canonicate at Saint-Pierre of Liège left vacant by the death of Simon Mauricii (q.v.). In October he reserved the rectorate of Saint-Sauveur of Bruges (Tournai). In August 1348, as *capellanus capelle*, he requested canonicates at Tournai and Laon, and in December of that year he sought the rectorate at Carvin (Tournai). In late 1349 and early 1350, Johannes was engaged in acquiring a canonicate and the title of cantor at Saint-Pierre of Lille (Tournai). In the fall of 1352, he acquired the canonicate of Saint-Piat at Seclin (Tournai) once belonging to Johannes Gervasii (q.v.). In April 1354, he was attempting to augment his holdings at Lille, by adding the dignity of the *scolastria*. He received the office of *scriptor* of penitential letters upon the death of Petrus de Moncoulon (q.v.) in September 1358. After having been given this title, Johannes vacated the canonicate at Saint-Pierre of Lille; and in January of the following year, he gave up his prebend at Seclin. He was dead by 30 May 1361, at which time his title of *scriptor litterarum penitentiarum* was bestowed on Johannes

Ademari (q.v.). About a year and seven months after this date, Dionysius Fabri (q.v.) obtained the rectorate of Carvin once held by Johannes Clementis de Brullio.
(AVB 1: 215, no. 868; 329, no. 1243; 339, no. 1281; 374, no. 1407; 374, no. 1408; 392, no. 1465; 478, no. 1840; 512, no. 1969; 645, no. 2476; 652-53, no. 2507. AVB 5: 117, no. 435, fn.; 504-5, no. 1230; 512, no. 1249; 684, no. 1676; 685, fn.; 737, no. 1824. AVB 7: 137, no. 463. AVB 9: 233, no. 640. AVB 10: 220, 221, 229, 232-33, 236. AVB 17: 53, no. 123, Clercx: 14 fn. *OKS*: 63, 64. *Lettres, Urbain V*, vol. 1: 192, no. 2049. Informatique: S03700037, fol. 6.)

## JOHANNES COLINI
He is said to have been a *cantor* when on 4 October 1372 he was deprived of his stipend because he struck the *magister capelle*. He must have remained in service at least through the early part of 1373 since he was absent from the chapel from 20 April to 25 April 1373. Nothing more is known about him. He might have been the Johannes Colini de Grimonte (or Gumonte), a cleric of the diocese of Toul, named in the rotulus of poor clerics made 28 November 1378 during the return of the pope from Fondi to Spelunga. In this document he requests a canonicate with expectation of a prebend at the church of Saint-Paul of Liège. He held a chaplaincy at the cathedral of Metz in 1383/84.
(Haberl: 212, AVB 8: 550, no. 2019. ASV, *Coll.* 457: fol. 21. *RG* I: 74.)

## JOHANNES COSSARDI (POSSARDI)
On 26 January 1364 he was received into the group of *capellani sive cantores capelle*. In this document he is called priest of the diocese of *Rochen*. This is probably better transcribed as *Rothen* and should then be expanded to *Rothomagensis*, or Rouen. His name appears in the papal documents one more time, on 27 November 1365, as *capellanus capelle intrinsece*. He should be identified with the singer employed by the Aragonese royal family, Johan Cossart. In February 1353, the chaplain and almoner of King Peter IV of Aragon, Jerart Bru, came back from Avignon with four singers for the royal chapels. Two were paid from the king's account; the other two were incorporated into the chapel of the queen. These last two were Johan Avenell and Johan Cossart. Though paid from the king's account for part of 1353, the records show that Johan served in the chapel of the queen from 1354 until 1356. A rotulus submitted by Queen Eleanor of Aragon on 15 December 1362 for her chaplain, familiar, and domestic, Johannes Cossardi, calls him *precentor capelle Alienore regine*. In that document he reserved a canonicate and the provostship, parsonage, or some other office at the cathedral of Lerida in Spain. For this he offered to resign a benefice at the church of Saint-Martin at Vesly (Rouen) while keeping a benefice at the cathedral of Tarragona.
(Schäfer III: 28, 145. Gómez Muntané: 85-88. Informatique: S03601121, fol. 126.)

## JOHANNES DE CRUCE (CRUCA)
On 4 July 1388, this cleric from the diocese of Cambrai requested a benefice at the monastery of Saint-Ghislain (Cambrai). On 13 November of that year, in a rotulus of Cardinal Pierre de Cros (†16 November 1388), Johannes de Cruce, chaplain of the cardinal's chapel, added a benefice at the Benedictine abbey of Saint-André-du-Câteau (Cambrai) to the above request. Several years later, as familiar of Cardinal Jean de Brogni, he submitted a supplication bearing the date 31 May 1392, in which he solicited for an unspecified benefice. On 9 August 1393 in a rotulus of students of the city of Avignon, this cleric was more specific in his request, this time asking for a canonicate at the church of Sainte-Croix at Cambrai. By 16 October 1394, Johannes had received this canonicate and added to it a canonicate, prebend, and the secular abbacy of Châtel-Censoir (Autun). At the time, as familiar of Cardinal Jean and student in the third year of canon law, he was seeking a canonicate at Saint-Géry of Cambrai. On 11 August 1403, when Benedict XIII gathered his chapel members at Pont-de-Sorgues, the name of Johannes de Cruce was listed among those present. On the following 13 October, he asked for and was given a canonicate at the cathedral of Cambrai. At the time he held the rectorate of Senuc (Reims), and canonicates at Saint-Didier of Avignon and Saint-Géry of Cambrai (instead of Gaurain, as the document states). He served the chapel of the pope at this time and at least until 8 November 1404. He probably did not remain in the chapel

during the pope's first journey to Italy, but instead, rejoined the entourage at Marseille sometime in 1407. In a supplication dated 18 June 1407, he is again called *capellanus capelle*. At the time, he sought to obtain the archpresbyterate of the collegiate church of Capdrot (Sarlat) that belonged to one Hugo Chanelli, who at the time was familiar of Cardinal Jean de Brogni. By 4 August, however, Johannes de Cruce was dead.

(AVB 13: 236 fn.; 278, no. 1517; 286, no. 1571; 356, no. 2002; 376, no. 2153, AVB 19: 100, no. 228; 205-6, no. 542. AVB 26: 60, no. 179; 515, no. 2412; 803, no. 3629. Günther I: 192, 193, doc. 5.)

## JOHANNES DESRAME

He was paid on 21 June 1405 in the city of Genoa for his service as *cantor*. Although there seems to be no relation between the two, a cleric from the city of Paris, bearing the same name, received a canonicate and expectation of a prebend at the cathedral of Meaux on 26 November 1362. He was a student in he arts, and this was his first benefice.

(Günther I: 194. Günther II: 42. *Lettres, Urbain V*, vol. 1: 417, no. 3700.)

## JOHANNES DURANDI

There is only one extant payment to Johannes for chapel service, that made in 1336. But it is likely that he is identical to the Johannes Durandi who in 1332/33 was *scriptor* and *clericus intrinsecus* of Pope John XXII. He is again cited as *scriptor* and *clericus* for the year 1333/34, and he was also prefect of the papal library from 28 May 1333 until the death of Pope John (4 December 1334). In May 1337, he vacated the rectorate of Puydaniel (Rieux) by accepting the deaconate of the Marian church of Villeneuve-lès-Avignon. On 28 February 1338, he acted as testamentary executor of a commensal chaplain. He is noted as having been engaged in wine purchases for the pope, especially for his dealings with the vinyards at Villeneuve, in the years 1343, 1344, and 1346. Also during 1343, a Johannes Durandi acted as the procurer in the diocese of Thérouanne for Guillaume Roger, nephew of the pope. During this year he was involved in a certain financial transaction on behalf of the Holy See. On 20 August 1348 a Johannes Durandi appears as a relative *(consobrini)* of the legation to Alexandria.

(Schäfer I: 261, 272, 273, 597, 602. Schäfer II: 44, 200, 269, 295. *Lettres, Benoît XII*, vol. 1: 392, no. 4190. *Lettres, Clément VI*, vol. 1: 159-61, no. 1077. AVB 10: 81. Göller II: 127. Mohler: 332, 410. Ehrle: 175, 731. *OKS*: 62, 63.)

## JOHANNES FABRI (ANEQUINUS FABRI, ANEQUI LO FABRI, ENEQUI, FRARE JOHAN FABRE, FABRA)

Translated into any language, the name "John Smith" is always surrounded by the aura of anonymity. Though it is most often ill-advised to identify all appearances of any one name with the same personality, the documentation seems to indicate that here we may be dealing with one person. He was a cleric from the diocese of Tournai who was said to be *de capella* of Cardinal Pedro de Luna (the future Benedict XIII) in a rotulus dated 15 November 1378. In the document, Johannes asked for and received a canonicate at Saint-Pierre of Cassel (Thérouanne). He might have been with the cardinal when Pedro made his journey to Spain as papal legate in 1379 and where he remained for 11 years. Sometime during that time, he probably passed into the service of Cardinal Guillaume de Chanac, O.S.B., bishop of Mende († Avignon, 30 December 1383). By 5 May 1384, he was under the protection of the royal house of Aragon. On that day, he (Enequi) and Johannes Rogerii (q.v.) were among those who received clothing. On 8 November 1384, brother Johan, *lo petit monge qui fou xantre del Cardinal de Mende*, entered the chapel of Duke John of Gerona, heir to the throne of Aragon. Probably small or young, a diminutive form of his name appears in the chapel records, i.e., Anequi lo Fabre. Here he served during the years 1384 and 1385. Sometime after Cardinal Pedro settled back in Avignon, Johannes Fabri was again his familiar. On 24 January 1392, through the intercession of his patron, he received a rectorate at the parish church of Dottignies (Tournai). According to the accounts of the diocese dated before 1 August 1393, Johannes had failed to take possession of this benefice. In October 1394, approximately one week after the election of Pedro to the papacy, Johannes, long-time familiar *(antiquus familiaris)* of the new pope and cleric of the diocese of Tournai, requested a benefice in the diocese of Paris. At the time, he already held a chaplaincy at Ronque (Tournai) and the curate of the parish church of Eyne (Tournai). It is worth mentioning here that his supplication comes between those of Richardus de Bozonvilla (q.v.) and Johannes Hanini (q.v.). On 12 April 1395, he is listed as clerk of the papal chapel and bears the name Anequinus Fabri. Still a papal familiar on 28 September of that year, he asked for a chaplaincy at Le Collège des Bons-Enfants in the city of Paris. On 17 December, under the name Johannes Fabri, he was listed among the chapel members and had officially taken the oath to be admitted *in clericum dicte capelle*. Still a chapel cleric on 8 April 1398, he was made *scriptor*. By mid-October 1403, he had changed several of his benefices. At that time, he held a canonicate at Beauvais, the rectorate at Eyne, was *scriptor* of apostolic letters, and was seeking a benefice at the Benedictine priory of Saint-Eloi in the city of Paris. Around that time, he also requested a canonicate at Saint-Germain-l'Auxerrois (Paris). In this same rotulus appears the name of Jacobus de Pratis (q.v.). A document dated 11 June 1406 indicates that he received the rectorate at Saint-Pierre-de-Arsis near the royal palace in Paris, for which he was required to abandon the benefice at Saint-Eloi. During the years 1413 through 1416, a Johannes Fabri was responsible for transporting and repairing the organ for the pope. On 27 October 1413 he was paid 18 florins, 20 solidi for having the organ transported from Peñiscola to Tortosa and back and for reparations made on the organ. On 11 July 1414, the same trip was reported. On 21 February 1415, the records tell us that he moved the organ to and from San Mateo. In 1414 the cost was 23 Barcelonan solidi; in 1415 the cost was 2 florins, 8 solidi, and 8 denarii in unspecified currency. On 11 May 1416 he was also paid *pro vadia*. This information leads us to suspect that Johannes might have served as the organist at this time. Though there is some indication that he was a Benedictine early in his life, Eubel calls this Johannes a member of the Dominican order. He might also have been the *fra* Johan Fabre cited as *capellá mr.* (*maestro?*) of the king of Aragon on 9 March 1416. He is listed as a singer for the monarch again in 1420 and in 1422. It is not certain if this Johan is the same as the papal chaplain. The Johannes Fabri from Tournai, however, was still alive in May 1427, when he vacated the rectorate of Eyne. A Johannes Fabri served Benedict XIII as *pulsator campane* in 1404, 1405, and 1412. At the present time he cannot be identified with the Johannes Fabri from Tournai.

(AVB 8: 46, no. 152. AVB 10: 566, 567. AVB 13: 722-723 no. 2082. AVB 14: 186, no. 498. AVB 19: 80, no. 183. AVB 26: 9, no. 10; 499-500, no. 2373; 520, no. 2430; 543, no. 2557; 649, no. 3045; 790, no. 3595. Günther I: 188, 189, doc. 4. Konrad Eubel, "Aus den Ausgabebüchern der Schismapäpste Klemens VII. und Benedikt XIII.," *Römische Quartalschrift für Altertumskunde und für Kirchengeschichte*, 18 (1904): 339-40. Higinio Anglés "La música en la corte real de Aragón y Nápoles durante el reinado de Alfonso V el Magnánimo (1421-1458)," *Scripta musicologica*, vol. 2. Rome: 1976, pp. 975, 979. Higinio Anglés, "Spanien in der Musikgeschichte des 15. Jahrhunderts," *Scripta musicologica*, vol. 2. Rome: 1976, p. 879. Gómez Muntané: 93, 107; 202-203, no. 238. OPKA: 106-7 fn.)

## JOHANNES FOLIOMERI

He and Johannes de Manso (q.v.) accepted payment as papal chaplains on 25 January 1408 in Savona.
(Günther II: 43.)

## JOHANNES GERVASII (alias LE PICART)

On 8 July 1338, as domestic, commensal, and familiar of Cardinal Gaucelme de Jean, this priest was given the rectorate of the church of Montières now in the city of Amiens. Continuing in service to the cardinal, he retained his benefice at Amiens while, on 22 May 1342, adding a canonicate at Saint-Pierre of Aire (Thérouanne). On 5 June 1344, he received what appears to be his first stipend as *capellanus pape*. He is listed as a papal chaplain throughout 1346, during which year he became canon at Saint-Piat of Seclin (Tournai) and canon at the cathedral of Liège. In a notice from 1349, he is called *servitor capelle intrinsece*. His duties as *servitor* are unknown. Johannes continued to be called familiar in 1351, when he was given a canonicate at Saint-Pierre of Cassel (Thérouanne)

but not in 1352, when he exchanged his canonicate at Saint-Jean of Liège for the deaconate at Saint-Pierre of Aire and perpetual chaplaincy of Marck (Arras) belonging to Jacobus Comitis (q.v.). Although he was still alive on 16 March 1352, by 24 November of that year he was dead. At that time, his canonicate at Seclin was given to Johannes Clementis de Brullio (q.v.). At his death, he was listed as papal familiar and, several months later, is referred to as *olim capellanus domini Clementis VI...capelle intrinsece.* Johannes Gervasii, the papal chaplain, should not be confused with Johannes Sanctus (de Sonti) alias Pipelart (Pipelardi) who held the deaconate of Aire before Jacobus Comitis (q.v.). Nor should he be identified with the priest from Montélimar who acted in a matter of finance for the pope in 1341.
(Schäfer II: 265. *Lettres, Benoît XII,* vol. 2: 20, no. 5414. AVB 1: 280, no. 1079; 280, no. 1081; 286, no. 1100; 568, no. 2195; 607, no. 2346; 652-53, no. 2507. AVB 5: 4, no. 10; 174, fn. 2; 228, no. 545; 357, no. 842, fn. AVB 6: 6, no. 19. AVB 10: 159, 203. AVB 17: 53-54, no. 123; 295, no. 869. OPKA: 98 and fn.)

## JOHANNES GIRARDI LATHOMI
His name appears among those of the members of the papal chapel only on 5 October 1394 and in the form Johannes Lathomi. He is probably identical to the Johannes Gerardi Lathomi, cleric of Reims who reserved a chaplaincy at the cathedral of Paris on 22 August 1363. He was expecting a benefice at the convent of Sainte-Marie-aux-Moniales (Soissons). Neither married nor in Holy Orders, on 19 September 1365 he received the office of *tabellionatus.* Johannes reserved a perpetual chaplaincy at Wahagnies (Tournai) on 25 April 1369. At the time he held a chaplaincy at Origny-Sainte-Benoîte (Laon) and awaited action on a benefice at Paris. A document reveals that on 3 May 1370 he was a student of law who had written some secret minutes for the pope. It appears as though he had been engaged in such activity for some time, since, from a request for a benefice at Amiens written 26 January of the following year, we learn that he served the apostolic camera for three years writing the secret minutes. On 13 July 1374, he received a canonicate and semiprebend at the cathedral of Meaux. He held the benefices in the diocese of Tournai and Laon, a newly received rectorate at Jouarre (Laon), and awaited a benefice at Amiens. On 15 November 1378 Cardinal Gilles Aycelin de Montaigut submitted a rotulus for his associates, chaplains, familiars, and domestics. Among those listed was Johannes who requested and was granted an unspecified benefice at Tournai. At the time, he retained his semiprebend at Meaux, chaplaincy at Wahagnies, and had a rectorate at Le Crotoy (Amiens) in litigation. About one week later, called a student of canon law in a rotulus of students of the city of Avignon, Johannes requested that his semiprebend at Meaux be changed into a full prebend. Under Clement VII he served as an *abbreviator litterarum.* He could also be the Johannes Lathomi, *magister,* who was cited in a document concerning the University of Paris on 17 May 1389. Whatever the case, Johannes Lathomi was certainly held in high regard, since the appearance of his name in fourth position on the list of chaplains indicates a relatively long period of service in the *capella.*
(Günther I: 187, doc. 4. Haberl: 213. AVB 8: 69, no. 229; 334-335, no. 1112. AVB 11: 125, no. 242. AVB 12: 62, no. 205. AVB 15: 218, no. 2355; 327-328, no. 2541; AVB 20: 597-98, no. 2748. *Lettres, Urbain V,* vol. 4: 479, no. 15422; vol. 7: 84, no. 21197; vol. 8: 61, no. 23287; vol. 9: no. 27073. Informatique: S04000476, fol. 62. Logoz: 215 fn. Opitz: 179.)

## JOHANNES GODINI
Canon of the cathedral of Gap, on 14 May 1361 he collected a payment from the abbot of the monastery of Sainte-Marie of Forest-Montier (Amiens). He is called *capellanus capelle* when on 1 September 1361 his canonicate became vacant through his death.
(AVB 5: 717-18, no. 1172. Hoberg II: 88, no. 308.)

## JOHANNES GONTERII
He was chaplain of the pope in 1335, 1336, and 1337. He held the rectorate of Saint-Aubin-en-Charolais (Autun) on 14 February 1336 when the canonicate of Saint-Géry (Cambrai) was conferred upon him. He died before 7 July 1338.
(Schäfer II: 26, 44, 60. *Lettres, Benoît XII,* vol. 1: 264, no. 2863; vol. 2: 19, no. 5410.)

## JOHANNES HANINI (HANNU, ANETI, HANETUS)

This cleric from the diocese of Thérouanne was a familiar of Pierre-Raymond de Barrière, bishop of Autun from 22 April 1377 until his elevation to the cardinalate 16 December 1378. Exactly one month before his patron received the red hat, Johannes submitted a request for a canonicate at the Marian church of Nesle (Noyon), and was allowed to hold the chaplaincy of Saint-André at the church of Saint-Omer. In August 1393, he seems to have been named again in a papal document. This time, in a rotulus submitted by the lord (bishop?) of Amiens (Jean de Boissy), he received an unspecified benefice. On 5 October 1394, he appears as Hanetus on the list of chaplains of Benedict XIII. Eight days later, as *capellanus capelle*, he asked for a canonicate at either Thérouanne or Saint-Omer, and he held the rectorate of Coucklare (Tournai) though he had not officially taken possession of it. On 12 October of the following year, he retained the rectorate at Coucklare. In this document he is granted a canonicate at Thérouanne regardless of his *defectus natalium*. He was paid for his service in the chapel up to 12 April 1396. He abandoned the rectorate of Coucklare at the beginning of August 1397. At this time he is called familiar of the pope and treasurer of the cathedral of Thérouanne.
(AVB 8: 101, no. 329. AVB 13: 377, no. 2160. AVB 19: 1, no. 2; 64, no. 155. AVB 26: 9, no. 11. Haberl: 213. Günther I: 187, 188, doc. 4.)

## JOHANNES DE HEYS DE RANCOVADO (RANCONADO, RAUCOVADO, RAUWES, RENWEZ)

On 8 December 1362, this priest of the diocese of Reims and canon of Troyes held chaplaincies at Troyes, Reims, and a rectorate at Faverolles (Reims). At the time he was chaplain for Raoul, lord of Louppeyo, governor of Dauphiné. In February 1363 Johannes resigned a chaplaincy in the cathedral of Reims in order to receive a canonicate at Troyes. He is listed as *capellanus et cantor capelle intrinsece pape* on 19 June 1365. During August of that year and February of the next, Johannes acted as an official and proxy in several transactions. He maintained his benefices at Troyes and Reims until 24 April 1366, when, in order to convert his half prebend at Reims to a full prebend, he gave up his chaplaincy at Troyes. He traveled with Urban V to Rome. At St. Peter's on 5 November 1367, he and Ancelmus Martini (q.v.), were reimbursed for renting two horses for the pope's journey from Viterbo to Rome. He remained in the papal chapel the following year, and after his death, which probably occurred before 7 February 1370, his canonicate and half prebend at the cathedral of Reims were given to Johannes Lehoudain (q.v.). At this time, he was called *capellanus capelle pape*.
(Schäfer III: 30. Kirsch: 69-70. AVB 15: 349, no. 2575. *Lettres, Urbain V*, vol. 1: 194, no. 2060; 432, no. 3837; vol. 4: 115, nos. 13598-13599; vol. 5: 48, no. 16177; 67, no. 16265; vol. 7: 161-162, no. 23851; vol. 9: no. 25725; no. 27552. Informatique: S03600867, fol. 97; S03701807, fol. 221.)

## JOHANNES JOHANNIS

He was probably the chaplain who served Philippe Cabassole, bishop of Cavaillon, and remained in his service when Philippe was made Patriarch of Jerusalem. This Johannes appears as such in documents dated 11 August 1360, 22 March 1361, and 22 March 1362. In a supplication dated 11 November 1362, as papal chaplain, he offered to abandon a canonicate at *Rocheurbarum* (Aix?) and the chaplaincy of Saint-Martin at Château-Renault (Tours) in order to receive canonicates at L'Isle-Jourdain (Toulouse) and at the cathedral of Lavaur. He hoped to retain a rectorate at the church of Saint-Orens-de-Gameville (Toulouse). In another supplication from 16 December of that year requesting his prebend at Lavaur, he is called priest from Toulouse and chaplain of the papal chapel. He served in the *capella pape* in 1363, and from three payments made 14 June, 16 August, and 27 September 1365, we learn that Johannes not only continued as papal chaplain but was also responsible for certain acts of charity made on the pope's behalf. He was paid on 11 May 1368 in the *officium elemosinarii* for acts of charity made when Urban went from Rome to Montefiascone. Evidently, he was one of the chaplains who journeyed to Rome with Urban. Nothing more is known about him.
(Schäfer III: 330, 332, 333. Hoberg I: 327, 351, 394. Kirsch: 136. Informatique: S03600208, fol. 25v.; S03601097, fol. 123v.; S04001357, fol. 169v.)

## JOHANNES LEHOUDAIN (HOUDAIN)

He first appears with Urban V at Rome on 17 April 1368 when he is called priest from the diocese of Reims and *capellanus capelle intrinsecus*. Besides his activity in the chapel, on 7 October 1370, he is paid for his activities as assistant private almoner of the pope *(viceelemosinarius secretus pape)*. In June of that same year, he was required to remit his benefice at the parish church of Ardeuil (Reims) when he was given the canonicate and half prebend at Saint-Géry of Cambrai, available through the death of Johannes de Heys de Rancovado (q.v.). On 9 January 1371 he is called familiar of Gregory XI and former almoner of Urban V in Italy *(ultra montes)*. At that time, he held a canonicate and half prebend in the cathedral of Reims and a canonicate in the church of Saint-Géry (Cambrai). On the fifteenth of the month, he was admitted into the group of singers. He was granted the rectorate at the church of Saint-Pierre-le-Vieux (Reims) and was awaiting a full prebend at Saint-Géry on 27 January 1372. On 3 May 1372 he abandoned his half prebend at Reims in order to receive the canonicate and full prebend once belonging to Johannes de Machaudio. He eventually had to give up his benefice at Ardeuil, and two weeks later, on 25 April 1375 he acted as a procurer in a transaction. In the last document in which he is named, dated 12 June 1375, Johannes was still *capellanus capelle pape* but by then had also received the title *scriptor pape*. At that time, he gave up his benefice at Saint-Géry for a canonicate in the cathedral of Coutances.
(Schäfer III: 34, 343, 368. AVB ll: 39, no. 46. AVB 15: 347, no. 2575. AVB 20: 20, no. 1431; 84-85, no. 1585; 634, no. 2821; 634, no. 2822. AVB 25: 57, no. 3109; 68, no. 3135; 108, nos. 3228-3229. *Lettres secrètes et curiales du Pape Grégoire XI (1370-1378) relatives à la France*, L. Mirot and H. Jassemin, eds. Paris, 1935: 256-57, no. 765. *Lettres, Urbain V*, vol. 9: 27552.)

## JOHANNES LENFANT (dictus LENFANT)

This name first appeared in the list of chaplains who were paid for their service up to 22 January 1385. On 18 March, Johannes presented a rotulus on behalf of another, and on 6 May he himself was provided a canonicate at the cathedral of Thérouanne. He was probably the priest from the diocese of Thérouanne who served as chaplain and singer of Duke Louis I of Anjou in 1377 and 1378 and who, as *cantor* of the church of Saint-Laud at Angers, received a canonicate at the cathedral of Angers on 17 November 1378 by *motu proprio*.
(AVB 8: 148, no. 468. AVB 13: 199, no. 1119; 551, no. 972. Günther I: 184 and fn., 185, doc. 2. Ursula Günther, "Bemerkungen zum ältern französischen Repertoire des Codex Reina (PR)." *Archiv für Musikwissenschaft* 24 (1967): 242.)

## JOHANNES DE LOVANIS

He was paid for his service as papal chaplain in 1342.
(Schäfer II: 159.)

## JOHANES DE MANSO

He makes his first appearance on 25 January 1408 when, as *capellanus*, he shared the responsibility for paying the other chaplains their wages. He is again noted among the members of the chapel on 20 March 1408 and again during the year 1408/09 when he was paid at Perpignan. The last reference to Johannes is dated 28 May 1415, at which time this priest from the diocese of Tournai, still *capellanus capelle* to Benedict, requested a benefice at Cantalpiedra (Salamanca) to add to his chaplaincy at the altar of Saint Thomas of Canterbury in the cathedral of Barcelona.
(AVB 26: 835, no. 3718. Günther II: 43.)

## JOHANNES DE MOLEYO (MOLEIO, JEHAN DU MOLOY, DU MOLEY)

He makes his first appearance as a papal chaplain in the payment made 19 September 1379. Though he also served in the papal chapel in 1384 and 1387, he does not seem to have been in the chapel at least for certain periods during the years 1382 and 1385. He began his tenure as *magister capelle* in December 1388. Documentation for this period is quite incomplete and we only know of his presence in 1391 and August 1392, though it is assumed that his service was fairly continuous until this time. Johannes is absent several times from the chapel during the following years and, while it is clear that he continued to hold the title *magister*, some of his duties must have been assumed by Richardus de Bozonvilla (q.v.). The documents tell us that Johannes was indeed present for the payments made to the chaplains in December 1393, April 1394, and, under the new pope Benedict XIII, in October 1394. On 21 October he submitted a request for his *dilectus*, Johannes Syron, a cleric probably from the diocese of Chartres. Within the year, Johannes de Moleyo was replaced by Richardus as master of the papal chapel. He held the title of *cantor* at the cathedral of Chartres when on 4 April 1399 he was brought into the chapel of Duke Philip of Burgundy. He replaced Johannes Fillon (q.v.) as first chaplain, a position equivalent to that of the papal *magister capelle*. He lasted less than one year in this post. But on 20 February 1401 he was hired as chaplain to serve at the *bonnes festes*. He remained until the funeral of Philip in June 1404. (Haberl 213. Günther I: 182 fn., 184, 187 fn. Ehrle: 731. AVB 26: 177, no. 678. Konrad Eubel, "Aus den Ausgabebüchern der Schismapäpste Klemens VII. und Benedikt XIII.," *Römische Quartalschrift für Altertumskunde und für Kirchengeschichte* 18 (1904): 338. Wright: 74 and fn., 225, 227-30. BN, Coll. Bourg., vol. 23: 90v.)

### JOHANNES MONTERII
He was among the six chaplains of Urban V paid on 27 November 1365. (Schäfer III: 145.)

### JOHANNES DE NOILHACO (NOBILIACO, NOALHACO)
He was paid for his service in the papal chapel on 3 August 1342, during the year 1343/44, and again on 5 June 1344. It is possible that he is the papal *scriptor* who, on 27 June 1353, acted as agent in a collection from the diocese of Embrun. In December 1362, called canon of Langres, Johannes *scriptor pape* from the diocese of Tulle, acted as a proxy for Cardinals Hugues de Saint-Martial and Guillaume d'Aigrefeuille. On 16 February 1363, he acted as an agent of Cardinal Guillaume. On 5 May he appears as an official in a papal document concerning Cardinal Elie de Saint-Yrieix (cardinal ca. May 1363-†10 May 1367). Though Johannes probably continued as papal *scriptor* through 1370, from 19 June 1363 until 7 January 1367, he is also listed as treasurer of Cardinal Elie. On 13 January 1371, Johannes became *magister cere* of the new pope, and as such, he was responsible for the candles and the illumination of the papal palace. He held this office until his death in April 1374. (Schäfer II: 203, 234, 265. Schäfer III: 14, 97, 146, 174, 365, 367, 373, 405, 414, 425, 431, 477, 489, 538, 554, 555, 618. Hoberg: 471, Hoberg II: 70, no. 254. Guillemain: 403 fn. *Lettres, Urbain V*, vol. 1: 157, no. 1834; 158, no. 1839; 189, no. 2029; 237, no. 2345; 396, no. 3533; vol. 3: 123, no. 9460; 160-161, no. 9652; vol. 4: 60, no. 13329; vol. 6: 123, no. 19346; vol. 9: 25713. Informatique: S03601153, fol. 130; S03601720, fol. 171. *OKS*: 64.)

### JOHANNES PETRI DE ATTIGNIACO
His name is found in the accounts on 30 January 1361 when he received a prebend for a benefice at Saint-Pierre of Cassel (Thérouanne). This is somewhat puzzling since the date on the supplication for this benefice is 26 June 1361. At that time, Johannes was clerk of Cardinal Francesco degli Atti de Todi. The document also calls him cleric of the diocese of Reims. The cardinal died on 25 August 1361. A little over a year later we find Johannes as familiar, domestic, commensal, and *tenor capelle* of Cardinal Hugues Roger, brother of Clement VI. In November 1362, while already in possession of a canonicate at Cassel, a canonicate at Saint-Donatien of Bruges (Tournai) was conferred on him for which he resigned the rectorate of the parish church of Vinassan (Narbonne). Whether or not he remained in the employ of Hugues until the time of the cardinal's death (21 October 1363) is not known. We next find Johannes in the service of the pope as *capellanus et cantor capelle* on 19 May 1365 and again in November of that year. Still serving in papal chapel on 19 March 1366, he exchanged his canonicate at Cassel for a canonicate at Saint-Symphorien of Reims and for the rectorate of Montmarin (Reims). He is said to have received his prebend at Bruges in 1367, at which time he was chaplain of Cardinal Guillaume de la Jugie. He died before 29

August 1369, t Rome. His benefice at Bruges was given to Theobaldus Furnerii (q.v.).
(Schäfer III: 30, 145, AVB 5: 697, no. 1715. AVB 7: 33, no. 78; 627, no. 1633. AVB 9: 42, no. 92.
AVB 10: 179. AVB 15: 256-257, no. 2423. *Lettres, Urbain V*, vol. 8: 86, no. 23400, Informatique:
S03602385, fol. 232.)

## JOHANNES ROGERII alias DE WATIGNIES (VATIGNIES, WATIGHIES)

Though Wright has claimed that Johannes came from Lille (Tournai), all of our documents calling
him a priest from the diocese of Cambrai would indicate that he was from a different place. On 15
November 1378, as canon of the church of Saint-Symphorien of Reims and chaplain of the parish
church of Enghien (Cambrai), he asked for a canonicate at the cathedral of Laon. At the time he
was priest of the chapel and commensal of Cardinal Pedro de Luna (the future Benedict XIII). He
might have left the employ of the cardinal while Pedro was papal legate in Spain, beginning in 1379.
It is highly likely that he, along with Johannes Fabri (q.v.), entered the chapel of Duke John of
Gerona where he was cited as *capellá* both in a list of those receiving clothing on 5 May 1384 and
among those paid for chapel service in 1384 and 1385. Sometime after this date he went to Avignon,
where he was hired into the chapel of Duke Philip the Bold of Burgundy on Easter Sunday, 26
March 1391. He is recorded as ducal chaplain for the years 1391 and 1392. On 5 October 1394, he
appears as a member of the chapel of his former patron, now pope, but he did not remain long as a
*cantor pape*. In a supplication dated 13 October, as *devotus orator, olim capellanus capelle et
servitor, nunc capellanus capelle* and *subelemosinarius* of the duke of Burgundy, he requested a
canonicate at either Laon or Reims. At the time he was canon at Saint-Donatien of Bruges
(Tournai) and at Saint-Symphorien of Reims, and also rector of Saint-Eloi at Ferrières-en-
Gâtinais (Sens). Johannes explained in the document that he might also appear listed in a rotulus of
papal familiars since, at the time of its composition, he was indeed a papal chaplain. There is more
information about him a supplication bearing the date 16 October, though it may have been written
before the previous one. In it Johannes is called *servitor* and papal familiar, but *olim capellanus
capelle*. He asked for a canonicate at either Laon or rras, similiar to the previous request, and added
to his list of benefices the one at Enghien. It is probable that at this time Johannes was, in fact,
working out a special relationship with both the papal court and the court of Burgundy. According
to the Burgundian records, he was in Avignon again in 1395. During the winter of that year he was
involved in acquiring that much-desired canonicate at Laon which he succeeded in obtaining
before spring 1395, and for which he abandoned his benefice at Enghien. In a document submitted
sometime between 22 October 1394 and 1 November 1395 in which he made a request on behalf of
another, he calls himself chaplain of the papal chapel and (*ac*) of the lord duke of Burgundy. This
vascillating service and Johannes' presence in both the chapels of Burgundy and Avignon is more
indication that both courts at times apparently shared chaplains. In a supplication from July 1395
requesting a chaplaincy at Reims, he again calls himself chaplain *olim pape nunc ducis*. He served
in the papal chapel for the two months prior to 12 April 1396 and was paid for this on 2 May. On 30
June of that year, probably in a move to clear up what must have been a bureaucratic mess, possibly
not without some controversy, the following was decided: [*Johannes*]... *recipiatur in capellanum
capelle pape et in familiarum pape, ac eidem Johanni conceduntur omnes et singuli exemptiones,
immunitates, franchisie ac libertates capellanorum et familiarium hujusmodi*. This, among other
things, allowed Johannes to retain his benefices *sine cura* and to receive his prebends in absentia. In
August of that year, he received a canonicate at Saint-Nicolas-au-Cloître at Amiens by *motu
proprio*. Evidently he was still in papal service at this time. But on 22 November of that year, he
resigned his benefices *extra curiam* (probably back in the service of Burgundy) for the purposes of
permutation. The Burgundian records show that he bought houses first in Paris in 1398 and then at
Amiens in 1401. He was employed as subalmoner, and he served in the chapel of Burgundy, until
Duke Philip's interrment in June 1404. However, when Benedict escaped from the palace at
Avignon and drew his chapel together at Pont-de-Sorgues on 11 August 1403, the name of
Johannes Rogerii was again recorded among those of the papal singers. He probably served only
one two-month period, since, in a document written between 13 and 16 October of 1403, he

submitted a request for a benefice at Tournai as a chaplain of the chapel of Duke John of Berry! (The other chaplains of Berry who submitted supplications at this time were Stephanus Canis, Robertus Souvent, Henricus Fabri, Stephanus de Maresco, Eustachius Pouchon, Symon Arnulphi, Johannes Caritatis, and Robertus Paindavaine.) The new benefices that Johannes possessed included the canonicates at Laon and Amiens, a canonicate and treasurership *(capiceraria)* at Sainte-Opportune of Paris, and the chaplaincy of Saint-Léonard in the church of Saint-Jean at Grave (Liège). Still associated with the House of Burgundy, he was placed in the chapel of Duke Louis of Guienne during the years 1414 and 1415. There probably was another Johannes Rogerii, priest of Cambrai, who was *cantor* and commensal of King John I of Aragon according to a supplication dated in mid-October 1394. His benefices in no way resemble those of our Johannes. Johannes Rogerii alias de Watignies is a prime example of a chaplain who, while in the service of a Spanish duke, three French dukes, at least one cardinal, and a pope, must have carried with him some of the musical practices and liturgical traditions of each chapel. If he was not desired for his musical ability, he, nevertheless, possessed some facility at diplomacy, if not on an international level, then most certainly on a personal one.

(AVB 8: 45-46, no. 147. AVB 19: 28, no. 62; 34, no. 73; 42, no. 93. AVB 26: 15, no. 3; 25, no. 66; 47, no. 133; 197, no. 762; 464-65, no. 2221; 473, no. 2257; 493, no. 2343; 523, no. 2444. Günther I: 187, 188, 192, doc. 4. doc. 5. Haberl: 213. Wright: 62, 63 and fn., 65, 92, 218-230. BN, Coll. Bourg., vol. 23: 154v. Gómez Muntané: 93. *See also* AVB 26: 90, no. 317.)

JOHANNES RUFFI DE ROQUIGNIES (ROQUENI, ROQUENIE)

When he reserved a canonicate and minor prebend at Sainte-Walberge of Furnes (Thérouanne) on 5 June 1372, this cleric from Laon was called familiar of the pope and *cantor capelle*. By that time he already held a chaplaincy at the chapel of Sainte-Marguerite at Suippes (Reims), and he was awaiting action on a benefice in the diocese of Laon. He *cantavit et celebravit* his first mass on Quasimodo Sunday, 24 April 1373, in the presence of the pope and was given 12 francs on 4 May as a gift. He was twice absent from the chapel. On 2 November 1372 he left with Theobaldus Furnerii (q.v.) and returned 8 November. In 1373 he, Theobaldus, and Guido de Lange (q.v.) were absent from the chapel beginning 5 November until 11 November. The reason for their absence is not indicated, however we might conjecture that they were sent on missions for the pope. On 24 November 1373, as papal familiar and chaplain of the chapel, he was granted a canonicate at Sainte-Croix of Liège. He never actually took possession of this benefice but instead attempted to exchange it for one at the parish church of Avernas-le-Bauduin (Liège). On 10 July 1374 a canonicate at Saint-Pierre of Liège was conferred upon him, and approximately one month ater, he received the benefice at Avernas-le-Bauduin. He continued to retain the latter and a canonicate at Saint-Pierre of Liège, when he resigned the position at Furnes in order to receive a chaplaincy at Esen (Thérouanne). This occurred on 4 March 1375, at which time he was called *capellanus capelle pape*. In December 1376 he was granted a canonicate at the cathedral of Cambrai, and eleven months later he was given one at the cathedral of Tournai. For this, Johannes was required to resign his benefice at Esen. He evidently continued as familiar and chaplain of the papal chapel up to this time; consequently, we must assume that he made the journey to Italy with Gregory XI. On 9 September 1379, he appears in the service of Clement VII, when he is called *devotus orator* of this pope and *capellanus capelle* of Gregory. At that time he asked to be named parson or officer of the church at Laon. He continued to hold his canonicate at Saint-Pierre of Liège and at the cathedral of Tournai while retaining his benefice at the parish church of Avernas-le-Bauduin. There is a reference to a Johannes Ruffi who, in December 1373, was paid on behalf of the sacristan of Notre-Dame-des-Doms for the ringing of the bells on three anniversaries of the death of Pope Clement VI (†6 December) and for returning the gold cloth that was placed on the catafalque. This Johannes is called chaplain of the sacristan of the cathedral.

(Schäfer III: 425, 453, 478. AVB 8: 675, no. 2476. AVB 20: 106-7, no. 1635; 434, no. 2387; 596, no. 2745; 627-28, no. 2806. AVB 25: 37, no. 3063; 37, no. 3064; 406, no. 3812; 497, no. 3983. Günther: 177, fn. Haberl: 212 fn.)

JOHANNES DE SANCTO QUINTINO

In 1317, this priest from the diocese of Noyon was serving Pope John XXII. He held the office of *scriptor litterarum penitentiarum* from 1329. He was among the first of the chaplains of Benedict XII and received payment for his service in 1335 and 1336. On 23 January 1336, when he was given the rectorate of the parish church of Saint-Germain at Prémony (Noyon), he was called *scriptor et capellae Pontificiae cantor*. His stipend as a chaplain was again paid to him in 1337 and 1339. In July 1339 he was reimbursed for the purchase of large pieces of parchment from Carpentras. Again, at the end of the month of December the following year, he is recorded as having purchased similiar sheets of parchment *pro libris pape transcribendis*. Johannes served in the papal chapel during the years 1340 and 1342 according to the accounts. On 18 September 1344 he received the rectorate of the church of Saint-Christophe at Vallerauge (Uzès). At this time he still served as *scriptor*. Almost six years later, on 9 September 1350, he resigned the benefice at Vallerauge. He had long been in service to the popes of Avignon. He also seems to have been a protege of Guillaume de Mandagout, bishop of Uzès, in 1336.
(Schäfer I: 337. Schäfer II: 26, 44, 60, 94, 120, 159; 108, 134. *Lettres, Benoît XII*, vol. 1: 286, no. 3135. *Lettres, Clément VI*, vol. 1: 192, no. 1117. AVB I: 539, no. 2071. Guillemain: 364. *OKS*: 62, 63, 64.)

JOHANNES DE SINEMURO

He was chaplain of the pope on 3 August 1342 and during the year 1343/44. His canonicate at the cathedral of Sens was requested by Johannes de Bralli (q.v.) on 1 September 1348, after his death. He might also have been canon of Paris in 1340.
(Schäfer II: 203, 234. AVB I: 377, no. 1414, fn.)

JOHANNES SRELVIT (FREVLIT?)

From the diocese of Amiens, he was admitted to the papal chapel on 11 June 1395.
(Günther I: 189, doc. 4. ASV, *Coll.* 457: fol. 257.)

JOHANNES SYMONIS alias HASPROIS (ASPROYS, DE HASPRA)

This name first appears in a rotulus dated 16 November 1378 as a *dilectus* of the king of Portugal. At that time, Johannes requested full title to the rectorate of San Martín at Sister (Lisbon). Günther claims that he was in the service of King Charles V of France two years later.

He is said to have worked as a *petit vicaire* at the cathedral of Cambrai in 1384, and we do know that he received a prebend within the diocese of Cambrai during the year 1388/89. Called Johannes de Haspra in a document written between 1 August 1388 and 1 August 1390, he received a rectorate at the parish church of Liessies (Cambrai). During the interval between 1 August 1390 and 1 August 1393, he abandoned this benefice. The first reference to his service in the papal chapel comes from the payment made 30 October 1393. After the death of Pope Clement VII, he passed into the service of Benedict and is cited among the chaplains in the list of 5 October 1394. About one week later, he submitted a request for a canonicate at Arras. At the time he is called priest from the diocese of Cambrai, rector of the church of Saint-Nicolas-sur-les-Fossés (Arras), and had been deprived of the rectorate of the Marian church of Nijlen (Cambrai) *per antipapam*. On 21 October he submitted a supplication on behalf of a Jacobus Prepositi, cleric of Cambrai. Johannes was again paid for his chapel service for the period up to 12 April 1396. His name again appears in the list of chaplains which was compiled at Pont-de-Sorgues on 11 August 1403. It is uncertain how long he remained in the service of Benedict. A document dated 24 September 1404 in which he resigns a canonicate at the church of Saint-Laurent at Rozoy (Laon) makes no mention of his chapel service. Given the astrological expertise of several musicians at this time and the link between music and astrology in the quadrivium, our Johannes Symonis may very well have been the author of an essay that appears in BMA, ms. 1020: f. 112: *Anno fluente 1417, die, 17 augusti, completa 5 hora post meridiem cum 6 gradibus celi, magister Johannes Symonis, etc., proposuit talem questionem: Si in brevi et ante utilitatem Domini fiet electio pape et si sic infra quantum*

*tempus habebitur electio pape in concilio generali Constancie.* He is thought to have been the Johannes Symonis, *litterarum apostolicarum scriptor,* who died before 12 May 1428 in the Curia, freeing a canonicate and prebend at the cathedral of Cambrai. Johannes Symonis bore a very common name, and there was more than one musician by that name. Though the papal haplain might have played a musical instrument, we believe that any identification of Hasprois with a minstrel should, for the time being, be avoided. Four compositions are attributed to him in the manuscripts Ch, Mod, BL, and O: three ballades and one rondeau, all three-voice.
(Günther I: 186-188, 192, doc. 3-5. Haberl: 213. AVB 8: 606, no. 2279. AVB 10: 446, 527, 587. AVB 14: 249, no. 657 and fn. AVB 19: 159, no. 403. AVB 26: 10, no. 14; 178, no. 682. Ursula Günther, "Johannes Symonis Hasprois," *Grove 6,* vol. 8, pp. 276-277.)

## JOHANNES DE TREGROSSIO (TREGOS, CREGROSSIO)
He was required to abandon the perpetual vicariate at the parish church of Poussan (Maguelonne) in February 1336, but he evidently still retained his position when he was named rector of the church of alcrose (Uzès) early in 1339. He was paid as chaplain of Benedict XII in 1336, 1337, 1339, 1340, and 1342. One of the few chaplains to have continued in papal service under Clement VI, Johannes was cited as *capellanus capelle intrinsece* on 3 August 1342, and as *capellanus capelle* on 6 August 1342 and during the year 1343/44.
(Schäfer II: 44, 203, 204, 234. *Lettres, Benoît XII,* vol. 1: 286, no. 3137. *Lettres, Benoît XII,* vol. 2: 137, no. 6595; 152, no. 6737.)

## JOHANNES DE ULMO
On 19 November 1362 several documents concerning a Johannes de Ulmo were composed. At the time, this cleric from the diocese of Le Puy was a familiar of Cardinal Elie de Saint-Yrieix, notary public, and clerk to the cardinal's chamberlain. He held a canonicate at Saint-Genès in Clermont, and he requested a canonicate at Saint-Géry of Cambrai. Another document bearing the same date has him supplicating for a benefice at the church of Saint-Outrille at the castle of Bourges. Improbable as it may seem, another rotulus submitted by the same cardinal on the same day requested a canonicate at Meaux for Johannes de Ulmo, priest of Meaux, chaplain and *cantor* of Elie. At the time, he already had the rectoate of Monteriaco (Meaux) and was made to abandon the chaplaincy of Blessed Mary that he possessed in the church of Saint-Georges at Crécy (Meaux). The first Johannes de Ulmo is undoubtedly another person and does not concern us here. Cardinal Elie was transferred to the important see of Ostia, and a little over one month later, on 12 June 1363, Johannes was admitted to the papal chapel. A document from March of that year calls Johannes de Ulmo a priest who owned a *hospitium* though, there is not enough information given to be able to determine which Johannes de Ulmo this is. On 27 September 1365, Johannes received payment for expenses incurred as *administrator capelle.* Sometime before this date, he assumed the responsibility for the management of the chapel without assuming the actual title of *magister.* In February 1366 he acted as procurer in a transaction, and is referred to as chaplain of the altar of Saint-Denis in the church of Saint-Martin-des-Champeaux-en-Brie (Paris). By about the end of June he had officially become *magister capelle intrinsece pape.* Along with his familiar Stephanus Pictoris, a cleric from the diocese of Sens, he was instrumental in transporting the items of the papal chapel to Rome with Urban V. Although we have no accounts for the journey back to Avignon, Johannes presumably was engaged in similiar activities. On 8 July 1367, he was given a canonicate at Saint-Omer (Thérouanne) for which he vacated his chaplaincy in the diocese of Paris. He served as *magister* of Gregory XI and was sworn in as such on 3 January 1371. Six days afterwards, he received a canonicate at the church of Saint-Martin-des-Champeaux where he once held a chaplaincy. On 15 April 1372, he resigned this canonicate for the treasurership of the cathedral of Meaux. He functioned in the chapel of the pope as late as 31 October 1375. However by 23 May of the following year, the canonicate at Saint-Omer, vacant through his death at the curia, was conferred on Theobaldus Furnerii (q.v.).
(Schäfer III: 28, 112, 156, 182, 183, 242, 243, 367, 488, 541, 603, 622, 623. Kirsch: 12-13, 24, 45, 95-96, 143. Hoberg: 472 ff. Ehrle: 269 f. AVB 5: 207, no. 497. AVB 7: 14, no. 24. AVB ll: 39-40, no. 47.

AVB 15: 70, no. 2105, AVB 20: 20, no. 1430, fn.; 30, no. 1452; 33, no. 1457; 63, no. 1518. AVB 25: 323, no. 3628. *Lettres, Urbain V*, vol. 1: 41, no. 949; vol. 2: 163, no. 6140; 272, no. 6923; vol. 5: 49, no. 16182; vol. 6: 73-74, no. 18985; vol. 7: 76-77, nos. 21161-21162. Informatique: S03602217, fol. 218v.)

## JOHANNES VALENTIS (VALHANT)

This chaplain came from the town of Vendrest (Meaux). He first enters the service of the pope on 16 November 1349 when he was named *servitor capelle intrinsece*. He replaced the deceased Johannes Gervasii on 26 November 1352 as a *capellanus et servitor capelle*. On 29 July 1355 he held a benefice at the church of Pont-sur-Yonne (Sens) and the chaplaincy of Saint-Eloi at the cathedral of Auxerre, when he resigned a canonicate at the cathedral of Senlis in order to acquire one at Saint-Paul of Liège. On 21 November of that year, when he added a canonicate at Saint-Barthélemy of Liège to the above benefices, he was called *capellanus capelle intrinsece*. Still acting as chaplain in September 1357, he submitted a supplication for a benefice either at the rural church of Poissy (Chartres) or at Sens. On 5 May 1358 as chaplain of the chapel, Johannes received a canonicate at Saint-Merri (Paris). He sought the curateship of Alken (Liège) in January 1359, but if that could not be provided, he would accept a canonicate at the cathedral of Meaux. On 7 January, as chaplain of the papal chapel, he submitted a supplication on behalf of his nephew. At the end of October of this same year, Johannes asked the pope to grant 1 year and 40 days indulgence to those who visit Notre-Dame at Pont-sur-Yonne on Christmas, Epiphany, Easter, Ascension, Pentecost, Trinity, the four feasts of Mary, and All Saints. The church needed funds for restoration after *invasiones inimicorum*. On 21 June 1361, the nephew requested the canonicate at Saint-Barthélemy vacant by the death of his uncle in the curia. Johannes was one of the chaplains to receive an almuce on 3 June 1356. There is no indication that he should be identified with the composer Jehan Vaillant.
(Schäfer II: 625. OPKA: 98, and fn. AVB 5: 3, no. 5 fn.; 282, no. 663; 319-320, no. 752; 394, no. 945; 516, no. 1260; 570, no. 1394; 690, no. 1697; 698, no. 1718; 707-708, no. 1745. AVB 17: 364-365, no. 1091; 405, no. 1215. Ursula Günther, "Johannes Vaillant." *In Speculum musicae artis: Festgabe für Heinrich Hussmann zum 60. Geburtstag*. Munich: Wilhelm Fink, 1970, pp. 174-78.

## JOHANNES DE VENDA (LAVANTA)

He was already *capellanus capelle intrinsece* on 21 November 1355 when he was provided a canonicate at the Marian church of Maastricht (Liège). At that time, he already held benefices at Saint-Pierre of Marigny (Coutances) and Saint-Gervais of Paris. The following June, he received an almuce as papal chaplain. He might have been the *capellanus capelle Palatii apostolici* (probably commensal chaplain) who died before 21 August 1363 when a canonicate at Evreux became vacant.
(Schäfer II: 625. AVB 5: 319, no. 750. AVB 17: 405, no. 1214. *Lettres, Urbain V*, vol. 1: 281, no. 2635.)

## JOHANNES VINYAS (VINHAS)

Received into the chapel on 15 June 1407, at which time he was called priest and vicar of Saint-Etienne of Villemoustaussou (Carcassone). He was paid in the city of Perpignan and served in the chapel during 1408/09.
(Günther II: 43. ASV, *Coll.* 457: fol. 257v.)

## JOHANNES VITRARII (VITRASSI, VERRERII, VERDERII, JEAN DE VEREDY, DE VELLERY)

We first discover Johannes (Jean de Veredy) in 1387 serving as *valet de chambre aux deniers* for the duchess of Burgundy. This deacon from Reims received a perpetual chaplaincy at the church of Beaurevoir (Cambrai) by *motu proprio* on 12 July 1391. At the time, he was a *capellanus* in the papal chapel. It seems that this benefice was originally reserved by Matheus de Sancto Johanne (q.v.), but since Matheus was dead when the benefice became available, the pope decided to bestow

the prebend of Johannes. In 1392 he became involved in obtaining a canonicate at the cathedral of Angers, though not without considerable difficulty. His name appears in the list of chaplains drawn up on 30 October 1393, and on 5 October 1394 he is among the *cantores* of Benedict XIII. By 18 October, however, he was called chaplain of the chapel of Duke Philip of Burgundy, and in a supplication bearing this date, he solicited for a canonicate at Saint-Géry of Cambrai or one or two benefices at Sens and Nevers. On 2 May 1396, he was again included among he members of the papal chapel. By 21 April 1398 Johannes (Jean de Velery or Vellery) was employed as clerk of Pierre de Monsberraut, the treasurer, councellor, and governor of the finances of Duke Philip. On that date Johannes became *valet de chambre aux deniers* for John, count of Nevers, and oldest son of the duke. By 1 July of that year he was installed as *valet de chambre aux deniers* for Philip which he held through 1399. According to the accounts, he served again as *capellanus capelle pape* for at least some of the time after 11 August 1403 and preceding November 1404. By 19 December 1406 he was in the employ of John the Fearless, duke of Burgundy and might have been residing in Paris. In a supplication bearing that date submitted by King Charles VI of France, he is called familiar of Duke John, canon of Saint-Géry (where he was seeking the office of the *scolastria*), chaplain in the castle of Brieulles-sur-Bar (Reims), and he expected a benefice at Nevers and had one in litigation at Angers. Early in 1406 we find Johannes still in Paris, serving John as *valet de chambre aux deniers*. His service was probably continuous at least until 6 January 1408 when he added the title *secretaire du duc* to the above. He is found at the Burgundian court again in 1411, 1413, 1414, 1416, and 1419. No doubt due to his long service in the ducal household by 25 May 1422 he held the position of *conseiller et valet des comptes* for Duke Philip the Good.
(Günther I: 186-188, 192, 193, doc. 4, doc. 5. Haberl: 213, AVB 10: 527, 551. AVB 13: 342, no. 1912. AVB 19: 199, no. 520. AVB 26: 110-11, no. 413. *Pouillés*, vol. 3. *La Provence de Troyes*: 212. BN, Coll. Bourg., vol. 23: 145v.; vol. 25: 52, 61v., 63v.)

JOHANNES VOLKARDI (VOLCARDI, VOLCARDE) alias dictus YMMESOENS
On 1 May 1368 he reserved a canonicate at the Marian church of Antwerp (Cambrai) bestowed exactly 13 months later. At that time he was serving as almoner of Cardinal Anglic Grimoard, bishop of Albano and brother of Urban V. The document tells us that he came from the city of *Oerderensis* in the diocese of Cambrai, "at a distance of one league from Antwerp, or thereabouts." On 12 January 1371, by which time he was ordained to the priesthood, he was given a canonicate at Saint-Hermès of Renaix (Cambrai). He was then called familiar and commensal of Cardinal Anglic and canon of Antwerp. The benefice at Renaix was granted on 12 October 1374. Several weeks later, on 7 November, he was officially received into the papal chapel. On the following 15 May, he exchanged his benefice at Antwerp for other canonicates in the same church. In August, this familiar and *capellanus capelle* sought a canonicate at the church of the Holy Apostles at Cologne, and two months later, having received this benefice, he requested a canonicate at Saint-Servais of Maastricht (Liège). On 12 February 1377, still serving in the papal chapel, Johannes resigned his canonicate at Cologne in order to receive the rectorate of Oerbecke (Liège) and a canonicate and cantorate at Saint-Germain of Tirlemont (Liège). On the same day, he rather audaciously reserved a canonicate at the church of the Apostles at Cologne, left vacant by his accession to the *cantoria* of Tirlemont. On 27 April of that year, there was some question as to the legality of his acceptance of this position. From a document of Pope Clement VII dated 28 November 1378 we find that Johannes was stripped of his benefice and prebends at Tirlemont because of his adherence to the Roman Pope. Subsequently, he was deprived of all his titles because of infidelity to the Avignon line. He was cited as *magister capelle* to Urban VI in June 1380, therefore, he probably continued in service throughout the reign of Gregory XI and into the pontificate of the Roman Pope. After 18 February 1381 he was named deacon of Antwerp by Urban and at that time was still serving as his *magister capelle*. He made his will in 1377 and died towards the end of 1396.
(AVB 8: 673-74, nos. 2472-2473. AVB 11: 78, no. 131. AVB 13: 58, no. 391, fn. AVB 15: 238, no. 2387, fn. AVB 20: 660, no. 2878, fn. AVB 25: 82, no. 3164. 140, no. 3296; 179, no. 3374; 418-19, no.

3838; 419, no. 3839; 442, no. 3891. AVB 29: 83, no. 88, fn. *Lettres, Urbain V*, vol. 8: 142, no. 23784. Seidlmayer: 218-19.)

## LAURENCIUS DE ABBATISVILLA (LAURENTIUS DE ALLUNSVILLE)

Coming from the diocese of Amiens, he was chaplain in the chapel of Clement VI from 11 June 1348 until at least 7 March of the following year. During this time he was engaged in reserving a canonicate at Saint-Pierre of Aire (Thérouanne).
(AVB 1: 387, no. 1448; 410, no. 1522. Clercx: 14, fn.)

## MARCIAL COBRERII

From the diocese of Nîmes, he was inducted into the chapel of the pope on 24 June 1363.
(Schäfer III: 28.)

## MARTINUS DE PRATO

He became a singer of Pope Gregory XI on 3 January 1371, but probably had an earlier association with the pope. On 13 February he received payment for certain robes and shoes necessary to Petrus Terrini and Johannes Batalha, former clerks or singers (also called *pueri*) of the chapel of the pope when he was still cardinal. These two were sent to the *studium* in Montpellier. Through 1372 up to 11 January 1373 Martinus was responsible for these two students. On 11 October 1373 he was paid the remainder owed him for the expenses incurred by familiars and servants of the pope while Urban V was transporting the Curia from Italy to France. He acted as procurer on 22 November 1374. He is said to have possessed many benefices, though we have determined only that on 7 October 1377 he abandoned a benefice at Sens in order to obtain one at Amiens.
(Schäfer III: 364, 368, 394, 406, 476, 480. AVB 20: 690-91, nos. 2938-2939.)

## MATHEUS DE BARBINO

A cleric from the diocese of Amiens, he is said to have entered the chapel of the pope on 7 June 1348.
(Clercx: 14, fn.)

## MATHEUS DE LONGARIGA (LONGHARIGHA)

In a supplication dated 5 November 1372, this priest is called chaplain and familiar of Cardinal Guillaume d'Aigrefeuille. He held a rectorate at Paillencourt (Cambrai) when he sought the chaplaincy of Saint-Nicaise in the Benedictine church of Montivilliers (Rouen) that once belonged to Philippus Servonhi (q.v.). Six years later on 3 November 1378, Matheus was familiar and *capellanus capelle* of the pope. He was then given a canonicate at the cathedral of Laon. His name appears in the list of papal chaplains compiled on 19 September 1379, and he is again reported to have received monies for his chapel service in the fall of 1382. Because of an illness suffered in 1383, he was not able to accept payment due him until sometime after the wages were officially given. He is again listed among the chaplains that served during the two months prior to 22 January 1385. He continued to be active as chaplain and familiar of the pope at least until 3 June 1388 when he was granted a canonicate at the cathedral of Cambrai. After his death *extra curiam*, before 14 May 1393, this benefice went to Guillelmus de Ultraaquam. He seems to have been a chaplain and familiar at the time of his death.
(AVB 8: 5, no. 14. AVB 13: 634, no. 1518; 764, no. 2348; 765, no. 2355. AVB 20: 194, no. 1858. Günther I: 180, 182 and fnn., 185, doc. 2.)

## MATHEUS PETRI

He was *clericus cerimoniarum* under Benedict XIII from 1411 until 1423. He then went on to serve Eugene IV and Nicholas V in the same capacity from 1431 until his death in July 1450.
(OPKA: 108.)

## MATHEUS DE SANCTO JOHANNE

A cleric from the diocese of Thérouanne, he first appears as *clericus* in the chapel of Duke Louis I of Anjou on 17 November 1378. At this time he was ordained to minor orders and was seeking a

canonicate at Laon. Besides having served the duke, Matheus reminds the pope that *etiam eidem Sanctitati Vestre fideliter servivit.* He was listed among the chaplains of the pope in documents from 30 October and 20 December 1382. Maintaining his status as familiar, on 4 August 1384 he received the canonicate at Saint-Piat of Seclin (Tournai) vacant throught the death of Thomas la Caille (q.v.). Cited again for service rendered before 22 January 1385, Matheus continued in the papal chapel at least until 26 March 1386. In a document bearing that date, he received a dispensation from having to be ordained to the priesthood within three years of his acceptance of the canonicate at Seclin. He apparently reserved a chaplaincy at Beaurevoir (Cambrai) that he never received because he was no longer alive by the time it became available. It was conferred instead on Johannes Vitrarii (q.v.) by *motu proprio,* 12 July 1391. Matheus as therefore dead by this date. The documents written between the years 1382 and 1389 show, however, that Matheus was attempting to exchange the rights to this benefice for those at a certain church *in lingua Occitana.* This might be taken as a further clue to his whereabouts at this time. Günther proposes that he came from the monastery of Saint-Jean in the diocese of Thérouanne and might be identified with the "Mathieu de monastere Saint Jean" who was chaplain at the court of Queen Joanna of Naples in 1363. Günther also asks if he may be the Mathieu who was in the service of Duke Louis of Orléans in 1389. Though we do not know where he was at the time of his death, we know that he did die *extra curiam.* There are several extant pieces attributed to Matheus found in Ch and Mod: One five-voice motet, *Are post libamina,* one three-voice and one four-voice rondeau, two three-voice ballades and one four-voice ballade. Included in this is the ballade in praise of Clement VII, *Inclite flos orti Gebenensis.*
(Günther I: 180, 185 and fn., doc. 2. AVB 8: 109, no. 347. AVB 10: 351, 446, 527, 551. AVB 13: 189, no. 1065; 574-75, no. 1119. Ursula Günther, "Matheus de Sancto Johanne," *Grove 6,* vol. 11, p. 820.)

## MATHEUS VALETA (dictus VOLTA)
He is cited as chaplain of the pope in 1342, 1343/44, and on 5 June 1344.
(Schäfer II: 203, 234, 265.)

## NICOLAUS BENEDICTI (=NICOLAUS BERNARDI? q.v. =NICOLAUS BERTRANDI? q.v.)
He was papal chaplain in 1336.
(Schäfer II: 44.)

## NICOLAUS BERNARDI (=NICOLAUS BENEDICTI? q.v.)
He was called chaplain of Benedict XII in 1337.
(Schäfer II: 60.)

## NICOLAUS BERTRANDI (=NICOLAUS BENEDICTI? q.v.)
He served as chaplain to Benedict XII in 1337, 1339, 1340, and 1342.
(Schäfer II: 60, 94, 120, 159.)

## NICOLAUS DE BONDEVILLA alias DE SPEDONA (BOUDEVILLA)
On 8 November 1362, during the reign of Urban V, Nicolaus was called *capellanus capelle* of Innocent VI. At the time he was canon of Saint-Aignan outside to walls of Orleans, chaplain at Ablis (Chartres), provost of Sigalonia attached to Saint-Aignan, and held the rights to the rectorate of Gumery (Sens). Three days later, as chaplain of Urban he reserved a canonicate at the collegiate church of Saint-Martin-des-Champeaux-en-Brie (Paris) and offered to resign the posts at Gumery and Ablis. On 20 September 1363, as papal chaplain, he requested a rectorate at Maceriis (Rouen). He was agian listed as *capellanus capelle* on 27 November 1365. In September of the following year, when he acted as proxy in a transaction, Nicolaus was referred to as a priest from the diocese of Chartres. Still faithfully serving Urban in November 1369, this canon at the cathedral of Orléans was made to give up his benefice at Paris. By mid-July 1379 he seems to have passed out of papal service, though not without having spent a considerable amount of time at the

Curia. In a supplication of Pierre d'Auxy, bishop of Tournai, it states that Nicolaus was *successive capellanus* to *trium summorum pontificum ac etiam plurium dominorum cardinalium*. At that time he abandoned a canonicate at the cathedral of Noyon, one at Saint-Pierre-des-Filles at Orléans, and the recotrate at the parish church of Saint-Laurent outside the walls of Orléans in order to assume the *cantoria* of the cathedral of Auxerre.
(Schäfer III: 145. AVB 8: 665-66, no. 2448-9. AVB 12: 221, no. 799-800. *Lettres, Urbain V*, vol. 1: 132, no. 1673; 391, no. 3498; vol. 5: 108, no. 16461; 109, no. 16463; vol. 9: no. 25627; no. 27496. Informatique: S03602188: fol. 216v; S04001104, fol. 134.)

### NICOLAUS DE NASIACO (NOISIACO, NORSIACO)
He was paid as chaplain of the pope in August 1342, during the year 1343/44, and in June 1344. (Schäfer II: 203, 234, 265.)

### NICOLAUS RAIMUNDI
He was among the first chaplains of Benedict XII in 1335.
(Schäfer II: 26.)

### NICOLAUS VACHERII
After the death of Johannes Broulette (q.v.) which occurred before 2 November 1405, this priest and papal chaplain reserved the rectorate at the Benedictine monastery of Saint-Vaast (Cambrai) vacant by Johannes' death. At the time, he possessed two perpetual chaplaincies at the church of *Beata Maria de Marcatuli* at Pamiers. On 6 September 1406, Nicolas transferred his rectorate to Petrus Sellerii (q.v.) through the procurer Gerardus Gerardi (q.v.). He seems to have still been in the service of the papal chapel at this time.
(AVB 19: 187, no. 488; 195, no. 509.)

### PASCASIUS DE BRIELLA
In 1405 he was cited as *scholaris capelle pape*. He might have been a choirboy.
(OPKA: 105 fn., 106 fn.)

### PETRUS BANIARDI (BOMARC)
He was one of the papal chaplains to receive an almuce on 3 June 1356. There is no information for the following year, but we find him again in 1358, serving as *capellanus capelle*. In May of that year, he filed a supplication requesting a canonicate at Saint-Servais of Maastricht (Liège). On 1 August 1358, before action was taken on the above supplication, he was involved in procuring a canonicate at the cathedral of Tournai. During this time, he held a canonicate in the cathedral of Toulouse and a benefice at the church of Montgaillard (Narbonne). When he died, before 19 August 1361, his canonicate at Toulouse was sought by Alanus Avis (q.v.). At the time of his death he was serving as papal chaplain.
(Schäfer II: 625. AVB 5: 462, no. 1124; 488, no. 1188; 710, no. 1751.)

### PETRUS BATAILLE
As early as 18 June 1384, Petrus is cited as papal familiar, thouth the reason for such an appellation is unkown. On that date, this cleric of the diocese of Tournai was given the rectorate of the parish church of Esquelmes (Tournai) and is recorded as having paid various fees for its bestowal. During the year 1384/85 he was given the right to be ordained to the priesthood, probably required because of a "defect of birth." On 18 July 1391, as familiar of Cardinal Niccoló Brancaccio, he resigned his rectorate. Five months later, in the month of December, he was given a perpetual chaplaincy at the church of Beghine in the city of Bruges (Tournai). He appears as "Bataille" in the list of papal *cantores* compiled on 5 October 1394 after the election of Benedict XIII. A little over one week later, in a supplication for a canonicate either in the cathedral of Tournai or in Saint-Pierre of Lille (Tournai), he is said to have had a rectorate at the church of Jeancourt (Noyon), the chaplaincy at Bruges, and also a rectorate at Saint-Gilles of Bruges and a chaplaincy at the altar of Saint-Nicolas in the church of Saint-Pierre of Lille, both of which were

not yet officially in his possession. Though he was absent from the papal chapel in the spring of 1396, he is cited again as chaplain and familiar of the pope on 3 December 1397. At the time, this subdeacon, as he is called, was given a perpetual chaplaincy at Saint-Pierre of Lille by *motu proprio*.
(Günther I: 187, doc. 4. Haberl: 213. AVB 10: 379, 556, 563. AVB 13: 528, no. 838; 566, no. 1073; 708, no. 1987; 717, no. 2043. AVB 19: 74, no. 172. AVB 26: 10, no. 13.)

### PETRUS CAPUCII
This priest from the diocese of Rouen was admitted to the papal chapel on 24 March 1396, and he was paid on 2 May of that year for service up until 12 April.
(Günther I: 188, doc. 4.)

### PETRUS DE GODESCAUT (GODESCALC, GODESCANT)
As early as 1387 this priest is called *servitor magistri capelle pape*. On 28 March 1392, he was noted as possessing the rectorate of *Estacuria* (Equancourt?) in the diocese of Noyon, when he asked for another at the parish church of Thun-l'Evêque (Cambrai). Again in 1394 he is in papal service, this time as *servitor capelle pape*.
(AVB 13: 725, no. 2099. AVB 26: 178, no. 684. OPKA: 106.)

### PETRUS DE GUERMINI (GHIERMEGNY, QUERMINI)
On 15 December 1360, this priest from the diocese of Tournai was named in a supplication as familiar, clerk, and commensal of Elie Talleyrand de Périgord, the cardinal of Albano. In this document he requested a benefice under the jurisdiction of the abbot of the Benedictine monastery of Saint-Ghislain (Cambrai). In December of the following year, by which time he was awaiting action on the above-named benefice and on one at the parish church of Villeneuve-en-Chevrie (Chartres), Petrus is called subdeacon and familiar of Cardinal Talleyrand. He was asking for the canonicate of Saint-Jean-le-Rond at the cathedral of Paris. The cardinal died on 7 January 1364, and in less then three weeks Petrus moved into the chapel of the pope where he is called *capellanus sive cantor*. On November 1365, he is again listed with the chaplains.
(Schäfer III: 28, 145. AVB 5: 643-44, no. 1580; 742, no. 1839.)

### PETRUS DE MONCOULON (MONCOLO, MONTECOLONO)
On 11 March 1353, Petrus was called *elemosynarius secretus*. Several years later, on 3 June 1356, he received an almuce as papal chaplain. He was *scriptor* of penitential letters and almoner when he died in the Curia, sometime before 14 September 1358. His title was sought by Johannes Clementis de Brullio (q.v.).
(Schäfer II: 625; 529, 533, 551, 577, 603, 613, 640, 693. AVB 5: 504-5, no. 1230. Ehrle: 733.)

### PETRUS ROSSELETI
This cleric from the diocese of Poitiers entered the chapel of Benedict XIII on 25 October 1404. He is named on payment lists dated 24 April and 3 July 1405.
(Günther I: 194, 195 fn. Günther II: 42.)

### PETRUS SALTETI DE MIMATIS
On 14 January 1367, "sufficiently learned in grammar and logic," Petrus received the secular priorship and rectorate of he rural church of Saint-Martin at Aurillac (Lodève). At the time he held a benefice at the cathedral of Mende called *superpellicium*. By 19 January 1369 he was *clericus capelle*. He probably served in this capacity continuously until a papal mandate dated 24 October 1372; *De mandato domini pape, dominus camerarius privavit et suspendit dominos clericos capelle, videlicet Petrum et Pontcium [de Curte q.v.)] de vadiis usque ad mundatum pape.* The exact reason for this suspension is unclear. For the following 10 years we know nothing of the whereabouts or activities of Petrus. However, after the office of chapel clerk was reinstated, he is once again cited as serving in this capacity. We find him listed in the payment records of 30 October and 20 December 1382, 22 June 1385, and 30 October 1393. He entered the service of

Benedict XIII, and he is included in the first list of chapel members of this pope, compiled 5 October 1394. He seems to have left the service of the papal chapel sometime after this, since in the spring of 1396 he is replaced by Anequinus [Johannes] Fabri (q.v.). However, after Benedict regrouped his chapel members at Pont-de-Sorgues, he is again cited as a clerk of the papal chapel. The last two references that we have found place him in the chapel on 11 August 1403 and for the period ending 27 September 1404. He is said to have served as *clericus cerimoniarum* from 1403 until 1408/09 when he transferred his allegiance to the council of Pisa. Under Pope Martin V, he held several benefices in the diocese of Uzès where he probably died ca. 1432.

(Schäfer III: 35. *Lettres, Urbain V*, vol. 6: 49, no. 18867. ASV, *Coll.* 457: fol. 21. Günther I: 180, 185-87, 192, 193, doc. 2-5. *ZKM*: 96, fn. OPKA: 104-5, fn.)

### PETRUS SAUMATI alias DE MONTEACUTO (SAMATI, SANATI, MONTAGUT)

He was chaplain and familiar of the pope as early as 22 June 1355. This cleric from the diocese of Clermont, who held a perpetual chaplaincy at the chapel of Mary in the palace of Corbie (Amiens), was granted a canonicate at the church of Saint-Géry at Cambrai. During the month of November, he asked for a canonicate at the cathedral of Lisieux. At that time, he held a canonicate at Saint-Géry (though he may not have realized the prebend), and chaplaincies at Corbie, Hal (Cambrai), and Saint-Nicolas beyond the walls of Brussels (Cambrai). He was also awaiting a benefice under the jurisdiction of the abbot of the Benedictine monastery of Saint-Pierre of Ghent (Tournai). Five months later he supplicated for a canonicate at Badajoz in Castile. Still called chaplain of the pope in April of the following year, he exchanged his benefice at Hal for a canonicate at the cathedral of Reims. He is last named in a document dated 30 January 1361 in which he was involved in an attempt to exchange his canonicate at Saint-Géry with one at Nesle (Noyon). He died as a papal chaplain before 25 April 1361, at which time Egidius Quadrati

(q.v.) sought his canonicate at Reims. He was one of the papal chaplains to receive an almuce on 3 June 1356.

(Schäfer II: 625. AVB 5: 276, no. 648; 321, no. 759; 560, no. 1370; 586-87, no. 1433; 624, no. 1530; 651, no. 1597; 669, no. 1639. AVB 7: 272, no. 810; 352, no. 1015. AVB 9: 378, no. 903; 585, no. 1296. AVB 17: 359, no. 1074.)

### PETRUS SELLERII (SELLIER, SELHERI, SOLERII, SOLIERI, SALERII)

This name seems first to appear in papal documents dating from October 1379. On 15 October as *capellanus*, he extracted an evangel from the lower treasury for use in the papal chapel. Again on 29 October, he had dealings with the keepers of the papal book treasure. At that time, he withdrew approximately one ounce of blue pigment that was to be used for illustrating some papal books. In that notice, Petrus was referred to as *clericus capelle ipsius domini nostri pape*. His name is not found in the papal documents again until 1393. On 9 August of that year, in a rotulus submitted by the "lord of Alet" (Bishop Henri Bayler?) this acolyte from the diocese of Cambrai was given an unspecified benefice. Two documents bearing the date 13 October 1403 provide more information. In one, he appears as *servitor et familiaris in capella* for Pope Benedict; in the other, he is called *capellanus capelle*. Both notices specify that he holds the rank of deacon, that he has a chaplaincy at the cathedral of Cambrai, and that he requested and received a canonicate at Saint-Géry (Cambrai). The discrepancy in title can be explained by the following notice. On 23 April 1404, in the city of Marseille, the deacon Petrus Sellerii was officially sworn in as a member of the papal chapel. The situation in 1403 indicates that although ot officially a member of the chapel, he did carry out chaplain-like duties, enough so that he could be called chaplain by mistake. He is named in the list of chapel members that was drawn up on 23 September 1404. By 9 March 1405, he had been ordained to the priesthood. In a number of documents dating from around that time, we learn that Petrus, still serving as a papal chaplain, had to resign the canonicate at Saint-Géry in order to obtain the rectorate at Esperaza (Alet). On 16 September of that year, he gave up his chaplaincy at the altar of Sainte-Maxellende that he held at the cathedral of Cambrai. It was given

to Robertus Creque (q.v.). On 16 September 1406, called a papal familiar, Petrus received the rectorate of Saint-Vaast that belonged to Nicolaus Vacherii (q.v.); Nicolaus, in turn, received the rectorate of Esperaza. Gerardus Gerardi (q.v.) acted as procurer in the transaction. Evidently Petrus had not given up Saint-Géry as indicated in a document from the previous year. His whereabouts and actions after this date are unkown, and his name is no longer found in the records of the papal chapel. It is difficult to explain the 24-year hiatus in his service between 1379 and 1403. Perhaps there were two clerics by that name active in the chapel.
(AVB 13: 378, no. 2168. AVB 19: 100, no. 227; 171, no. 439; 171, no. 442; 173, no. 444; 184, no. 483; 195, no. 509. AVB 26: 515, no. 2413. Günther I: 193. Williman: 668-669. ASV, *Coll.* 457: fol. 257v.)

PETRUS SINTERII alias BARDONERII (SAINTERII, SANTERI, SENTERII, SENCCERII, SAYNTERII, BARDARIAS)
Paid for 53 days service on 11 February 1335, this cleric from the diocese of Mende was one of the first chaplains of Benedict XII. By the following January, he was listed at the head of the list. There he appears in 1337, 1339, and on all subsequent registers. Just after the election of Benedict, Petrus received a canonicate at the cathedral of Clermont. At the time, he was called papal familiar and already held a canonicate at Saint-Pierre of Clermont and rectorate at the parish church of Saint-Martin at Cantal (Clermont). On 7 November of that year, he was granted the fruits of his benefice in absentia. On 16 May 1336, while still possessing his canonicate at Clermont, Petrus resigned the rectorate at Cantal in order to receive one at the rural church of Saint-Hyppolite at *Villarifargaris*, today in the city of Narbonne. In a document that contains accounts for the year 1340, he is referred to as *magister capelle*. By 1341 he had already assumed responsibility for the expenses of the chapel, and we know that he officially held the title of *magister* before 24 July 1342. Petrus retained this position and his canonicate at the cathedral of Clermont until his death, which occurred after 25 May but before 20 November 1350. Raymundus de Anglade (q.v.) was executor of his testament.
(Schäfer II: 26, 44, 60, 94, 120, 140, 159, 165, 166, 199, 201, 203, 204, 212, 213, 234, 245, 252, 265, 273, 290, 302, 306, 319, 324, 338, 373, 390, 401, 421, 426, 434, 454. Hoberg: 103-7, fn. Mohler: 411. AVB 1: 555, no. 2144. *Lettres, Benoît XII*, vol. 1: 49, no. 393; 158, no. 1672; 232, no. 2577; 238, no. 2634; 242, no. 2670; 264, no. 2863; 278, no. 3041, 396, no. 4225; vol. 2: 19, no. 5404. Guillemain: 363.)

PHILIPPUS ROBERTI
In 1373, this priest was designated as chaplain, commensal, and long-time familiar (*antiquus familiaris*) of Cardinal Robert de Genève, the future Clement VII. At the time he held a chaplaincy at the church of Saint-Colomban (Saint-Pol-de-Léon), another in the parish church of Bernot (Laon), the rectorate of *Bonchosiacum* (Sens), and he awaited action on a canonicate at the cathedral of Paris. In the aforementioned document, he requested a canonicate at Saint-Pierre of Aire (Thérouanne). Listed among the familiars of the new pope, he requested a canonicate at the cathedral of Sens on 3 November 1378. Five days later the one at Saint-Donatien at Bruges (Tournai) was bestowed on him. His name appears among those of the chaplains of Clement VII who were paid on 19 September 1379. We know of no other reference to him serving as *capellanus*. On 13 October 1380 the benefice at Saint-Colomban was realized. He died outside of the curia before 22 January 1384, when the records declare vacant his canonicate at Aire.
(AVB 8: 4-5, no. 13. AVB 12: 27, no. 100. AVB 13: 504, no. 685. AVB 20: 456-57, no. 2426; 457-58, no. 2427. Günther I: 182 fn.)

PHILIPPUS SERVONHI (SERVANI, SERNAIN, SERVOINH, SERNARII, SERNAM, SERVAIN)
On 30 October 1361, he submitted a request for either the rectorate of the parish church of Valles (Tarragona) or for the one at Morannes (Angers). At that time, he is called *clericus capelle intrinsece*, held the parsonage of Schellebelle (Cambrai) that he received nine months earlier and

two perpetual chaplaincies: one in the Benedictine monastery of Montivilliers (Rouen) and the other in the manor of the bishop of Bayeux at Douvres. Although the pope did not respond to this request, Philippus had acquired the rectorate at Morannes by 11 November 1362. On that date, as *clericus* of the Apostolic chapel, a canonicate at Saint-Martin of Tours was conferred on him. For this, he abandoned his benefice at Schellebelle in March 1363. On 25 September 1364 he is called *capellanus et cantor capelle intrinsece pape*. He is again listed among the chaplains on 27 November 1365. He acted as proxy in a transaction of 22 April 1368. On 9 January 1371, Pope Gregory XI granted him a canonicate at the cathedral of Cambrai. In the document he is called chaplain of the chapel of the pope, one who served both Innocent and Urban for ten years, canon of Saint-Germain-l'Auxerrois (Paris), and rector of Morannes. Before he accepted the prebend of Cambrai, he was required to divest himself of the canonicate at Tours and the rectorate at Morannes. On 15 January 1371, he is listed among the *cantores* of Gregory. The following January, the chamberlain let it be known that Philippus was familiar of the pope since his election and, as such, was entitled to the prebends due him although he be absent. In a document dated 30 June 1374, in which he reserved a benefice under the jurisdiction of the bishop of Cambrai, he calls himself a former commensal chaplain of Cardinal Guillaume de la Jugie (†28 April 1374) whom he served for more than 20 years (!). At that time, Philippus was canon at Cambrai and Paris. On 11 June 1375 he was given a canonicate at Noyon, and in October of that year, he was called familiar of the pope. On 5 May 1376, he was accorded the right to have a portable altar on which to celebrate Mass. He was still alive on 24 April 1379, when he relinquished his canonicate at Cambrai for the rectorate of the parish church of Assche and a chaplaincy in the leprosarium at Soignies (both Cambrai).
(Schäfer III: 29, 145, 368. AVB 5: 734, no. 1817. AVB 7: 7, no. 9; 233, no. 720. AVB 9: 30, no. 51; 262, no. 696. AVB 11: 38-39, no. 45, fn.; 383, no. 918; 405, no. 976; 564, no. 1366, fn. AVB 12: 208, no. 778. AVB 20: 584, no. 2730. AVB 25: 177, no. 3370-71; 311, no. 3604. *Lettres, Urbain V*, vol. 1: 220, no. 2133; vol. 2: 294, no. 7055; vol. 7: 57-58, no. 21074. Informatique: S03602189, fol. 216v.; S03800450, fol. 45. Guillemain: 370.)

## PONTIUS DE CURTE

The first document concerning Pontius is the only one that we have found in the papal correspondance. On 7 May 1364, this cleric from the diocese fo Mende, neither married nor constituted in Holy Orders, was admitted into the curia as a scribe (*tabellionatus*). By 27 November of the following year, he was serving the *commensales* as their *clericus*. By the end of April 1367, when Pope Urban was about to leave Avignon for Rome, he had become one of the two unspecified *clerici capelle* serving both the *commensales* and the *intrinseci*. In the records of the payments made at this time, he was paid for recovering with silver an evangel that the pope was to take. By 16 September of that year he first appeared as a papal *scriptor*, and was often referred to as such throughout the period ending 3 August 1375. He acted as procurer for the Holy See at Montefiascone in the spring of 1370. As *clericus capelle* and *scriptor* he received payment for lamps, oil, and cord, and also for a pair of keys necessary during the conclave of cardinals that convened after Urban's death. Under Pope Gregory, on 24 October 1372, the office of *clerici capelle* was suspended for some unspecified reason. Although we do not know what the other clerk, Petrus Salteti (q.v.) did after this mandate, Pontius continued to be active in papal affairs. There is an extant deposition compiled by Pontius which gives damaging testimony concerning the underhanded dealings of Bartolomeo Prignano before and after the conclave of 1378. He was a firm supporter of Clement VII and served the papal chancellery in the late fall of 1378. Sometime during the early days of the pontificate of Clement, the office of *clericus capelle pape* was reinstituted, and we find our clerk again working there according to the payments of 30 October and 20 December 1382. His service was probably continuous throughout the pontificate of Pope Clement, since his name is on lists dated 22 January 1385 and 30 October 1393 as well. There were several powerful ecclesiastics attendant at Clement's deathbed. Pontius was among them. By this time he is said to have acquired canonicates at Mende and Rodez, and was probably

still a *scriptor*. His service as clerk extended into the first years of the reign of Benedict, and we find him paid with the other chapel members on 5 October 1394 and 12 April 1396. His whereabouts after this date are unknown.
(Günther I: 180, 185-88, doc. 2-4. Schäfer III: 145, 203, 375. Kirsch: 6. AVB 15: 329, no. 2543; 346, no. 2573. Logoz: 35-36, 173 fn., 216 fn. Opitz: 180. Seidlmayer: 309-10. *Lettres, Urbain V.* vol. 3: 563, no. 12076; vol. 9: no. 27540; no. 27548. ASV, *Coll.* 457: fol. 21. OPKA: 104 fn., 105 and fn. OKS: 64.)

### PRIVATUS PASTORELLI
On 10 January 1335, this cleric from the diocese of Mende was awaiting a benefice at Saint-Pons-de-Thomières (Saint-Papoul?) and was in possession of a vicariate in the parish church of Monferrand (Saint-Papoul). He appears among the chaplains of Benedict XII who were paid in 1337, 1339, 1340, and 1342, but he probably began his service sometime in 1336. In March 1339 he is called papal familiar and rector of the parish church of Seyne (Embrun). At that time, he held a perpetual chaplaincy in the church of Monferrand which he was forced to give up. One of the few chaplains of Pope Benedict to have continued in service under Clement VI, he was paid as chaplain during the year 1343/44 and on 5 June 1344. He died in 1348 as a papal chaplain.
(Schäfer II: 60, 94, 120, 159, 234, 265. *Lettres, Benoît XII*, vol. 1: 107, no. 1118; vol. 2: 141, no. 6643; 145, no. 6680.)

### RADULPHUS
He became *cantor* of Gregory XI on 3 January 1371.
(Schäfer III: 368.)

### RADULPHUS COSSARDI (=RAOLINUS COSSART, RADULPHUS TAFARDI)
He was called chaplain and familiar of the pope on 21 May 1342, when he submitted a request for a canonicate at the church at Saint-Omer of Saint-Omer (Thérouanne). By that time, he had already obtained a license in law, the chaplaincy at the chapel of the count of Eu in the monastery of Saint-Denis (Paris), and a benefice in the parochial church of Crecy-sur-Serre (Laon). He is again listed among the papal chaplains on 3 August 1342, during the year 1343/44, and on 5 June 1344.
(Schäfer II: 203, 234, 265. AVB 1: 1, no. 4. Gasparrini: 3, no. 7.)

### RADULPHUS RICARDI
He was chaplain of the pope in 1342 and during the year 1343/33.
(Schäfer II: 203, 204, 234.)

### RAIMUNDUS DE ANGLADE (ANGLADA, ANGLADIS, LAGLADA)
He was paid as chaplain of the pope in 1335, 1336, 1337, 1339, 1340, and 1342. He is probably identical to the Raimundus de Anglada who gave up the rectorate of the parish church of Saint-Apollinaire at Les Assions (Viviers) in February of 1336. He was involved in a financial transaction on behalf of the pope in 1340. In December 1349 he was still *capellanus capelle pape* and was a prebended canon at Lodève. On 20 November 1350 he acted as testamentary executor of Petrus Bardonerii (Sinterii) (q.v.).
(Schäfer II: 26, 44, 60, 94, 120, 159. *Lettres, Benoît XII*, vol. 1: 286, no. 3138. Göller II: 159. Mohler: 441, 583.)

### RAIMUNDUS ARNULPHI
Priest from the diocese of Limoges, he was accepted into the chapel as *magister organorum* on 8 July 1405. He was sworn in as a member of the chapel and as such received the wages of chaplain.
(Haberl: 213.)

### RAIMUNDUS SEGUINI
Rector of the church at Condat (Périgueux), on 9 January 1335 he was given a canonicate at Saint-Front (Périgueux), and in May 1336 he was granted permission to receive his prebend in

absentia. On 12 October 1337, the rectorate of the parish church of Antioque (Mirepoix) was conferred on him. In December of the following year Raimundus acted as procurer for the chapter of Saint-Front. He is listed among the first chaplains of Benedict XII, and was paid as such again in 1336, 1337, 1339, 1340, and 1342. It seems that this same person also called Raimundus Seguini de Altigiis held canonicates at the cathedral of Paphos in Cyprus, at the cathedral of Agen, and rectorate at Murrenchis (Condom) in November 1362. By the following fall he was said to have been licensed in law and archdeacon of Paphos. During 1363 he acted as an official in several transactions. It is possible that he might have been the Raimundus Seguini who, in September 1316, was granted a benefice at Saint-Vincent at Le Mas d'Agenais (Agen) as rector of Castillonenès (Agen) and familiar of Cardinal Arnaud de Pellegrue.
(Schäfer II: 26, 44, 60, 94, 120, 159. *Lettres, Benoît XII*, vol. 1: 49, no. 397; 305, no. 3362; 408, no. 4337; vol. 2: 154, no. 6757. *Lettres closes et patentes intéressant les pays autres que la France*. J-M. Vidal and G. Mollat, eds. Paris, 1950: 233, nos. 886-887. Göller II: 30. *Jean XXII. (1316-1334). Lettres communes analysées d'après les registres dits d'Avignon et du Vatican*. Mollat, ed. Paris, 1904: vol. 1: 28, no. 269; 81, no. 797. *Lettres, Urbain V*, vol. 1: 139, no. 1716; 571, no. 4939; vol. 2: 2, no. 4954; 382-383, no. 7852.)

## RAIMUNDUS SERVIENTIS
He was paid as papal chaplain in the years 1335, 1336, 1337, 1339, 1340, and 1342. A Raimundus Servientis is twice cited in papal financial accounts of 1337 as chaplain and familiar of Jean de Cojordan, bishop of Avignon.
(Schäfer III: 26, 44, 60, 94, 120, 159. Göller II: 60, 64.)

## REGINALDUS DU HOUX (DE HOS, REGNAULT DU HOULX)
He makes his first appearance when, on 13 May 1391, he and Johannes de Bosco (q.v.) received the wages on behalf of the chaplains. He is listed among the members of the chapel on 30 October 1393. On 5 October 1394, after the election of Benedict XIII, his name appears among those of the *cantores*, and he was probably still in the service of the pope when Duke Philip the Bold of Burgundy hired him on 8 June 1395. The duke was in Avignon during May and June of that year and was engaged in negotiations with Benedict. Reginaldus served in the Burgundian chapel throughout the reign of Philip. He was given financial assistance in order to buy a house on one occasion and, in 1402, was again aided by the duke when he sought to have his two nieces married. Soon after the interrment of Philip, Reginaldus returned south and, on 5 August 1404, reentered the chapel of Pope Benedict. At the time, he was recorded as having possessed a canonicate at the cathedral of Meaux, his diocese of origin. He continued in the service of the papal chapel at least until 23 September 1404 but seems not to have made the journey to Italy with the pontiff.
(Günther I: 186-87, 193, doc. 4. Haberl: 213. Wright: 64 and fn., 85, 221-30. ASV, *Coll.* 457: fol. 257v.)

## RICHARDUS (I)
He was admitted *in cantores* on 3 January 1371.
(Schäfer III: 368.)

## RICHARDUS DE BOZONVILLA (BOUZANVILLE, BOUSONVILLA, BOUSANVILLA, BOSSAUVILLA, BOUSAVILLA, BUSANVILLA, incorrectly, BONNEVILLE)
On 20 March 1364, Morandus de Bargunelz exchanged canonicates with Nicolaus *dictus* Marsaulz. Nicolaus was allowed to keep his perpetual chaplaincy of Saints Mary Magdalene and Katherine the Virgin that he possessed in the episcopal palace of Toul. The procurator in the transaction was a Johannes Pauli, canon of Saint-Paul at Liège. Several years later, on 13 January 1371, Richardus de Bozonvilla, *cubicularius* (chamber valet) of Cardinal Jean de Blauzac, was granted a canonicate at the church of Saint-Paul of Liège. He asked to be allowed to retain his chaplaincy in the episcopal palace of Toul. On 10 July, Richardus realized his prebend at Liège through the death of one of the canons, Johannes Pauli. The document tells us that he

was permitted to the *perpetuam capellaniam S. Katherine in capella palatii episcopalis Tullensis.* There seems to have been a definite relationship between Richardus and the clerics mentioned above. However, three years later, on 27 July 1374, still as familiar of the cardinal, Richardus had to give up this chaplaincy in order to assume a canonicate at the church of Saint-Dié in the city of Saint-Dié (Toul). He came to the attention of Clement VII in a supplication dated 19 November 1378. In that document, the pope's sister, Margaret, countess of Geneva, asks for a canonicate at the collegiate church of Saint-Dié for one of her favorites, even the one held by Richardus, she further specifies, *si eam interim vacare contigerit per assecutionem pacificam alterius beneficii cujuscumque per eundum Richardum faciendam.* The pope gave his sister's *dilectus* an expectation of prebend. Cardinal de Blauzac died on 8 July 1379. On 11 August 1379, several members of the college of cardinals, specifically, his executors, submitted a rotulus for his familiars. Two of these were the cubiculars Richardus and Johannes de Bosco (q.v.). As canon of Saint-Paul of Liège, Richardus wished a plenary indulgence written up, *si placet,* under the seal of Cardinal Anglic Grimoard. Although only his first name is given, we can be relatively certain that it was Richardus de Bozonvilla who was listed last in the account of the payment to the papal chaplains made 19 September 1379. He probably was not long a member of Clement's *capella intrinseca.* He is listed as *capellanus* in payments made 30 October and 20 December 1382, and again in a list for service rendered up until 22 January 1385. Richardus seems to have been in constant service throughout this time. At the end of 1392, he began to substitute for the *magister capelle,* at least in so far as he came to be listed first among the *capellani.* The same situation occurred at the end of October 1393. After the death of Clement VII, Richardus passed into the service of Pope Benedict XIII as a *cantor sive capellanus capelle.* In a supplication from 13 October 1394, the titles of *capellanus capelle et lector Biblie* are applied to Richardus. (The task of reading the Bible during the papal meal was assigned to the *magister capelle* by 1409, but he could have designated one of the singers to perform this duty on his behalf. Evidently, the task belonged to Richardus at this time, whether or not it was supposed to have been reserved for the *magister.*) Though deprived of the canonicate at Liège by the Roman *antipapa,* he did have one at the cathedral of Embrun, another at Saint-Dié, and he held the rectorate of the parish church of Blachières (Viviers). In that supplication, Richardus asks for a canonicate at the cathedral of Chartres or at the church of Saint-Martin of Tours. Eight days after the above document was submitted, another request was filed, this time on behalf of Johannes Hobaut, cleric from the diocese of Cologne, familiar of Richardus de Bozonvilla. The post of *magister* was held by Richardus from sometime after this date. We find him again listed first among the *capellani* on 23 December 1395 and on 2 May 1396 but only find him officially bearing the title of *magister* from February 1397. Though there are no chapel records for the next several years, we can say something about Richardus's activities. During part of the year 1400 and for several years preceding, Raymond de Bretennes had been provost of the cathedral of Apt. But sometime during the year 1400, he was raised to the see of Lombez. Richardus then filled the position at Apt. According to the notarial acts of the chapter, Richardus was present at over two score of meetings during the subsequent three years. The following information was taken from ADV, GII 58*, *Actes notairiés pour le Chapitre: Colin Brisson, notaire.*

| folio | date present | folio | date present |
|---|---|---|---|
| 1v. | 4 June 1400 | 35v. | 28 October |
| 3 | 2(...) | 36 | 29 |
| 3v. | 6 September | 37 | 5 November |
| 4 | 12 | 37v. | 17 |
| 5 | 9 | 38 | 19 |
| 6 | 9 December | 39 | 2 December |
| 6v. | 23 | 39v. | 17 January 1402 |
| 7v. | 15 January 1401 | 41 | 27 |
| 8v. | 29 | 42 | 4 February |

| | | | |
|---|---|---|---|
| 9 | 5 February | 43v. | 28 |
| 9v. (prov.) | 27* | 45 | 24 |
| 10v. | 15 March | 47 | 6 March |
| 11v. | 26 | 47v. | 8 April |
| 13 | 9 April | 50 | 12 June |
| 15v. | 11 May | 53v. | 28 |
| 16v. | 27 | 54v. | 28 |
| 25 | 27 | 59 | 19 September |
| 29 | 18 June | 60 | 30 |
| 30v. | 10 August | 44v. | 13 November† |
| 31v. | 3 September | 63v. | 26 January 1403 |
| 33 | 14 or 17 | 65 | 9 March |
| 34v. | 7 October | | |

* prov.=provost was present. Name not given.
† The document is ADV. Apt, Etude Pondicq 59. *Brèves de Louis de Rocha*. (1402-1403).

The next reference to Richardus occurs after Benedict's escape from Avignon. On 11 August 1403, the pope had reassembled his chapel members at Pont-de-Sorgues. In the records that have come down to us, Richardus again headed the list. No other document contains his name until the entry of 8 November 1404 when he appears first among the *capellani*. He was still serving as the master of the chapel according to a document dated 24 January 1405. At that time, the pope conferred on him by *motu proprio* a canonicate and the precentory of the cathedral of Carpentras. He continued to hold the rectorate of the parrochial church of Saint-Julien at Blachières (Viviers), the provostry of Apt, and he expected an official title at the cathedral of Cambrai. Five days later, while residing with the curia in the city of Nice, Richardus de Bozonvilla died. At the time of his death he left some 2,000 écus with his niece and with the convent of Sainte-Catherine at Avignon. Although the pope accorded Richardus the right to make a will and to dispose of the totality of his goods as he saw fit, this right usually extended only to some charitable legacy or to a bequest to familiars. The Apostolic Camera probably took possession of this money. At the time the will was drawn up, 27 March 1391, Richardus was referred to as *scriptor litterarum apostolicarum*. He had probably come to be favored somewhat, first by his having been permitted a will, and second by his having become the "substitute" master of the chapel by the end of 1392. On 22 April 1405, Olivarius de Solerio took possession of the provostry of Apt. On 6 October of that year, papal *scriptor*, Nicolaus de Hubantus, and canon of Embrun Johannes Haubaut (Hobaut), probably familiar of Richardus up until his death, acted as executors of the last will and testament of the late *magister* before the chapter of Apt. Richardus left 125 florins *currentes* for *una, duobus, aut pluribus* anniversary masses to be said for his soul and for the benefit of his executors. The Masses were to be said 29 January, 29 May, and 29 September with the vigils and nine *lectiones mortuorum*. The first payment from his legacy was made the following day and appears as follows:

> *Item die mercuri VIIa dicti mensis* [*octobris*] *fecimus cantarum pro domino Richardi* (!) *de Bonavilla preposito Aptensis ecclesie qui legavit centum francos anniversariis dicte ecclesie et primo solvi pro illis qui pulsarunt campanas*, 2videlicet.............................x.ss.

Richardus seems to be the most likely candidate for the link between a sophisticated musical center and the appearance of the manuscript Apt 16 bis in the basilica of the city. He might also be the person responsible for the presence of a polyphonic hymn to St. Anne, the patroness of Apt, in a small volume, Apt 9.

(Schäfer III: 368. Haberl: 213. Günther I: *passim*. AVB 8: 171-172, no. 543; 670-71, no. 2463. AVB 11: 150, no. 87; 428-29, no. 1035. AVB 19: 174, no. 446. AVB 20: 605, no. 2760. AVB 26: 9, no. 9; 177-78, no. 679; 746-47, no. 3430; 751, no. 3441; 790-91, no. 3596. *Lettres, Urbain V*, vol. 3: 574, no. 12182; 574, no. 12183. Favier: 258, fn. *Gallia Christiana*. Paris, 1715, col. 375, BMA, ms. 1780-81:

"Histoire écclesiastique de la ville et du diocèse d'Apt par M. d[e] R[emerville] S[aint]-Q[uentin]."
Manuscript copy of Edouard Cartier. Apt, 1844, pp. 421, xxxii. ADV, Apt, Etude Pondicq 100:
*Brèves, Colin Brisson* (1404-1406, 1414): fols. 103-103v. ADV, Apt, Etude Pondicq 59: *Brèves de
Louis de Rocha* (1402-1403): fols. 44v., 111, 120. ADV, G II 58* *Actes notairiés pour le chapitre*:
(1400-1403), Colin Brisson, notaire: *passim.* ADV, G II 84*: *Livre de recettes et dépenses*, 1405: fol.
19.)

### ROBERTUS
Admitted among the singers of the pope on 2 January 1371, he might possibly be identified with
Robertus Pisson (q.v.).
(Schäfer III: 368.)

### ROBERTUS CREQUE (RUBERT CREQUA, CREQUO)
He was a chapel singer of King John I of Aragon during the year 1394. On 16 September 1405, he
was given the perpetual chaplaincy of Sainte-Maxellende in the cathedral of Cambrai after it was
resigned by Petrus Selleri (q.v.). At the time, he already possessed the rectorate at the parish church
of Beaucaire (Alet) and a canonicate at Saint-Pierre de Douai (Arras). In a supplication dated 30
November 1406, he was listed as a clerk of the papal chapel and seems to have entered papal service
as *clericus cerimoniarum* one month earlier. He requested the canonicate at Le Mans vacant
through the death of Johannes de Bosco (q.v.). Robertus appears to have worked for the pontiff
through 1407. He received the payment for the clerks and chaplains that was made on 4 May 1408.
(AVB 19: 184, no. 483. AVB 26: 796, no. 3611. Günther II: 43. Gómez Muntané: 91. *ZKM*: 130.
OPKA: 105 fn.)

### ROBERTUS NYOT (NIOTI, RUBINET NYOTY)
He served as a chaplain of King Peter IV of Aragon from 1379 to 1380. On the list made
immediately following the election of Benedict XIII, he appears among the chaplains. This
citation, dated 5 October 1394 may indicate that Robertus was in the service of Benedict when he
was cardinal, though this is speculative. He is named as a chaplain of the pope in the payment
record made 2 May 1396. Nothing more is known about him.
(Günther I: 187, 188, doc. 4. Haberl: 213. Gómez Muntané: 93.)

### ROBERTUS PISSON
He appears as *cantor* according to Haberl. However, all we have been able to ascertain is that on 26
October 1374 a Robertus Pisson *recessit*, or left papal service, much in the manner of Guido de
Lange (q.v.), Johannes Colini (q.v.), Johannes Roquenies (q.v.), and Theobaldus Furnerii (q.v.). If
he was indeed a *cantor*, he might have been the Robertus (q.v.) who entered the chapel in 1371.
(Haberl: 121. ASV, *Coll.* 457: fol. 21.)

### SIMON CHAUVIN (CHAUWIN)
As *capellanus capelle*, Simon submitted a request on 22 November 1378 for a benefice on behalf of
another. He was included in the chapel according to the list compiled 19 September 1376.
(AVB 8: 396, no. 1329. Günther I: 182 fn.)

### SIMON HAQUETIN (HACQUETYN, ACQUETINI, LACQUETI)
The first reference to Simon is from 6 September 1379. On that date, as *magister capelle*, he
withdrew a book from storage. On 19 September, he headed the list of chaplains that were paid.
Simon is cited as master of the chapel during the years 1382, 1385, and seems to have held the office
continuously from at least the time of the first reference. On 27 August 1388 he obtained a receipt
for the accounts that he rendered which were verified by cameral officials. This is the last reference
to Simon acting as *magister*. Though he seems to have relinquished his duties and title by
December of that year, on 3 January he still was listed as papal familiar. In a papal letter bearing
that date, Simon is called treasurer of the cathedral of Auxerre, canon at Noyon, and at Saint-

Germain-l'Auxerrois (Paris), rector of Marchellpot (Noyon?), and chaplain at the church of Brie (Noyon). At that time he was granted a canonicate and prebend at Saint-Pierre (Tournai). (Günther I: 180, 182 fn., 185, doc. 2. Favier: 84-85. Ehrle: 731. Williman: 668, 669. AVB 13: 646, no. 1591.)

## SIMON MAURICII

He was granted a perpetual chaplaincy at Saint-Pierre of Lille (Tournai) in May 1342. He appears among the chaplains of the pope who were paid 3 August, and in October of the same year he received a canonicate at Saint-Pierre of Liège. As cleric of Notre Dame of Paris, Simon was also given a canonicate at Saint-Denis of Liège. He was again listed as papal chaplain during the year 1343/44, and as papal familiar in 1342, 1344, and 1347. He died in the Curia before 27 August 1347. (Schäfer II: 203, 234. AVB 1: 2, no. 8; 143, no. 622; 166, no. 701; 329, no. 1243. AVB 6: 3, no. 11; 184, no. 568; 393, no. 1123; 416, no. 1197.)

## STEPHANUS DE CHAULAGETO (CHAULHAGUETO, CAULHAGUETO)

He was a member of the papal chapel from June 1344 at the latest. On 11 March 1347, as canon of Compostella, he sought a canonicate at the cathedral of Thérouanne. He received the right to enjoy the fruits of his benefices in absentia. By 13 February 1351, when he received payment for expenses as *magister capelle*, he had assumed full responsibility for the chapel. Still alive sometime after 10 April 1353, he was dead by 25 August, at which time the rectorate of La Fouillade (Rodez) became vacant. (Schäfer II: 205, 265, 445, 454, 502-3, 529. Hoberg: 153, 156. AVB 1: 307, no. 1169. AVB 5: 125, no. 317. AVB 10: 129. *Clément VI (1342-1352). Lettres closes, patentes et curiales se rapportant à la France*. E. Déprez, J. Glénisson, and G. Mollat, eds. vol. 2. Paris, 1958: 329, no. 3230.)

## STEPHANUS TURQUETI

He received his first payment as a singer in the papal chapel on 17 September 1381. On 14 October of that same year, he was granted a canonicate at Senlis by *motu proprio*. His service in the papal chapel seems to have been continuous since he appears on all the extant lists in 1382, 1384, and 1385. The next reference to Stephanus is dated 30 October 1393, at which time he received payment for chapel service on behalf of all the singers and clerks, a task usually reserved for the *magister capelle*. However, on 2 November 1394, shortly after the death of Pope Clement, he was brought into the chapel of Duke Philip the Bold of Burgundy. In 1397 he was involved in acquiring a canonicate at the cathedral of Beauvais with the assistance of his patron. He served in the chapel of Philip through 1400. By 1403 he had received the canonicate at Beauvais, and evidently was doing his residence there. He was still alive in July 1418. (AVB 13: 134, no. 826. Günther I: 180, 182, 184-87, doc. 2. Wright: 63 and fn., 65, 67, 68 fn., 69, 221-26.)

## STEPHANUS DE UCIS

A priest from the diocese of Maguelonne and a papal familiar, on 28 January 1335 he sought benefices at Frontignan (Maguelonne) and Castelnau-le-Lez (Maguelonne). During the year 1355, he worked for the *buticularia* by purchasing oil, wine, and salted meat. In October of that year he is called *capellanus intrinsecus*. He first received payment as chaplain of the papal chapel in 1336. The following year he submitted a request for a benefice at the parish church of Dourbies (Nîmes) and again was paid as chaplain. Stephanus continued to act as *capellanus* in 1339, 1340, and 1342. He was involved in a transaction with the sacristan of Notre-Dame-des-Doms on the last day of February 1342. He last appears in papal employ in July of that year. (Schäfer II: 15, 16, 26, 28, 29, 44, 60, 94, 120, 159. *Lettres, Benoît XII*, vol. 1: 113, no. 1182; 408, no. 4335. Göller II: 103, 191. Hoberg: 52.)

## STEPHANUS VERGONIO (BORGONIO, BERGONHO)

As *magister capelle* he drew up the first accounts for the chapel on 11 September 1361. The payment made to him was for the period beginning 24 July, therefore, his tenure as master of the

chapel must have begun around that time. There is no indication that Stephanus belonged to the papal chapel before his appointment as *magister*. On 19 July of that year, this cleric from the diocese of Clermont supplicated for a canonicate at the church of Saint-Pierre of Aire (Thérouanne). Besides the title of *magister capelle*, he was also called *helemosinarius*, and held a rectorate at the parish church of Puiseux (Laon). He received his prebend at Aire as early as 29 August 1361. On 22 April 1363, he requested, and was granted, a canonicate at Saint-Pierre of Lille (Tournai). On this date he also received a prebend of a benefice at the secular priory of Vatan (Bourges), though in a list of his benefices which contained a canonicate at Aire, one at Arras, and a rectorate at Cassagnes-Bégonhès (Rodez), this one at Vatan was not included. He was active as *magister* at least until the last week of November 1364. He seems to have relinquished his title not long after this date. On 21 February 1372, Stephanus abandoned the canonicate at Lille in order to accept the *cantoria* at the cathedral of Arras. At that time, he still held canonicates at Arras and at Aire. Johannes de Ulmo (q.v.) was procurer in this transaction.
(Schäfer II: 817. Schäfer III: 75, 76. Hoberg: 180, 187, 210, 325, 397f. AVB 5: 709-10, no. 1750, fn. AVB 7: 256, no. 768. AVB 9: 308, no. 748. AVB 10: 180, 238. AVB 20: 30, no. 1452; 33, no. 1457. *Lettres, Urbain V*, vol. 1: 220, no. 2224; vol. 2: 280, no. 6970. Informatique: S03801463, fol. 162v. S03801464, fol. 162v.)

## TEODORICUS CANDELERII
He was paid in the city of Perpignan for his service as chaplain during the year 1408/09.
(Günther II: 43.) THEOBALDUS FURNERII This cleric from the diocese of Le Mans was a familiar of Cardinal Etienne Aubert in January 1364. On 27 October 1367 he was admitted as *capellanus et cantor capelle intrinsece pape*. Two years later on 29 August 1369, he was called papal familiar and *clericus* of the papal chapel. At that time, a canonicate at Saint-Donatien of Bruges (Tournai) was bestowed on him. He already held canonicates at Saint-Martin-des-Champeaux-en-Brie (Paris) and at Bayeux. Theobaldus was admitted *in cantores* of Gregory XI on 15 January 1371. However, in a document of 9 January, he was called *clericus capelle pape*. He was granted a canonicate at the cathedral of Le Mans, where he served *in divinis* for more than six years, and he continued to hold his benefice at Bruges. He was out of the chapel from 2 November until 8 November 1372, when he was presumably sent on business along with Johannes Ruffi de Roquenies (q.v.). He was again absent from 5 November until 11 November 1373, when he and Johannes were accompanied in their mission by Guido de Lange (q.v.). In December of that year, Theobaldus reserved a benefice at the parish church of Duncherie (Reims), which was conferred on 31 May 1374. At that time, he continued to serve as *capellanus* while maintaining his canonicates at Bruges and Le Mans. On 14 October 1374, he vacated his title at Bruges in order to accept a similiar one at Sainte-Walberge of Furnes (Thérouanne). Papal records note that both Theobaldus and Guido de Lange left the service of the chapel on 30 October of that year, though the date of their return is unknown. On 3 June 1375, as priest, familiar, and chaplain of the papal chapel, he was given the rectorate of the church at Souday (Le Mans), while t same time maintaining both the canonicate in the diocese's cathedral and also the one at Saint-Omer (Thérouanne) that once belonged to Johannes de Ulmo (q.v.). This is the last reference to Theobaldus as *capellanus* that we have been able to find. He appears to have been still alive between the years 1388 and 1390, when he resigned his canonicate at Saint-Omer.
(Schäfer III: 32, 368. AVB 10: 455, 532. AVB 11: 40, no. 48, and fn. AVB 15: 256-57, no. 2423. AVB 20: 443-44, no. 2402; 567, no. 2697; 661, no. 2880; 662, no. 2881. AVB 25: 102-3, no. 3215; 323, no. 3628. *Lettres, Urbain V*: vol. 3: 84, no. 9264; vol. 8: 86, no. 23400. Haberl: 212. Günther I: 177, fn.)

## THOMAS LA CAILLE (LE, DE, QUAILLE)
When a canonicate at Seclin (Tournai) was conferred on Thomas in January 1371, he was familiar and commensal of Cardinal Gui de Boulogne (†25 November 1373). At the time, he had been negotiating for a benefice at the monastery of Mouzon (Reims), but none existed. On 3 July of the same year, as familiar, commensal, and *clericus capelle* of Gui, he was given a canonicate at the

church of Saint-Dié at Saint-Dié (Toul) and already had acquired one at Saint-Piat of Seclin (Tournai). The prebend of the former seems only to have been realized on 23 June 1375 throught the death of Arnulphus de Maseriis (q.v.). At this time, Thomas was familiar of Cardinal Robert de Genève, the future Clement VII. Yet another document conferring the benefice at Seclin, dated 8 April 1376, was composed. In this one, some precious information is given: Thomas is said to have been *in vicesimo tertio etatis sue anno* (23 years old) at that time. This would have made him 18 years of age at the time of our first notice, when he was serving as clerk in the chapel of Gui. In a rotulus of familiars compiled soon after the election of Cardinal Robert to the papacy dated 3 November 1378, Thomas requested the parsonage or other office at the church of Sainte-Walberge of Furnes (Thérouanne). In the document that officially confers the above benefice, he is called *scriptor ac familiaris*. He appears in the list of papal chaplains paid on 19 September 1379. He died before 4 August 1384, at which time the papal familiar Matheus de Sancto Johanne (q.v.) was granted the canonicate of Saint-Piat left vacant through the death of Thomas outside of the curia. (AVB 8: 5, no. 15. AVB 11: 66, no. 102; 422-23, no. 1023. AVB 12: 10, no. 34. AVB 13: 189, no. 1065; 532, no. 861. AVB 25: 116, no. 3244; 294, no. 3570. Günther I: 182 fn.)

## THOMAS MILONIS

When he was admitted to the chapel on 15 May 1396, he was called rector of the parish church of Saint-Maurice at Angers. He is cited as a chaplain on two more occasions: on 9 August 1403, after the pope regrouped his chaplains at Pont-de-Sorgues, and on 23 September 1404 at Marseille. (Günther I: 192, 193, doc. 5.)

## THOMAS MULTORIS

On 12 January 1371, this familiar of Cardinal Guillaume d'Aigrefeuille was granted a canonicate at Saint-Donatien of Bruges (Tournai). At the time, he was called bachelor of arts and evidently had taught (*rexit*) grammar and logic for 10 years. In the service of the cardinal as familiar, domestic, and commensal on 15 May 1374, he was also called priest and *abbreviator litterarum apostolicarum* in a supplication for the rectorate of Tatinghem (Thérouanne). He was still familiar of the cardinal when he realized his canonicate at Bruges on 25 January 1376. He appears on a rotulus of papal familiars compiled 3 November 1378 as *capelle capellanus* and *abbreviator*. In this document, he requested and received a canonicate at Saint-Pierre of Lille (Tournai). In a supplication presented 15 November by Cardinal Guillaume, he is called *capellanus capelle* of the cardinal. The date on this document is wrong, or at least it contains a request that was made at least several weeks earlier, since in papal letter of 3 November he was given the benefice that was requested (a canonicate at the cathedral of Arras). For this benefice he was ordered to give up either the rectorate at Tatinghem or the canonicate at Saint-Pierre "given today." Thomas appears on the list of papal chaplains dated 19 September 1379. In July 1380 he took possession of the rectorate at Le Maisnil (Thérouanne), and on 19 September of that year he is named in a rotulus submitted by King Ferdinand of Portugal. Still a papal chaplain, Thomas requested and was granted a canonicate at Saint-Omer (Thérouanne) at that time. Nine days later, he abandoned the canonicate at Lille. He continued to serve in the papal chapel according to payment lists from 30 October and 20 December 1382 and 22 January 1385. Thomas was still in the papal chapel in March 1386 and from September 1387 through June 1388 he served as chaplain, *abbreviator* of apostolic letters, deacon of the cathedral of Arras, and canon of Saint-Omer. He is named as a papal familiar in a document dated as late as 10 June 1390/93, at which time he received his prebend at Saint-Omer. He does not seem to have been in the service of Benedict XIII in any capacity. (AVB 8: 5, no. 17; 41, no. 127. AVB 10: 454, 516, 530, 570, 571, 643. AVB 11: 75-76, no. 124. AVB 12: 11, no. 35; 11, no. 36. AVB 13: 79, no. 494, 133, no. 820; 416, no. 139-40; 424-25, no. 195-96; 440, no. 293; 575, no. 1121; 616, no. 1404; 616, no. 1406; 635, no. 1522. AVB 20: 556-57, no. 2680. AVB 25: 250-51, no. 3499. Günther I: 180, 182 fn., 185, doc. 2.)

## THOMAS TAURI

On 16 March 1368 he was admitted to the *capella intrinseca* as *capellanus*, and he was received among the *cantores* of Gregory XI on 3 January 1371. Thomas was still serving in the chapel at the end of January 1374 when he reserved a canonicate at the cathedral of Beauvais. He became *magister capelle* after the death of Johannes de Ulmo (q.v.), and drew up his first accounts for the chapel on 12 June 1376. It was his responsibility to transport the chapel items to Rome with the return of Gregory. The last reference to this *magister* dates from 2 October 1376 and provides no further information about him or his duties. He might have died during the journey or have entered the service of the Roman pope in 1378. In any case, he is never again named in the documents of Avignon popes.

(Schäfer III: 34, 368, 656, 672. Kirsch: 178, 181, 191. AVB 20: 484, no. 2484.)

## WALTERUS DE VASTONIA (WASTONIA, BASTONIA)

On 14 August 1353 he was named as a familiar, domestic, and commensal of Cardinal Bertrand de Déaux (†21 October 1355). At that time, this cleric from Liège was awaiting a benefice at Visé (Liège) and had requested a canonicate at the church of Saint Stephen at Mainz. The following May, still in the service of the cardinal, he sought a benefice at the cathedral of Liège. By 12 December 1357, he had entered the service of Cardinal Jean Duèse de Caraman (†1 August 1361) as familiar and commensal. At that time, he held a canonicate at Mainz, awaited a benefice at the cathedral of Liège, and requested a canonicate at Maastricht (Liège). On 23 October 1360 he exchanged the canonicate at Mainz for the office of *matricula* at the Marian church of Eyck and for the perpetual chaplaincy at the altar of Saint-Blaise in the church of Saint-Sepulcre at Nivelle (Liège). He expected a benefice at Saint-Servais of Maastricht and possessed the chaplaincy of Saint-Laurent in the cathedral of Liège. It is not known whether he was still in the service of the cardinal at this time. On 11 November 1362, in a rotulus addressed by the college of cardinals for Walterus, who continually served and resided with them in the conclave, a request was made for a benefice in the diocese of Liège. Walterus's list of benefices at this time included a canonicate at Saint-Piat of Seclin (Tournai), the altar of Saint-Laurent at Liège, and the expectation of a benefice at Maastricht. In this document, he is called *clericus capelle*. To accept the new benefice, he resigned the chaplaincy at Liège. He abandoned his canonicate at Saint-Piat on 20 September of the following year for a benefice at Liège, probably a canonicate and prebend. During the year 1364, Dionysius Fabri (q.v.) sought the vacant canonicate at Saint-Piat, once held by Walterus. He continued to serve as *clericus capelle* at least until 24 May 1364. At the time of his death, which occurred sometime before 25 August 1385, he possessed prebends at Saint-Paul of Liège and at Sainte-Gertrude of Nivelle (Liège). (AVB 5: 118, no. 306; 187, no. 453; 418, no. 1009; 638-39, no. 1568. AVB 7: 7, no. 10; 383, no. 1091; 449, no. 1226; 481, no. 1297. AVB 9: 30, no. 52; 398, no. 941. AVB 10: 232, 241, 243. AVB 13: 213-14, no. 1182; 214, no. 1185. AVB 29: 313-14, no. 236; 489, no. 581. Informatique: S03700744, fol. 89v.; S04001266, fol. 156v.)

**Addenda to Index of Benefices**

AGEN. *Agen:* Cathedral—(can.) Raimundus Seguini
CHARTRES. *Poissy:* Johannes de Ayras(?)
CONDOM. *Murrenchis:* Raimundus Sequini
LANGRES. *Langres:* Cathedral—(can.) Johannes de Noalhaco.
ORLEANS. *Orléans:* Cathedral—(can.) Nicolaus de Bondevilla.
PAPHOS. *Paphos* (Cyprus): Cathedral—(archdeac.) Raimundus Seguini.
PARIS. Saint-Eloi—Johannes de Ayras(?)
REIMS. *Reims:* Johannes de Heys de Rancovado.
REIMS. *Faverolles:* Johannes de Heys de Rancovado
ROUEN. *Marceriis:* Nicolaus de Bondevilla.
SOISSONS. *Sainte-Marie ad Moniales:* Johannes Girardi Lathomi.
THEROUANNE. *Aire:* Franciscus de Goano (can.).
THEROUANNE. Saint-Pierre—(can.) Franciscus de Goano.
THEROUANNE. *Vieil-Hesdin:* (can.) Franciscus de Goano.

**Addenda to Other Service**

*Bishops*
Guillaume d'Aigrefeuille, relative of Pope Clement VI; cardinal priest of s.Maria Transtiberim, 17 December 1350-17 September 1367; cardinal bishop of Sabina until †4 October 1369. Eubel: XXIII₁₇.
—(Johannes de Noalhaco 1362)

Gilles Aycelin de Montaigut
—Franciscus de Goano 1362.

Hugues de Saint-Martial
—Johannes de Noalhaco 1362.

Francesco Tebaldeschi, cardinal bishop of Sabina, 22 September 1368-†20 August or 6/7 September 1378. Eubel: XXV₁₂.
—Franciscus de Goano 1375.

Gérard de Dainville, bishop of Cambrai, 6 June 1371-†18 June 1378. Eubel: 160.
—Franciscus de Goano 1372.

*Secular Authorities*
King John II of France (1350-1364)
—Johannes Carnoten from 1359(?).

Duchess Margaret of Burgundy (1369-1405)
—Johannes Vitrarii 1387.

Duke Philip the Good of Burgundy (1419-1467)
—Johannes Vitrarii 1419(?), 1422.

Raoul, Lord of Louppeyo, Governor of Dauphiné
—Johannes de Heys de Rancovado 1362.

# Bibliography

d'Agnel, Arnaud. "Le Trésor de l'Eglise d'Apt." *Bulletin archéologique* (1904):329-35.

Albanès, Joseph-Hyacinthe. *Entrée solennelle du pape Urbain V à Marseille en 1365. Programme de la fête, dressé par le conseil de la ville, texte provençal inédit du XIV$^e$ siècle, notes historiques et pièces justificatives.* Marseille: Boy-Estillon, 1865.

————. *Gallia Christiana Novissima.* Vol. 1, *Aix, Apt, Fréjus, Gap, Riez et Sisteron.* Montbéliard: Société anonyme d'imprimerie montbéliardaise, 1899.

————. *Gailia Christiana Novissima.* Vol. 7, *Avignon.* Valence: 1920.

Aliquot, Hervé. "Les livrées cardinalices de Villeneuve-lès-Avignon." *Avignon: Genèse et débuts du Grand Schisme d'Occident.* Paris: 1980, p. 317-28.

————. "Les livrées cardinalices de Villeneuve-lès-Avignon." D.E.S. d'Histoire médiévale, Université d'Aix, 1976.

Analecto Vaticano-Belgica. First series, Documents relatifs aux anciens diocèses de Cambrai, Liège, Thérouanne et Tournai. Brussels: Institut historique belge de Rome, 1908-1976.

Andrieu, Michel. "L'Authenticité du 'Missel de la Chapelle papale.'" *Scriptorium* 9 (1955):17-34.

————. "Le Missel de la Chapelle papale à la fin du XIII$^e$ siècle." *Miscellanea Fr. Ehrle II.* Rome: Biblioteca Vaticana, 1924. pp. 348-76.

————. *Les Ordines romani du haut moyen âge.* Vols. 1-5. Louvain: 1931-1961.

————. *Le pontifical romain au moyen âge.* Vol. 2. Studi e testi 87. Rome: 1940.

Anglès, Higini. "Els cantors i organistes Franco-Flamencs i Alemanys a Catalunya els segles XIV-XVI." *Gedenboek aagenboden aan Dr. D. F. Scheurleer (70sten).* The Hague: Martinus Nijhoff, 1925, pp. 49-62.

————. "Cantors und Ministrers in den Diensten der Könige von Katalonien-Aragonien im 14. Jahrhundert." *Bericht über den Musikwissenschaftlichen Kongreß* in Basel, 1924. Leipzig: Brietkopf & Härtel, 1925, pp. 56-66.

————. "*Dè cantu organico,* Tratado de un autor catalán del siglo XIV." *Anuario Musical* 13 (1958):3-24.

————. "Gacian Reyneau am Königshof zu Barcelona in der Zeit von 139.. bis 1429." *Studien zur Musikgeschichte, Festschrift für Guido Adler zum 75. Geburtstag.* Vienna: Universal-Edition, 1930, pp. 64-70.

————. *Historia de la música medieval en Navarra.* [Pamplona]: Disputación Foral de Navarra, Institución Principe de Viana, 1970.

———— *Hygini Anglés, Scripta Musicologica.* Edited by José López-Calo. 3 vols. Storia e letteratura, nos. 131-33. Rome: 1976.

————. "El músic Jacomí al servei de Joan I i Martí I durant els anys 1372-1404." *Homenatge a Antoni Rubió i Lluch; miscellanía d'estudis literaris, històrics i linguistics.* Vol. 1. Estudis universitaris catalans nos. 21-22; Analecta sacra Tarraconensia no. 12. Barcelona: 1936, pp. 613-25.

———. "La música sagrada de la capilla pontificia de Avignon en la capilla real aragonesa durante el siglo XIV." *Anuario Musical,* 12 (1957):35-44.

Apel, Willi, ed. *French Secular Music of the Late Fourteenth Century.* Cambridge, Massachusetts: Mediaeval Academy of America, 1950.

———, ed. *French Secular Compositions of the Fourteenth Century,* 3 vols. Corpus Mensurabilis Musicae, vol. 53. [Rome]: American Institute of Musicology, 1970-1972.

Artonne, André; Guizard, Louis; and Pontal, Odette. *Répertoire des Statuts synodaux des diocèses de l'ancienne France du XIIIᵉ à la fin du XVIIIᵉ siècle. Documents, Etudes et Répertoires.* Vol. 8. Paris: Centre National de la Recherche Scientifique, 1963.

*Atlas historique: Provence. Comtat Venaissin, principauté d'Orange, comté de Nice.* Paris: 1969.

Attwater, Donald. *The Penguin Dictionary of Saints.* Harmondsworth, England: Penguin Books, 1965.

Avril, J. T. *Dictionnaire Provençal-Français.* Apt: Edouard Cartier, 1839.

Baldelló, Francisco de P. "La música en la casa de los Reyes de Aragón." *Anuario Musical* 11 (1956):37-51.

Baluze, Etienne. *Vitae paparum avenionensium.* Guillaume Mollat, ed., 4 vols. (1693). Paris: Letouzey et Ané, 1914-1928.

Barroul, Jean. *Sainte-Anne d'Apt d'après une documentation nouvelle.* Apt: Reboulin, 1964.

Batiffol, Pierre. *History of the Roman Breviary.* Trans., Atwell M. Y. Baylay. London: Longmans, Green and Co., 1912.

Batlle y Prats, Luis. "Juglares en la corte de Aragon y en el municipio de Gerona en al siglo XIV." *Estudios dedicados a Menéndes Pidal.* Vol. 5. Madrid: Consejo superior de investigaciones cientificas, 1954, pp. 165-84.

Baudet, J. "Cérémonial," *Dictionnaire d'Archéologie chrétienne et de Liturgie.* Fernand Cabrol, ed. Vol. 2, 2nd part. Paris: Letouzey et Ané, 1910, col. 3296-97.

Baumstark, Anton. *Liturgie comparée.* 3rd edition. Chevetogne, Belgium: Editions de Chevetogne, 1953.

Bayerri Bartomeu, Enrique, and Eguíluz López de Murga, Angel. *Un Gran Aragonés (El Papa Pedro de Luna).* Barcelona: Porter Libros, 1973.

Berlière, Ursmer. *Un ami de Pétrarque, Louis Sanctus de Beeringen.* Rome: Institut historique belge de Rome, 1905.

Besseler, Heinrich. "Hat Matheus de Perusio Epoche gemacht?" *Die Musikforschung* 8 (1955):19-23.

Bibliothèque des Ecoles françaises d'Athènes et de Rome. Paris: E. de Boccard, 1892- . (Cited in the text as BEFAR.)

Billioud, Joseph. "Les manuscrits liturgique provençaux du XIVᵉ siècle." *Mémoires de l'Institute historique de Provence* 1 (1924):58-71.

Binns, L. Elliott. *The History of the Decline and Fall of the Medieval Papacy.* Hamden, Connecticut: Archon Books, 1967.

Bofarull y Sans, Francisco de. *Animals in Watermarks.* Hilversum, Holland: 1957.

Borren, Charles van den. *Le Manuscrit Musical M.222 C.22 de la Bibliothèque de Strasbourg.* Antwerp: E. Secelle, 1928.

Bosco, Henry. "Sur un Diner offert au Pape Clément V, en 1303 par le Cardinal 'di Pelagru.'" *Annales d'Avignon* 2 (1913):113-27.

Boyle, Leonard E. *A Survey of the Vatican Archives and of Its Medieval Holdings.* Toronto: Pontifical Institute of Medieval Studies, 1972.

Braun, Georg. *Civitates orbis terrarum.* Reprint edition. Cleveland: World Publishing Co., 1966.

Brentano, Robert. *Rome before Avignon.* New York: Basic Books, 1974.

Bridgman, Nanie. "La musique dans la société française de l'Ars nova." *L'Ars nova italiana del trecento.* Certaldo: Centro di studi sull'Ars nova italiana del trecento, 1959, pp. 83-96.

Briquet, C.M. *Les Filigranes: Dictionnaire historique des marques du papier.* Second edition, reprint. New York: Hacker Art Books, 1966.

Brun, Robert. "Annales Avignonaises de 1382 à 1410: Extraites des Archives de Datini." *Mémoires de l'Institut historique de Provence* 12 (1935):17-104, 105-42; 13 (1936): 58-105; 14 (1937): 5-57; 15 (1938): 21-52, 154-92.

Burnham, Philip E. Jr. "Cultural Life at Papal Avignon 1309-1376." Ph.D. dissertation, Tufts University, 1972.

*Bulfinch's Mythology: The Greek and Roman Fables Illustrated.* New York: Viking Press, 1979.

Caanitz, Mechthild. "Petrarca in der Geschichte der Musik." Doctoral dissertation, Albert-Ludwigs-Universität, Freiburg-in-Breslau, 1969.

Cappelli, A. *Cronologia Cronografia e Calendario Perpetuo.* Milan: U. Hoepli, 1969.

Carreri, F. Ch. "Chronicon parvum avinionense de schismate et bello (1397-1416)." *Annales d'Avignon* 4 (1916):161-74.

Casimiri, Raffaele. "L'antica *Schola cantorum* romana e la sua fine nel 1370." *Note d'archivio per la storia musicale* 1 (1924):191-99.

*The Catholic Encyclopedia.* Vols. 1-16. New York: 1907-1914. (Cited in the text as *CE.*)

*Centenaires pontificaux, 1352-1952.* Exposition catalogue. [Avignon: 1952].

Chevalier, U. *Repertorium hymnologicum.* Vols. 1-6. Louvain and Brussels: 1892-1920.

Chobaut, H. "Documents inédits sur les peintres et peintres-verriers d'Avignon, du Comtat et de la Provence occidentale de la fin du XIV$^e$ au premier du XVI$^e$ siècle." *Mémoires de l'Académie de Vaucluse* 4 (1939):83-145.

Cingria, Hélène; Barnicaud, Philippe; and Tournois, Bernard. *La Chartreuse du Val de Bénédiction, Villeneuve-lès-Avignon.* [Paris]: Caisse nationale des Monuments historiques et Sites, 1977.

Clercx, Suzanne. *Johannes Ciconia. Un musicien liégeois et son temps (vers 1335-1411).* [Brussles: Palais des Académies, 1960.]

_____. "Propos sur l'Ars nova." *Revue belge de musicologie* 10 (1956):154-60.

Clercx-Lejeune, Suzanne. "Les débuts de la Messe unitaire et de la *Missa parodia* au XIV$^e$ siècle et principalement dans l'oeuvre de J. Ciconia." *L'Ars nova italiana del trecento.* Certaldo: Centro di studi sull'Ars nova italiana del trecento, 1959, pp. 97-104.

Colombe, Gabriel. "La Chapelle clémentine, vue de l'intèrieur." *Mémoires de l'Académie de Vaucluse* 35 (1935):79-100.

_____. "La Chapelle pontificale 'du nord' annexée à la Métropole." *Mémoires de l'Académie de Vaucluse* 18 (1918):45-73.

_____. "La Fenêtre 'de l'Indulgence' au Palais des Papes d'Avignon." *Mémoires de l'Académie de Vaucluse* 10 (1910):33-40.

_____. "Le Porche devant l'Audience: L'Escalier montant à la Grande Chapelle." *Mémoires de l'Académie de Vaucluse* 5 (1940):11-27.

_____. "La Salle 'de Jésus' au Palais des Papes," *Mémoires de l'Académie de Vaucluse* 19 (1919):49-63.

_____. "La statue mutilée du portail de la Grande Chapelle." *Mémoires de l'Académie de Vaucluse* 33 (1933):4-10.

*Corpus iuris canonici.* Part 2, *Decretalium collectiones.* Emil Friedberg, ed. Leipzig: 1928.

Coville, Alfred. "Gilles li Muisis." *Histoire littéraire de la France,* vol. 36. Paris: 1937, pp. 250-324.

_____. "Philippe de Vitry." *Romania* 59 (1933):324-30.

Cummings, Anthony M. "Toward an Interpretation of the Sixteenth-Century Motet." *Journal of the American Musicological Society* 34 (1981):43-59.

Déprez, Eugene. "Les funérailles de Clément VI et d'Innocent VI d'après les comptes de la cour pontificale." *Mélanges d'Archéologie et d'Histoire* 20 (1900):235-50.

Despy, Georges. "Note sur les offices de la curie d'Avignon: les fonctions du *magister capelle pape.*" *Bulletin de l'Institut historique belge de Rome* 28 (1953):21-30.

De Weese, Malcolm Leslie, Jr. "A Study of Decision Making in France During the Reign of Charles VI (The Rejection of the Avignon Papacy 1395)." Ph.D. dissertation, University of Washington, 1975.

Dufourcq, Norbert. "Orgues comtadines et orgues provençales." *Mémoires de l'Académie de Vaucluse* 34 (1934):61-172.

――――. "Orgues comtadines et orgues provençales (supplément)." *Provence Historique* 5 (1955):111-28, 232-47.

Duhamel, Leopold. *Inventaire-sommaire des Archives communales antérieures à 1790 de la ville d'Avignon.* Série AA. Avignon: Bernaud, 1906.

――――. "Testament du Cardinal Jacques de Montenay (28 avril 1391)." *Annales d'Avignon* 4 (1916):147-59.

Dykmans, Marc. *Le cérémonial papal de la fin du moyen âge à la Renaissance.* Vol. 1, *Le cérémonial papal du XIIIᵉ siècle.* Bibliothèque de l'Institut historique belge de Rome, fascicle 24. Brussels: 1977. Vol. 2 *De Rome en Avignon ou le cérémonial de Jacques Stefaneschi.* Bibliothèque de l'Institut historique belge de Rome, fascicle 25. Brussels: 1981.

――――. "D'Avignon à Rome, Martin V et le cortège apostolique." *Bulletin de l'Institut historique belge de Rome* 43 (1968):203-309.

――――. "Mabillon et les interpolations." *Gregorianum* 47 (1966):316-42.

――――. "Les palais cardinalices d'Avignon: un supplément du XIVᵉ siècle aux lists du Docteur Pansier." *Mélanges de l'Ecole française de Rome* 83 (1971):389-438.

Ehrle, Franz. "Die Chronik des Garoscus de Ulmoisca Veteri und Bertrand Boysset (1365-1415)." *Archiv für Litterature- und Kirchengeschichte des Mittelalters* 7 (1900):311-420.

――――. *Historia Bibliothecae Romanorum Pontificum tum Bonifatianae tum Avenionensis.* Vol. 1, Rome: 1890.

――――, ed. *Martin de Alpartils Chronica actitatorum temporibus domini Benedicti XIII.* Paderborn: 1906.

――――. "Zur Geschichte des päpstlichen Hofceremoniells im 14. Jahrhundert." *Archiv für Literature- und Kirchengeschichte des Mittelalters* 5 (1889):565-602.

Elling, Alwin. "Die Messen, Hymnen und Motetten der Handschrift von Apt." Doctoral dissertation, Göttingen, 1924.

Elze, Reinhard. "Das *Sacrum Palatium Lateranense* im 10. und 11. Jahrhundert." *Studi Gregoriani* 4 (1952):27-54.

Eubel, Conrad. "Aus den Ausgabebüchern der Schismapäpste Klemens VII. und Benedikt XIII." *Römische Quartalschrift für Kirchengeschichte* 18 (1904):339-40.

――――. *Hierarchia catholica.* Vol. 1. Münster: 1898.

Fabre, Paul and Duchesne, L. eds. *Le liber censuum de l'église romaine.* BEFAR, 2nd series, vol. 6, 6. Rome: 1910, 2 vols.

Fallows, David. Review of Craig Wright. *Music at the Court of Burgundy, 1364-1419,* published in the *Journal of the American Musicological Society* 34 (1981):545-52.

Faucon, Maurice. *La librairie des papes d'Avignon.* BEFAR, fascicles 43 and 50. Paris: 1886-87.

Favier, Jean. *Les finances pontificales à l'époque du Grand Schisme d'Occident: 1378-1409.* BEFAR, fascicle 211. Paris: E. de Boccard, 1966.

Fellerer, Gustav. "La *Constitutio docta Sanctorum patrum* di Giovanni XXII e la musica nuova del suo tempo." *L'Ars nova italiana del trecento.* Certaldo: Centro di studi sull'Ars nova italiana del trecento, 1959, pp. 9-17.

――――. "Zur Constitutio *Docta SS. patrum.*" *Speculum musicae artis.* Munich: Wilhelm Fink, 1970, pp. 125-32.

Finke, Heinrich. "Mossen Borra in Deutschland." *Homenatge a Antoni Rubió i Lluch.* Vol. 2. Barcelona: 1936, pp. 149-60.

Fischer, Kurt von. "The Manuscript Paris, Bibl. Nat., nouv. acq. frç. 6771 (Codex *Reina* = PR)." *Musica Disciplina* 11 (1957):38-78.

――――. "Reply to N.E. Wilkins' Article on the Codex Reina." *Musica Disciplina* 17 (1963):75-77.

Font-Réaulx, J. "Les sources de l'histoire d'Apt." *Provence Historique* 18 (1968):121-27.

Fournier, Paul. "Pierre Roger (Clément VI)." *Histoire Littéraire de la France,* vol. 37. Paris: 1938.

Fox-Davies, A.C. *A Complete Guide to Heraldry.* Revised edition. London: Thomas Nelson and Sons, 1969.

Gagnière, Sylvain. *Eglises et Chapelles d'Avignon.* Avignon: Rullière, 1953.

_____. *The Palace of the Popes at Avignon.* Third Edition. Paris: Caisse Nationale des Monuments Historiques, 1977.

Galinsky, Karl G. *Aeneas, Sicily and Rome.* Princeton Monographs in Art and Archaeology, vol. 40. Princeton, NJ: Princeton University Press. 1969.

Gasparrini Leporace, T. *Le suppliche di Clemente VI: (19 maggio 1342-28 maggio 1353).* Rome: 1948.

Gastoué, Amédée. *Inventaire des anciens manuscrits liturgiques conservés dans l'église d'Apt.* Avignon: Aubanel, 1900.

_____, ed. *Le manuscrit de musique de trésor d'Apt.* La Société française de Musicologie, series 1, vol. 10. Paris: E. Droz, 1936.

Gattico, J. C. *Acta selecta caeremonialia sanctae romanae ecclesiae.* Vol. 1. Rome: 1753.

Girard, Joseph. "Les Aménagements du Palais des Papes pour le Couronnement d'Innocent VI." *Mémoires de l'Académie de Vaucluse* 1 (1950-52):5-19.

_____. *Evocation du vieil Avignon.* Paris: Les Editions du Minuit, 1958.

_____. "L'Exposition des manuscrits à miniatures du Musée Calvet, (19 mars-1$^{er}$ mai 1927)," *Mémoires de l'Académie de Vaucluse* 1 (1950-52):5-19.

Girard, Joseph, and Requin, H. "Le couvent des Dominicains d'Avignon." *Annales d'Avignon* 1 (1912) 81-96.

Glasfurd, Alexander L. *The Antipope Peter de Luna, 1342-1423: A Study in Obstinacy.* New York: Roy, 1966.

Gómez Muntané, María del Carmen. *La música en la casa real catalano-aragonesa durante los años 1336-1432.* Vol. 1, *Historia y Documentos.* Barcelona: Antoni Bosch, [1977].

Grant, Michael. *Roman Myths.* New York: Charles Scribner's Sons, 1971.

*The New Grove Dictionary of Music and Musicians.* Edited by Stanley Sadie, 20 vols. London: Macmillan, 1980. (Cited in the text as *Grove 6.*)

Guillemain, Bernard. *La cour pontificale d'Avignon (1309-1376).* BEFAR, fascicle 201. Paris: E. de Boccard, 1962.

Günther, Ursula. "Eine Ballade auf Mathieu de Foix." *Musica Disciplina* 19 (1965):69-81.

_____. "Bemerkungen zum ältern französischen Repertoire des Codex Reina (PR)." *Archiv für Musikwissenschaft* 24 (1967):237-52.

_____. "Das Manuskript Modena, Biblioteca estense, α.M.5,24 (*olim* lat. 568 = *Mod*)." *Musica Disciplina* 24 (1970):17-67.

_____, ed. *The Motets of the Manuscript Chantilly, musée condé, 564 (olim 1047) and Modena, Biblioteca estense, α.M.5,24 (olim lat. 568).* Corpus Mensurabilis Musicae, vol. 39. [Rome]: American Institute of Musicology, 1965.

_____. "Die Musiker des Herzogs von Berry." *Musica Disciplina* 17 (1963):79-91.

_____. "Problems of Dating in the Ars nova and Ars subtilior." *L'Ars nova italiana del trecento.* Certaldo: Centro di studi sull'Ars nova italiana del trecento, 1975, pp. 289-301.

_____, secretary. "Round Table: Die Rolle Englands, Spaniens, Deutschlands und Polens in der Musik des 14. Jahrhunderts." In *Bericht über den neunten internationalen musikwissenschaftlichen Kongress, Salzburg 1964,* vol. 2, pp. 188-200. Kassel: Bärenreiter, 1966.

_____. "Zur Biographie einiger Komponisten der Ars subtilior." *Archiv für Musikwissenschaft* 21 (1964):172-99.

_____. "Zwei Balladen auf Bertrand und Olivier du Guesclin." *Musica Disciplina* 22 (1968):15-45.

Gushee, Lawrence. "New Sources for the Biography of Johannes de Muris." *Journal of the American Musicological Society* 22 (1969):3-26.

Haberl, Franz X. *Wilhelm du Fay,* vol. 1, Bausteine für Musikgeschichte. Leipzig: Breitkopf & Härtel, 1885.

―――. "Die römische *Schola cantorum* und die päpstlichen Kapellsänger bis zur Mitte des 16. Jahrhunderts." *Vierteljahrsschrift für Musikwissenschaft* 3 (1887):189-296.

Halecki, Oskar. *Un Empereur de Byzance à Rome.* Warsaw: 1930.

Haller, J. "Zwei Aufzeichen über die Beamten der Curie." *Quellen und Forschungen aus italienischen Archiven und Bibliotheken* 1 (1898):1-38.

Hamm, Charles. "Manuscript Structure in the Dufay Era." *Acta Musicologica* 34 (1962):166-84.

Harder, Hanna, and Stäblein, Bruno. "Neue Fragmente mehrstimmiger Musik aus spanischen Bibliotheken." *Festschrift Joseph Schmidt-Görg zum 60. Geburtstag.* Bonn: Beethovenhaus, 1957, pp. 131-41.

Harrison, Frank Ll. "Music and Cult: The Functions of Music in Social and Religious Systems." *Perspectives in Musicology.* New York: W. W. Norton, 1972, pp. 307-34.

―――. *Music in Medieval Britain.* 4th ed. Buren, The Netherlands: Frits Knuf, 1980.

Hayburn, Robert F. *Papal Legislation on Sacred Music.* Collegeville, Minnesota: The Liturgical Press, 1979.

Hayez, Anne-Marie. "L'érection de trois églises paroissiales avignonnaises en collégiales au XIV^e siècle." *Bulletin philologique et historique* (1979):99-120.

Hayez, Michel. "Avignon sans les papes (1367-1370, 1376-1379)." *Avignon: Genèse et débuts du Grand Schisme d'Occident.* Paris: 1980, pp. 317-28.

Hirshberg, Jehoash. "The Music of the Late Fourteenth Century: A Study in Musical Style." Ph.D. dissertation, University of Pennsylvania, 1971.

Hoberg, Hermann. *Die Inventare des päpstlichen Schatzes in Avignon, 1314-1376.* Studi e testi 111. Vatican City: 1944.

Holder-Egger, Oswald, ed. *Monumenta Erphesfurtensia Scriptores Rerum Germanicum.* Hanover: 1899.

Hoppin, Richard H. "The Cypriot-French Repertory of the Manuscript Torino, Biblioteca Nazionale, J.II.9." *Musica Disciplina* 11 (1957):79-125.

―――. *Medieval Music.* New York: W. W. Norton & Co., 1978.

―――. "Some Remarks a propos de Pic. (B.N. coll. de Picardie vol. 67, folio 67)." *Revue belge de musicologie* 10 (1956):105-11.

―――, and Clercx, Suzanne. "Notes biographiques sur quelques musiciens français du XIV^e siècle." *Les colloques de Wégimont* no. 2. Paris: Société d'Edition "Les Belles Lettres," 1959, pp. 61-91.

Hucke, Helmut. "Toward a New Historical View of Gregorian Chant." *Journal of the American Musicological Society* 33 (1980):437-67.

Huizinga, Johan. *The Waning of the Middle Ages.* New York: Doubleday, 1954.

Hunter, Dard. *Papermaking, the History and Technique of an Ancient Art.* New York: 1947.

Jeffery, Peter. "Notre Dame Polyphony in the Library of Pope Boniface VIII." *Journal of the American Musicological Society* 32 (1979):118-24.

John, Eric. *The Popes.* New York: Hawthorn Books, 1964.

Johnson, Mildred Jane. "The Motets of the Codex Ivrea: Volume I: Commentary. Volume II: Transcriptions." Ph.D. dissertation, Indiana University, 1955.

Jordan, Karl. "Die päpstliche Verwaltung im Zeitalter Gregors VII." *Studi Gregoriani* 1 (1947):111-35.

Jungmann, Joseph A. *The Mass of the Roman Rite: Its Origins and Development.* Translated by Francis A. Brunner. Vols. 1-2. New York: Benziger Brothers, 1951-1955.

Kirsch, Johann Peter. *Die Ruckkehr der Päpste Urban V. und Gregor XI. von Avignon nach Rom, Auszüge aus den Kameralregistern des vatikanischen Archivs.* Quellen und Forschungen herausgegeben von der Görresgesellschaft, vol. 6. Paderborn: 1898.

Labande, L.-H. "L'Avignon papal d'autrefois." *L'Art* 62 (1903):454-63.

_____. "Le cérémonial romain de Jacques Cajétan." *Bibliothèque de l'Ecole des chartes* 54 (1893):45-74.

_____. "Les manuscrits de la Bibliothèque d'Avignon provenant de la librairie des papes du XIV$^e$ siècle." *Bulletin historique et philologique* 1-2 (1894):145-60.

_____. *Le Palais des Papes*. Vol. 1. Marseille: F. Detaille, 1925.

_____, and Girard, Joseph. *Catalogue général des manuscrits des bibliothèques publiques de France*. Vols. 27-29, *Avignon*. Paris: 1894-1897. Vols. 40, 44, 49, *Supplément*. Paris: 1902-1951.

Lauer, Philippe. *Le Palais de Latran*. Paris: 1911.

Leroquais, V. *Les sacramentaires et les missels manuscrits des bibliothèques publiques de France*. Vol. 2. Paris: 1924.

Le Roy Ladurie, Emmanuel. *Montaillou: The Promised Land of Error*. Translated by Barbara Bray. New York: Vintage Books, 1979.

Lewis, Charleton T., and Short, Charles. *A Latin Dictionary*. Oxford: Clarendon Press, 1879.

*Liber Sextus decretalium d. Bonifacii papae VIII. Clementis papae V. Constitutiones extravagantes tum viginti d. Ioannis papae XXII. tum communes*. Venice: 1615.

*The Liber Usualis*. Tournai: Desclée, 1961.

Logoz, Roger Ch. *Clément VII (Robert de Genève)*. Lausanne: Payot, 1974.

Loÿe, Georges, de. "Réception du Pape Clément VI par les Cardinaux Hannibal Ceccano et Pedro Gomez à Gentilly et Montfavet, 30 avril-1 mai 1343 (ou 1348)." In *Actes du Congrès International Francesco Petrarca*. Avignon: Aubanel, 1974.

McKinnon, James W. "Representations of the Mass in Medieval and Renaissance Art." *Journal of the American Musicological Society* 31 (1978):21-52.

Madan, Falconer. *Books in Manuscript*. 2nd edition, revised. London: Kegan, Paul, Trench, Trubner and Co., 1920.

Maier, Anneliese. "Die *Bibliotheca minor* Benedikts XIII. (Petrus' de Luna)." *Archivum historiae pontificiae* 3 (1965):139-91.

_____. "Der Katalog der päpstlichen Bibliothek in Avignon von Jahr 1411." *Archivum historiae pontificiae* 1 (1963):97-177.

_____. "Ein Leihregister aus der Bibliothek des letzen Avignoner Papstes Benedikt XIII. (Petrus de Luna)." *Rivista di storia della Chiesa in Italia* 20 (1966):309-27.

_____. *Der letzte Katalog der päpstlichen Bibliothek von Avignon (1594)*. Sussidi Eruditi 4. Rome: Editioni di Storia e Letteratura, 1952.

Marbach, Karl, ed. *Carmina Scriptuarum*. Strasbourg: 1907.

Martene, Edmundus. *Thesaurus novus anecdotorum*. Vol. 4. Paris: 1717.

Migne, J.-P., ed. *Johannes XIII papa. Epistolae et decreta*. Patrologia Latina 135. Paris: 1849, cols. 951-1000.

_____, ed. *Johannes XIX papa. Epistolae et diplomata*. Patrologia Latina 141. Paris: 1853, cols. 1150-1160.

_____, ed. *Ordo romanus XIII... XIV... XV*. Patrologia Latina 78. Paris: 1849, cols. 1105-1368.

_____, ed. *Wilbertus. Sancti Leonis Vita*. Patrologia Latina 153. Paris: 1854, cols. 457-504.

Mollat, Guillaume. *The Popes at Avignon 1305-1378*. Translated from the 9th edition by Janet Love. London: Thomas Nelson and Sons, 1963.

Monfrin, Jacques. "La Bibliothèque des rois aragonais de Naples." *Bibliothèque de l'Ecole des chartes* 114 (1956):198-207.

Montault, Barbier de. "Les manuscrits liturgiques provençaux du XIV$^e$ siècle." *Mémoires de l'Institut historique de Provence* 1 (1924):61-65.

Morganstern, Anne McGee. "Pierre Morel and Sculpture in Avignon during the Period of the Schism (1378-1417)." Ph.D. dissertation, New York University, 1970.

Mošin, Vladimir A., and Traljió, Seid M. *Filigranes des XIII$^e$ et XIV$^e$ siècles*. Vols. 1-2. Zagreb: 1957.

Muratori, Ludovico. *Antiquitates Italicae Medii Aevi*. Vol. 3. Milan: 1740.

_____. *Rerum italicarum Scriptores*. Vol. 3, part 2. Milan: 1734.

Nabuco, J., and Tamburini, F. *Le cérémonial apostolique avant Innocent VIII.* Rome: 1966.
*New Catholic Encyclopedia.* Vols. 1-15. New York: McGraw-Hill, 1967. (Cited in the text as *NCE.*)
Opitz, Gottfried. "Die Sekretärsexpedition unter Urban V. und Gregor XI." *Quellen und Forschungen aus italienischen Archiven und Bibliotheken* 33 (1944):158-98.
Pansier, Paul. "Annales avignonaises de 1370 à 1392, d'après le livre des mandats de la gabelle." *Annales d'Avignon* 3 (1914):5-72.
_____. "Les Confréries d'Avignon au XIV$^{me}$ siècle." *Annales d'Avignon* 20 (1934):5-48.
_____. *Histoire du Livre et de l'Imprimerie à Avignon du XIV$^{me}$ au XVI$^{me}$ siècle.* Vols. 1-3. Avignon: Aubanel, 1922.
_____. *Les Palais cardinalices d'Avignon aux XIV$^{me}$ et XV$^{me}$ siècles.* Vols. 1-3. Avignon: J. Roumanille, 1926-1931.
Parker, James. *A Glossary of Terms Used in Heraldry.* New edition. Rutland, VT: Charles E. Tuttle, 1970.
Pelzer, Auguste. *Addenda et Emendanda ad Francisci Ehrle Historiae Bibliothecae Romanorum Pontificum tum Bonifatianae tum Avenionensis.* Vol. 1. Rome: 1947.
Piola Caselli, F. *La costruzione del palazzo dei papi di Avignon (1316-1367).* Milan: 1981.
Pirro, André. *Histoire de la musique de la fin du XIV$^e$ siècle à la fin du XVI$^e$.* Paris: H. Laurens, 1940.
Pirrotta, Nino. "Church Polyphony a propos of a New Fragment at Foligno." *Studies in Music History: Essays for Oliver Strunk.* Princeton, New Jersey: Princeton University Press, 1968, pp. 113-26.
_____. "Il codice estense lat. 568 e la musica francese in Italia al principio del '400." *Atti della reale Accademia di Scienze, lettere e arti di Palermo* 5 (1945):101-54.
_____. "Music and Cultural Tendencies in 15th-Century Italy." *Journal of the American Musicological Society* 19 (1966):127-61.
_____. "Scuole polifoniche italiane durante il sec. XIV: Di una pretesa scuola napolitana." *Collectanea historicae musicae,* vol. 1. S. Olschki, 1953, pp. 11-18.
Pognon, E. "Ballades mythologiques de Jean de le Mote, Philippe de Vitri, Jean Campion." *Humanisme et Renaissance* 5 (1936):385-417.
_____. "Du noveau sur Philippe de Vitri et ses amis." *Humanisme et Renaissance* 6 (1938):48-55.
Pons, André. *Droit ecclésiastique et musique sacrée.* Vol. 3. St. Maurice, Switzerland: Editions de l'Oeuvre St. Augustin, 1960.
*Pouillés.* Recueil des historiens de la France. Vols. 1-10. Paris: Académie des inscriptions et belles-lettres, 1904-1972.
Reaney, Gilbert. "The *Ars nova* of Philippe de Vitry." *Musica Disciplina* 10 (1956):5-12.
_____. "The Manuscript Chantilly, Musée Condé 1047." *Musica Disciplina* 8 (1954):59-113.
_____, ed. *Manuscripts of Polyphonic Music (c. 1320-1400). RISM,* vol. BIV². Munich: G. Henle, 1969.
_____. "A Postscript to 'The Manuscript Chantilly, Musée Condé 1047'." *Musica Disciplina* 10 (1956):55-60.
*Regista Pontificum Romanorum.* Philip Jaffé, ed. Vol. 1. Leipzig: 1885.
*Repertoire international des sources musicales.* Munich: G. Henle, 1960-. (Cited in the text as *RISM.*)
*Repertorium Germanicum.* Vols. 1-3. E. Göller *et al.,* eds. Berlin: Preussischen historischen Institut in Rom, 1916-1935.
Rose, E.-V. *Etudes historiques et religieuses sur le XIV$^e$ siècle, ou Tableau de l'Eglise d'Apt sous la cour papale d'Avignon.* Avignon: Aubanel, 1842.
Ross, William Braxton Jr. "A Study of Latin Letters at the Court of Avignon in the Time of Clement V and John XXII, 1309-1334." Ph.D. dissertation, University of Colorado, 1964.
Roux, Augustin. *La cathédrale d'Apt d'après des documents inédits.* Apt: Reboulin, 1949.

Rubio y Lluch, Antoni. *Documents per l'historia de la cultura catalana mig-eval.* Vol. 2. Barcelona: 1921.

Ryan, Granger, and Ripperger, Helmut, trans. *The Golden Legend of Jacobus de Voragine.* New York: Arno Press, 1969.

Sanders, Ernest H. "The Early Motets of Philippe de Vitry." *Journal of the American Musicological Society* 23 (1975):24-45.

Sauerland, H. V. "Itinerar des [Gegen-] Papstes Klemens VII. von seiner Wahl bis zu seiner Ankunft in Avignon (1378 Sept. 20-1379 Juni 20.)." *Historisches Jahrbuch* 13 (1892):192-93.

Sautel, Joseph. "Apt." *Dictionnaire d'histoire et de géographie ecclésiastiques.* Vol. 3. Paris: 1924, cols. 1080-1087.

_____. "Catalogue descriptive des manuscrits liturgiques de l'église d'Apt." *Annales d'Avignon* 6 (1919):53-111.

Sauve, Fernand. *Histoire d'Apt.* Rognes: [1980]. Reprint of 1903 edition.

Schäfer, K. H., ed. *Die Ausgaben der apostolischen Kammer unter Benedikt XII., Klemens VI. und Innocenz VI. (1335-1362).* Vatikanische Quellen zur Geschichte des päpstlichen Hof- und Finanzverwaltung 1316-1378, vol. 3. Paderborn: 1914.

_____, ed. *Die Ausgaben der apostolischen Kammer unter Johann XXII., nebst den Jahresbilanzen von 1316-1375.* Vatikanische Quellen zur Geschichte des päpstlichen Hof- und Finanzverwaltung 1316-1378, vol. 2. Paderborn: 1912.

_____, ed. *Die Ausgaben der apostolischen Kammer unter den Papsten Urban V. und Gregor XI. (1962-1378).* Vatikanische Quellen zur Geschichte des päpstlichen Hof- und Finanzverwaltung 1316-1378, vol. 6. Paderborn: 1937.

Schimmelpfennig, Bernhard. "Die Funktion des Papstpalastes und der Kurial Gesellschaft im päpstlichen Zeremoniell vor und während des grossen Schismas." *Avignon: Genèse et debuts du grand Schisme d'Occident.* Paris: 1980, pp. 397-408.

_____. "Die Krönung des Papstes in Mittelalter." *Quellen und Forschungen aus italienischen Archiven und Bibliotheken* 52 (1974):192-270.

_____. "Die Organisation der päpstlichen Kapelle in Avignon." *Quellen und Forschungen aus italienischen Archiven und Bibliotheken* 50 (1971):80-111.

_____. *Die Zeremonienbücher des römischen Kurie in Mittelalter.* Bibliothek des Deutschen historischen Instituts in Rom, vol. 40. Tübingen: 1973.

_____. "Zum Zeremoniell auf den Konzilien von Konstanz und Basel." *Quellen und Forschungen aus italienischen Archiven und Bibliotheken* 49 (1969): 273-92.

Schofield, Bertram. "The Adventures of an English Minstrel and His Varlet." *Musical Quarterly* 35 (1949):361-76.

Schrade, Leo. "The Chronology of the Ars nova in France." *Les colloques de Wégimont* no. 2. Paris: Société d'Edition "Les Belles Lettres," 1959, pp. 37-59.

_____. "A Fourteenth-Century Parody Mass." *Acta Musicologica* 27 (1955):13-39.

_____. "The Mass of Toulouse." *Revue belge de musicologie* 8 (1954):84-96.

_____. "Philippe de Vitry: Some New Discoveries." *Musical Quarterly* 42 (1956):330-55.

_____, ed. *The Roman de Fauvel, The Works of Philippe de Vitry, French Cycles of the Ordinarium Missae.* Polyphonic Music of the Fourteenth Century, vol. 1. Monaco: Editions de L'Oiseau-Lyre, [1956].

Schuler, Manfred. "Die Musik in Konstanz während des Konzils 1414-1418." *Acta Musicologica* 38 (1966):150-68.

_____. "Zur Geschichte der Kapelle Papst Eugens IV." *Acta Musicologica* 40 (1968):220-27.

_____. "Zur Geschichte der Kapelle Papst Martins V." *Archiv für Musikwissenschaft* 25 (1968):30-45.

Schwarz, Brigide. *Die Organisation kurialer Schreiberkollegien von ihrer Entstehung bis zur Mitte des 15. Jahrhundert.* Bibliothek des Deutschen historischen Instituts in Rom, vol. 37. Tübingen: 1972.

Seidlmayer, Michael. *Die Anfänge des grossen abendländischen Schismas.* Spanische Forschungen der Görresgesellschaft, 2nd series, vol. 5. Münster in Westfalen: 1940.

Shepherd, William R. *Historical Atlas.* Ninth edition. New York: Barnes & Noble, 1964.

Sherr, Richard Jonathan. "The Papal Chapel ca. 1492-1513 and Its Polyphonic Sources." Ph.D. dissertation, Princeton University, 1975.

Smet, J.-J. de, ed. *Recueil des Chroniques de Flandre.* Vol. 3. Brussels: 1856.

Smoldon, William L. *The Music of the Medieval Church Dramas.* London: Oxford University Press, 1980.

Stäblein-Harder, Hanna. *Fourteenth-Century Mass Music in France.* Musicological Studies and Documents, vol. 7. [Rome]: American Institute of Musicology, 1962.

————, ed. *Fourteenth-Century Mass Music in France.* Corpus Mensurabilis Musicae, vol. 29. [Rome]: American Institute of Musicology, 1962.

Stapleton, Michael. *A Dictionary of Greek and Roman Mythology.* London: Hamlyn, 1978.

Stevenson, Allan H., ed. *Briquet's Opiscula.* Hilversum, Holland: 1955.

Terris, Paul de. "Recherches historiques et litteraires sur l'ancienne liturgie de l'église d'Apt." *Société littéraire, scientifique et artistique d'Apt. Mémoires,* new series 1 (1874):171-248.

————. *Sainte-Anne d'Apt, ses traditions, son histoire d'après les documents authentiques.* Edited and shortened. Avignon: Seguin, 1876.

Thomas, Antoine. "Jean de le Mote, trouvère." *Histoire littéraire de la France,* vol. 36. Paris: 1937, pp. 66-86.

Valls i Subirà, Oriol. *Paper and Watermarks in Catalonia.* Vols. 1-2. Amsterdam: 1970.

Valois, Noël. "Essai de Restitution d'Anciennes Annales Avignonaises (1397-1420)." Offprint from *Annuaire-Bulletin de la Société de l'Histoire de France.* Paris: 1902.

————. *Le Grand Schisme d'Occident.* Vol. 2. Paris: 1901.

Van Dijk, S. A. "Historical Liturgy and Liturgical History," *Dominican Studies* 2 (1949):161-82.

Van Dijk, S. J. P. *Sources of the Modern Roman Liturgy.* Vols. 1-2. Leiden: E. J. Brill, 1963.

Van Dijk, Stephen J. P. and Walker, Joan Hazelden. *The Ordinal of the Papal Court from Innocent III to Boniface VIII and Related Documents.* Spicilegium Friburgense, vol. 22. Fribourg: 1975.

————. *The Origins of the Modern Roman Liturgy: The Liturgy of the Papal Court and the Franciscan Order in the Thirteenth Century.* Westminster, Maryland: The Newman Press, 1960.

*Vatikanische Quellen zur Geschichte des päpstlichen Hof- und Finanzverwaltung 1316-1378,* in Verbindung mit ihrem historischen Institut in Rom herausgegeben von der Görresgesellschaft. Paderborn: 1910-1967.

Weakland, John Edgar. "The Pontificate of Pope John XXII: Problems of Church Reform and Centralization." Ph.D. dissertation, Case Western Reserve, 1966.

Wilkins, Ernest Hatch. *Life of Petrarch.* Chicago: The University of Chicago Press, 1961.

Wilkins, Nigel. "Some Notes on Philipoctus de Caserta (c. 1360?-c. 1435)." *Nottingham Mediaeval Studies* 8 (1964):82-99.

Williman, Daniel Henry. "The Books of the Avignonese Popes and Clergy: A Repertory and Edition of the Book-Notices in the Vatican Archives, 1287-1420." Ph.D. dissertation, University of Toronto, 1973.

————. *Records of the Papal Right of Spoil: 1316-1412.* Paris: Editions du Centre national de la recherche scientifique, 1974.

Wooldridge, H. E. *Oxford History of Music.* Vol. 1, 2nd edition. Oxford: 1929.

Wright, Craig. *Music at the Court of Burgundy, 1364-1419: A Documentary History.* Musicological Studies, vol. 28. Henryville, Pennsylvania: Institute of Mediaeval Music, 1979.

Wrigley, John. "Studies in the Life of Pierre Roger (Clement VI) and of Related Writings of Petrarch." Ph.D. dissertation, University of Pennsylvania, 1965.

Young, Karl, *The Drama of the Medieval Church.* Vols. 1-2. Oxford: 1933.

_____. "Philippe de Mézières' Dramatic Office for the Presentation of the Virgin." *Publications of the Modern Language Association* 26 (1911):181-234.

Zaslaw, Neal. "Music in Provence in the Fourteenth Century." *Current Musicology* 25 (1978):99-120.

Zonghi, Aurelio. *Zonghi's Watermarks*. Hilversum, Holland: 1953.


**Addenda to the Bibliography**

Chiffoleau, Jacques. *La comptabilité de l'au-delà. Les hommes, la mort et la religion dans la région d'Avignon à la fin du moyen âge (vers 1320-vers 1480)*. Rome: Ecole française de Rome, 1980.

Caillet, Louis. *La papauté d'Avignon et l'église de France*. Paris: Presses universitaires de France, 1975.

Dykmans, Marc. "Les pouvoirs des cardinaux pendant la vacance du saint siège d'après un nouveau manuscrit de Jacques Stefaneschi." *Archivio della Società Romana de storia patria* 104 (1981): 119-45.

Favier, Jean. "le niveau de vie d'un collecteur et d'un sous-collecteur apostolique à la fin du XIV$^e$ siécle." *Annales du Midi* 75 (1963): 31-48.

Guillemain, Bernard. *Histoire d'Avignon*. Aix-en-Provence: Edisud, 1979.

_____. *Les recettes et les dépenses de la chambre apostolique pour la quatrième année du pontificate de Clément V (1308-1309)*. Rome: Ecole française de Rome, 1978.

Hayez, Anne-Marie. "Comptes du Palais sous Innocent VI (1352-1362) d'après le registre des Archives." Typescript. [Avignon]: [1982?].

Ward, Tom Robert. "The Polyphonic Office Hymn from the Late Fourteenth Century until the Early Sixteenth Century." Ph.D. dissertation, University of Pittsburgh, 1969.

# Index

during solemn Pontifical Mass, 106; sing *missa coram papa,* 107; standing of, 67-73, 79, 85-86, 91; quartered at VILLENEUVE, 83; participation at Vespers, 113-16; wages of, 64, 72, 83, 87, 91-93, 182n. 77; abandon Pope BENEDICT XIII, 44, 68. *See also* the biographical index
*Capellani commensales,* 40, 45, 47, 49, 51, 53, 54, 61, 63, 73-74, 94, 96-99, 107, 109, 111, 162n. 122, 168nn. 4,5, 169n. 7, 170n. 19, 171n. 36, 187n. 71; assist at *missa coram papa,* 107; duties of the office of; execution of lections at Easter Vigil, 110; participants at solemn Pontifical Mass, 106; participation at Vespers, 113, 115, 116; termination of office of, 26; of Pope CLEMENT VII; *See also* PHILIPPE DE VITRY
*Capellani honores,* 96. *See also* PIERRE OLLIER
*Capellani intrinseci,* 48, 50, 55. *See also* GAUFRIDUS ISNARDI, *Capellani capelle*
*Capellania* (dormatory), 47, 48, 49, 53, 72-73, 79, 86, 177n. 128
*Capellanus domini pape. See* AMATUS
Cardinal of Pamplona. *See* MARTIN DE SALVA
Cardinals, 3, 38-39, 44, 58-58, 82, 120, 172n. 50, 186n. 44, 188n. 109; activities at Vespers, 113-14; at feast for Pope CLEMENT VI, 16; dead in plague (1361) 21; intone antiphons at Lauds, 110; bishops: 113, 184, n. 12; as chaplain of the pope, 47, 108, 113, 186n. 48; assist at solemn Pontifical Mass (prior), 106; perform *Gloria,* 106, (second), 106, (third), 106, 113; chapels of, 8, 25, 164n. 149; deacons: 113, assist at solemn Pontifical Mass, 106; perform *Gloria,* 106; livreys of. *See* AVIGNON, VILLENEUVE-LES-AVIGNON; priests: 113, 118; as chaplain of the pope, 186n. 48; assist at solemn Pontifical Mass (prior), 106, 108; as patrons of the arts, 16, 25-26; retinues of, 2, 5, 8, 43, 58, 67, 95, 157n. 29
CARPENTRAS, city of, 6, 16, 44, 50, 125, 193n. 35; cathedral of; canon and precentor. *See* RICHARDUS DE BOZONVILLA
Carthusian order: church and monastery. *See* VILLENEUVE
*Cassola,* metal case for coals used in censing, 77, 78
CASTILE, kingdom of, support for Pope CLEMENT VII, 41-44; king of, exequies for, 186n. 58. *See also* JOHN I, HENRY III

CATALONIA, 140. *See also* ARAGON
Cathedra, 78. *See also* Faldstool
CAUMONT, 44
CAVAILLON, city of, 44, 125, 194n. 53; bishop of. *See* PHILIPPE DE CABASSOLE
Cemeteries. *See* AVIGNON, Churches
Ceremonials, curial, 81, 96, 97, 103-4, 117; from the former cathedral of VAISON (ca. 1370), 155n. 5
CHAISE—DIEU, Monastery of (O.S.B.), 12
Chamberlain *(camerarius),* 104; papal, 108, 122; dines with *capellani capelle,* 121. *See also* ARNAUD AUBERT, FRANÇOISE DE CONZIE
CHANTILLY, music manuscript at, 26
Chanting. *See* Singing
Chapels: in episcopal palace of *AVIGNON (Saint-Denis, Saint-Etienne, Saint-Jean, Saint-Michel),* 8; in city and churches of *AVIGNON. See* AVIGNON, chapels
Chaplains: of cardinals, 156n. 29, 164n. 149
CHARLES IV, Holy Roman Emperor, at ROME, 24, 125
CHARLES IV, King of FRANCE, 12, 14; *notaire* of. *See* PHILIPPE DE VITRY
CHARLES V, King of FRANCE, the Dauphin, 29
CHARLES VI, King of FRANCE, withdraws obedience from Pope BENEDICT XIII, 44
CHARLES II, Duke of ANJOU, 3; chancellor of. *See* Pope JOHN XXII (JACQUES DUESE)
CHARLES II, King of NAVARRE. *See* JACOB DE SENLESCHES
CHARTRES, cathedral of, *cantor. See* JOHANNES DE MOLEYO
*Chassa. See Caccia*
CHATEAUNEUF-DU-PAPE, papal residence at, 31, 44, 109
CHATEAURENARD, 44
CHIRAC, Monastery of (O.S.B.), 21
Choirboys, serving in chapels of cardinals, 176n. 119; at feast for Pope CLEMENT VI, 17; of Cardinal PIERRE ROGER DE BEAUFORT, 25. *See also* PASCASIUS DE BRIELLA
Christmas, 2, 29; donation of the *presbyterium,* 48, 169n. 7; Mass celebrated: Midnight, 106, 187n. 76; Dawn, 106, 187n. 76; Day, 106; Vigil of, 168n. 5. *See also* Canonical hours, Mass
Circumcision (1 January), 50; Mass celebrated, 106. *See also* Canonical hours
Cistercian order, 9, 50, 54
Clerics, 157n. 32; attached to households of cardinals, 156n. 16; behavior of, 155n. 6, 156n. 15, 165n. 150